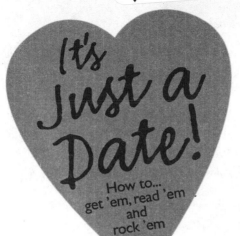

It's
Just a
Date!

How to...
get 'em, read 'em
and
rock 'em

Also available:

He's Just Not That Into You: The No-Excuses Truth
    to Understanding Guys
by Greg Behrendt and Liz Tuccillo

It's Called a Breakup Because It's Broken: The Smart
    Girls Breakup Buddy
by Greg Behrendt and Amiira Ruotola-Behrendt

Greg Behrendt and
Amiira Ruotola-Behrendt

It's
Just a
Date!

How to...
get 'em, read 'em
and
rock 'em

HARPER

HARPER

An Imprint of HarperCollins*Publishers*
77–85 Fulham Palace Road,
Hammersmith, London W6 8JB

First published by HarperCollins*Publishers* 2008

1

A catalogue record for this book
is available from the British Library

ISBN 0-00-723320-5
ISBN-13 978-0-00-723320-5

Printed and bound in Great Britain by
Clays Ltd, St Ives plc

Mixed Sources
Product group from well-managed
forests and other controlled sources
www.fsc.org Cert no. SW-COC-1806
© 1996 Forest Stewardship Council
FSC

contents

Part Two
CARPE DATEM—SEIZE THE DATE!

introduction

A Call To The Winner Dater Within

So your dating life is in the crapper and you've just about given up on the idea altogether at this point. And seriously, what's with guys, right? Why don't they ask women out? Why does it have to be so damn hard to date? Or what ever happened to dating, for that matter? Used to be that a guy would ask a girl out. Then he'd pick her up at her house, take her out for dinner, a movie, or a cup of coffee and some conversation. Then both parties would decide if they wanted to do it again next week. There was protocol. A courtship. A standard set of guidelines to follow for this age-old ritual outlined by our "Foredaters". Now who even knows what dating is?

WHAT IS A DATE?

If you hook up at a bar and go home together are you dating? If he text-messages you, "what are you wearing?" are you dating? If he tells you where he's going with his friends after work and tells you to bring your friends, are you dating? It's not cut and dried anymore—in fact it's become completely absurd. Sadly, dating has become somewhat obsolete, having been edged out of the line up by hooking up, hanging out and casual sex. Why is that? Because both men and women have said by their actions and willingness that they don't need the formality of a date to give their time, the privilege of their company and sometimes even their body. We've become a world of non-daters and, judging from the masses of unsatisfied singles that we hear from and about, we'd surmise that the whole non-dating thing's not going that great. It's too confusing, too casual, too grey and not enough black and white. Courtship has gone so far astray that it's come down to proximity and laziness. Like if you stand next to someone long enough at a party then eventually you'll pair up and be in a relationship with them without any actual effort, action or decision having been put into it.

BACK TO BASICS

It's time for a change and, aside from non-dating, the only other option to dating would be arranged marriages or marriage by lottery system. So it seems like now's the time to figure out how to date again, because you may not like ending up with #4 8 15 16 23 42. You obviously like yourself enough to pick up this book and consider the idea of improving your dating or non-dating life, and for that we love you. Hooray, we just hugged! Now, having said that, we will not coddle you. This is not a touchy-feely "you're great so everyone should think you're great" book. This is a "how bad do you want it and to what lengths will you go to achieve what you truly deserve and then be willing to throw it all away because after all It's Just a F*#king Date?!" kind of book. We have made our living being straight with you about our experiences and we've done it wrong ourselves enough times. But ONLY after you've done it wrong so many times will you have that moment of awakening, of clarity, where you admit, "I do it wrong. I need to do it differently."

By reading this book you are entering a no-bullshit area. Unlike some of your friends we will not sign off on your questionable behavior and will continually demand better of you. We will not be buying the rationalizing that you do to make it okay nor the excuses you make for yourself or someone else that's giving you less than you deserve. Now is the time to redefine what kind of dater you are and how you date. So buckle up ladies because you've come to the right place. You know what we've got? We've got answers and we've got plans for you.

REALITY CHECK!

The reality of dating is that almost every date you go on is not going to work out or turn into a lasting and meaningful relationship. In fact every date and relationship won't work out until you find the one that does. That's how it works. That's how life works and dating works. There are no shortcuts or loopholes and absolutely everyone is in the same boat as you. The only difference is how you approach these dates, the attitude you have when you get there. You can continue to dread them, be annoyed by the whole process, have expectations that are sure to disappoint you and project the futility you feel about the whole thing. OR you can let go of all of it, tell yourself that *It's Just A Date!* not the rest of your life, that it probably won't work out in the long run but might be fun nonetheless. With those expectations you'll have a much better time than you thought you would. Because *that* actually is the point of dating: an opportunity to spend time one on one to see if there's a spark. That's it. Dating was never meant to be a tortuous obstacle course that you had to suffer through, nor the culmination of all our dreams that aren't being fulfilled crashing down again when it doesn't work out. And if that's what dating is for

4

you—then you've got to ask yourself why are you doing that to yourself? Then you have to tell yourself to knock it the f*#k off. You control how you date, not anyone else—including the person you're on the date with. So let go of the old dating patterns that aren't working for you and embrace the ideals of dating like a winner and being the best you that you can be.

MY NAME IS AMIIRA AND I'M A BAD DATER

It seems like I should have figured that I was doing it wrong after the fiasco of my first marriage. Want to talk about going fast? I met him and it was love at first sight ... except for the fact that he had a girlfriend. It was a matter of months before they broke up and we got together, so to make up for lost time we spontaneously got married in Vegas by an Elvis impersonator. That's good, right? I had never been to his home, we hadn't met each other's families and probably didn't know each other's middle names. We did have similar record collections, so that, along with our young love, should have been enough. Well, not surprisingly it turns out that we didn't really know each other that well among other biggies that eluded us like similar values and the desire for children. So that didn't work out but I learned my lesson about jumping in too fast. Right? Or did I, as my next relationship went straight from "Nice to meet you" to "We should go to Barbados on vacation." At least I had seen his house before packing my bikinis and we did have similar record collections. But ultimately we got too intense too quickly and it we burned out on each other. Strike two! It'd be nice if there wasn't a strike three but there he was and who could resist the best friend that proclaims his love after too many Heinekens? Not I. So into instant boyfriend I fell. You know what happens when you go from being best friends to instant boyfriend/girlfriend? You realize that you probably weren't meant to be boyfriend/girlfriend but are trapped in a relationship with a person you love but "not in that way." That didn't end well. So at this point I was recognizing that speed was my foe and the way I dated wasn't working for me. The relationships I got myself into were plagued by the lack of certainty from rushing myself or someone else into feelings that weren't fully there. Then I met Greg Behrendt, who must have been doing the same thing in his life because he was Mister Take It Slow. Nice. We went out on our first date, which was very good, in fact we decided that we would go out again while still on the date. But then I broke up with him. Huh? It's a long story involving an ex-boyfriend that wouldn't go away. However he said the most amazing thing upon hearing my true but cocka-mamie sounding story about the ex-boyfriend on my lawn, "It's also okay if you don't like me like that." What?! Who the hell was this completely self-possessed guy? I told him truly that I didn't know yet whether I liked him but would be interested in finding out. So we dated, the old-fashioned way. He called ahead, asked me out, plans were made and we went on dates. We also dated other people while dating each other. There was no hopping in the sack, no racing to lock it down, no panic about what the other was thinking, feeling, doing. Then one day he said something mind-blowing, "I'm not going to date other people. I only want to go out with you but I don't expect you to do the same until you're ready to." What?! Who the hell is this guy who is going to stop dating other people but not demand I do the same? So we continued dating and soon after I came to the same conclusion that he had ... I didn't want to date other people. So there we were as boyfriend and girlfriend because we both truly wanted to be that and had figured it out at our own pace. Revolutionary! Then shortly thereafter he says those three magic words followed by the even more magical words that I had never heard before, "I Love You. But you don't have to say it back. You don't have to be at the same place emotionally that I am but I know that I love you and I wanted you to know it." Holy crap!! Are you kidding me? Where did this alien creature come from that is so comfortable in his own feelings that he can allow me to have my own feelings? That's how foreign the idea of taking things slow and actually figuring your feelings organically was to me. Normally at this point in a relationship I would have felt obligated to blurt it right back and hope that I grew into the feelings later, but because he was so self-possessed it made it effortless for me to be too. That being said, when I actually experienced having a relationship in real time, on my time, it became the one that has lasted the longest and burns the brightest because it's real and taking place in actual time. We're on this journey together side by side instead of one dragging the other behind. Our story is the reason that we decided to write this book because we know what is possible if you learn to do it right.

THE GOOD THE BAD & THE SKILLET OR WHY I TRIED DATING by Greg

The decision to start dating was a simple one. It started with a skillet. Not even a nice one, but one of those gun metal grey now singed black, workhorse skillets that you burn fried eggs with. "Wait Greg, are you telling me the interested reader that a dirty skillet got you dating? I'm not convinced." Yes I remember thinking as the greasy black pan was heading towards my skull, "This might not be the right relationship. I'm not choosing the right lady for me." Here's what happened. I was newly "drinks free" (I like that better than sober because it almost sounds like free drinks and that makes people happy) and had been set up with a girl who was also "drinks free". She was foxy and funny with a little edge. Anyway we went on two dates, one a formal dinner and the other we hung out at a thing then had awkward sex too soon and became girlfriend-boyfriend. We didn't really know each other but because we had had sex we felt beholden to one another and after all, this is how most of my relationships started in the past. Why should this be any different? Ever since college the recipe had been the same. Meet someone, take them out twice, have sex on the third date, become a couple, then fight until done. Ding! It wasn't either person's fault it was how the game had been set up. I had a pattern, it didn't work and I was sticking to it ... until the skillet. I remember calling my mom that day and saying "... you know what? Maybe I don't end up with anybody. Maybe I'm just destined to be a bachelor. And if that is the case then I'm gonna bachelor the shit out of it." I went at it like a sporting event. I got my own apartment. Taught myself how to cook and to clean. Picked out my own furniture. I went to movies by myself, ate at restaurants by myself and bought my own clothes. I began to teach myself to live as though I might never meet someone but if I did they'd be blown away by how self-sufficient I was and by my matching bamboo end tables. Like *Field of Dreams*. If you build it they will come. And then the weirdest thing happened: I started meeting girls. Everywhere. Department stores, flower shops, cafés, softball games and hair salons. See a pattern, fellas? Go to where the girls are. But don't go just to go. The fact that I was now not actively looking for a relationship made me appear to just appear. And for the first time in my life I had the opportunity to date more than one person. And I took it. I'd never done that, so why now? Well, I was at my parents over a Thanksgiving break and I was in my mom's office looking for something when I came across an old date book of hers from when she was dating my dad. I flipped through it and I noticed something almost revolutionary. She had begun dating my dad in May. I know this because his name appears periodically through out the month. Thursday Richard. Saturday Richard. But there are also two other names that appear throughout the month. Steve and Aaron, but as we get to June Aaron drops off like a stone and Steve's name appears less and less until it fully goes away in July. My dad kicked some dating ass, but the real lesson was my mom wasn't limiting her options until she was sure. I asked her if my dad knew about the other guys. "Not at first. But you didn't ask in those days. It was just assumed that you were dating." "Assumed you were dating? And he was cool with that?" "He didn't love it but he respected it and in some ways I think it made getting me all the sweeter." Dating!? What a great f*#king idea. Imagine, just going out with someone a few times to see how you really feel about them. So I decided to give it a try. And I found that I liked it and that I was pretty good at it. Were all the dates good? Hell no! There were some nightmares you will read about later on in the book. Did you get your heart broken? Not as badly as if I had tried to turn them into relationships. But it led to the best relationship I ever had with another person on this planet. And that's why I wanted to write this book. There is an option out there and it's the only one we have besides arranged marriages. Wait—we don't have arranged marriages. But I have supplied a petition at the back of the book if you want to lobby for arranged marriages. So why go on a date? Because they work, because dating is the best way to get to know someone you don't know and someone you do, because it's a great way to set the tone and speed for a relationship, because there are snacks, because you might make a friend or meet a future business partner, because you might have the worst night of your life and that could lead to you writing the next great novel, because you'll never know if you don't, because it's just a f@#king date.

WHERE WOMEN BLOW IT by Amiira

Women always have and always will continue to date a man's potential instead of his reality. We can't help ourselves. It's in a woman's nature to be hopeful and to see the possibilities, the greatness that people possess. Hooray for us, aren't we lovely? We are, but dating someone's potential is probably the biggest mistake women make in relationships and certainly the one that leads to our romantic downfall. That's because there are three types of men: the ones that find our faith in their potential to be appealing, the ones that find our faith in their potential to be a burden … and the ones that find it appealing at first then are crushed by the burden of their un-reached potential and resentful of the woman they once adored for that very faith.

The problem is that we don't know which of the three the man of our dreams is going to be until it's often too late. Once you've *unintentionally* crushed a man's ego (read: once he decides that he doesn't want to reach the potential *you* have for him) it's hard for him to be excited about you anymore. Then it's just a matter of time before the sex starts diminishing, there's bickering where there wasn't any before and the distance between you begins an expansion that is unwieldy.

More often than not, dating a man's potential is the long road to disaster—so listen to who he says he is and take him at his word. If you can love who he is now and not have your attraction be based on who he might become then you're in good shape. If you're not, well then you best keep looking because most people have different aspirations than you might have for them.

Love isn't swimming upstream.

part one

prepare yourself for dating excellence

! WARNING!

You are now entering a new way of dating and living. Old habits are not welcome and failure is not an option. Those not willing to make some serious changes should turn back now and get a few cats to keep you company.

the principal principles of dating for winners

The 8 Super Extraordinary Principles For Ultra-Successful Winner Dating™

You probably were skulking around the bookstore mumbling to yourself, "My dating life's a mess—I sure wish I had some guidelines for dating more successfully." Well today's your lucky day, so buck up Sugarpot because that's exactly what we have for you! Super Extraordinary Strategies for Ultra-Successful Winner Dating™. We know that dating has become a confusing mess for most single folks out in the world, and quite honestly it shouldn't be that way. Dating was one of the most well structured, well thought out things that our generation inherited. How we managed to f*#k that one up is a mystery. Or is it? In fact it's not a mystery at all. In our natural evolution as humans and as we've become a more liberal society we've rid ourselves of ideas or thought processes that don't work. Certainly there are formalities and expected behaviors that do need updating and revising to keep up with the contemporary times, but dating, as it turns out, may not have been one that needed much. The radical revision of dating that followed the sexual revolution and its continual morphing that has come with the advances in communication technology (like emails, texting, etc. ...) has turned dating into a blur of booty calls and ambiguous hanging out. And the result is a lot of unhappy and unclear people that are in complete disharmony with their romantic universe.

What women are craving is the formality of dating because of the clarity that it would provide for them. Think about the collective sigh of relief from just the knowledge alone that when you're asked out that you're actually on a date. Instead of spending the time trying to figure out if you're on a date, just hanging out as friends or being sized up as a candidate for casual sex. Dating is something that *YOU* have control over so if you want it to change, if you want to take control of your dating life you have to take it upon yourself to be very serious about and completely committed to HOW you date. You have to have a set of standards that you live and date by *without* exception. Which means formulating a dating strategy and instituting dating policy for yourself, then sticking to it. It sounds ridiculous but it's not. In fact, had you done it earlier you might be in a very different place with your love life and been able to save that $19.95 (or whatever this book costs) you spent on this fantastic piece of literature, put it into a high yielding mutual fund and turned it into at least $1,047 billion dollars by the time you retire. (These numbers are guess-timations made by two book writers that have no experience or financial expertise and cannot be held accountable for the way you spend your money.)

We know the word *strategy* in relation to dating can sound like an underhanded manipulation of another person and that is NOT at all what we're talking about. **Strategy**, in the dictionary, is defined as: **1.** The science or art of planning or conducting a war or military campaign. (Nope!) **2.** Carefully devised plan of action to achieve a goal or the art of developing or carrying out such a plan. (Wrong again!) **3. An evolutionary theory, a behavior structure, or other adaptation that improves viability.** AHA! Bingo! Now we're talking!

There's an element of strategy in everything that we do in life and there's nothing wrong with that. There are choices, actions and consequences. That's what everything in life is and dating is no exception. Like the time you agreed to let the drummer for "Mighty Lemon Phillipshead" come up for a nightcap—that's a choice. Then woke up the next morning to find him in your roommate's bed—that's a consequence. To be fair, it was dark in your apartment but still … No, no, no that's just another excuse you make to cover for making bad choices. The truth is you actually liked him and hoped to go out on a second date and *had you said goodnight at the front door you might've had a chance*. So let's embrace the idea of creating a strategy for dating and your life so that the choices you make are better. As they say in that popular book that features that guy Jesus, "Faith without works is dead." Meaning **you can believe you want a better dating life but unless you're willing to do the work, nothing will change.** "Wow you got all serious on me. I didn't think Jesus went on dates." Well now you know why people got so mad about *The DaVinci Code*. But let's get back to you …

If your experiences are anything like the throngs of emails and letters we get complaining about the state of dating then you know that for most men you encounter, dating is something they only *have* to do if they can't get away with hanging out under less formal circumstances (or they can't get you to fool around with them at the bar). It's probably the single most frustrating thing we hear about in all of our varied "What's the deal with men?" conversations. The deal is that *THEY FOLLOW YOUR LEAD*. That means if you give them the easy way out, that's what they'll take.

It's important to recognize that while you can change the way a man dresses, you can't change the way he approaches dating. You can only inspire him to want to change that for himself so that he gets to spend time with you. *The thing you determine is the value of your time, the value of your company and how you date*. Those are the *only* things you are in complete control of, but that's enough to turn the tide. Think about it ... it's only when you set the value of your time low and you agree to non-dates that they can exist for you. However, if you maintain a high standard for how you date and you don't accept the premise of quasi-dating, non-dating and hanging out then you leave him with only two choices: to ask you out on a proper date or to do without your company. And if he chooses the latter then you're better off anyway because getting to spend time with you is a gigantic prize.

People need to start dating again and not participate in the non-dating if they want to find a real relationship rather than someone to have confusing sex with. "But how do I date amongst all the confusing confusion of dating?" We're glad you asked, because there is a definite right and wrong way to date and if you want to get good results you have to start dating smarter and better. There's a reason why you're not having success: it's because what you're doing isn't working for you. It's time to change your game. "But I don't like playing games. Dating should not be about game playing." Yeah, yeah ... We've heard it. The reality is that there is a game to be played when dating and it's called *RESTRAINT*. Quite frankly, when you *reject* that idea you yourself are playing your own game. It's a game of refusing to look at human nature and the things you already know about friendships, work, eating and every other thing in life where you take the time to responsibly think to yourself, "I need to do this right.

There's an order in which everything happens. If I mess with the order the whole thing will fall apart." Why would you single out dating as the place to say, "Ah, f*#k the order! I'm not going in order. I'm going to just tell them now that I love them, blow them in the bathroom (or whatever impulsive thing that you know you shouldn't do), because that will either make him want to be with me more or bail *but at least I'll know now!*" It makes no sense. You don't walk into a job interview and ask where your desk is. You don't make a new friend then, after week one, tattoo their name on your neck. You don't eat shitty all week and wonder why your pants don't fit. Do you see where we're going with this? There's an order to things and dating is no exception.

So what we've devised is a set of guidelines, or rather Super Extraordinary Guidelines For Ultra-Successful Winner Dating™. These are the key to turning your dating life around and setting the new standard for HOW you date. Like we stated earlier, **you get to determine** the value of your time, the value of your company and, most importantly, how you date and how you absolutely *do not* date. Grab a fork and dig in, sister, because you've got some dating to do!

Here's a preview of what dazzling principles you're going to have drilled into that pretty little head of yours.

The 8 Principles of dating success:

✓ **Like yourself and know you're worthy**
Start with giving your thighs a break. Why can't you just like them for once after all these years they've supported you?

✓ **Get a life, have a life ...**
... and don't throw it away when every Tom, Dick and Agnes comes along.

✓ **Pretty is as pretty does**
Get real about what you're putting out into the world.

✓ **Don't accept less than an actual date**
Seriously. Stop hooking up with bozos when you're drunk.

✓ **Don't freak people out with your need**
Crazy + Sexy doesn't always = Cool

✓ **Doormats finish last and end up in the dirt**
Have some standards and ditch the deal breakers.

✓ **Don't show the movie before the trailer**
Make sex an event, not a given.

✓ **Not every date is going to turn into a relationship**

And a worthwhile one is a journey, not a race.

HERE'S THE DEAL ...

It's Just A F*#king Date! It's a philosophy and an attitude all rolled up into one great big package. It's the difference between expecting something to happen and being surprised when it does. It's letting go of the whole process but not letting go of you. There are things in life you can change. Your weight, your appearance, your mindset, etc. ... but there is one thing you cannot change and that is *other people*. Try as we might we cannot get people to love us. Even when we are the coolest, best version of ourselves someone is going to say, "Not for me." But if we feel good about ourselves we shrug it off and say, "It's Just A F*#king Date" and know that there will be others.

When you really want something and you're doing everything you can to make it happen and it's not coming to fruition, you have to **let go of the result and do the work anyway**. You can't live inside of a result because it will always disappoint. But if you work towards the goal and *let go* of the result then you'll not only get what you wanted but will probably get something that's better and different than how you had imagined it. That's how life works. Life comes in a different package than you expected it to. The same goes for dating. You need to show up and see what happens. Well now, that doesn't sound so hard—but in fact it is.

This book is going to demand two things from you that may seem to conflict. We are going to ask that you be vigilant in your attempts to better yourself AND not take dating so damn seriously. "So does that mean I have to get all dressed up and try even if I'm not supposed to care about what happens?" Exactly. And you'll be a better person for it.

So pull it together woman, and let's get ready to date!

principle #1: like yourself and know you're worthy

Find Your Inner Cheerleader, Rock Star, Physicist And Some Self-Esteem

Last year this woman in her mid-twenties came to us because she was having terrible luck dating. She hadn't had a boyfriend or decent date since high school and couldn't get arrested by a single dude much less get one to ask her out and pay for dinner. She was cute, had a good personality, definitely had some sex appeal but it was as if she had actually been deflated. Her whole energy was sad and dejected. She said, "If I had known that high school was going to be the best it was going to get for me, I would have enjoyed it more or nailed down a guy for the future." She really thought it was over for her at the age of 26. We asked her what was different in high school? Why did she think she peaked romantically then?

She thought about it and responded that she had been a cheerleader in high school. She was happy, popular with a lot of different social groups, was lusted after by teenage boys, celebrated by the football team, got special privileges during school to do cheerleader things like decorate the jocks' lockers, prepare for pep rallies and whatnot, and she was in the spotlight performing at halftime, getting to wear her uniform to school on game days, etc. ... It was an idyllic high school existence and now she no longer even felt like the same person and certainly wasn't living the same kind of life.

We thought about what she was telling us, what we know of cheerleaders and it instantly became clear to us. Cheerleaders are sexy and confident, they're kind of hot shit around the halls of high school and they carry themselves like they're hot shit. Now she was wearing a frumpy outfit that was the antithesis of confident cheerleader, which she told us was how she dressed every day. When we asked her, "Why are you hiding that cheerleader?" it all came pouring out then. Tears streamed down her face as she admitted that she had put on some weight since high school, she didn't like her body, she had been dumped hard by not even a good guy but a totally shitty one in her freshman year in college and she didn't even feel like herself anymore. The truth is she didn't like herself or feel at all worthy of having good things in her life. She no longer felt those great things about herself that she did back in high school so she didn't carry herself out in the world with the same self-confidence or self-worth. Basically her self-esteem was completely shot. This girl needed to find her inner cheerleader—she needed to find her confidence again. And as bad as we felt for her, it was a story we have heard countless times from women of every age and we had to bring down the hammer. This is the gist of what we told Boo Hoo the Cheerleader ...

Happiness is hard work. It always has been since the beginning of time. It takes diligence to continually set yourself up to win—not competitively but personally— and winning is the kindling for the brightly burning fire of self-esteem and happiness. When your self-esteem is heightened you carry yourself with more assurance, your energy is more vibrant, people respond to you more positively and you are more magnetic so you attract opportunity. Basically, you walk differently, talk differently, rock differently and in the words of the late, great Justin Timberlake you're bringing sexy back. (To the best of our knowledge Justin Timberlake is very much alive but we just wanted to see if you were paying attention.) When your self-esteem is lessened you feel badly about yourself so you avoid things and people, your energy is heavy and sad, people are less likely to respond to you well and you repel opportunity (including prospective dates!). If you like yourself, if you love yourself, if you feel good about yourself, if you value yourself, you will feel worthy of good things and you will get good things (like a rockin' boyfriend. Maybe even Mr. Timberlake himself).

The whole concept of winning on a personal level is simple but not necessarily easy to do. The key is to *constantly* put yourself in a position to feel great about you and keep out of harm's way. This translates into stopping your bad behavior, staying away from the people that provoke your bad behavior, or people that make you feel anything less than good about yourself. Otherwise your self-esteem pays the price. Personally winning is finding a way to keep yourself in the personal space where you're being the best you, the biggest you, the most vibrant you instead of the smallest you. That is the secret to success in anything you want to do in life. That means not comparing yourself to anyone else and concentrating on you. Because when your self-esteem is in the shitter and you don't feel worthy you look to others for validation, you settle for crappy things and all you get is crappy things and who wants that?

Let's break it down for a moment before we sum it up in a fancy gold-plated nutshell with rims for you. (For those of you who haven't seen any hip-hop videos lately, "rims" are like jewelry for your car wheels—the fancy flashy bits in the middle of the tire that often spin counterclockwise or blind you with their shine and ornamentation.) You started out with so much promise with endless possibilities for what you can do with your life and who you can become. From the moment you come out of the womb, you have the potential to be anything from Mayor McCheese to running the Free World, who knows?! (By the way, the McCheese gig pays better and is much less stressful but damn is it hot in that hamburger suit.) From early on we are encouraged, applauded even for our first accomplishments, be it learning to walk, saying our first words, actually making it into our mouth with the spoonful of bananas instead of down our front. The ovation continues for you lucky ones who grow up surrounded by people that love and support you and whose greatest joy is to build you up after every foul ball, good try or embarrassing failure. *The great promise that we're talking about is simply the existence of self-esteem.* When you're older you can find it for yourself, but for many it is what you are given, brick by brick, every time you are told that you are good, the world is your oyster, you can do anything you put your mind to or you're much prettier than your cousin Laura. (What a sea hag she is.)

So you have this self-esteem, this self-worth all stored up but then at various points along your journey to here you've lost some of the value you once had for yourself because that's part of the experience of this life. That's the rub. We all have events that reduce our self-esteem and disappointments that make us question our worth be it socially, academically, professionally or romantically. It only takes getting your heart smashed when your boyfriend dumps your for a younger girl, a leggy blonde, a sports model, your best friend, that guy from the bowling alley (you didn't see that one coming didya?) or just simply someone else to send you into a self-esteem spiral that can last for years. Then we end up in an ongoing cycle of losing romantically because every time a relationship or even a first date doesn't pan out you blame yourself. The thought that runs through your head is, "There must be something wrong with me because I wasn't good enough for them to love me." When what your thought should be is, "I'm only responsible for my half of it not his. It wasn't a match for me because it takes both halves for it work so I'm better off for it ending now." Do you know why that should be your thought? **BECAUSE YOU CAN'T LOOK FOR SOMEONE ELSE TO GIVE YOU YOUR VALUE!** You have to do that for yourself, you *CAN* do it for yourself and you certainly f*#king should.

Self esteem, self-worth and confidence are something you have to constantly rebuild until you get to the place where those things can no longer be shaken from you. But these things are only are gained by a series of tiny victories that, once accumulated, start making you feel better about yourself. You can't wait for the world to drop these opportunities in your lap, you have to go and create those victories for yourself. "How do I do that?" Easy, create small accomplishable victories that you can do on a daily basis and that you will under no circumstance deviate from. Personal hygiene is a great place to start. Every morning wash your face, Victory! Brush your teeth, Victory! Floss, Victory! See you've only been awake for 10 minutes and are already winning. Boom, more victories for you my friend! What we are talking about here are good choices, many of them in a row, which make you feel good about your self, thus blowing up your sagging self-esteem. Exercise, travel, find something that makes you feel great and do it—volunteer at a charity or take on a challenge that you can do. But consistency is key. Tiny victories are what will nourish you back to the promise you once had. You have to do this or some version of this every day as a way of honoring who you are and how you operate. Your unwillingness to compromise will be your greatest asset because that is what tells you and the world that you care about yourself (which we all know is a huge turn-on). Tiny victories are actually the cornerstone of almost any successful person you know, because when all else fails at least you flossed.

The key to Ultra Successful Winner Dating is that you can't date what you are not. You will not attract great things by wishing for them, seeing a psychic or buying magic rocks. You only get Great by being Great, and Greatness takes work!

BUT GREG, I HAVE QUESTIONS

But What If I'm Not Worthy?

Dear Greg,

I was supposed to get married two Christmases ago to my boyfriend of three years but about six months before the wedding he changed his mind. He said he didn't think he was in love with me. He's not with anyone else but I can't get past the idea that there's something wrong with me. Why else would he break our engagement to be alone?

Kate

Bath, England

Dear Wedding Crashed,

It sucks to get dumped when you thought you had your whole life worked out but what he actually did was the excellent service of not marrying you when he recognized that he wasn't in love with you. Despite what may have been in the past, things change and it sucks. However it also means that you were released to move on to your next great thing but you are holding up the bus by blaming yourself, sinking your self-esteem and being an all-round bummer. The only thing wrong with you is that you can't see your value and that's going to take some work, possibly even counseling, but it's time to revisit the girl you were when you were at your best. Possibly right before you met the wedding smasher. Hang in there Hot Stuff, your story ain't over yet.

But What If I Can't Rebuild My Self-Esteem?

Dear Greg,

My last boyfriend cheated on me with some girl from his office. The boyfriend before that cheated on me with a mutual friend and the boyfriend I had before that was just an asshole. I don't know why, but I stayed with all of these men for long after I had identified their problems. I don't know how to rebuild my self-esteem after so many blows to the ego.

Claire

Minneapolis, MN

Dear Loser Magnet,

Holy smokes! You do have the winning ticket to the loser lotto. Do you know the phrase "Water seeks it's own level"? The same goes for losers. That doesn't mean that I'm calling you a loser but what I am saying is that you are comfortable with them and you allow them to be the losers they are in your company. What that does mean is that there's something in your mechanics that tells you that you don't deserve better than this and whatever that is needs a fixing. To rebuild your self-esteem you need to surround yourself with people that make you feel good and bring out the best in you, take care of your well-being without exception and line up some tiny victories. It's only when you get to the place where you think you're worthy of a good relationship that you'll find one. So kick the losers to the curb and get some help for whatever's ailing your self-worth.

But What If I Do Like Myself?

Dear Greg,

I'm 42 years old, I own my own company, I have a lot of great friends, a great relationship with my family and I've lost over a hundred pounds in the past year so I'm in fantastic shape for the first time in my life. In other words I'm not f@#ked up. But I'm starting to feel like I'm going to spend my life alone. I go to clubs, bars, cocktail parties, dog parks, you name it but no one seems to notice me and I can't get asked out. What do I do? I'm really lost in this part of my life.

Anika

Ft Lauderdale, FL

Dear Weighed Down,

Firstly, congratulations on doing so many things right in your life and taking control of your health and weight. Bravo to you. Here's what I think is happening, you're used to being overweight and probably have been overweight your whole life. So even though you like yourself and have shed the extra pounds you still feel like the fat girl and probably carry yourself as such. That means you're projecting old ideas about yourself onto the new you and taking those out into the world and people respond thusly. People aren't noticing you because you don't feel noteworthy still. So let's stop that business right now because you didn't do all of that work to lose. If it means standing in front of the mirror every day or leaving yourself a voice message that says, "I am now a new person, have you seen my butt?" then do it, because like every person reading this you're great and you deserve to be in a great relationship, but it will only happen not only if you like yourself and feel worthy of it but also project that out into the world as well.

But What If There's Nothing To Like?

Dear Greg,

What's wrong with me, why can't I catch a break? I always get "downsized" at jobs, dumped after the first date or completely overlooked because my best friend is prettier than me. I'm the person that has to be thankful for bad luck otherwise I'd have no luck at all. Now there's this guy who I really like and he only knows me as the girl who dropped her new phone in the toilet at work. Why would he even like me much less want to go out with me? For once I just wish something good would happen to the girl standing next to the pretty girl.

Florence
Quebec, Canada

Hey Flo,

Hard on yourself much? Look, being clumsy is fine, in fact it can be cute, but being clumsy or having bad luck is not your problem. You're treading water in a personal crisis because you don't even kind of like yourself or think you deserve good things. If you're running for the title in the Miss Victim Of Her Own Life you definitely have a good shot but I'd suggest you step down from that pageant and try to get involved in the Miss I Like

Myself competition. And by the way, who cares if your best friend is prettier than you and why is it that you like her better than you like yourself? If you want anyone including the guy at work to like you, you have to start liking yourself first. As for the catching a break part, you have to make your own breaks and optimize those before the universe will start dropping them at your feet. So next time you drop your mobile phone down the toilet just turn to the guy you like at work and playfully say, "Which do you think is hotter, that I dropped my phone in the toilet or that I went in after it?" Or "I'd offer you my phone so you can call my voicemail to ask me out but it's on vacation in the ladies' room." Be confident, have a sense of humor about life's little trials and see if you can't give yourself a break!

FROM THE OTHER SIDE OF THE FENCE

But What If It's Not Me It's Them?

Dear Greg,

Women never like me so dating sucks. I'm the assistant manager of a small women's boutique so I'm around women all the time and I overhear their conversations about men. You should hear the load of crap they say. They talk about not caring if guys have money and just wanting to be taken out on a real date. And then in the next sentence they talk about their expensive dates with the guys with money going to a fancy restaurant in town. They're all phonies. Where's the girl who is going to be super excited to go out for McRibbs with me in my Honda when she could be out with some guy with money and a cool car? Seriously f*#k it.

Brad
Fargo, ND

Dear Bad Braditude,

I hear you and I get what you are saying and I think you are right. You don't have enough money, so give up and stop dating altogether, then you'll have more time to pick out the small apartment where you are destined to die alone. (Make sure it has no windows or a view of the alley where the dumpsters are.) Or you can A) not worry about girls who are only interested in guys with money, B) figure out ways to be creative with the money you have and C) figure what kind of life you want to have. But before you do all that I'd say you should take a good long look at how you feel about women because from your letter it seems like you hate all of them *as well as yourself*. With all due respect I don't know anyone that would sign up with someone with that attitude and lack of self-esteem. You're surrounded by women all day— that's a giant opportunity that not all guys have and if you took advantage of it and learned how to be charming and funny instead of pissed off at all the women you're surrounded by you'd probably be in high demand for dates instead of being rejected by them. *And by the way there are far more attractive things than money, like for instance confidence.* You should try to get some of that. It'll get you further in life than a wad of cash.

THE CHICK THAT ROCKED IT

I'm not going to pretend that I've never been the kind of guy that doesn't take advantage of a good opportunity with girls. I don't know if it's a "Daddy" thing or what but some girls let you walk all over them or treat them like shit. When we were still in college the guys would all sit around and compare notes about it. So after college I expected that it would probably be different once I was in the business world working with professionals instead of sorority girls. But even the most successful women are so starved for male attention that they'll let you go all the way without even promising them a phone call. It's wild. So I was riding the wave of no strings attached for many years until I met Susan. Susan wasn't having any of my bullshit and wasn't even kind of amused by it. For the longest time I couldn't figure out what it was that made her different but I was so fascinated by her. She was smart, sexy and confident, which is great, but I had been with women like that before. She was pretty-ish but had a good size nose that she should have been self-conscious about but wasn't. I couldn't stop thinking about her and she couldn't care less about me. I tell you I have never worked so hard for a first, second or third date as I did to get Susan to go out with me. The more time I spent with her the more I was intrigued by her, but it wasn't until years later when we were living together that I finally figured out why she was different from every girl I had ever dated before. She liked herself and didn't need my approval in the slightest bit. So I married her before she could realize that I lacked those qualities myself and I hope that I somehow get to learn them from her before she figures me out. Why women settle for scraps I'll never understand, but as long as they do guys are happy to reap the benefits from it.

Tim

Denver, CO

IT WORKED FOR ME!

I met you guys at a singles mixer for "It's Called A Breakup Because It's Broken" in Seattle. During a Q&A session I told you about my last relationship with a verbally abusive man and the subsequent breakup of it and you were both very supportive of my decision to leave (a decision I was regretting at the time). When you spoke to me one of you said that I didn't think I deserved anything better than being in an abusive relationship and I told you that you were wrong. You continued to challenge me on that idea and it really hurt my feelings because I like to think of myself as a pretty together person who likes herself. But when I got home that night I looked at the pictures in frames around my house, seeing images of myself as a little girl with my parents and at various stages of my life and I burst into tears. I cried for a long time and it was a therapeutic crying jag but during it, or maybe what caused it, was the realization that you were right. If I really felt like I deserved better I wouldn't have stood for the abuse as long as I did and it wouldn't have been hard to leave. So it's a few years later now and I've been doing a lot of work on myself and seeing a therapist to try to figure out why I constantly compromise myself for others that wouldn't do the same for me. I feel like a different person, a clearer person and a more confident and valuable person. Today I'm happy to write to you to tell you that I've met a wonderful man who loves and reveres me as much as I do myself and we're getting married this fall. (Please see the enclosed invitation.) I hope you can attend because you really did change my life, but no need to bring a gift as you've already given me one.

Mavis
Kirkland, WA

FIRST PERSON SINGLE by Amiira

I settled for pieces of the pie for a long time in my romantic history. If there was a guy with only few of the qualities I was looking for but loads of the ones I wasn't, then I was on board! Or better yet, if there was a guy who wasn't ready to commit but could muster up just enough effort to string me along, then sign me up! That's my man! But don't tell him he's my man because it might scare him off. Anything that felt bad and made me insecure was worth the effort because if I could just get the person who doesn't love me to love me then I would know for sure that I am good enough. Good enough for what? Seriously. What is it that I'm looking for and why do I think that this asshole that makes me feel less than or inadequate is not only better than me but has the answers? Why does someone else hold the key to my self-esteem? That's the revelation I finally had after yet another disappointing quasi-relationship with someone who had such bad qualities that it was almost comical. It takes one of those to give you the proverbial smack up side the head so that you can give your brain a good shake and get all the self-loathing out. You have to continually hit the reset button on your life to make you consciously start making better choices because no one else can do it for you. Look, it's hard to be in a relationship where there's an imbalance of feelings. I know it because I've been on both sides of that imbalance and neither of them is really that comfortable. At least when you're the one least invested you don't feel the panic and inadequacy of when you're on the losing end of the "Please Love Me Enough" equation. But being uncomfortable in your relationship is symptomatic of not only that you're in the wrong relationship but that you aren't in a good space with yourself. Continuing to be in bad relationships where you feel not good enough, unloved, and insecure or anything other than consistently great is like having a gambling addiction. Every day thinking the next will be the turning point where things will stabilize and be great is the same thing as thinking that the next hand of cards is going to make you the big winner when in fact you're just slowly giving yourself away. It's denial in a truly profound sense because you participate in it daily and you know it even if it's only on a gut level that shows itself in the discomfort you feel being riddled with self-doubt.

It's hard to say why it took me so long to like myself enough to gracefully refrain from engaging in self-doubting relationships, but once I had figured it out it was an undeniable truth that I could not turn back from. No one knows better than I do about me and because of that I don't need anyone to validate me. I am free. I am powerful. I am worthy. I am lovable. And people around me know that I *know* that about myself. It only took me ten years to get there but because I got there I found the best relationship for me and now I get the rest of my life to feel good.

THOUGHTS FROM MAN CITY

What attracts a man to a woman? Cleavage! The End.

Okay that's not really what I want to say. It's really an almost impossible question to answer. Probably because the answer lies in what each individual man is looking for. There are things we know for sure, sex appeal is very high if not at the top of the list. Men are visual creatures (see the Internet for details). Confidence is also high on our list because it can almost completely make up for any shortcomings a person has in the looks department. Then there are things like personal style, work ethic (yes, contrary to popular belief some men like a woman they have to compete with), religious beliefs and favorite bands. But my note to you ladies is, **WHO GIVES A SHIT?** Finding out what we like won't help you unless you like it too. If you want to be in a great relationship then I suggest having a great relationship with yourself. We are only going to like you if you like you, and if you don't we can tell. And some of us will prey on those weaknesses for our own pleasure. Do I have to explain or do you get it? When you compromise *your* values or *your* needs for *our* pleasure or attention we will always sense it and eventually leave. It works both ways. Anytime I ever gave up who I was to procure sex or attention it always ended badly (see *It's Called A Breakup Because It's Broken* for further details). The only reason a person compromises themselves is because they don't feel strongly enough about themselves and are looking for another person to fix it for them either sexually or emotionally. That's why it is imperative that you get to a place where you like yourself even if just for the added bonus of weeding out the creeps.

 **DATING FORTUNE COOKIE**

Sexy beats cute, smart takes sexy, funny wins the pot ... and confidence body-slams them all.

WORST DATE EVER 😞

I never understood what I was doing wrong on dates until I went on a date with myself. Let me explain. About a year ago I met this guy on a chair-lift skiing in Lake Tahoe. It was a long ride and on it I learned that he lived in San Francisco like I did. He asked me out or rather hinted that he would like to ask me out but he said he was too shy. I thought it was a kind of a cute way of asking/not asking me out. I know how you guys feel about that stuff but he was really cute so I helped him ask me out and we went on a date. It was the worst date I'd ever been on. We had dinner at this really nice restaurant in the Embarcadero in San Francisco. It was all going okay but he was very down and hesitant about things and everything he said about himself was negative like, "I don't know, I'm not really that smart" "I used to be fit but now I'm in terrible shape" "My life's not really that interesting" or "You're probably used to dating better looking guys." Here he was this handsome skier with a great job in real estate and all he could do was tell me what a loser he was while putting away drink after drink and getting more and more depressed. It bugged me a lot but then I finally realized that it bothered me because I had been guilty of doing the same thing for as long as I could remember. Constantly selling myself short, putting myself down for God knows what reason and falling apart on dates. You know what I found out? It's a big turn-off. No one wants to date a conceited ass but who wants to date the person that thinks so little of himself? It was the very first time in my life that I realized that *I'm a beautiful skier with a great job and despite what I've spent years telling date after date after date, I'm kind of a catch.* I didn't see him again but I did see me and what a terrible date I had been for the first time, so the date wasn't a total loss.

IT'S JUST YOUR F*#KING HAPPINESS

Your happiness is the most important thing in this life. If you are not happy you are of no use to anyone else. Look, no one is happy all the time but if you are at least in the pursuit of happiness then that is what ultimately will make you appealing to the kind of man that not only wants to stick around but is also fun to be with. The point is you have to figure out how to be happy no matter what the cost and we can tell you right here and now that happiness won't come from another person. It will come from the tiny victories and the big goals. And ultimately if you find happiness you may find that you don't need a man in your life, or if you do find one he is simply an addition to a life well lived.

The Original World Famous Winner Dater's Workbook

It's time to get serious about reclaiming your self-esteem. Whatever your personal zenith was, whatever the time in your life where you were totally ruling, winning and firing on all cylinders—*that's where the answers are to reclaiming your self-worth.* That's where your self-esteem was the highest, when you were projecting that into the universe and having the most personal success. You have to go back to the point in your life where you felt the very best about yourself and figure out how you got there, what was going on for you then that isn't now and how to get yourself back into that space. To find a great relationship it's imperative that you of all people believe all the best things about yourself again and figure out why those beliefs went away in the first place. Seriously, if you don't feel them then why would anyone else be able to feel that about you?

Bust out your laptop, a notebook and cocktail napkin or whatever you can find. It's personal inventory time. Fill in the blanks in the most specific terms you can. Let's see if we can't go and find the super you!

1. When was the best period in your life?
2. What was going on that made it great?
3. What was different about you then?
4. How did you feel about yourself then?
5. When did things change and what changed?
6. How do you feel about yourself now?
7. What can you actively do to get back into that space?

Let's build on the good stuff you already have going for you

1. Why are you special?
2. What makes you different from everybody else?
3. Why are you a person of value that others should get involved with?
4. What are your best qualities?
5. What are your lovable flaws?
6. What are the tiny victories you're going to line up for yourself?

principle #2: get a life, have a life …

And Don't Give It Up For Every Tom, Dick And Agnes That Comes Along

Dating someone new is always exciting. The rush of feelings you get accompanied by the desire to spend every minute together basking in the yummy gooey feelings of "first like" are awesome. It's like you've entered this Utopian little existence where the two of you are in this bubble totally connected by these bursting emotions. You talk constantly, see each other daily, run home from work to get to him five minutes earlier, blow out your friends, go into work late, leave early, skip your yoga class and everything is great … until it all bites you in the ass. When you give up your life to devote all of your time and energy to a new romance you suffocate the other person. The feelings go from being "Wow, she's amazing" to "I can't get enough of her" to "She's a little needy and wants to spend every second with me" to "I can't get rid of her" to "How can I avoid her?"

You can feel the shift when someone is willing to give you all of their attention, and though at first it's flattering, shortly thereafter it becomes burdensome. It's those shifts that cause you to back off, or to have someone back off from you. We've all done it or felt it. People don't want you to give up your life for them, even if they think they do at the beginning. Those that do want you to give yourself up for them are the ones that later will stalk you.

Many dating books, experts, websites, crystal balls suggest that you appear busy, ignore phone calls, pretend you have plans and generally play a game called "I don't have time for you, please fall in love with me." And while this may appear like sound or at least strategically sound advice, it is ultimately encouraging you to start off your relationship by being dishonest and has the faint smell of something … what is it? Oh, right, manipulation. That's how all of the great love stories start, right? Wrong. So why does it seem like the game of "I don't have time for you, please fall in love with me" would work? Well, it has a certain logic to it, being that you are hard to get and thusly more desirable, and because everybody wants what they can't have it makes sense that if you're unavailable then they'll want you more. But pretending you have a life is just pure game-playing and misery. Well, then, what is your magnificent suggestion, guys? Ready? Wait for it

... GET A LIFE SO YOU WON'T HAVE TO PRETEND YOU HAVE ONE. Actually be busy. Have unbreakable plans with your friends because they are as important as your love life. Be on time for work because it matters to you. Don't bail on your responsibilities, family, dreams, values or well-being for the next Jett, Kingston or Maddox that comes along.

People like a little mystery. People like to get to know you over a period of time and they like to think about you and wonder what you might be doing. Wonder why you might have to leave early, why you like your job, why your friends are so important or why you're so close to your family and think, "Wow, she's got other priorities than me and a very cool life." Having a life that's important to you and not dumping your friends, job, plans, interests and current schedule for someone new will serve BOTH of you well.

You must have a life! A full one that does not stop every time a potential boyfriend or girlfriend comes into the fray. And if you don't have one you need to ask yourself why that is, and what the f*#k you're waiting for? Seriously. There are people that live lives that people admire and there are people that watch people live those lives. Why are you being a watcher instead of a doer? It's actually quite simple to get a life. For instance, let's say it's Thursday, and you don't have plans for Friday but you think the person you have your sights on might call to ask you out. The old you would have just waited to see if they called, then be disappointed if they didn't and have missed the boat on whatever opportunities you might have had besides a date. But the new you, being the doer that you are, will not sit by the phone but instead will make any variety of plans that will enrich your life or create an interesting experience to retell over coffee, like meeting up with old friends, trying a new restaurant, going to see a great new band at that club you've never been to or attending an art opening. By getting out in the world and doing things instead of waiting for someone to take you into their world you become a person who is living a fuller life. Are you not more interesting when you have experiences to share? Are you not more appealing if you have events to talk about? Are you not more fascinating if you have a valuable life instead of a disposable one?

People are attracted to winners and movement. We love and are inspired by people who move gracefully through this world with a sense of purpose. People who don't ask permission to live their lives but actually just do it regardless of what others think. When you have a full life, not only will you attract the things you want but you'll also still get to have the things you have.

BUT GREG, I HAVE QUESTIONS

But What If *His* Schedule is Hard To Work Around?

Dear Greg,

I've been going out with a guy for a couple of weeks who works a lot. He can't plan ahead that often for dates so I've been really cool about keeping my schedule open in case he can see me. My friends are getting all pissed off at me because I either won't commit to plans with them or bail to see the new guy. What's the trick to this sticky situation?

Clara

Notting Hill, England

Dear Calendar Girl,

Let me put it this way. I fly with a particular airline because I like them and they are dependable. However they don't wait for me to call to decide when they are going to fly. They have a schedule to keep so I fly only when it's right for both of us not just them. Sometimes I have to change my plans so I can catch a certain flight because I don't want to fly with anyone else. I also know that if I decide not to fly they are going to fly anyway and that doesn't mean they don't like me. It means they've got a job to do and that's why I fly them in the first place. Plus they are just a really sexy airline. Do you see where I'm going with this? You are the airline. You should keep your flights—that means plans with your friends and your own schedule—and he can come fly with you when he can but you aren't holding up the plane or your life for him. Because flying with you is better than flying any other airline and the right guy will figure that out.

But What If I'm Happy To Give Up My Life?

Dear Greg,

When I like someone, I like them a lot. I can't help the way I feel and I'm not going to deny myself all those great feelings when you like someone new and are completely inseparable. I'm happy to give up my life because what I get in return is worth the price. I'm guilty of smothering guys but I've been smothered too and it's not the worst way to figure out that you're not in the right thing. That's how I roll and it just makes sense to me that when I find the right guy we'll be all over each other and know we're in the right place when neither of us gets tired or smothered. That sounds like paradise to me. Every relationship is a gamble and I'm a girl with a stack of chips and a taste for gambling. So put that in your pipe and smoke it.

Brooke

Los Angeles, CA

Dear Smoking Aces,

Right on. Can't wait until your book comes out. Sounds like you and the guys you attract have a lot going for you.

P.S. The next time you smother someone do it with a pillow, that way they'll never go away.

What If Not Canceling My Plans Doesn't Work?

Dear Greg,

I went on this fabulous first date with a sports writer. This was on a Monday. I felt we really connected. We both like South Western cooking, the outdoors and especially camping. He actually said something like, "We should go camping sometime." Which I thought was both promising and sweet. So I said, "... let me check my schedule." We laughed about it. Two nights later her took me to a baseball game and the night after that we went dancing. Both times he brought up the camping thing, even saying maybe we could go that weekend. I told him I had a cousin who was having her baby shower but maybe the weekend after that. He said that he was going to be on the road and that this was the only chance he'd have for awhile. I told him I wasn't going to break my plans but would block out some time when he got back. He agreed but I never heard from him again. Did I blow it? I really liked him.

Emily
Pittsburg, PA

Dear Camp Emily,

You did blow it. Not only should you have told your cousin to shove it, you should have also quit your job, bought a tent and camped out in front of his place. No, you didn't blow it! You did exactly what you should have done, which is stick to your plans. You had already seen him three times that week. The fact that you never heard back makes me think that the sports writer just wanted to get you naked in a tent. Otherwise he would have gladly waited for the pleasure of your awesome company. Besides, how upset would you be had you disappointed your cousin, gone camping and then he never called again? Just keep doing what your doing, kiddo, because you're batting a thousand

What If He Has No Life?

Dear Greg,

Okay here's a tough one. I've been seeing this very cool guy for a little over a month. He did everything right, in fact he is just that into me. Ha! He calls, he shows up when he says he's going to, he's affectionate, he's interested in my work (I'm a barrister) and he likes my friends and family. So what's the problem? I feel so bad even writing this, but he's too available. I was so afraid he was going to be like so many guys I had dated before who weren't interested in my life, but this is just the opposite. He's almost too interested in my life, not only that but aside from his job (he's a systems analyst) he doesn't seem to have a life of his own. How do you tell someone to get a life? I don't want to ruin this. How do I fix it?

Cerys
Cardiff, Wales

Dear He's Just Too Into You

You just have to tell him the truth today because this is a relationship killer. Here's how you do it: you tell him all the good things you just told me about him and that this relationship has real potential, but in order for it to go the distance he shouldn't feel the need to devote so much time to you. Tell him that you'd love to do more things with his friends and family and that you also require a little alone time to recharge your battery. One of two things will happen: he will be excited at the possibility of bringing your two worlds together or you'll find out for sure that he has no other life. If the latter is true then you will have to tell him that your requirements for a great relationship include both people having a full life and that he's got to find other things in his life besides his job and you to bring him happiness. Hopefully he will understand. You may be doing him a giant favor but you have to be clear that this relationship will not work unless he does that. Sorry Hot Stuff, but it just won't.

FROM THE OTHER SIDE OF THE FENCE

Where Can I Find A Life?

Dear Greg,

I heard you on the radio the other day talking about getting a life but you didn't say exactly how one should do that. Here's my problem. I moved recently for work and within a week I met the girl who would become my girlfriend. We spent all kinds of time together but now I can tell she's getting kind of sick of me. I don't want to be that guy who has no life. The problem is I don't know anyone here except my boring office mates and most of my social life revolves around her. Help.

Burton
Roswell, GA

Dear This Boys Life,

Softball, guitar lessons, charity work—just do something. Look, moving is a big adjustment let alone adding a new relationship to the mix. So do some deep thinking. Get a piece of paper and write down all the things you have always wanted to try or do. Anything from starting a band to losing weight is an excuse to get you out the door and into the world. Plus don't be afraid to spend some time alone. Trust me, as a married father of two, I read your letter with a spot of envy. I love my life like no other, but there are days when I'd eat a bee's nest for a couple hours alone. Okay, that's not entirely true, but you get my meaning.

THE CHICK THAT BLEW IT

Sienna and I worked for the same Internet marketing company for about two years but I only ever spent time around her at company functions, retreats, team-building events, etc. ... Then I got promoted and ended up being in charge of her division. I thought, "Cool, now I'll get to know her better." So I asked her out and we went on a few dates that were great. I realized that I really liked her a lot and I wanted to see her all the time. I'd call her from business meetings and ask her to sneak out to meet me during work hours, but she wouldn't. It was delicious torture. We'd meet up after work a couple times a week but that was it. Her sister and she do dinner together on Tuesdays, she has Pilates on Thursdays, does her laundry and housekeeping on Sunday and had just signed up for a pottery class Saturday morning. She was pretty scheduled out so that didn't leave that much time for me. Finally a girl with a life of her own, how sexy is that? I was really getting into her and loved having to juggle my own schedule to match any openings she had. It made the time we did spend together really valuable. But then it's like she flipped a switch and just ditched everything to hang out with me all the time. She even blew off her Tuesday dinners with her sister and was just always there. All the things that made her so interesting and almost unattainable were just gone. I tried to hang in there but when she stopped doing all those things she stopped being the girl I was so attracted to and became totally dependent on me to fill her time. It was too much pressure and I bailed after three weeks.

Enzo

Berkeley, CA

IT WORKED FOR ME!

I spent years being unfulfilled by my life, my job, my boyfriends and my friend-friends. I just couldn't get everything in sync to a place where it all felt good instead of just okay. So now I'm here. I love my job and get great satisfaction from doing it well. I've narrowed down my friends to just the ones where the friendship is effortless, secure and supportive. I have a dog who keeps me busy and well loved and have my little rituals that I do, be it bubble baths, crossword puzzles, Sunday matinees with the girls or riding my bike to work once a week that make me feel pretty happy on a daily basis. Things felt better than good because I liked my life. So when Mitchell and I started dating I was really reluctant to give any of it up because I had worked so hard to find the perfect balance in my life. It was the first time ever that I wasn't trying to escape from my life into a relationship. But Mitchell not only didn't want me to give up my life, he liked that about me and even had his own that he didn't want to give up. What a concept! Because we both had lives that we liked we didn't just rush into spending all our time together and have really built our relationship slowly. The time we spend together is time we're dying to spend together because we have so much to tell each other and have had time (even if it's just been a day) to miss each other. It's the best-feeling relationship I've ever had and it's because my boyfriend is part of my life, not my life.

Gerilyn

Edmonton, Canada

FIRST PERSON SINGLE by Amiira

I like being alone, in fact I love it, so when I was single it was a great luxury for me to get to design my life around the basic parameters of work, friendships and spare time. Though I've never been one to go to the movies or dinner at a restaurant on my own (not because I was afraid to but because it never occurred to me) I was always up for a solo adventure in the city and found that I often preferred being alone to having plans. How antisocial, right? Maybe or maybe not ... The thing about having things that are important to you and that don't depend on anyone else's availability or interest is that you can fuel your life and happiness without others. That in my estimation is a very powerful thing to be able to do. I'm very in touch with what makes me feel good, less than good, powerful and pathetic. Filling my life with things, people, events, pastimes and hobbies of value made my life and my time valuable. It also made it something worth building on instead of scrapping every time I had a good date. Not only that, I didn't need a man in my life to make my life great and found quite a few of them actually just complicated and detracted from it, which was definitely not a bonus to what I already had going on. My advice to anyone who is living a life that they don't love is to change it! If you don't like your job, find another one that you will like. If you don't like your wardrobe, get creative and make it better (Project Runway anyone??). If you don't like your friends, the color of your apartment, the stuff you put in your fridge, the way you go to work, whatever the hell it is—it's up to you to improve it and mold it into something that you genuinely like. It's only when you get a good life, have a good life and maintain a good life that you'll find a man worth spending time away from it.

THOUGHTS FROM MAN CITY

I like the chase. I always have, the more challenging the course the more rewarding the catch. I don't care if it's an antiquated thought. And I believe it to be true for most men. When I've told women this they always respond with, "Well I don't want to come off like a bitch who doesn't have time for the guy I like." You don't have to be a bitch about it. There is a nice way of letting someone know your life matters to you. If I look back the great loves of my life they were always women who were self-possessed, confident and goal-oriented. They were women who challenged me. I remember I dated a painter who when she was working on a painting wouldn't see me until it was done. Sometimes that would take weeks. Weeks! If I were lucky she'd let me visit her at her bar-tending gig where she would make out with me for 10 minutes in the utility closet before sending me home. That's it. But I was fascinated with her. So why didn't it work with any of the other women? Because usually I'd end up giving my life away or being okay with seeing someone for only ten minutes a week in a utility closet. See, for a relationship to really work it has to be the coming together of two great very valued lives that over a period of time merge while staying true to who they are. It's great when we fall in love with you, but it's even better when we fall in love with your life as well.

DATING FORTUNE COOKIE

You are the architect of your own life, so build one that you love living in ... and put in a pool and a walk-in closet while you're at it.

WORST DATE EVER

Every year my girlfriends and I go to Las Vegas for our girls' weekend. I know it sounds a little corny but I love blackjack and a good martini. I'm not a big partier, I'm a lab tech at a veterinary hospital and I'm studying to be a vet. So needless to say I really look forward to our girls' getaway and last year was no exception, as my father had passed away and I really needed to do something fun. Well, about a week and a half before our big event I met Kurt when he brought his dog Cheech in for some x-rays. He was very handsome and talked to me like no man had spoken to me in some time. Since my divorce I've really spent the last few years working on myself and not really dating. Anyway I was pretty taken with him. He took my number and we talked on the phone every night. I even came into work late a few times because I'd only gotten off the phone hours before. He was all I could think about. He finally asked me out and I'll bet you can guess for when. Exactly, Greg! The same weekend as our Vegas trip. I told him I was so conflicted. He even said we could do it when I got back. I called my girlfriends and they all said the same thing. "He'll be here when you get back." That's why I'll never understand why I did what I did next ... I called him and told him I'd gladly break my plans to see him. Now that you know the deal you can only imagine how stupid I felt when he told me at dinner that he wanted to be clear that this was just a friend thing. A F@#%ING FRIEND THING! My girlfriend just now texts me that she's sitting next to Britney at the Palms—and he wants to be friends? How much worse does it get Greg? Trust me, I've learned my lesson.

IT'S JUST A F*#KING ART MUSEUM

It's all out there waiting for you, kid. Museums, gyms, friendships, charities, travel, etc. ... all you have to do is put one foot in front of the other. These are the things that make you attractive, these are the things that give you stories to tell on dates and this is the life that awaits you. It is the life you must have in order to be in a successful relationship, so start taking some risks. You are not going to love everything you try, but do it anyway because you never know who else has signed up for that formula one racing class.

The Original World Famous Winner Dater's Workbook

It's time for you to get a life—and if you already have one, it's time to make it an even fuller and more kickass one. We are put here on this planet to explore and enjoy it, so let's get you out into it and doing things so that next time you get asked out you'll have to check your schedule *for real*.

Make a list of things that you want to do and start scheduling them regularly so that you are getting the most out of your life while this time is still yours alone to use. We'll give you a few ideas to start but it's up to you to think of more, then go do them regularly.

List 5 things you'd like to do weekly

1. Take a yoga class
2. Do the Sunday Crossword puzzle
3. Take the dog on a walk
4.
5.

List 5 things you'd like to do every other week

1. See a movie
2. Wander around Primark for half an hour
3. Have dinner with a friend
4.
5.

List 5 things you'd like to do monthly

1. Get your car washed
2. Try a new restaurant
3. Take a tennis lesson
4.
5.

4

principle #3: pretty is as pretty does

What's The Message You're Sending To The World?

So as it turns out, this world here that we've been living in happens to be a visual medium. How totally random is that? Not random at all, actually. The reason we have eyes is to see the world around us and the people in front of us. To give our brains images and information so that it has things to process so that we can form opinions and ideas about what and who we see. But what does that mean in a dating book? Glad you asked, because we've been meaning to talk to you about this, and it's a bit awkward but … it's time to get real about what you're putting out into the world. We all have blind spots and don't necessarily see ourselves the way others see us, and we don't always care about the things that others care about. But the undeniable truth is that how you present—that means what you look like, how you're groomed, what you wear, how you smell, how you act and how you carry yourself—speaks volumes to those that we come in contact with. We know, we know ... people shouldn't be judged by the way they look but rather by what's on the inside. You're totally right and also totally in denial about how the world works.

Like it or not, men are visually stimulated creatures. Do you really think that when a guy sees two women; one of them styled out and groomed and feeling great, the other not particularly caring about what she looks like, that he thinks that the un-styled one must have a great personality? NO! He thinks the styled out girl might be interesting and the other one doesn't really care so why should he? It's not about being pretty, it's about telling the world that you care about yourself. There's a million different ways to style out and make the effort; not everybody has to look like Agyness Deyn. And not looking like Agyness Deyn isn't a good excuse to not care how you look.

Here are a few things to keep in mind ...

FEELING PRETTY IS PRETTY

If you know that plucking your eyebrows and shaving your legs make you feel prettier, then do it! If shaving your legs opens up your wardrobe to wearing skirts more often, then do it! Maybe you don't wear make-up because it adds time to your morning routine but when you do wear mascara and lip gloss you look prettier, more notice-able and carry yourself with a little more sparkle. Men notice sparkle! So take the extra five minutes and then you won't have to wait until you're stuck in an elevator during a city-wide blackout for someone to take an inter-est in getting to know you.

DON'T FORGET YOU'RE A WOMAN

Men like you to look nice and smell good otherwise they don't get to be distracted from their stupid problems when you walk by. They like to see your legs, catch a glimpse of your cleavage, watch you brush your hair away from your eyes and, most of all, *they like to know that you know that you're a sexual being.* Any hint of sexuality or sensuality is golden with men.

... BUT NOT A PROSTITUTE

Men want to see your body BUT not too much of your body! Do you know what we're talking about? There's a difference between making an effort to style out with your appearance and dressing *too sexy.* Some outfits tell a guy "Hey, it's cool to call me at 4 a.m." and others say "You are going to have to work for it if you want to be a part of this spectacularness!" Yes, spectacularness is a new word.

DATING ALERT!

Dressing too sexy is a very real problem for a lot of women trying to attract someone that wants to *date* them. It's a fine line between dressing provocatively and dressing too sexy. When you fall on the side of too sexy you attract guys that just want to get laid and think you're the gal for the job. How can you tell if you're being too sexy? Well, are you revealing *all* of your physical assets? Is there enough skin to shock your father? That may be too sexy. Unless you're on stage performing at the Grammys, a burlesque show or in a Vegas chorus line, you needn't give away the North *and* the South poles. We suggest you choose a sexy part to feature instead of showcasing them all. Do you know how much sexier you are if a guy has to imagine what might be under those clothes? If he can see it, he doesn't have to imagine it, which means he's not getting the opportunity to really think about you.

IT'S NOT *JUST* ABOUT YOUR BODY

Take a good look at your life. What does the state of your car say about you? Is it clean and orderly or can you write your name in the dirt and make a killing with the recycling in the back seat? What does your home look like? Is it cluttered, messy and reeking of old take-aways or is it clean, organized and an inviting space to be in? What does the top of your desk at work look like? The reason we ask you to look at these things and take an honest inventory about what state they're in is because all of those things— your appearance, your home, your car, your dress, your office—all these things tell someone not only what your life looks like but who you think you are and whether or not you value and like yourself. That's what people are going to base their opinions of you on, whether what you're projecting is an accurate representation or not. If the guy of your dreams walked into your apartment would he be impressed to see the piles of stuff on every surface and seventy-five framed pictures of your ex-boyfriend? Would super-handsome bachelor #1 be turned on by your teddy bear collection and candyfloss pink sheets? Would your dreamboat delight in the idea of canoodling on a sofa covered in cat hair? How would it make you feel if you had a great date then he walked in to your home, took a look around and decided that he didn't like your life? Everyone's sofa tells a story. What's your sofa saying? So with that said, what is it that you could be doing better? What is it that you need to change or work on?

This is a really hard chapter to write because no one wants to tell another human being that they're not good enough as is. And that's not the message of this chapter because we do think you're good enough as is, but if you're reading this book it's because you're having trouble finding the right guy that echoes that same sentiment.

It's hard enough to find each other in this world, so step up your game so that the message you project is "I might be the one" instead of "don't notice me" or even the popular trend of "I'm easy to get in the sack." We know you are smart, funny, cool, loyal, dorky, successful, compassionate, great in bed and all the other things that are important to be and, yes, that should be enough to find the right guy. And we agree that in a perfect world we all have laser beam vision or retinal scans where we can see into each other's hearts, souls and minds and find each other that way, but until that technology is perfected you're going to have to make the effort the old-fashioned way. What if the right guy for you can't find you among the sea of other women that don't try to stand out to him? Then what happens?

The image you project is important. Think about it … They don't make James Bond movies about a guy in flip-flops.

BUT GREG, I HAVE QUESTIONS

What If The Thing I'm Putting Out There Attracts The Wrong Guys?

Dear Greg,

So after my last breakup I really took stock and realized that while I hadn't picked the greatest guy around I also had some areas that needed work. So I joined a gym, got a new apartment and started seeing a therapist. My old boyfriend used to complain that I wasn't sexy enough and in retrospect I have to agree. I was overweight and dressed dowdy but now that I'm slimmer I've started to dress sexier. I even highlighted my hair blonde. I definitely feel pretty great about my transformation but now the problem I'm having is that when I go to clubs, bars and the like I always get the guys that want to only have sex with me. What's a girl to do, Greg?

Portia

Stockholm, Sweden

Dear Stocks and Blondes,

First, I hope you can see that I'm holding up a huge banner that says Portia Kicks Ass! I applaud your very smart response to the dissolution of your last relationship. It's so great to hear someone acknowledge her part in a breakup. Yes, he was the wrong guy but I love that you were interested in what you could be doing better. Now it's just a matter of refinement. Look, since I have no idea what you look or dress like, let me just say this. There is sexy (Eva Mendes, Gwen Stefani, Beyoncé, Sophia Lauren) and there's "What time is the porn shoot?" I'm all for personal freedom in dress, but try and understand what you are putting out into the world. If you just wanna get laid then rock the house. But if that's not what you're going for, and I assume it's not, then ask a good friend. "Is this dress gynecologically short?" or "How much of my nipple is too much?" Look in magazines and find looks you like and try and replicate them. At the very least it's your right to tell men "Hey, if you want to see more you're going to have to work a lot harder than that. This is the trailer for a movie that opens in a month."

But What If I'm Not Pretty?

Dear Greg,
I am no Angelina Jolie. You can dress me up, put me in hair and makeup and I'll look fine, but as soon as the "costume" comes off you are stuck with plain old ugly me. So why should I pretend to be what I am not ... pretty? At least this way men know what they're getting so they are not disappointed later.
Danica
Perth, Australia

Dear Costume Party,
Whatever works for you, Danica, but what doesn't work for me is how you feel about yourself. My guess is makeup or no you are not a lot of fun to be around. We all look different without our hair gel, good pants, makeup or whatever. I think it's generally understood that most people don't look as good wet from the shower as they do when they arrive at the party, but that's not what people respond to. People don't fall in love with or even want to ask out your eyeliner, they simply notice you because you wore it, but your winning (read: not surly) attitude is what makes them like you.

But What If I'm Stylistically Impaired?

Dear Greg,

I know I'm supposed to style out more, I get that, but I hate shopping and I have no sense of style. Seriously even if I had all the money in the world I'd just buy jeans and sweats. Where I live polar fleece is as fashionable as anything else. I have a decent body but I'm not a girly girl and I'm lost in a department store. It bums me out because I know what you are saying about looks and personal presentation mattering, but I am clueless in this area.

Kendra

Seattle, WA

Dear Styleless In Seattle,

Man I wish I could help you, but I can't because I don't live near you—but you know who does? The jillions of people employed by department stores and other such establishments whose sole purpose is to help you find something to wear. There are people in hair salons, gyms, yoga studios and makeup counters whose whole lives are dedicated to making you look and feel better. So ask for help from people who can help you. Maybe you have a real stylish friend who would just jump at the chance to rock the mall with you. And do some research, look through one of those glossy fashion magazines or music magazines and start tearing out things you respond to. Even if you are not a girly girl there is something called Tomboy Chic. Avril Lavigne anyone? Get going, kiddo.

But What If The Image I'm Trying To Project Is Eclipsed By My Wheelchair?

Dear Greg,

Hey smart guy. Here's a question for you. I am paralyzed from the waist down so obviously I'm in a wheelchair. I'm a very positive person and a super fun hang but let's get real, I am definitely at a disadvantage in the looks department just by virtue of my situation. It's hard to get psyched to go out when you won't even be a consideration in the first place. What does a girl like me do?

Violet

Baltimore, MD

Dear Wheels Of Steel,

I would give the same advice to you as I would give to anyone else. What is the most rocking version of you? How do you look best? What's the coolest chair you could have? Have you changed your hair lately? I can't begin to imagine what your life is like but I'm guessing you have to work harder in all areas of your life and dating is for sure going to be one of them that will require the same hard work. I have in my travels met and seen some very foxy wheelchair-bound ladies so I know it's possible to achieve, and here's another thing to think about—all that is the easy stuff, as you've already done the hard work by being so positive.

FROM THE OTHER SIDE OF THE FENCE

What If The Girl Of My Dreams Is Beautiful But Her Life Is A Mess?

Dear Greg,

So dude I've been seeing this girl for a couple of weeks now. She is really hot. I mean f&*king Maxim magazine hot. But there's something about her that bums me out. The first few times we went out I drove but then last Friday she wanted to take me out so we took her car. Greg, it was a dump on wheels. Seriously, I've never seen so much crap in a car—it's like she's homeless and I don't mean that to be mean. I even asked her if she really had an apartment. Then I began to notice other stuff, stuff like her re-wearing the same skirt three days in a row even when it had a stain on it. Look I'm no neat freak but I actually pulled gum out of her hair the other day. The thing is she's really funny and I'm falling for her but I'm afraid when I see her apartment I'm going to want to run. Advice bro?

Travis

Nome, Alaska

Dear Gum Picker,

Wow, I feel you, man. I had a similar situation with a girl I dated right after college. Your instincts about her apartment are probably right on. Her car is telling you not only what her apartment may look like but really the inside of her head. The two things I can tell you are: do not overlook this hoping it will just go away; and you can't change another person—they will only change when they want to. Because you are a good guy your instinct is probably to rush in there and save this beautiful disaster, but you can't. The best thing you can do, and I know this will be hard, is tell her you think her car is too messy. You can offer to help her clean it. But if you are really connecting with her, tell her it bums you out and you can't hang with it. That may be the wake-up call she has been needing.

THE GUY THAT BLEW IT AND THE CHICK THAT ROCKED IT

Jules and I have been friends for five and a half years. She's my best girl friend, she's like a sister to me and we hang out all the time. We go to clubs together, rock shows, movies, you name it we do it and she's always my "Wing Man", helping me pick up chicks and telling them how great a guy I am. So about three weeks ago when we were out she met this guy that she liked and the next thing you know she's completely changed the way she looks. This is a girl who has never worn a dress in the five plus years that I've known her and now she's in dresses and high heels. She's wearing cute little Natalie Portman outfits, wearing makeup, wearing her hair down and she's HOT! Like really hot. Like not the same person hot. Now I like her differently and I'm jealous that she's dressing up for some other guy and not me. I've never even thought about Jules and I being together but now it's all I can think about. She's already my best friend so it's not like I only like her for her looks but I just see her so differently now that it makes me feel differently about her. I think I'm in love with my best friend now and she's hot for someone else.

Joey

Glendale, AZ

IT WORKED FOR ME

You can go ahead and say, "I told you so" because you were right. The way you look matters. There, I said it. I was one of those too-cool-to-care-how-I-looked girls that wanted to prove the world wrong by not trying to make myself look pretty to get the guy. So I slugged out that brilliant plan for a few years and suffered about a million disappointments when the guys I liked only liked me as a friend. So I decided to do a little experiment and change one thing about what I wear and one thing about how I look. So instead of wearing loose-fitting jeans and a loose-fitting t-shirt I started wearing a cute and better fitting (not super tight!) tank top. Instead of wearing no makeup I started wearing lipgloss. Almost immediately guys started responding differently. So then I started wearing better fitting jeans with my cuter tops and wearing mascara and a little eyeliner. Now guys that didn't give me the time of day were giving me free coffee at the coffee shop and totally flirting with me. And I not only like how I look and how looking prettier makes me feel, but I also still feel like me. It's not like I had to radically change who I am and become some hoochie to get a guy's attention. I just feel like a cuter version of me that's still being me and it only takes like a few minutes more to look AND FEEL good. I truly didn't think a tube of lipgloss and better fitting clothes would make any difference but I was wrong because I feel different and people see me differently and, all in all, I'm happier now.

Mallory

Puerto Vallarta, Mexico

FIRST PERSON SINGLE by Amiira

I met Greg Behrendt three times before I really noticed or remembered him, even though he always remembered me. The first time was at a party and I was decked out all cute, the second time I was at a music convention for work so I was kind of hipstered out, but the third time I met Greg was at a hair salon on a weekday morning at 10 a.m. Now when going to a hair salon for a cut and color on weekday morning at 10 a.m. you don't usually shower since you're about to get your hair washed anyway. You also don't usually worry about your attire as you will be changing into a robe upon arrival or draped in a smock. So here I am, rolling into the salon on a day off from work unshowered and kicking it casual, because it's not like I'm going to be seeing anyone I know—it's a work day, right? Nope. I'm there for all of five minutes before I feel someone staring at me. I look up and see Greg Behrendt's smiling face and he says, "Hey, I know you." I don't recognize him (again) so he explains how I had come to a party at his house with a mutual friend and then how we had met again in Seattle at the Bumbershoot festival. So we exchange pleasantries and are chatting away and I'm thinking that he's pretty funny and easy to talk to. Well, since we were both getting highlights in our hair we both spent hours at the salon. Sometimes sitting side by side under hair dryers while our colors processed, others separated by the distance between our respective hairdressers' workstations. Now take a moment to picture me (not that he was any different or better): I've got my hair separated into sections and wrapped in foil, a clear shower cap over the foils with cotton balls unrolled and placed along my front hairline and I'm draped in a black nylon smock that comes down to my knees. So basically my feeling hot factor wasn't off the charts and I was carrying some pretty severe aesthetic obstacles. But because I don't ever leave the house unless I feel a little cute (because who wants to go into the world losing from the get go?) I had taken the time to put on a little mascara and lipgloss and from the waist down my outfit had some personality. So between having a little cuteness in my holster which gave me some confidence that I might not have had in that situation combined with a healthy dose of conversation and "get to know you time" and *despite* having with my hair in foils, covered in a shower cap while sitting under a hair dryer wearing a black nylon smock, he asked me to come see him do standup later that night.

THOUGHTS FROM MAN CITY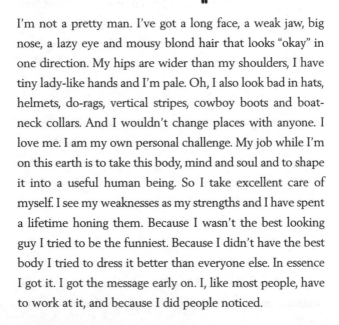

I'm not a pretty man. I've got a long face, a weak jaw, big nose, a lazy eye and mousy blond hair that looks "okay" in one direction. My hips are wider than my shoulders, I have tiny lady-like hands and I'm pale. Oh, I also look bad in hats, helmets, do-rags, vertical stripes, cowboy boots and boat-neck collars. And I wouldn't change places with anyone. I love me. I am my own personal challenge. My job while I'm on this earth is to take this body, mind and soul and to shape it into a useful human being. So I take excellent care of myself. I see my weaknesses as my strengths and I have spent a lifetime honing them. Because I wasn't the best looking guy I tried to be the funniest. Because I didn't have the best body I tried to dress it better than everyone else. In essence I got it. I got the message early on. I, like most people, have to work at it, and because I did people noticed.

We, as in we men, notice you. We notice what you look like, we notice what you wear, we notice when you're laughing, we notice when you care about yourself. We notice when you take the time to look good and we love it when you do. When you don't take the time, when you don't put the effort into how you look, then usually we don't notice you. It's as simple as that.

DATING FORTUNE COOKIE

You don't have to be pretty to be attractive.

ONE OF GREG'S WORST DATES EVER

When I first moved to San Francisco after college I met this beautiful girl who lived on my block. She was a playwright and waitress. I asked if she wanted to go for a late cup of coffee one night. She agreed and asked if I'd stop by her place to pick her up. I arrived when she asked me to at nine o'clock and she came to the door in a robe saying she'd just woken from a nap. She invited me in and said she wouldn't be a moment. He apartment was a mess—and when I say that I don't mean mess in the traditional sense of busy young bohemian with a lot on her plate messy, I mean indoor junkyard "are those eyeballs in those jars?" messy. I mean "what's that smell and does it have its own driver's license?" messy. And I kid you not, she walked down the hall in her robe and picked up the panties that were lying on the floor by a soiled plate and slid them on. This is before we've had a formal hello. Now, look, I didn't expect every person I dated to feel the same way about hygiene as me. I wasn't even a neat freak back then, but this was a lot to ask a person you don't know to be okay with. I got a peek into her world that I wasn't ready for. I judged her because of it and I'll tell you why, most of the people I know who live like that are really sad and messed up and I saw it as a warning sign. The fact that I think she forgot we were even supposed to go out made our first date our last. Wherever she is now I hope at least she has some clean underwear.

IT'S JUST A F*#KING PULLING IT TOGETHER

Look, you really can't argue against looking better regardless of what your version of you looking good is. Yes, it takes a little effort but so does practically everything else in life that's worth having. Besides, when you look good, you feel good, and when you feel good, you attract good things. But more importantly, when *you* think you're worth the effort and you make the effort—so will others. Try it our way and see if you don't agree. There is a fantastic version of you in there and we want to see it go on a date. Even at the end of the day (date or no date) you still honored yourself and pulled yourself together so it wasn't a complete loss.

The Original World Famous Winner Dater's Workbook

Have you ever had a friend tell you, "I'm doing everything I can but I'm just not finding anyone" but when you look at them you know they're not doing everything they can? They might be overweight, they might not be a good listener, they might have stinky breath and bad manners. In essence you know what their problem is and if you had the guts you'd tell them, but you don't want to hurt their feelings or upset them. We've all been there. Now we're asking you to turn that mirror on yourself and be honest about it ... could you use a mint?

1. Do you put the time into your appearance that you should?
2. Is the image you project to the world one that says, "I'm worth getting to know?"
3. What could you be doing better to make yourself more interesting to the people you want to attract?
4. What is it that you need to change or work on?

Once you've truthfully answered these questions you'll be able to see where you need improvement to better yourself and your chances for attracting the guy that's been out there looking for you. So get your act together, shave your legs, pluck your brows, put on some heels and let them know you're here!

principle #4: don't accept less than an actual date

Stop Selling Yourself Short!

There are dates ... and then there are things that appear to be dates, feel like dates or even have elements of a date but **ARE NOT** dates. We know you know what we're talking about because that's what you and your friends have been settling for, then trying (unsuccessfully) to parlay into a relationship. So unless you're having a yard sale where you're selling yourself short, as of now you will not be going on NOT-dates, quasi-dates, half-assed dates or semi-sort of couldabeen dates ever again. (*This includes hooking up, hanging out, drunken make-outs, group gatherings, tagging along or talking all night at a party or bar.*) Why, you ask? Well there are many reasons so we'll give you a few: because a date signifies an intent that is clear for both parties, because a date infers that you have a busy and exciting life that would require scheduling to fit someone new in, and how about the best reason of all which is that *It's Just A F*#king Date and you deserve to be asked on one*! Quite honestly, if some guy isn't motivated enough to ask you out, and you've given him the opportunity and encouragement to do so, he doesn't deserve to get to hang out or hook up with you. Simple as that.

We're aware that most of you are less likely to get asked out on a date than asked to hang out. The quasi-date is vastly popular with guys for obvious reasons. Hanging out doesn't require an actual plan and is a more nebulous proposition. But with a hang-out you don't actually know if you're on a date and of course there's the possibility that you may end up going "Dutch" to said unnamed hang-out destination. There may or may not be other people involved in the hang and it's often at one's house where there's a bedroom nearby and you know what that means. Actually you don't because when hanging out leads to having sex you still don't know where you stand. Does it mean that now you're dating because you had sex on your hang-out? Or are you now the girl that he gets to have sex with without the pesky process of having to get to know you? Enough already—Just stop it!

We're not suggesting that you stop living your life spontaneously or veto advances from cute boys, but it's up to you to be clear about the kind of woman you are. The key to finding a great relationship is to stop settling for less. You get to set the value of your time and company— not anybody else—and by participating in less than an actual date you set your value low. The longer you deval- ue yourself the longer others will too. Here's the wildly obvious secret that you should remind yourself of daily— guys like hanging out, hooking up, getting it on and mak- ing out BUT it means more to them if they have to earn it. That's just part of their nature. Hell, it's a part of human nature!

By partaking in this lame epidemic of Non-Dating, you are positively reinforcing that the lack of effort is good enough for you; that not stepping up to the plate, putting your ass on the line, declaring your attraction and treating a woman right will be greatly rewarded. Constant reward- ing for minimal effort over time equals the poor state of dating today. Women are as responsible as men for Non- Dating and it's time for you to demand more of yourself and the men you choose. This is why we say Don't Settle For Less Than An Actual Date And Stop Selling Yourself Short.

However, because we're realists, we know that a casu- al invitation to hang out or join a pre-existing event is the safest way for a guy to gauge your interest in him. Therefore we're not going to hold the hard line that says you absolutely under no uncertain circumstances should EVER hang out or join a preplanned event for others if you ARE interested in someone. But what we do say is there's a strategy for how to do it right. You must set limits, be very clear that *it's not a date* and have a clear exit strategy. By setting limits we mean:

✓ Make this a one-time thing. You hanging out once is plenty reinforcement that you're interested; the next time he sees you should be when he's asked you on a date.

✓ No hanky panky. Not to be too prudish but if he gets the prize without the effort he won't make the effort. Yours is an exclusive club and memberships don't come that easily.

✓ Leave the room early. The one-time hang-out is like a trailer of a movie. This is a preview of all the things they'd get to see if they paid the price of admission, which is asking you out on a date.

Example: John tells you that he and the guys are meeting over at Skee-lo's Sportatorium to get a few pitchers and watch the World Series and that you should come.

Low Self-Esteem Laura would drop by, drink a few beers, get a buzz on and watch the game then head off with him for a bite afterwards then back to his place for a make-out party and/or drunken sex.

But Super Winner Dater Stella might drop by on her way elsewhere, watch the game with John and the guys over a beer. Then when the game is over excuse herself to get back to her previously scheduled plans (and very full life). When asked if she wants to grab a bite she will flash her flirtiest smile and let him know that she can't tonight but if he'd like to ask her out to dinner another time she'd love to go on a date with him. Then give him a little hug or a kiss on the cheek, wave goodbye to his friends and turn on her heel and exit with all eyes on her.

After that kind of exit strategy a rocking lady would be way more likely to get asked out on a date than had she woken up at his house hung-over and trying to find her shoes. Look, if you just want to have casual sex or be the kissing bandit when you're hopped up on Margaritas, then hooking up, hanging out and quasi-dates is fine. But then why are you reading this book? Busted!

The point of this book is to redefine how you date if you're looking for a serious relationship. Rare is the couple that turns the hook-up into a fifty-year marriage. Common is the couple that turns the hook-up into a six-month relationship that fizzles out because one of them realizes they never really wanted to be in the relationship in the first place. It is the most common outcome of the relationship started from anything other than absolute intention—one realizes that they were never really into it. Let's be honest about these non-dating relationships ... women generally think that if they're agreeable to less than dating and they ride it out that it will eventually lead to something more serious. Whereas many guys think that if women are agreeable to less than dating that it's the shortcut to having sex without the responsibility of a relationship. See the difference? So when these relationships, built on an imbalanced foundation of hope for her and sex for him, falls apart it's generally the hopeful party that it really sucks for.

That's why the fourth Super Extraordinary Principle for Ultra Successful Winner Dating is Don't Accept Less Than An Actual Date And Stop Selling Yourself Short if what you're looking for is a serious relationship. That means no more hooking up, hanging out and quasi-dating. Take a stand and read on, because we're going to show you how to get guys to ask you out and how to change the way you date. After all, It's Just A F*#king Date and you deserve to be asked out on one!

BUT GREG, I HAVE QUESTIONS

But What If Dating's Too Much Pressure?

Dear Greg,
Why can't I just hang out? Why does it have to be so official? It's not the Age Of Innocence where you have to marry me before you get in my corset. Hanging out is a much easier way to get to know someone because there's no pressure, where dating is like going on a job interview.
Amanda,
Marina Del Rey, CA

Dear Job Applicant,
It doesn't have to be official if you like things vague or are just looking for a good time. But if not you have to ask yourself why you don't want to be clear about it? Besides, what kind of guy can't handle the pressure of a date? Can I get him a cold compress while he lies down? Most women think that by asking for some level of certainty about a man's interest, i.e. a date, will scare him off. But to begin editing what you want for fear it might scare someone off or molding yourself into something different to accommodate another's reluctance to

step up is a losing and dishonest approach. Look, it makes sense to not run a formal agenda past a person we've just met, but it doesn't make sense to not be clear with yourself about what you want or what you're worth. Men will be as vague as you let them be, so it's up to you to decide what level of ambiguity works for you.

But What If He's Too Shy To Ask Me Out?

Dear Greg,

In my circle of friends there's this guy that I've been hanging out with that I really like. His friends tell me he likes me too but he's really shy and never asks girls out, he just hangs around until the girl makes the first move, then they're boyfriend and girlfriend. Every relationship he's ever had has started like this, so how do you get the shy guy to ask you out when the closest he's ever come is, "Is this seat taken?"

Hannah
Dublin, Ireland

Dear Shy By Night,

   Oh goodie, the shy guy question! The rules are no different for the shy guy. If he has the ability to be in a relationship with other people, certainly he has the ability to ask you out. Next time he approaches you at a friend-fest and asks the magical question, "Is this seat taken?" Tell him, "I'm saving it for the guy that's going to ask me out tonight. Is that you?" If he can't manage to nod yes to that, then you have to ask yourself if he's really the kind of guy you envision yourself in a relationship with.

But What If I've Already Had Sex With Him?

Dear Greg,

   I met this guy at a friend's BBQ who was really good looking but not boyfriend material. We flirted the whole time then ended up hooking up. It was just a sex thing the first couple of times but now that I know him better I'd really like to date him for real. I've made a few jokes about us going on a date but he never asks me out, he only offers to bring over a pizza. We obviously get along well and he knows the sex is good so why won't he ask me out? Have I blown it?

   Elle

   Melbourne, Australia

Dear BBQ-ed,

We never know at first how we're going to feel about someone new, but we do know the difference between thinking you might want to be in a relationship with someone vs. thinking you might want to go skinny dipping with them. But certainly you have the right to change your mind once you've gotten to know a person. However, by hooking up on day one and positioning it as a casual sleep-around thing you limit the way he perceives you. Guys tend to compartmentalize things and booty calls and potential girlfriends are two different compartments. The only way to shift gears is to reposition yourself as something other than a booty call. When he calls you have to be unavailable for a booty call but offer an opening for Sunday morning if he'd like to take you to brunch. He won't see you as anything other than the girl he has casual sex with unless you make him. That means that you have to take away the casual sex and that's generally not a well-received development in the booty call dynamic. It's really hard to go from having sex to holding hands, because once you've had the dessert, breakfast doesn't seem so appetizing.

What If In College All You Did Was Hang Out?

Dear Greg,

In college there is no real "dating", it's a much more casual process. People hang out in groups in the dorms, pair off, hook up at fraternity parties and generally do everything but date. All my past relationships started that way and it's hard to really get into the mode of one-on-one dating when it seems almost archaic compared to what's worked for me, what I'm used to and what's actually happening in the dating world. Why is a real date such a big deal and how does one make the leap to dating, let alone get the men to do the same?

Kila

Cambridge, MA

Dear Dorm-ed if you do and Dorm-ed if you don't,

Hey, I went to college so I get it. But the post-collegiate world calls for you to make some adjustments in your lifestyle. In college you go to keg parties at fraternity houses and wear your pyjama bottoms to class, but your boss probably wouldn't think you to be quite an impressive lady if you rocked your PJs to work or showed up at the office party with a beer bong. You adapt to your environment and surroundings so that you can win, and dating is no different. Real dates are a big deal because they let prospective guys know that your time is precious and you don't have the time to hang out, so if they want to get involved with you they gotta work on your schedule and within the framework of your life. It puts you in the driver's seat and makes you seem like a huge f*#king prize! Plus, dating can be awesome. And in case they didn't teach you this in college—guys like the girl who is the huge f*#king prize! The how-to is simple, just keep a few key phrases locked and loaded. Like "If I had time to hang out I'd be spending it with my friends, but I would consider having dinner with you if you want to ask me on a date" or "Are you asking me on a date? Because I'm not into hanging out, but if this is a date, I'd like to go."

FROM THE OTHER SIDE OF THE FENCE

Why Should I If I Don't Have To?

Dear Greg,

Why should I ask girls on a date when I don't have to? Dating costs money and won't get me any more laid than I can already get not dating.

The Anonymous Asshole at the bar down the street,

Your Town

Dear Ass-hat,

Dude, you shouldn't ask anyone out EVER. Dating is for guys who like women and themselves; clearly you don't. But to be fair, the women who go out with you either A) Just want to get laid (nothing wrong with that) or B) Don't value themselves any more than you do so it's a perfect match. For me asking women out and pursuing them was one of the greatest pleasures in life. Hopefully someday you will meet a girl you really like who you will have to ask out because she accepts no less and you will come to understand the pleasure of dating an awesome chick!

THE GUY THAT BLEW IT AND THE CHICK THAT ROCKED IT

I'm all about hooking up or any form of not dating that I can get away with. The only exception to my not dating policy was if there was a dance or function that I needed a date for. Then and only then would I actually call someone in advance and book a date, everything else was as casual as casual gets. You can believe me when I tell you that there are plenty of girls that I could get to hang out any night of the week. Then I met Rebecca at a friend's party. Rebecca was different, she wasn't the most beautiful girl I'd ever seen but there was something about her. I tried every approach in the book. I talked to her, flirted with her, offered to drive her home, walk her home, take her home, get her a drink, take her outside for some "air", see if she wanted to hit another party, everything. She was nice, she was confident and she was definitely out of my league. Nothing happened that night or the next few times we were at the same parties. Finally I asked her what I had to do to spend some time with her. Her answer was, "You'd have to ask me out on a date." Here's where I blew it—I asked her back, "What kind of date?" She laughed and said, "It's not going to work. You're just a boy and I date men." I must have tried a dozen times after that to ask her on a date but she never would go out with me. Then I met her new boyfriend and I asked him, "How'd you get Rebecca to go out with you?" Get this, he said, "I asked her out." I still keep things casual with most girls but when I meet one that I might really like ... I don't even try to get her to hang out with me, I just straight up ask her on a date. Know what? Asking a girl out on a date actually makes me feel like more of a George Clooney super-suave kind of guy. Like I'm the shit. I don't know why but it just does.

Patrick
Newark, NJ

IT WORKED FOR ME!

For years I've been the most accommodating and least demanding potential date for every guy I've shared a decent conversation, drunken kiss or romp in the hay with. I've always thought if I wanted to actually be taken on a date instead of just hanging out that guys would think I was high maintenance and not want to be with me. So basically I was agreeable to all forms of not dating. None of these "relationships" (and I use that term very loosely) ever lasted very long and a lot of times I was the only one that even thought it was sort of a relationship. I was starting to feel really crappy about men and myself, plus I was at the point where I was wondering what was wrong with me. I hadn't been asked on a date in over six years. Then I met this guy I really liked who had a girlfriend, so obviously I didn't do anything other than talk to him the few times we came across each other. But I always thought that he was the kind of guy I'd like to go out with. Cut to six months later after I've taken a vow in front of my best friend and a Margarita that from now on I'm *only* going out on dates—I run into him. After catching up and finding that he and his girlfriend are no longer he says that we should hang out some time. The old me would have agreed and hoped he even remembered to text me, but the new improved vow-in-front-of-a-Margarita me said, "I'm not really a hanger-outer. But I bet if you asked me on a date I'd say 'Yes'." Not only did I completely surprise myself with how ballsy I was, but for the first time in six years I felt really good about myself. And you know what? He asked me out right there on the spot, told me he liked my confidence and has continued to ask me out for the last three months. So I'm here to say that being the kind of gal that doesn't accept less than a date really works!

Kristie

Taos, NM

FIRST PERSON SINGLE by Amiira

I used to like hanging out with guys because it seemed so much easier and less formal than dating … except when I really liked someone and realized that it's not easy at all. In fact it's completely consuming with the whole fuzzy nebulous "what are we doing, how can I turn this into a date and how can I tell if he really likes me?" thoughts that overtake your brain. It's having enough of those experiences and also, if I'm being honest, reaching a level of maturity that makes you not like hanging out anymore. Or at least that's how it was for me. Many of my relation-ships started as hanging out then became something more but I have to be clear that I was kind of a prudish hang. I didn't do a lot of messing around or sleeping around. I wasn't a girl you were going to score with easily because I had downed a few wine coolers, because even drunk I would rather talk to a cute boy about his record collection than have my tongue down his throat. I don't know why that is and certainly there are some boys that I should have had sex with. But as I got older and became clearer about who I was and what kind of people I wanted in my life—be it friends, business associates or boyfriends—I found myself detaching from people that were cloudy about their lives. It's almost a cliché but some days you just wake up and don't want your relationships to be so difficult, delicate or tenuous. In this period of moving through life with real direction and clarity, an interesting thing happened. I started getting asked out on dates by guys that had their shit together as well as being asked to hang out by guys that had girlfriends, local bands, no ambition and bad reputations. So I went on actual dates and declined the hang-out invitations. A funny thing hap-pened then ... the hang-outers started asking me on dates too when I wouldn't hang out with them. I had a dating renaissance and it rocked. Not because every date was spectacular or even good, but because I was clear about what his and my intentions both were when going on the date. Clarity about who I am, how valuable my time is and how I date became my compass, and ultimately led me to the right man for me.

THOUGHTS FROM MAN CITY

I don't speak for all men, I can only speak for me and about the conversations I've had with my buddies. My experience was always that if I didn't have to put a name on it, I didn't. Meaning if a lady would let me just hang out or drop by or rock the booty call, I would. If I could just meet her out with her friends, have a couple of drinks and go back to her place, that was great. But it was *never* something I was serious about. Then if she happened to mention to someone that we were dating I would always be surprised because I thought that we were just hanging out WHICH IS NOT DATING. Dating to me has always implied a seriousness and an intent to pursue a relationship. It only really happened when I was really taken with someone so much that I was willing to work for it. However I was on the opposite side of it as well, where I was with a girl who really never wanted to do anything but hang out and have sex. Sounds ideal, right? It would have been if I hadn't liked her so much and wanted more.

Here's the truth about men: Men want to have relationships too, and when we do, we act like it and ask you on dates.

 DATING FORTUNE COOKIE

You determine your worth. If a non-date is what you will settle for, then a non-date is all you will get.

WORST DATE EVER

I met this totally awesome guy while I was interning at a law firm in San Francisco. He was this hot blond bartender named Taylor who worked at the yuppie pub down the street from my office. I worked long hours and usually stopped in to say "Hi" during last call. I could tell he liked me because I don't think I paid for a drink but maybe one time. Sometimes I would hang out with him and the rest of the bar staff after closing hours and we'd usually end up making out. After about a month of this I remember thinking how awesome it was to kind of have a boyfriend. I finally got hired at the law firm full time and I wanted to take Taylor out to celebrate. I made reservations at a great restaurant, surprised him at work and took him out to blow my first paycheck. At dinner I told him my news and that I wanted to celebrate with the guy I'm dating. He stopped me dead in my tracks and said, "Wait a minute. We're not dating because I've never asked you on a date."

I thought he was being playful so I batted my eyes and asked him if he'd like to ask me on an official date and he said, "Not really. I only ask girls out that I really like." I was stunned. So I asked him what that made me and he told me, "I don't know, a girl that lets me feel her up in the bathroom."

IT'S JUST A F*#KING DATE PT.1

What's the big deal? It's not like you are being unreasonable. It's a date. And don't you deserve to go on one? Our answer is yes. If he can't muster up the energy or the imagination to at least take you to coffee, then he's in not available to receive a membership to Club You. The philosophy of this book is simple: going on the actual date shouldn't be such a big deal, but getting to go out with you sure as heck is. So set your standards to 'DATE' mode and rock the house.

The Original World Famous Winner Dater's Workbook

Congratulations, you are no longer a person that just lets dating happen to them. You are in the driver's seat and today is the day that you are finally on your way. Mark it in your journal; this is the first day of your New Dating Policy! "Dating policy? Journal? C'mon. You don't really expect me to write a dating policy, do you? I thought you guys were the anti-self-help, self-help guys?" Kiddo, you can do whatever you want, but we've found, as many have, that it really makes a difference when you plot your own course on paper. It gives you something tangible to remind yourself of who you are trying to be and how you want to honor yourself on those days you can't remember or want to cave on the standards you've set for yourself because it seems too hard. Plus we just bought a lot of stock in a notepad company and are hoping to make a killing. Need some help? Read the sample below and then create your own using the words you like.

I *write your name* am a person who goes out on dates. If I like someone and I think there may be a chance that I might really want to be with them, then I will take the time to get to know them by dating them. I don't give my time away because it is precious. I don't hang out, hook up or compromise what's important to me. This makes me a sexier and more interesting person because I know my value and it is sky-high, motherf*#kers!!!! So let's date!

Okay, you get the idea, so give it a try. Ready, Steady, Go!

principle #5: don't freak people out with your need

Crazy + Sexy doesn't always = Cool

Don't Be Needy. Sounds simple. Sounds easy. Yet, this will be the most difficult thing we will be asking you to do because need is a cagey little bastard. No one likes to think of himself or herself as being needy. Needy is not sexy. Needy is not attractive. Needy is not the one you ask to move in with you and spend lazy Sundays with. You are not normally a needy person, are you? You probably aren't (most of the time) but dating can bring out the only insecure fiber in the most confident being and wreck them and any potential relationship that lay in front of them (Google Lisa Marie Nowak for living proof. She's that astronaut that ditched her family and drove cross-country in a diaper to try to kidnap her boyfriend's new lover.) It's true. Dating is not something you can control and overwhelming feelings are not something that are easy to control, so it's a combustible recipe. It's torture when you put yourself out there and open yourself to another human being who will either embrace you or reject you and you only get to know what's going on in your head and heart. It's scary being that vulnerable, so you want to know sooner rather than later if you're going to be rejected. You NEED to know so you can protect yourself and keep your emotions in check. How do you go about finding out sooner? You rush things. Push for definition. Get obsessively analytical about every aspect of every date, email, text or phone call to try to decipher where you stand with the other person and what's going to happen next. Abracadabra! You're playing emotional chess (which is a bad dating game) and trying to force someone to either "mate" you or retreat. Once you're in that mode you're not even really dating each other anymore. You're dating the version of the person that's under pressure to figure out how they truly feel at an accelerated pace. They're dating the version of you that you're pretending to be to make them feel the things you want them to feel in order to commit to you. Ultimately it's a mess, because neither of you are actually genuinely being yourselves, nor are you experiencing your emotional responses in an organic nature or at the pace that is right for you as individuals. Next thing you know you've become a crazy person.

If you take just one piece of advice from us let it be this, needing constant reassurance manifests itself in ways that will surely cause the person you're newly dating to think you are an insecure freak and depart your company quickly. YOU MUST SHOW SOME RESTRAINT. Under no circumstances is it a good idea to plan the wedding after the first date, call him 20 times a day, analyze the relationship non-stop, or be desperate for definition before you know his middle name, because that's what a crazy person does. Even when you think you have your need in check, it is often subconsciously motivating us to act on an impulse. That's why you have to actually work diligently at all times. Like, say you're on a date and you have an uncontrollable urge for him to reassure you that you're pretty ... instead of fishing for the compliment, stuff your mouth with pats of butter, breadsticks or your napkin until the urge passes. Run to the bathroom and splash cold water on your face, then lock yourself in a stall until you can resist, borrow his phone then excuse your-self to make an important phone call to yourself, then leave yourself a voicemail on your mobile phone begging you not to blow it—that way you can recheck that message all night long if you need to. See how there are solutions right in front of your face? Only you can stop the crazy, needy girl in your head.

We know that you don't want to play games when dat-ing, but there is a very important game to be played and it's called **Don't Freak People Out With Your Need.** It's not a game of tactics and deception (like waiting two or three days to call back and pretending to have got busy) or "how can I be different so I can trick them into liking me?" or "how can I manipulate this person into loving me?" Those of you who refuse to acknowledge that there is a *right* game to be played are the least likely to succeed because you're actually playing another game called, "I'm ignoring the rules of engagement and I don't care what you think or feel about it."

Love feels unlike anything else on this planet with the small exception of the Cadbury Creme Egg. It is glorious, magnificent and reassuring. Love makes you feel confident and powerful, secure in your place in this world. The road to love feels considerably less good than that, as it is paved with fear of getting hurt and "What if he doesn't like me, like me?" It's unknown territory and thus you want constant around-the-clock reassurances that you're going in the right direction and that everything is going to be okay. You want to define things, know where you stand, know how much they like you and whether or not this is going to be the one. You find yourself wanting to call the person regardless of the fact that you've only gone out with him twice (three times if you count meeting him and his buddies at the beer garden) and say, "Hey is this gonna happen or not? Cause I'm losing my shit over here" even though the rational part of you knows that asking for definition this early in the relationship will backfire. Our insecurities create the most difficult emotions to manage, so people get caught up in the result rather than in building the relationship. The need for definition overrides Better judgment—it's the biggest pitfall for today's daters.

This method of dating is backwards. As opposed to figuring out, "How can I get you to love me?" You should be thinking, "How about if I take a moment to actually see where I am with this and do I even like you?" That's a completely different mindset that implements a much different and healthy dating strategy.

A relationship is an evolution and it's much more enjoyable if you're actually experiencing it instead of just trying to get to the finish line. Sometimes the mind is no match for the feelings that rule us. So take a deep breath and get a handle on your bad self. Patience, young grasshopper.

BUT GREG, I HAVE QUESTIONS

But What If I Need To Know Where "It's" Going Because I Have To RSVP For A Wedding?

Dear Greg,

What's up with guys? This guy asked me out last year when I had a boyfriend so I politely declined but he kept emailing me occasionally to let me know that if I ever was single that he wanted the first date. So I'm finally single and we go out on a great date. He says it was completely worth the wait and we make plans for another. After a few more dates I asked him if he'll go to my cousin's wedding with me in two months (I have to send in the response card that far ahead because apparently it's of national importance that I reserve the correct number of dinners) and he goes completely strange on me. Granted him agreeing would presume that we'll be going out two months from now, but if it's already going so well and he waited for a whole year to go out with me in the first place, why's that such a stretch?

Sienna

Birmingham, England

Dear Houdini,

Ahhhh, the old wedding date trick. This one's been going around for decades and yet every woman I've ever talked to thinks she's the first one to find the loophole to locking down a relationship. It doesn't matter if it's your cousin's wedding, a trip to the Super Bowl, tea with the Queen or tickets to the Academy Awards—you can't bribe or coerce someone into a committed relationship and expect a good result. Dudes get freaked out when you try to rush them because it makes you seem needy and panicky. If you think you're not putting pressure on the other person because "it's no big deal" then you're just playing a game with yourself. If you were really confident in the future of the relationship you'd RSVP for two and invite them when it's closer to the actual wedding. And if they're not in the picture anymore then you take a friend who's happy to go since you didn't dump them for the bozo that dumped you before your cousin's wedding. A general rule is no locking down future plans until you've been together for an amount of time greater than the distance between now and the upcoming event, and a minimum of two months. A cousin's wedding ... really.

Why Does It Freak Him Out That We're Perfect For Each Other?

Dear Greg,

My friend Belinda set me up with her older brother Ryan because she thought we'd have so much in common. So Ryan and I decided to go out for Indian food and to see Amy Winehouse, which we had discovered we both totally loved. Dinner was great, our conversation couldn't have clicked any better and we have absolutely everything in common. We even joked about getting married because it was weird how completely alike we are and how good our date was going. The concert was amazing and by the end of it he was standing behind me with his arms wrapped tightly around me like I was his girl. We made out in his car for an hour and it was the best date I ever had so I fully expected that we were kind of going out (what with the wedding comment over dinner) and made some kind of joke about how when we get hitched I'm going to make both he and Belinda take my surname instead of taking theirs. The next day I called him and he was totally a different guy—really acting distant and non-committal about getting together. So I called Belinda to see if he had reported back to her after our date and she told me that he said that I was a little too excited about the marriage idea and it made me seem desperate for a boyfriend. Can you believe that? We had the best date ever, he even said that we're perfect

for each other, so I was excited by that, but desperate? C'mon. What I can do to make him think I'm not desperate so he'll go out with me again?
   Tabitha
   Leeds, England

Desperately Seeking Tabitha,
   Look, I wasn't there and I didn't hear the joke but I have to say that the word married is a loaded gun on the first date. Even if you meant it to be a pop gun and he mistook it for an Uzi. At some point in the midst of the world's best first date he took the marriage joke to heart and either sensed some real desperation, projected some desperation as an excuse to bail or maybe he scares easily. Or it could be that you are perfect for him and he's not ready to settle down so he's blowing you off and making you the fall guy. Dudes panic when things are going too well too soon, they think that there must be something wrong that they can't see. In any case this guy and you weren't as ideal a match as you had thought because if the date were as stellar as you say, he wouldn't have let a joke keep him from seeing you again. Sorry Sweet Potato, but you'd best move on and next time keep all marriage jokes under wraps until you're with your fiancé, because dudes are easily freaked by marriage. By the way, how was Amy Winehouse? I hear she's a little inconsistent.

What If I Wasn't Needy Then But I'm Feeling It Now?

Dear Greg,

Grant and I have been dating for about four months and though things are going really well I'm concerned. See, he was very clear up front about not wanting a serious relationship and feeling like he didn't want to be responsible for someone else, so I played it all casual and cool at the beginning. Not really caring about how often we saw each other or what our status as a couple was (or at least I pretended to). I didn't act needy or insecure at all I was completely nonchalant about the whole thing. Then when he was enjoying the benefits of our casual and uncomplicated dating, I started slowly moving a few of my things into his place. I took over a drawer for undergarments and reserve clothing in case I stayed over, put some of my toiletries in his medicine cabinet and started to stock the fridge with my brand of yogurt and breakfast foods, and I made myself a key to his place under the guise of being able to walk and feed his dog when he has to work late. I just kind of started staying over a few times a week to the point where we have become boyfriend/girlfriend, or at least I assume we are because I've made it kind of impossible for him to date anyone else. Now he seems to be pulling back from me a little, acting differently and getting really irritated with me. I think I'm in love with him and I'm afraid he thinks I tricked him into being my boyfriend and is reconsidering being with me. I can't seem to stop asking him for reassurance that we're good and I feel all panicky. What do I do?

Petra

Ottawa, Canada

Dear Sneaky Pete,

It sounds like you did trick him into being your boyfriend. He was clear with you at the beginning about not wanting a serious relationship and then you disregarded his feelings and moved yourself in. I can't say this enough—people get to their feelings at their own pace. So even if you manipulate someone into committing to something faster than he wanted to so that you could have what you wanted, you're screwed. Because you know that at the bottom of his heart he has doubts because he wasn't true to his inner emotional clock, he's not comfortable with what you need from him and you've tricked him into being in this relationship. So great, now you will always be wondering if he's going to change his mind because of that doubt, or worse look for something better. If you thought you needed reassurance before you were boyfriend and girlfriend, how's it going to feel now that the stakes are higher and you have to worry every time he leaves the house that he'll realize he doesn't want to be with you? Need is a dangerous thing to be in servitude to and it can make you crazy. You should be honest with your dude, tell him that you may have rushed him into this and are happy to back off and give him some space if he needs it to figure out his feelings.

Is There A Difference Between Being Needy And Being Honest?

Dear Greg,

I was on a first date with this new guy and it was going really well. We talked really easily, there was never a lull and he's really gorgeous. Here's where things go from well to not so well. I got a bit tipsy and laid my cards on the table and said something like, "I don't play games, this is who I am. I'm not going to pretend I don't like you so that you'll like me more. I like you a lot and think we'd be great together." I thought a guy like John would appreciate my honesty but that wasn't his reaction. He was like, "This is just a first date. I don't even know you yet and I certainly can't tell you that we're going to have a future together. Let's just see how we get through dinner because I'm not really ready to get tied down before dessert." I totally blew it and he never called again. I thought being honest was a good thing, what did I do wrong?

Kristen

Sydney, Australia

Dear Tipsy Roulette,

Being honest is a good thing, so let me be honest with you. What a bozo move that was! Before you are honest with someone else it's imperative that you be honest with yourself. You should have asked yourself, "Why do I need to know where this is going right now?" Or how about, "Is this person really ready for me to lay all my cards on the table right now?" Or "Do I want to ruin the good feelings I'm having and the ones he's having by trying to solidify an answer about the future?" or "Can't I wait until at least the end of the third date?" Or even, "Do I want to appear completely crazy?" Once you've answered these maybe you'll feel differently about being so honest. Look Kristen, using honesty as a reason to actually push someone away is a neat trick, because then you can pretend he's the bad guy. But there are better ways to push someone away and not get what you want. Hey, go easy with the drinks next time, they're not helping.

FROM THE OTHER SIDE OF THE FENCE

How Do I Make Someone Back Off A Bit So They Don't Wreck It?

Dear Greg,

I started dating a girl I met on the subway one afternoon, which seemed like a massive stroke of good luck at first. The thing is that after a couple of dates she started waiting for me on the subway platform so we could ride together every day. I know I should think it's nice but it feels claustrophobic, like I'm supposed to see her every day now. She doesn't say that but it's weird to ride home every day after work and have the "what are you doing for dinner?" conversation and not feel like she's waiting for me to ask her out. I can't tell whether she has no life or just digs me a lot, but either way it's more than I bargained for and it's freaking me out. How do I get her to back it up a bit?

Marcus,
New York, NY

Dear Subwait,

Wow. This is a tough one. It's almost like you want to shout to her "No, wait, don't ruin this." She probably has no idea that she is ruining it either. This is an example of freaking people out with your need and being too available. Even if she's not necessarily a needy person she's making you think she's got nothing better to do than wait around for you at the subway. While that should be flattering let's be real—it's a colossal turn-off. If she had done it once and surprised you, you would have been rocked by it, but by day five it's feeling more like stalker than rocker. If you really like her you should just tell her what's up. Try something like, "The He's Just Not That Into You guy told me that you'd appreciate my honesty so here goes ... I like you but I can't decide if I really like you because I see you too often. I need to not see you so that I can think about you and hopefully miss you waiting for me at the subway." Then jam your hands in your pockets and look at your shoes—girls love that. I think it's because you look vulnerable and boyish when you do that but it'll soften the blow and make it seem like it's your own deal not something she should be embarrassed about.

THE CHICK THAT BLEW IT

Why is it that every time I start dating a girl I like she turns into someone I can't deal with at the six-week mark? It's the same thing almost every time, it starts off great, we get along great, we're taking our time getting to know each other then six weeks into it she starts her descent into becoming the weirdly insecure version of her. I know it has everything to do with the fact that I have to travel every two months for work, so it never fails that I have to go out of town just when we're hitting our stride. I always make it a point to reassure her that I will call when I can but that I can't always talk during the day. I always send flowers with a note saying that I'll miss her. So when I started dating Ivy I was totally upfront about what has happened in the past and she swore that she was not like that at all. So I went away, like I told her I would have to do for work, and I couldn't call as much. At first it seemed okay but by the fifth day everything changed, instead of hearing, "Hey!" when I called I got the icy, "How nice of you to take time out of your busy schedule to call me." Or if I called to say goodnight it's like thirty minutes of having to assure her that I miss her and am thinking about her. Jesus! If I wasn't thinking about her I wouldn't have called, and now all I'm thinking was that I wish I hadn't called. Then there's the "Do U still miss me?" texts, "Just thinking about you" emails and the "Give me a call when you get a chance" voicemails that distract me from my work and make me feel guilty and kind of annoyed if I'm being honest. When I'm on a business trip I'm generally with my boss who is a very serious businessman, or with clients that don't love me taking time out to address my personal life. By the time I'm supposed to come home I don't feel the same way I did about her before I left because I've been driven crazy by a woman who either thinks I'm going to cheat on her or forget she exists. Then I'm the bad guy because she doesn't believe that I like her enough and instead of this being a great opportunity for me to miss her I'm completely irritated by her and then I can't get back to liking her again.

Tommy

Calabasas, CA

MAYBE YOU GUYS ARE RIGHT

I know that I can get insecure and needy when I like someone a lot and I'm not getting the total reinforcement that we're going to be together next month or next year. I can feel my uneasiness rising every time we are apart and I haven't heard from him in a day. A day seems like an eternity when you like someone too much and can't tell if they're just dipping their toes in the pool or jumping in with both feet. I've always been the type of person that likes someone too much too fast then wrecks it by scaring them off by needing to know what's going to happen next. It's only after the deed is done that I can see how totally desperate I must seem to them trying to turn a third date into a committed relationship. It's embarrassing to look back at some of the things I've done. So now that I'm thirty I've decided that I am no longer allowing myself to act on my needy impulses when dealing with a new guy. The rule is if you haven't made me your girlfriend, I am not going to be your problem. I can handle myself. Now that's all easier said then done and of course as soon as I made this declaration I met Bryan. But this time I was determined to keep my self-destructive impulses in control, so anytime I was feeling insecure and wanting to fish for reassurance I called my friends and had them talk me out of reaching out to him. Instead they sang my praises and kept reminding me that I would feel and be ten times more attractive if I just managed to keep my sanity. So Bryan and I are going on six months together and even though I had crazy feelings I never exposed them to him. Not only has he told me that the thing he loves most about me is that I'm the most independent and together woman he's ever dated, but he's also shared past horror stories of women pressuring him and being need freaks. (Some of whose actions I totally have been guilty of in the past! Shhhh!) Not only do I feel like a new person for conquering my need but I also *finally* got the guy!

Janessa

Chicago, IL

FIRST PERSON SINGLE by Amiira

I have felt both the crushing need of another and been the crusher myself. Neither one of those experiences are ones I'd like to revisit for any number of reasons. From what I can gather from my experiences there seems to be this invisible thread that connects Need with Respect. Or rather, the way someone handles their own need is directly proportional to how much respect they command from the person that they need so desperately from. You can't always muster up respect when dignity has left the building and desperation has surfaced in its place. It's hard to feel good about someone who's sudden panic has shattered their normal cool exterior and turned them into a Clinger. We've all been there in some degree or another when the person you're *kind of* going out with has that seismic shift and suddenly can't bear the idea of continuing in the ambiguity that is supposed to be dating for one moment longer. So they stick to you like glue or, worse yet, check up on you constantly making jokes about the future and fishing for assurance that you are on your way to being serious about them. It's the worst! I remember really liking a guy I had been seeing for a few weeks only to be completely turned off when his easy-going nature was overtaken by a sudden need to lock down our relationship. The constant having to talk about a future that I could not see coupled with his omnipresence was suffocating and ultimately the beginning of the end. Even worse is the knowledge that I've been the needy one before. Seeking validation and reassurance from someone who shrinks from you the more you persist. Even ten years later I can still recall how sucky it felt to be so weak and out of control of my own emotions and behaviors. We all learn from our past mistakes, that's why they say that hindsight is 20/20. So remember that the goal is to keep your self-respect above all and be someone that he will want to run to *not run from*.

THOUGHTS FROM MAN CITY

Look, it's pretty simple: guys don't like to be rushed into committing to anything bigger than what is for lunch. We especially don't like to be rushed when dating because when you rush us you've basically folded your cards and said, "I'm yours for the taking" and the chase is over. When you rush us into reassuring you that we like you, the flattery you want us to feel is completely drowned out by the hydraulics of the truck that's about to dump a pile of emotional responsibility into our laps. When you rush us things go all snowy and weird in our heads and the girl you couldn't wait to get undressed becomes the girl with an alarming amount of need. Even if you're not that, it's the panicked place that we go to in record time. The thing is we want to know you are busy and we'd be lucky to get to see you, so when you are willing to drop everything for us this early in the game we panic. We panic because it feels like suddenly we have to take care of you or that you are looking to us to make you happy and we don't know how to do that. That may not be your truth, you might just be excited and forthcoming with your feelings, but that's how we react. Here's the thing, once someone rushes you or has needs that you aren't sure you can handle, it makes you feel differently about them. You can go from worshipping someone to being completely unsure about that same person in the time it takes to say, "So are we boyfriend/girlfriend or what?" If you don't have a visual for what need feels like, it's like someone pulling your trouser leg when you are drowning and it's scary to men. Yes, we know that you've been there too but it's not like you ladies love the needy guy. Human beings don't like to be rushed up on, it's just how we are. It's not something that can be changed; it's a survival instinct. Hell, even dogs circle around each other a few times before they sniff butts. Now isn't that sexy?

 DATING FORTUNE COOKIE

The only thing less sexy than overwhelming need is shitting your pants.

WORST DATE EVER

I was on a date with a girl from work, we got along great on the job and as she was leaving to pursue another career I felt free to ask her out. We went to dinner at a comedy club. We got along okay but thank God there was someone else doing the talking. We were chatting and laughing but she seemed distracted and she kept looking back over her shoulder. Then finally she literally shouted, "If you are going to look at other f*#king women all night then why don't you take me home!" Seriously I was shocked. Hey, I'm no saint, I've looked at other women before when on a date, but even when I did I was pretty discreet. But that night I wasn't looking at other women, in fact I was pretty interested in my date and actually remember that I was trying to make sure I was making eye contact as much as possible. So I said as much and she paused a moment and then said, "See you're doing it again." And she slammed down her fork, and that's when I realized she was referring to my amblyopia or "lazy eye". Well, needless to say she was pretty embarrassed when I explained myself. She apologized and we had an okay time. I never asked her out again partly because I don't like yellers but mostly because that date was such a tour of her insecurities. I was completely attuned to my date and regardless of my body language or comments about how great she was, all she was concerned about was that there was an imaginary girl over her shoulder that was prettier and better than she was. I can only imagine if she needed that much reassurance during dinner what dating her further would be like. Plus I had my lazy eye at work, which she would have easily noticed had she paid as much attention to me then in broad daylight as she did in the dim corners of a comedy club.

HE'S JUST A F*#KING GUY

C'mon now. He's just a guy. That's it. And you don't need a guy to make you happy. Sure it's great to share your awesomeness with someone, but not any guy will do for you and in fact most of them won't. You are selective because you are not needy, and because you are not needy you get to decide who's lucky enough to take the ride with you. After all it's just a guy; it's not like it's cake.

The Original World Famous Winner Dater's Workbook

It's time to take control of yourself so that from now on you can be self-possessed when you're dating. To do that we must figure out what you're afraid of and why your need to know what someone else is thinking, feeling and doing is getting the best of you. We'd like you to do some reflecting and really think about these questions before you answer them.

1. When you like a guy, what do you feel?
2. At what point do your feelings of liking him make you more uncomfortable than excited?
3. What feels better, the anxiety of a "where's this thing going?" conversation or meeting your girlfriends for a pedicure?
4. Is it better to take your time figuring out what to order off of a new menu or be rushed by a passively impatient waiter? Why?
5. Is it better to try on a pair of shoes that you're going to wear a lot to see if they fit and are comfortable or just plop down your cash and hope they don't make your feet sweat or give you blisters?

6. If the guy that you like doesn't like you back do you:
a) Die of heart failure?
b) Turn to a life of crime on the streets?
c) Set his car on fire and spend sixty days in prison?
d) Be disappointed but get over it the next time a cute boy looks your way?
7. Would you rather go out with someone that's kind of into you or be single and still be looking for the guy that's totally into you? Why?
8. How much does it matter what he's thinking or feeling?
9. If he doesn't like you are you not a good person?
10. If he doesn't like you will you never have another chance of finding someone?
11. If he doesn't like you do you really want to go out with him?

Now write the following one hundred times on a chalk-board:

"I will not be needy or a crazy person. I will concentrate on how I feel because that's what's important."

Look, most guys you go out with aren't going to be the guy for you. It's just the way life works that we like many but only choose one. So you must understand that the *right* relationship is what you're trying to find and the *right* relationship won't make you a crazy needy person. So when you're having those dreaded feelings of need and insecurity they should be your first clue that this is probably not the guy for you because *HE* wouldn't want you to feel that way.

principle #6: doormats finish last and end up in the dirt

Setting Up Some Standards And Losing The Deal Breakers

Many people go through their lives setting unnecessary deal breakers that ultimately keep them from succeeding in the areas that they want success in the most. And yet they're the last person to see it, much less admit to it. They're the people that proclaim things like, "He's got to be taller than me and own his own home or I'm not interested." Really? Why is that? Because you're insecure about being seen with someone shorter than you? You sound really deep. Why can't he move into your home if things get serious? Oh right, you probably don't own one. That seems fair.

The deal breaker types are those that create a list of things that they want (and don't want) out of a mate then set parameters that someone must fall within in order to have real potential as a partner. This sounds like a good idea in concept, certainly it's better than having no idea at all about what you want or just playing drunken roulette and grabbing the first person you see at the "Lion's Den Bar & Grill Happy Hour and Hot Wing Wing Ding" in hopes that it'll pan out and become a relationship. The problem with the *idea* of deal breakers is that, *by setting them you are working against the very properties and nature of a great relationship* instead of encouraging one. **Setting parameters to determine someone's worth or viability as a romantic partner assumes that they don't have other areas of value that could possibly be more appealing than the ideas or wants that you have**. It also assumes that how they are in this moment in time is all they will ever be. What if the love of your life turns out to be a social worker who fights for the rights of children and raises loads of money for worthwhile charities but doesn't have much more than the shirt on his back and rents a tiny flat? You know Bill Gates wasn't always as wealthy as Bill Gates and Clive Owen wasn't always as hot as Clive Owen. Something to have a think about.

THE BIG DIFFERENCE BETWEEN STANDARDS AND DEAL BREAKERS

There's a difference between having standards and having deal breakers when dating, though many think they are the same thing. Having standards is completely different. "How?" We're glad you asked.

✓ *Standards are about how YOU LIVE YOUR LIFE, where Deal Breakers are about how YOU VIEW THEIRS.*

✓ *Standards are you living your life at a higher level and only accepting things that strive for excellence— it's living a life of quality choices and high self-worth.*

✓ *Deal Breakers are you QUANTIFYING another person's assets or attributes to validate your worth.*

✓ *Standards are not about hair color or record collections, height or financial worth. They are about tolerable behaviors, about the kind of relationship you want to be in and the way you want to be treated.*

✓ *Standards are you walking the walk. Deal Breakers are you talking the talk.*

Standards are defined as a level of quality or excellence that is accepted as the norm or by which actual attainments are judged. It's about how you live. Having a set list of personal Deal Breakers seems like a surefire way to save you from winding up in a bum relationship. However, the truth is that most of those people end up being either eternally single or end up "settling" for someone who they consider to be less than what they wanted in a mate. And how great for the person that they "settled" for—a relationship based on the thought that they, as a partner and a person, are better than nothing but still not as good as themselves. That must feel good for both parties. What a great story to tell your kids. The bottom line is that most Deal Breakers are unnecessary requirements that you've set to validate you and really don't have much to do with the other person. If a relationship is good and worthwhile the things you want will work themselves out anyway.

Still confused about the difference? Maybe this will help …

✓ Standard: *I don't date people that drink so excessively that it makes me uncomfortable.*

✓ Deal Breaker: *I don't date people that drink blue fruity drinks.*

✓ Standard: *I won't date men who consistently don't do what they say they're going to do.*

✓ Deal Breaker: *If he forgets to call me one time he's done.*

✓ Standard: *I won't date anyone who's emotionally unavailable.*

✓ Deal Breaker: *I won't date anyone less than six feet tall.*

Get it now? Standards are a level by which you live—or in this case, specifically, date—and which you will not compromise on. "How is that not a Deal Breaker?" you ask. Because they are not about hair color or record collections, height or financial worth, they are about *tolerable behaviors, about the kind of relationship you want to be in and the way you want to be treated.* Living with a set of standards tells the world "this is how I operate." Deal Breakers tell the world, "these are my requirements." People automatically assume that they already live by a solid set of standards and in truth they probably do ... except when it comes to dating. For some reason when it comes to dating people compromise their standards in hope that they will get something lasting in return. Don't you want your relationship to be of the highest quality? Shouldn't the person you share your life with and the relationship that you turn to in your best and worst times be of the highest standards?

Living and dating with standards means holding yourself and those around you to behavior that honors a higher caliber of life (and we're not talking about material things) ... it also weeds out the riff-raff so you really can't argue with us on this one. If you want a relationship with someone that honors and respects you and that you honor and respect, you must operate at a level worthy of such things. How do you do that? Well, let's think about it.

You will need to be ...

✓ *Someone that values himself or herself as much as they value the person they want to be with.* *('Cause who's the awesome catch that wants to get saddled with "Grabby can't let go" a needy partner that doesn't feel worthy of them?)*

✓ *Someone who is considerate and generous but expects consideration and generosity in return.* *(As in I scratch your back you run to market at 4 a.m. for a pint of Dulce de Leche.)*

✓ *Someone who is respectful and honest to others and accepts no less from others.* *(C'mon, this one's obvious right? It's not? Man, are you in trouble.)*

✓ *Someone who has a sense of purpose and attracts others who have purpose, not dead weight and co-dependents.* *(Coffee is for closers. See the movie* Glengarry Glen Ross *for more on this ... or don't. Just find a person with a sense of purpose and you'll see what we mean. You will find them in the super successful winner department of your local grocery store.)*

✓ *Someone who surrounds themselves with excellence that honors their worth, be it a clean house, a well-groomed appearance or a coterie of good friends. (Did you notice we didn't say a jobless slob with a Barbie doll head collection? Did we knock your socks off with the use of coterie?)*

✓ *Someone who elicits respect and doesn't endure those who aren't respectful, be it a date, a boss, a friend or a family member. (Doormats finish last and end up in the dirt. Sad but true—ask your doormat. By the way, if you have a doormat you are a person who honors themselves.)*

Think of what you stand for in life, what you represent in the world, how your friendships exist and what you want out of a relationship. Then know that the exceptions and excuses you make for people by lowering your standards will only bite you in the ass later. We know it from experience and we've got the bite marks to prove it.

BUT GREG, I HAVE QUESTIONS

But What If I Know What I Want Regardless Of What You Call It?

Dear Greg,

I know what I want out of life and a relationship and it's not negotiable. So when I'm on a first date I cut to the chase and tell the guy what I'm looking for—what my criteria is (i.e. must love travel, wants to get married, has to love cats, etc.) so that we don't waste a lot of time if we're not going to be compatible. I don't play games and some guys find my honesty off-putting but others are grateful for it and glad for the time I saved them. My girlfriends think I'm crazy and am ruining my chances of getting asked out on a second date. I think I'm saving myself from the heartache of getting attached to someone who doesn't share my goals. What do you think?

Josie

Manchester, England

Dear Must Love Cats

I think that's a great idea. I actually think you should also get a credit report, a field sobriety test, and ask for three references not including family. And while you are at it why don't you bring your cat on the date so that you can appear totally crazy and never end up with anyone except Whiskers? Look, I know it seems like you are trying to be smart about it, but what you are doing is driving people away and limiting your perception of yourself and any potential suitor to who they are today. And you are actually playing a game: you're playing a game called "How Can I Keep Myself From Being Vulnerable To Getting Hurt?" When you meet someone of quality that has their own interests, who's to say that that wouldn't expand YOUR interests or vice versa? The thing you're not taking into account is that people evolve when they come together if it's a good match, and when you cut someone off at the knees by limiting them to your narrow-minded version of suitability you're the one who's blowing it. Because they'll go on to find someone else that's more flexible and adventurous to evolve with while you stay lonely but protected. Besides, cutting someone off at the knees is something painful, bloody and, I'm assuming, in some states illegal.

Is It Ever Too Late To Have Standards?

Dear Greg,

How do I tell a guy that I've been going out with for two months that I'm not okay with some of the things I pretended to be when we first started dating? I really like him and he fits into my idea of what I want in a man (good job, doesn't do drugs, owns his own home and is really good looking) so I let some things slide that I thought weren't that big of a deal to me. It seemed like a good trade-off for what he did have at the time, but now it's not working for me. After our first date he suggested that it'd be easier for us to meet at restaurants instead of him picking me up since I live on the other side of town. I agreed because it seemed logical but now it makes me feel like I'm not worth driving fifteen minutes for. He told me that he doesn't like having me sleep over because he sleeps better in the bed alone and needs a good night's sleep in order to do his job well. So when we go back to his place and get intimate I always feel like he's watching the clock and waiting for me to leave. It sounds bad but the relationship is going well and I know he's not seeing anyone else but rather he's set in his ways. Do you think these are deal breakers and how do I renegotiate the terms of our dating life?

Arabelle

Paris, France

Dear Bait and Switcher,

Gotta come clean, kiddo. You set the bar low and now you are living at it. And as you pointed out it's not his fault. This is what he thinks is standard operating procedure for you and it works for him. It's what guys refer to as the old Bait and Switch. You've sold him this version of you that doesn't require some of the basics of dating. Now you are going to have to set him straight and tell him that you've changed your mind, then understand if he buckles at the idea of doing things differently. As far as things that don't work for him, like sleeping over, why are you letting him decide what's okay for you? Relationships are a negotiation where you get to have your needs met too. In the future, be clear about what you want from the beginning and you can't go wrong.

Is Religion A Standard Or A Deal Breaker?

Dear Greg,

I'm 29 years old, Jewish and single. My family is not conveniently Jewish as in we like an extra day off work; we are actively Jewish to the point that my mother is insistent that I marry a Jewish man or I will break her heart and the Torah will burst into flames or something else that's really bad. I'm not saying that I won't marry a Jewish guy but I am keeping my options open to finding the best man for me then dealing with religion later. Does religion fall under deal breakers or standards, and what defines the difference in this particular case?

Eliza
Oxford, England

Dear Torah Destroyah,

This is entirely up to you. Faith usually sets a standard by which we decide to live our lives. My own personal experience with it is this: I was not brought up in a spiritual home. When I was 33 I got sober and turned my life over to a "power greater than myself" and I live my life by a set of spiritual principles. For the longest time I would only date sober girls, figuring that they would be the only ones who would understand me. Well, that turned out not to be the case. Those actually turned out to be some of the most volatile relationships I'd ever been in. So I finally opened the door to dating others, and lo and behold I met some one more spiritually compatible than anyone I had met in my program. So I chose to pick the person who made me feel the most spiritually sound rather than of my particular faith. This may not work for you but the narrower we make the door, the fewer get in.

What If A Deal Breaker Is Unfair?

Dear Greg,

Matthew and I have been going out for seven months and I thought things were not only going well but that we were definitely headed for the altar. We are like two peas in a pod, we get along great, have the same sense of humor and the sex is the best I've ever had. So you can imagine how completely surprised I was when he broke up with me and cited the fact that I am taller than him as the reason that he doesn't want to get serious with me. What is that all about? How can my height be a big enough deal that he's ending a great relationship? It's not like I was short when we met and started dating then grew. I've been 5'11" since the first time he asked if he could buy me a drink, and I was even wearing heels that night. But he says he can't marry a woman who's taller than he is and that even though he loves me it's a deal breaker for him. What can I do?

Delphine
Madison, WI

Dear Delphine the devastated,

Sadly there are people in this world that let great relationships go because of some preconceived and narrow-minded idea about what the right person for them must be look or be like. Though it sucks to be on the other end of it, sounds like you got out at just the right time. Who wants to spend eternity with someone who willfully won't love you because of your height? Or maybe he feels small around you and can't get past it. We can't always help how someone makes us feel about our self. Either way it would have spelled out a miserable future even if your past together was a great one. The best things in life come in completely different packages than we expect them to, but some people resist that idea all the way to the grave. Just remember that some of the most beautiful women in the world are tall ones. Anyone ever heard of models?

FROM THE OTHER SIDE OF THE FENCE

When Should I Settle?

Dear Greg,

I believe there are girls you have fun with and girls you bring home to meet the folks, you know what I mean? As an equal opportunity dater I've been able to fine-tune my ideas of the perfect woman and when I find her I'll marry her. The perfect woman has her own job, life and income. The perfect woman can tell a joke, take a joke, play one-on-one hoop and know the difference between every major sport. She must love sex and be good at it but not have had it with more than two people a year after the age of 18. She's stronger than she looks (emotionally and physically), smarter than she is beautiful and loyal to her friends and family above all. My friends and I call this the Quest For The Perfect Ten but I've been coming up empty handed for a few years now. I've asked my sisters what points do they think I should settle on but they just rolled their eyes and dared me to ask you. So do I settle or hold out?

Lucas
Wichita, KS

Dear Dumbass,
You forgot about the kind of girls you let wash your pickup truck. I'm sure you're probably a perfect ten yourself ... except for being a little short on intelligence and endowment. Good luck with that.

THE CHICK THAT BLEW IT

So I had been kind of fooling around with this girl that I thought was amazing. She was beautiful, sexy, cool and really smart. We had so much in common and our chemistry was palpable. For months I tried to get her to promote me to being her boyfriend and take me and us seriously. She would always just tell me she couldn't entertain the idea of something serious now, she didn't have the capacity to devote the time and effort because she was so busy with work. I did everything right. I treated her like a queen, always did little things to let her know I was thinking about her and was nothing but available and interested. Then one night after a few too many of the drinkie-poos as she liked to call them (the only uncool thing about her) she finally fessed up that she could never really respect a guy that didn't make more money than she did and that's why she wouldn't be my girlfriend. That admission was like a punch to the solar plexus. Here I was in love with this girl and she didn't respect me because of money? At the time I was launching an Internet marketing company out of my studio apartment that she thought was an excuse not to have a "real job." So that was that and it was almost five years ago. Well, cut to last week and I see her at an event that my company's promoting and she makes her way over to ask how I've been. It was like the best moment of my life when I got to look her in the eye and tell her, "Things are great. I just sold my company for 20 million, bought a jet last week. How are you?" I'm telling you she went ashen. Then the next three weeks she left me seven voicemails and sent about thirty texts all of which went unanswered.

Jonah

Laguna Beach, CA

MAYBE YOU GUYS ARE RIGHT

Most of my relationships since college have been wildly unsuccessful and I think of myself as a relatively easygoing person. I've always been able to overlook a flaw or forty when it comes to guys if they're a good person. Then I finally realized that guys with forty or more flaws are actually not that great of a catch. So I decided that I needed to take a look at my standards and give them some updating. I figured out that my problem wasn't that my standards were low it was just that I wasn't sticking to them or, worse yet, I was letting other things override them or make up for things that were lacking. Like if I was dating a guy who had never been able to be monogamous but was really convincing when he said he thought he might be able to stay faithful to me then I'd make an exception on my "Won't date cheaters" standard. How do you think that one paid off for me? That was nine months ago when I recognized the error of my ways and decided that I was sticking to my guns with a new "No Bending" rule to my standards. I'm not going to lie that it's been slim pickings because most guys don't live their lives or make choices that rise to my level of standards, HOWEVER the few guys that I have met who do, are much better guys than I have ever dated before. It's a total quality over quantity reversal. Though I'm not currently in a relationship, I know that when I am it will be a good one because I will have finally chosen someone capable of having a good relationship because he too will live a life of standards.

Marissa,

Edinburgh, Scotland

FIRST PERSON SINGLE by Amiira

Compromising my standards used to be a full-time job for me. I'd do it for work, I'd do it for friends, I'd do it to fit in and I'd certainly do it for love, almost love and even like. Looking back at myself it's so clear the things I could not see or didn't want to see in the men I chose. Their blatant limitations, unfixable flaws in character or outright trespasses and my *choice* to not see them. I'm not blind or dumb about men ... I'm worse. I'm a deliberate over-looker. I will forgive you many sins if you make me laugh. A great sense of humor will get you everywhere with me and I'm not proud of it. But don't think I didn't suffer for being such a pushover because I was put through the ringer by some of these underdeveloped but funny boys. I was convinced that I could fill in the blanks for these guys or fix them or help them grow up or whatever it was that I had assessed them with a deficiency of. You know what I learned over and over again with every disappointment? You can't fix people or make them change, the only thing you can do is pack your shit and leave if it isn't working for you. Though I tested that "can't change people" theo-ry over and over again I found it to be true. So instead of trying to fix or change others I concentrated on what was going on with me. What I discovered was that my self-esteem had taken a few beatings, that I looked for valida-tion from broken men and that funny isn't enough on its own—it takes substance as well. I revisited all my past relationships and thought about those men, their limita-tions and flaws as well as my own and I made a mental checklist of places I wouldn't be going again. Emotionally unavailable or stunted would no longer be seeing my face. Compulsive liar and cowardly actions were off my Christmas card list. Can't get his shit together or dig his way out of a hole with a shovel and a map were plummet-ing down the charts. Wildly selfish and has no concern for others was tied to an anchor and sinking. But you know what made a big comeback? My own value, the things I truly see value in and a higher standard by which I choose to live and fill my life. That's when my life started to go from being good to great. You have complete control over the most important thing that will determine your path in life and that is the standards by which *you* decide to live.

THOUGHTS FROM MAN CITY

I have to admit I know a thing or two about standards. Probably because I really didn't used to have any. Well, let's be fair, I knew what tequila went best with tequila, and that at nighttime it's best to sleep indoors. Whose bed didn't really matter. Let me tell you this; a life without standards can end pretty badly, so when I was 33 I made the decision to get drinks free. (Remember?) That doesn't make me special, it's just the right choice for me. At one of the meetings that I attended in an effort to stay sober someone said the phrase "Stick with the winners." Meaning, I guess, hang with those who have what you want in life, the ones that live up to an ideal and principles you can identify with. That afternoon I was wandering around a mall looking at stuff I couldn't afford to buy when I met a winner. A toaster. "Drunk again?" you ask. No, quite the opposite actually, some people refer to it as a moment of clarity. I was looking at the window display of a housewares store when I saw, in all its polished glory, a beautiful four-slice, stainless steel, toaster. The kind with the two wide slots that, according to the salesperson, make the natural leap from toast to toasted sandwiches. For some reason this household appliance with all of its toasting dexterity struck me as extraordinary. I know that sounds insane and maybe it was but I was newly "drinks free" and I was hanging on by a very thin thread. It seemed to be the most evolved and full-blown version of a toaster that there could be. It had in its very design a sense of pride and dignity. This toaster wasn't just content to make toast—it was about a toaster lifestyle. By virtue of its aesthetic this toaster was challenging everything around it to the same standard of excellence that it was living at. I felt the toaster was asking me to answer questions like "Who's the man that owns this toaster and what's his life like? Who's the girl that dates the man that owns this toaster and what kind of life do they have when they are standing around the toaster eating toast and/or toasted sandwiches?" I felt that in its design this toaster was advocating a better life. I mean, after all, isn't that what great design is supposed to do? It was so inspiring, in fact, that for days it was all I could obsess about instead of wanting a drink. It moved me to write—which I had not, with the exception of my phone number on some cocktail napkins, ever done. I also got a job because I wanted to buy this toaster and also pay rent, which seemed of primary importance to my roommate. Roommates can be sticky like that. Over time I wrote a one-man show about it called Mantastic that eventually became an HBO special, in fact the same special that convinced my wife to go on a date with me. I sent her an advance copy, which I can't strongly enough suggest you do if you have one. And the four-slice, stainless steel toaster with the two wide slots that make the natural leap from toast to toasted sandwiches sits with great pride in my kitchen today, making toast for my girls every morning. But more than that it reminds me every day of who I am and who I want to be and the level my life needs to be lived at. It is the standard by which I live my life, because I'm the guy that owns it. Toast?

 DATING FORTUNE COOKIE

Live well and the world will open its doors. Live poorly and the world will slam them in your face and go back to playing cards with its buddies.

WORST DATE EVER 😦

I had been trying online dating since I hadn't had much luck in the real world dating pool, and had been having some pretty good luck. Lots of people read my profile and "winked" at me and I started emailing with a few of them. Eventually I narrowed the field (if you can call three a field) down to this one guy who miraculously fit into all the things I was looking for in a guy and I fit into all the things he was looking for (except that I'm blonde and he prefers brunettes) in a woman. We corresponded all the time and eventually moved to the phone and had an even bigger connection than online. I thought I had hit pay dirt. We talked about what kind of future we could have together and both got carried away with how perfect the whole thing was going. We decided to go out on a proper date so when he showed up I was relieved that he looked like his photo on his profile. We went out for dinner, which started out great except that he was rude to our waiter—really rude to the point that I left an extra twenty-dollar bill under my plate for him. Then we went to the movies but when we were in line for popcorn he was openly condescending about the guy working the conces-sion stand. Commenting loud enough so the guy could hear him about how slow he was and that the theater must have hired the "challenged". It was awful. I was so embarrassed and when we got to the front of the line I apologized to the guy behind the counter, who explained that they were having a glitch with their cash registers. My date got pissed off at me for undermining him then proceeded to bring it up over and over again during the movie, using a tone that I haven't heard since I got caught stealing in eighth grade. Then when we got "shhh-ed" for his berating me he told them to "Mind their own f-ing business" followed by a generalized sexual preference slur. It was mortifying. Here's this guy who I thought was everything I wanted in a guy—had my whole checklist covered—*something that has never happened for me before* and he was the worst guy I've ever met and shitty to every person that crossed his path. I hadn't even thought to put "Not A Shitty Person" on the list because I assumed that would be a given, but apparently not. Needless to say our date ended abruptly after that because I walked out of the theater in the dark and blocked him from my online profile and my mobile phone. As it turns out my standards of what's right for human behavior are more important than my deal breakers or wish lists.

IT'S JUST A F*#KING STANDARD

You know what you want. You always have. And if you don't remember, let us tell you. You want to be happy and you want to be in a relationship where you can feel comfortable with who you are because you picked someone who honors the very essence of you. Finding happiness is going to be harder for you if it's based on a height requirement. So set standards that are attainable for people striving for greatness regardless of hair color or yearly income. Trust us, your whole life goes better when you live by a set of standards because they teach people how to treat you.

The Original World Famous Winner Dater's Workbook

Now that you've read about the differences between Standards and Deal Breakers, let's see if you can spot which is which.

1. Must have tight red curly hair
2. Believes in God
3. Has traveled outside the country he was born in
4. Must believe in Bon Jovi
5. Doesn't eat red meat
6. Can speak more than one language
7. Owns his own home
8. Likes Indian food
9. Is under 45 years of age
10. Has a full head of hair
11. Likes my kids
12. Calls when he says he's going to
13. Doesn't do drugs
14. Has ambition
15. Can't have any female friends

Turn page upside down to see the answers below.

2, 11, 12, 13, 14 are all standards

1, 3, 4, 5, 6, 7, 8, 9, 10, 15 are all deal breakers

principle #7: don't show the movie before the trailer

Anticipation, Seduction And The Fine Art Of Waiting To Have Sex

Here's a great way to think about sex and dating. Think of yourself as a summer blockbuster movie or, more specifically, that having sex with you is a summer blockbuster movie. Now, with such a highly anticipated event you don't just open it at the theaters without any fanfare, right? What about a teaser? How about the trailer? Think about it. "Don't show the movie before the trailer" is a philosophy and a strategy all rolled into one. Close your eyes. Now imagine it's Christmas time and you're in the movie theater to see some holiday triumph of the human spirit flick. You're settled into your seat with your popcorn, Junior

Mints and Diet Pepsi … then the lights go dark, the curtains open then BOOM! a giant glowing version of the Batman bat logo slams against the screen. It vanishes as quickly as it arrived and then you see the numbers: 7. 6. 09. The whole thing lasts less than ten seconds but it's thrilling. It's the teaser and it's a wildly effective way of letting people know that something great is coming. Anticipation is the greatest aphrodisiac in the world, so if you like him and want him to stick around then don't show him the whole movie right away. Let him check out the teaser early on, like a long hot kiss and the mention of things to come. The teaser gives him the complete understanding that yes, you'd like to show him the feature but it's still a ways away from the opening. (Again, pun intended).

Then comes the trailer—a two- to three-minute preview of the most exciting, emotional and sexy parts of the movie cut together to tell you enough of the story as they can without revealing the ending in the hope that you won't be able to contain yourself until it opens. Making out in your underwear is a great trailer. The point of the teaser and the trailer is to make the actual movie (the first time you have sex) matter. No one is suggesting that you remain chaste until your wedding night, but what we are saying is there is real value in building up to the actual event instead of just doing it. When you have sex quickly you're overlooking the glory of foreplay and anticipation, which are some of the premiere parts of the sexual experience. You only get this part, the newness, the beginning of the relationship once—YOU CAN'T GET IT AGAIN. Why would you want to rush through it when you could draw it out and really savor it for all its deliciousness? There is only *one* first kiss, *one* first touch, *one* first time you have sex together—why not make each one memorable because there was some anticipation involved? Seriously. We don't know if you've heard the news, but going the speed of light only serves the space program.

Sex is where people get the most screwed (pun intended) in dating. If you have sex **too soon** with someone you really like, you have a pretty good shot of f*#king up the relationship. The problem is when people want to get into a serious relationship they have sex too casually hoping it will expedite the process and create intimacy when in fact it often has the opposite effect. Sex is an intimate act and you cannot underestimate the power it has on two people when they hardly know one another. Sex changes things, even if you don't want it to or continue to pretend that it doesn't. People feel differently about each other after they've done it. Sometimes they feel closer, sometimes they feel weirder, sometimes they feel confused and sometimes they feel the beginning of the end. That's why we suggest that you can't lose by waiting to have sex until you get to know someone better but you can totally blow it by having sex too fast. We've spoken to every guy we know and they all agree that having sex changes how they feel about a woman. (Wow, what a revelation.) But here's the interesting thing, many of the guys we talked to said that a lot of times when they have sex with a girl they don't know very well that as soon as it's done, they're over her and they don't know why it is because she's still all the things she was before they did it. People don't always know why there's an internal shift and it's not always intentional, but sex triggers the "get me out of here" button in many men (and women for that matter), but it happens less to those that go slower.

We are not now, nor have we ever been, against casual sex. In fact we think that's all you should have from college until your mid-forties. Okay, that's not true. We think if you are comfortable with having casual sex then rock the sheets and, if used properly, casual sex can be a great learning tool as you evolve into a person who eventually wants to get into serious relationships (and has some good moves in the sack). We are talking about two different things here so let's be clear. There's the "I really like this guy and I want to have sex with him." And the "I'm just looking for someone to have a naked party with." If you're falling into the earlier category you have to decide when is the right time for you to have sex. Is it before you know each other? (PROBABLY NOT/RESOUNDING NO!) Is it after you know each other a little better? (MAYBE BUT ACTUALLY NO.) OR is it after you're both emotionally invested enough that it won't freak one of you out or make it a relationship based on sex? (HELL YES!) We like the idea of setting up a mental checklist of things that you only know about a person after you've spent some quality time with them. Once you know the details of the things on your list and many other juicy nuggets of information, not only will you have a better knowledge of your future sex mate but probably a deeper fondness. And that will make the sex even more rocking!

Example

✓ How they take their coffee.

✓ Which commercials make them angry and which ones make them nostalgic.

✓ What they call their Grandma and what Grandma calls them.

✓ A detailed account of their high school formal dance.

✓ Their most embarrassing moment.

✓ What they really like to do on Sundays when they're not trying to impress you.

✓ What they can tell you about you. (Do they know what you do for a living? Can they spell your last name?)

✓ What they are like after 10 dates (gotcha on that one)

Look, guys can find a girl to just have casual sex with but you get to decide if you're that girl. If you really like someone and want to have a shot at having a great relationship with them ... DON'T BE THAT GIRL.

BUT GREG, I HAVE QUESTIONS

But What If I Waited and He Still Bailed?

Dear Greg,

Okay, I saw you and your wife on the Today Show and you said something about waiting to have sex with a guy if you really like him. Well I took your idea to heart. At the time I was falling pretty hard for this musician named Pete who was ridiculously hot. Greg I'm no dummy and I wasn't going to sleep with him right away just because he was in a band but then I heard you and decided to really make him work for it. We waited almost two months! He was on and off the road to be fair so it's not like it was completely because of my will. Well finally we did it and it was awesome. I was so glad we waited I hadn't ever done that. But guess what Greg? Three days after the big night he broke it off? What gives … I WAITED and he still bailed right after we had sex.

Nova,

New York City

P.S. His band totally sucked.

Dear Band Aid,

Obviously there are no guarantees in life and people, especially musicians, can be weird it's just a fact. (Look it up on Wikipedia if you won't take my word for it.) That said, aren't you glad you gave it your best shot? Would it have been better if you had slept with him on the third date and then never heard from him, always wondering what you could have done better? You respected yourself and the situation and for that you should feel great. You tried to get to know someone before getting intimate with him—that's just smart living. I know that doesn't take the pain away but some guys are only going to be in it for the sex—it just happens. But that doesn't mean that you aren't a great person. In the long run you have succeeded in becoming a person who runs their life differently and I suspect you will attract an even better man next time, or at least one from a better band.

But What If We Won't See Each Other Again For Two Months?

Dear Greg,

I met this terrific gentleman online. The problem is, and always seems to be, that we live in different towns. He lives in Libertyville, Illinois and I live in San Carlos, California. We were online for a month and then we switched to the phone, texting, and instant messaging. We communicate all day every day. We've seen multiple pictures of one another (all clothed ha ha) and we seem to be really attracted to each other. Here's my question. Obviously our texts and e-mails have gotten flirty and a little sexual. Now he's coming to visit me for the weekend. He's getting a hotel but I feel like we are going to both want to have sex even though this is the first time we've been in person together. Is that the wrong move? I don't want to lose this guy but is this too early? What if we can't see each other for another couple of months?

Bethany
San Carlos, CA

Dear Cyberdater,

No I don't think you should and here's why ... It's your first real date. Chances are the moment he steps off the plane it's going to become really real for both of you and possibly a bit awkward because that's when he becomes a person. In fact I bet you don't start feeling comfortable with one another until halfway through the trip and only then will you know if this is a person worth being with at all. Sex changes things, it just does, and right now you are on a winning streak. So keep it in check until the next time and if there is real heat I bet you guys don't wait two months to see each other.

But What If Sex Is The Only Way To Keep Him?

Dear Greg,

I really liked this guy Liam and we dated for about a month before it became clear that we were at a standoff. I really didn't want to sleep with him until he had stopped sleeping with other women and he wasn't ready to commit to being only with me. So things got tense between us and it seemed like it was all going to be ruined if I didn't give in. So I slept with him figuring that he would be so happy that I had given in that he'd like me even more then stop seeing the other women. Well that didn't happen and now I'm just one of three women he's seeing and I don't even know if I'm at the top of the three or the bottom. What do I do now that he's having his cake and eating it too?

Imogen
London, England

Dear London Bridges,

How come your London Bridges are always falling down? I don't need to tell you that you shouldn't have caved in for this guy. What I will tell you is that in the future if you want to be in a monogamous relationship then don't have sex until you have defined the relationship as such—NO EXCEPTIONS. As for the having and eating his cake, the only thing you can do is take it away from him and save it for someone who will truly appreciate you and not make you wonder if you're bringing home the gold, silver or bronze medal in ladyfest.

How Do You Turn Casual Sex Into Actual Dating?

Dear Greg,

My lab partner and I started hooking up during our lab sessions and now I'm screwed. We see each other all the time between class, lab session and extra curricular hooking up but every time I try to get him to ask me out on a proper date he shuts me down. He says dating is too much pressure and that he's not really into old school dating. We go to a very prestigious school so you'd think he'd be able to handle pressure a little better. What the f*#%! How do I convert this thing from being a casual sex thing into more of a dating exclusively thing?

Maggie

Vancouver, Canada

Dear Lab-orious,

Wake up Maggie I think I got something to say to you. You set the tone for this thing from the beginning and attracted the kind of guy who according to you can't handle the "pressure" of dating you. Let's see how he handles the pressure of not getting to have sex with you as you back off this ridiculous relationship you set up for yourself. If dating is what you want then dating is what you do and nothing else. Tell Grabby the lab partner that you've tested the theory and run the data but his lack of effort less than equals the glory of getting down with you. If the thought of getting to continue having sex with you at some point isn't motivation enough for him to ask you out then you have your answer (He's Just Not That Into You) and if you need back-up I'll send you my first book.

FROM THE OTHER SIDE OF THE FENCE

What Does Waiting To Have Sex Really Mean?

Dear Greg,

Okay so I'm a bloke and I've read your books so clearly I'm messed up. I've been seeing this woman for two months now. We have the best time hanging out, skateboarding and going to gigs. But she will not have sex with me. I feel like she likes me because we snog (she's a good kisser) and whatever (meaning things that could be considered foreplay) but she says she wants to wait to have sex. She's not a Christian or anything, in fact I know she's slept with some other guys that she dated before sooner. Maybe I misunderstood your book but is she not into me?

Blake

Bristol, England

Dear Sensitive Skatepunk,

I think you did misunderstand what I was saying in *He's Just Not That Into You*. In that book I said if someone isn't interested in being sexual with you then you might want to consider that they are not that into you. She is in fact being sexual with you, maybe the fact that she hasn't slept with you is that she really likes you and sleeping with guys too quickly in the past hasn't worked for her. If it's not working for you then break it off, but I say if you're still getting hot kisses and what not what's the hurry? You still ride a skateboard and go to concerts so you're young at heart at the minimum.

THE CHICK WHO BLEW IT

It's hard to say "No" to a girl who wants to have sex with you on the first date. It's always pretty fun but afterwards it's so weird. What does she think it means? Does she think that we're going out now? Should I sleep over or go? Will she be mad if I go? The sex on the first date is tough because obviously I liked her enough to ask her out but, and I know it's a terrible thing to say, once you have sex the cat and mouse is over. You've already gotten the cheese. So I had been really jocking this girl Chloe to go out with me and she was playing hard to get/couldn't care less for the longest time. Then I finally broke her down and she agreed to having lunch with me during the week. Is lunch on a Wednesday even a date? So I went to her house to pick her up and she wasn't dressed yet. She walked from her bedroom to her bathroom in her bra and underwear right in front of me and I was thinking, "Oh, man please put on some clothes because I really like you and we need to go out to lunch or I'm screwed." Well she didn't get dressed in fact she just threw on an open robe and came and sat on the couch and suggested we watch TV. TV turned into making out, which turned into having sex. I kept thinking, I can be different, this time will be different but the truth is that I tend to lose interest with women that sleep with me on the first date. It's such a terrible thing to say but I couldn't go out with someone who gives it up so easily because if they're giving it up for me, how many others have gotten in on the action too? I can't believe I'm admitting that to you. I sound like a shit. Sex is different than love and even though we love having sex we'd trade good, easy sex in for a great love.

Scott

Scottsdale, AZ

MAYBE YOU GUYS ARE RIGHT

Every relationship I've ever had started sexually before emotionally. I'm 28 now and have never had a relationship that lasted longer than three months because somehow the sexual relationship didn't translate into an emotional one on both sides. More accurately, the guys never got as invested as I did and things just kind of fizzled out. Then when I met Josh I decided to take your advice and wait to have sex with him. I thought that waiting four dates would seem like an eternity but when we got to date four I realized that I really liked how things were going and I wasn't ready to change the dynamic of it yet by having sex so I decided to wait until the sixth date. Then date six rolls around and he mentions something like, "… when you meet my parents you'll see what I mean." We had yet to have sex and he could see me meeting his parents in the future! Unheard of. So date six blows by and on date eight, when things are already going better than with any other guy I've ever dated he says that he'd like it if I was his girlfriend. You have no idea what that felt like for me. If I could have stopped time I would have so I could leap right out of my seat and do a happy dance. So date eight was the magic number and that night we had sex and it was the greatest first sex I've ever had in my life. If I had known how much better sex is when you have significant feelings (other than lust) for someone I would have waited way before now. I guess I thought that sex was the way to get a guy but what I learned is that it's not the way to keep one. Guys stay when they like more than just having sex with you.

Vivianne

New Haven, CT

FIRST PERSON SINGLE by Amiira

Not that I should be applauded for my sex life but aside from one exception, I've always been one to keep my pants on. Not that I'm a prude or don't enjoy sex but strong is my desire to keep the membership to my super secret private club lower than the number of digits in my phone number (including area code ... and international calling code. Wait, how many is that?) Keeping my number low was a source of self-respect and not surprisingly a crazy turn-on for the Don Juans applying for a membership. When I started dating someone new it wasn't until we really knew each other and were going out exclusively that I showed them the secret handshake and laminated their membership card. Then one time I threw out the winning recipe and slept with a guy that I really liked on the second date. I thought what the hell, why not? We're on the right track, he likes me, I like him what difference can it make? So we had sex then went out for breakfast the next morning, me thinking, "wow, this is nice. I guess waiting isn't all that necessary." Clearly I was thinking that he and I were on the same page, that I was a good judge of character and that we were probably pretty much going out after having slept together. He on the other hand wasn't even in the same book much less on the same page as me as he saw fit to take home an "exotic dancer" the next night who needed a ride and didn't resurface for three days. Not only did it hurt my feelings that he slept with someone else but I was totally embarrassed for being so wrong about what I thought it had been and what we were moving towards. It only took once for me to learn the lesson that sex upfront doesn't always pay in the end. Not only that but the sex wasn't good enough to out-weigh how shitty it made me feel. Now you may not think that all guys will be okay with waiting but let me tell you a story. I used to work in the music business so I worked with fledgling bands and rock stars, all of who are used to having ladies give up the goods shortly after the initial "Hey, great show." A good majority of those same (aspiring and established) rock gods delighted at the idea of nailing one of the chicks from the record company so even when I was married to my first husband I was propo-sitioned quite often. While it was flattering and a little lame at the same time I learned to deflect their advances and keep my job. A flirty little, "I don't think I can expense condoms and a hotel room but thanks for thinking of me" always did the trick and, interestingly enough, every time my rejected rockers came into town it was my office that they would park their asses in to try to make headway into my super secret private club. During these headway sessions what happened is that we got to know each other and so I was the one they would call from the road for advice about how to get rid of some other record compa-ny girl they had gotten busy with then pledge their love to me and tell me how it would be different if I finally gave in (which I didn't by the way). The thing that became clear to me was that even the most happening guy wants to be told "NO", and not only that, he is titillated to try to work harder for it. Seems to me that having sex early can be a rocking good time but isn't always the shortcut to a good relationship. More often than not it's the road away from one.

THOUGHTS FROM MAN CITY

You ladies run the show. I know many of you don't think you do but YOU DO! With the exception of some extreme assholes, we guys will pretty much do only what you let us. Example: If you let us come over at 4 a.m. for a "snack" then we're coming over BUT if you say we have to wait a few weeks until we know each other better then WE WILL WAIT. If we can't wait ... well then we only *ever* wanted to just have sex with you in the first place. Sorry ladies but it's the truth. I know you think you have to have sex with us or we're going to leave but if sex is all we want we're going to leave anyway. That's how I see it. I'm just me. Whenever I had sex with a woman too early on, here's what would happen: My head would be so clouded with the idea of having sex that I often wasn't sure whether I liked them or just wanted to "do it" because sex is on guys' minds much of the time. Then as soon as I would orgasm I'd realize "Oh, I only wanted sex" OR "Wow I don't even know this person!" It would be awkward and often I'd bail. Now I take full responsibility for my actions. It wasn't the girls' fault we had sex too early or that I wasn't emotionally able to handle it, but I think this is a common problem for many men. We are not sure which end of it we're on in the early stages, if it's sex or a relationship that we want. Since I believe that women are the gate keepers to sex I'd have to tell you that if you want to be sure a guy's there for more than sex— KEEP THE GATES LOCKED FOR A BIT. You might be interested to know that many of us want you to make us work for it. That there is great pleasure in not getting what you want right off the bat. It makes you work harder to get it. And along the way we get to know you better, know your taste in music, wine, clothes, how many cats you have, your brother's name and why we like you in the first place besides your smile and sweet-smelling skin. So if you like us and you're interested in more than just sex make it a challenge. And any guy who calls you a tease is a chump. It's not a tease, it is, as we discussed earlier in this chapter, a preview to a movie that we are so glad we got cast in.

 DATING FORTUNE COOKIE

Sex is the way to reach an orgasm not a commitment.

WORST DATE EVER

I liked this guy forever and thought he would never ask me out because I saw him all the time but he never even looked in my general direction. Then one night he walked over to me and my friends at the bar we all hang out at and told me with a smile that it really hurt his feelings that I hadn't asked him out yet. I laughed at his little pick-up line and we spent the rest of the night talking, drinking and flirting. Then he asked if he could come home with me and I know I shouldn't have let him but I did. So we went back to my place and had mind-blowing sex. We were up all night talking, having sex and then snacking naked at the fridge. It was one of my best nights ever. I had liked this guy from afar for so long and he was as great as I hoped he would be. So before going our separate ways in the morning we decided to meet back at the bar around 8 that night. I went to work and called every last one of my girlfriends and told them about my scandalous yet awesome night and invited them all to come meet us for drinks. So I get to the bar with my girlfriends and I'm waiting for him to show and it's 8 o'clock then 8:30 then 9 o'clock then 9:30 and there's no sign of him. At 10:15 he comes rolling in with another girl! So I go up to him and tell him that I've been waiting for him since 8 p.m. and he plays completely dumb like he has no idea what I'm talking about. So I say, "Are you going to introduce me to your friend?" Now I'm totally feeling like a crazy jealous woman trying not to lose my sh*t. And he says, "I would if I knew your name." Then he and his girl breezed past me like I was a nut job and sat in another room in a booth with its back turned to where I was so he wouldn't have to see me. I've never been so embarrassed and humiliated in my whole life.

IT'S JUST F*#KING SEX

Don't get us wrong, it is one of the more awesome aspects of being human. That's why it should be respected as such when it comes to love. Sex doesn't solve problems or solidify relationships. What we believe sex should be is an enhancement to what should already exist like friendship, trust and a mutual respect for the artistry of the Arctic Monkeys. Give sex its due and put it in its proper place and it will serve you better.

The Original World Famous Winner Dater's Workbook

It's time to make your checklist of things you should know about the guy (or gal) you're thinking about having sex with. The list must be comprised of things that you couldn't possibly know about him without having invested many dates and hours' worth of conversation to uncover. While you're at it why don't you make a list of things he should know about you before he gets to know what you look like in the buff? We'll start you off with a few, then you're on!

What I Want To Know About Him
1. What's one thing he's always wanted to try (that's not related to sex)?
2. Where did his parents meet?
3. Favorite band, favorite record, favorite song, favorite movie
4.
5.
6.
7.
8.
9.
10.

What I Want Him To Know About Me

1. What my favorite thing is on the menu at three different restaurants
2. Who my best friend is and what he or she looks like (that means he's got to meet your friends)
3. Favorite smell
4.
5.
6.
7.
8.
9.
10.

principle #8: not every date is going to turn into a relationship

And A Worthwhile Relationship Is A Journey Not A Race

There's nothing quite like the feeling of meeting someone new. Your whole body is awake and alive, your mind is buzzing—it's as if your entire being is vibrating at another frequency. The speed at which thoughts and ideas occur as you see flashes of your future is dizzying and thrilling, it's the exhilaration of new like and possibly future love.

There you are in line for a coffee when he asks for the time. You oblige with the information and blush when he admits to already having a watch and just using the time as an excuse to talk to you. Two hours later you're still at the coffee shop talking animatedly and kind of falling for this cute guy with an English pop star haircut that's asking you to dinner. He kisses you on the cheek after entering your digits into his mobile phone and cementing dinner plans for the next night. All the way home you nearly levitate with the giddiness of liking someone new that you "totally connect" with for the first time in a long time. For the next thirty-six hours until your dinner date with the cute guy from the coffee shop (or at least the ones that you're conscious for) you think about him, replay the kiss goodbye, think about what to wear, tell your friends about him, remember what his smile looked like, wonder where he grew up and whether his parents still live there, wonder if you'll like his parents, think about how cute you'll look together walking around the city on the weekends, wonder if he'll move into your place or you'll move into his, feel the relief of having a date for your sister's wedding, wonder if the wedding will get him thinking about marriage, debate keeping your own name or taking his when the two of you get married, replay the kiss goodbye, think about what you're going to wear to dinner, wonder if you'll get married in a church or outdoors, envision the two of you running amidst the pouring grains of rice to climb into the car with "Just Married" written in soap on the rear view window, replay the moment he admitted that the time was just an excuse to talk to you and on and on it goes until dinner with the dreamboat. The future looks bright ... then he never calls and your "end resulting" only results in being more crushed than necessary.

(End resulting being when you play a scenario so far out in the future in your head that you become invested in the future or end result instead of the present reality.)

There's something intoxicating about liking someone new and thinking that "this might be it." We can't help ourselves we just race into the future with our thoughts and desires because we want that thing that we don't have. We want to lock down our future happiness so we know that we're not going to miss out. It's the place where desire and desperation meet. It doesn't feel desperate because the rush of feelings is so yummy but the "end resulting" is a manifestation of fear that we might miss out. That's not to say that you shouldn't get the future that you want, just that you're less likely to it if you try to cement it prematurely. *People arrive at their true feelings at their own pace*. Rushing yourself or someone else into feeling something they're unsure of or bending and reshaping yourself to try to be what will get them to commit is the beginning of the end. We know it's exciting and anxiety riddled because you want so badly for it to work out. For something to be "the thing" that fills in the blanks you're leaving open, but you have to calm those feelings down. Take your time getting to know not only this person *but also you with this person*. Relationships are like desserts: they are to be savored and enjoyed otherwise you rush through them and get a headache, feel sick and wish you hadn't had one in the first place. Beside, what's the rush?

Think about this, when you find the "One" and decide to spend the rest of your life together, barring sudden death, *you're looking at a very long time.* Seriously. That's why people get cold feet before weddings, not because they think they chose the wrong china pattern it's because **FOREVER IS A LONG F*#KING TIME.** Spending the rest of your days with one person is a daunting idea and one that many cannot actually accomplish. All that second-guessing about "Are they the right person for me?" "Was I really being me when we fell in love or was I being who I thought they wanted me to be?" The reason the divorce rate is so high is because people rush into relationships so quickly and bend and reshape themselves into what they think the other person wants in an effort to nail something down. Then cut to years later down the road when the newness has worn off and they realize that they can't stay with this person forever. Or even worse, that they're not that person they pretended to be. **NOT EVERY RELATIONSHIP YOU HAVE IS MEANT TO LAST FOREVER**—that goes for friendships, romances and even family. Maybe that guy you're still hung up on that was the one that got away was only meant to last for two years and that's why it went so wrong in year three.

Even the best relationship is going to have parts that are dull beyond belief and not even noteworthy. The thing about a meaningful relationship is that it will continually change as the two of you change and become more attuned to each other. However, if you rush through the beginning to get to the middle of it you miss so much of the good stuff that you really need to make a relationship last. Most relationships end because one (or both) people are missing something, longing for something else, someone else, a new set of experiences. Let us make an analogy. Meeting new people, dating new people, having sex with new people, falling in love, feeling lust, anticipation—all of those experiences are like opening a box on Christmas morning. When you're in a long-term relationship as time goes on you don't get a lot of that "experiencing something new feeling" beyond the big events in your lives. Consequently, when you hit a big lull, rocky or dull patch you tend to crave something different, something new—you want to open a new box. When you race through the good stuff early on in the relationship like a kid tearing through their presents to see what they all are, you don't fully experience opening the boxes in a *memorable way*. So when you're in a bad place in your relationship and could use some reinforcement, you're unable to recall the memories and feelings of that rush of excitement of opening the "first time you kissed" box or the "first time you saw each other naked" box or the "first time you really missed each other" box or the "first time you robbed a bank together" box. It may sound trite but having those experiences and being hyper-aware of them as they're happening is what gets you through tough times in a relationship. It's those experiences *in the beginning* of your relationship that fuel your desire to persevere when things aren't spectacular instead of abandoning ship to find a new box to open. So if you motor through those moments, the opening of those new boxes when it's happening, they won't resonate as being the profound and excellent experiences that are the building blocks of a lasting union.

The goal is to have a relationship that rocks and lasts forever (which we've established is a very long time) so it's the decision you should be the most discerning and certain of. Think about how much time and thought you put into buying a car. You wouldn't just go to a car dealership, hand him a pile of cash and say, "I'll take the red one." No, you'd want to look at many cars, many models, test drive a few, compare prices, look under the hood, kick the tires and be sure, then double sure, then triple sure that you're making the right choice for you. And buying a car is a decision that you can change every few years! So why would you rush into a relationship without the same deliberation? Look, you're not always going to be in sync with the person you're dating. One of you generally gets in deeper sooner, but don't be afraid to arrive at your emotions at your own pace. Don't mistake having sex as a tool for locking down a relationship. And don't be rushed into being anything other than a Summer Blockbuster Movie! Slow down, be the real you and just be in the moment. The rest will take care of itself.

BUT GREG, I HAVE QUESTIONS

But Dating Online Goes Fast?

Dear Greg,

Okay, so I've been divorced for three years and I'm finally ready to start dating. I meet this guy online and we really hit it off. He sends me funny e-mails that are flirty and cute without being pervy. Finally we decide to meet and go dancing (we both like 70s disco) after about two weeks of corresponding. He's cute, we get along even better in person and everything seems great except for one thing, he's really anxious to lock down a commitment from me as though we've been dating this whole time and it's the first time we've met. I can almost feel his panic and it's turning me off. I never said anything to mislead him or even indicate that I didn't want to date others as well. We have so much in common and I really like him but I don't want to be pressured into a relationship. That's how my marriage started and that was a disaster. The flip side is I'm 38 and I don't want to end up alone. Help!

Sophia

Milan, Italy

Dear Panic At The Disco,

Lock this down immediately! 38 years old? How do you disco with your walker? Are discos even open at 5:30 in the afternoon? Old women like you should hang on to any warm body you can find! Am I making my point? Here's the great thing about your situation: You've been to the dance (literally as well as figuratively) already and this time you want to do it right. Trust that and stop worrying about your age. You set the pace on the Internet or anywhere else and all you've got to do is be communicative with him about how you intend to live your life post-divorce and that you need to take things slowly. If this dude is worth his salt he'll be down with that and if he's not then he's not the guy you want to dance with anyway. Now go eat your pudding, Grandma.

But What If A Situation Speeds It Up?

Dear Greg,

I'm dating this guy who is perfect for me but we've hit a bit of a patch. It started pretty casually just hanging out a couple times a week at the pub we met at then taking it back to my flat. Things heated up pretty quickly and he started sleeping over a few times a week and everything was great. Here's where it got wonky. His landlord just sold the building he lives in and the new owners just raised his rent excessively so he can no longer afford to live there. He's got less than a month to find a new flat so I said that he could move in with me temporarily until he finds one. I thought he'd be excited at the thought since I'm offering a place to stay rent free and we're already going out so he stays here anyway. But instead of being thrilled he has totally pulled back. What happened?

Sabina

Brussels, Belguim

Dear Rent Free Romance,

This is a classic case of scaring him off. What happened was you had established a relationship that you were both comfortable with in its frequency of seeing each other and the looseness of future commitment. But by asking him to move in, even temporarily, you made your intentions clear about stepping it up in the future before he was ready to go there. When you propose cohabitation, even out of consideration for his situation, the unspoken agenda is that you're getting more serious, exclusive and planning a future together. Call him back and tell him that you weren't trying to accelerate the relationship and that you'd love to help him find a place. Everybody likes you when you want to help them move.

But What If I Can't Help Myself?

Dear Greg,

Doug and I have been on six dates if you include the night we met. I count it because we talked all night and it lasted longer than many of my other first dates have. We just had sex for the first time on our sixth date and I think he likes me as much as I like him. I want him to be my boyfriend and I told him so after we had sex, well not that bluntly but I initiated the "Where is this thing going? / Are you seeing anyone else?" conversation. He was non-committal aside from reassuring me that he liked me a lot and that he likes the way things are progressing. What the hell does that mean? I know I shouldn't push him for more but I don't know if I can help myself. I haven't had a boyfriend in three years and I don't want to lose him and I don't want to seem desperate either.

Carla

Las Vegas, NV

Dear Borderline Desperation,

Wow, there is a lot going on here. So first things first, not to put too fine a point on it but I think it's best if you have the "Are you seeing any one else?" question before slipping out of your skivvies. It's just healthier. As for the "Where is this thing going?" question, again if you don't know maybe you shouldn't sleep with this person until you feel comfortable enough that he'll be around afterwards to watch Conan. Unless this is just a sexual relationship it's best to ask questions first then get your "get on" on later. As for his response that he "likes the way things are progressing," you've got your answer. He's not ready to commit but he's enjoying your sex on the sixth date rule. If you pressure him for more you probably will lose him because people like to arrive at the way they feel because they actually feel it, not because someone's making them feel bad about not feeling it fast enough. Take a deep breath, slow yourself down and try to stay present for the present and not worry about locking down the future. Even if you do end up locking down the relationship, you'll have missed the good stuff that got you there. If you find yourself losing control and wanting to pressure him then call a friend and ask her to tie you to a tree until the feeling passes.

But What If I've Already Rushed Into A Marriage?

Dear Greg,

I met Jackson at an all-day music festival two years ago this summer. It was love at first sight, lust at first sight, completely overwhelming at first sight. By the end of the day we were together and three months later we got married in Vegas. Things were magical for the first year, everything was perfect but sometime after that the magic wore off and it feels like we hardly even know each other. We really love each other and feel like we were destined to be together so we want to make this marriage work. How can we be so close but still feel like complete strangers some days?

Tally

Shreveport, LA

Tally, Tally, Tally,

The problem, my magical little elf, is that you and Jackson never dated so you don't really know each other. The whole reason dating exists is so that people can get to know each other and figure out if there's an attraction and compatibility that is *strong enough* for a long-term commitment. The truth of the matter is that you are married to a relative stranger and had you dated instead of running away to Vegas you would have had a better idea if there were something besides the cosmic connection that you both share or whether or not you can actually live with one another. You rushed through the yummy part and skipped to the middle and now it's not what you expected. I get it. So what do you do? Two things. One: go see a professional marriage counselor or therapist and see what they suggest. Two: Start dating your husband again. After trying these two things you may find that you aren't compatible and the marriage isn't meant to be. Sometimes the cosmos only want us to be together for two months, not a lifetime. And there's nothing wrong with that— we're all guilty of misreading the stars and romantic situations at some point or another.

FROM THE OTHER SIDE OF THE FENCE

But How Slow Is Too Slow?

Dear Greg,

I've been seeing this amazing girl for four weeks now and I'm totally out of my element. Usually I meet someone, go out once or twice, sleep together then stay with them for a few months before moving on. I know, not cool but that has been my pattern up until now. This new girl, Anonda, has heard tales about me so she's been really clear about not wanting to be another notch on my bedpost and wants to take it slow. So we've been dating for a month now and I'm afraid to kiss her. I really like her, more than any other girl I've met and I don't want to go too fast and make her think that I'm only after sex. How slow is slow enough??

Travis

Bellingham, WA

Dear Snail's Pace,

Man did you luck out! There is, in my not so humble opinion, nothing sexier or better than a woman who knows what she wants and that puts you off your "game". The best advice I can give you is, be honest and forthright with her. Just because she wants to go slow doesn't mean she wants you to not feel sexually towards her. Four weeks in, she might be wondering what's up so I'd simply tell her in your own way, "Hey I'm ready for that first kiss whenever you are." Have fun with it and, seriously dude, you will be so happy you guys went this route because you only get the first part of a relationship once so you might as well make it last.

THE CHICK THAT BLEW IT

I had a crush on this girl from college that I never had the guts to ask out. So years later when I saw her at a college friend's wedding I was determined not to miss my opportunity to go out with her. We started dating and she was as great as I had always imagined she would be and, believe me, I had thought about it a lot over the past nine years. So we're about two months into exclusive dating, I'm seeing her three or four times a week and we're really starting to get to know each other well. Things are great, she's great, I'm great ... then one night we're having dinner and she's quiet and standoffish. I ask her what's wrong and she says we need to talk about our future. She told me that she's going to be 32 soon and wants to get married and start having kids in the next year or so and if I'm not going to marry her that she doesn't want to see me anymore. What?! We've only been dating for two months! Sure I had thought about her a ton for years but didn't really know her or whether or not we'd actually be a good match. I told her that it was too soon for me to know. I really was into her and maybe even falling in love with her but I couldn't tell her for sure two months into dating that we're definitely going to get married and have kids immediately. This was very early on in our relationship, like before meeting each other's friends and family kind of early and she totally freaked me out. It wasn't that she asked, I think it's okay to be clear about what you want, it was her panic about it and demanding that I commit to something as big as marriage before we're even sure we're in love with each other that turned me off. I want to get married, I do and had she not rushed me with an unrealistic ultimatum we might have gone down that path naturally and maybe even gotten married and had kids in the time frame she wanted, but instead she dumped me. By the way ... she's still single and 34 now. How do I know that? Because she recently called to ask if she could see me again and I felt terrible when I had to tell her that I was engaged.

Aaron

Cleveland, OH

THE CHICK THAT ROCKED IT

Every relationship I've ever had has gone from zero to living together in like three months flat. Of course, none of those actually lasted because I finally figured out that it takes more than three months to really know someone. Until you've traveled together, nursed the other when they're sick and seen them at least at their semi-worst you have no business moving in together. I've changed apartments and boyfriends five times in the last seven years. So I decided to try something different the next time I got involved with someone: that I would self-impose an "opposite corners" rule. That meant no moving in and sleepovers were on an invite-only-basis, not a show-up-on-your-doorstep assumption. So when Bradley and I started dating, I took it slow for the first time ever, really slow. Normally my first dates last a week and a half but this time I let him kiss me goodbye outside the front door. The next time we went out I got food poisoning and spent the entire night vomiting, which isn't generally a very sexy or romantic second date. Bradley took care of me—I'm talking holding my hair back while I throw up, changing the cold compress on my forehead, renting me movies and going to the deli to get me soup, crackers and ginger ale. The whole weekend he took care of me only leaving to go home and shower and change clothes. He even did my laundry because I had spewed all over my sheets and pajamas. Bradley and I have been together for almost a year and a half now and I can confidently say that I know him better than anyone else in the world and he holds that same status with me. We've been talking about moving in together soon, which makes me laugh when I think of all the past relationships that I raced through to get to this stage and how little I knew those guys and how those relationships ended as fast as they started. Yesterday we went looking at apartments to see what was out there and we found the perfect place. You know how I knew it was perfect? Because he pulled a ring box out of his pocket and asked me to marry him by the fireplace in the empty living room of our new apartment.

Monica

Brooklyn Heights, NY

FIRST PERSON SINGLE by Amiira

At this point in my life I can say that I'm an authority on the shelf-life of relationships, or rather the authority on what the shelf-life *should* have been in hindsight. It's almost embarrassing how poor my judgment was until the age of thirty. There was the boyfriend that I had only intended on going out with for the two months before I moved away who then followed me across the country therefore obligating me (in my own mind) to stay with him for nearly two years. I knew from the beginning that I wasn't that into being in the relationship but I'm young so what's a little time, right? Shelf-Life: 2 months, Real Time Spent: 21 months. That'll teach me, though. Not at all. How about the guy who had a girlfriend when we met (though he pursued me anyway) who always without fail had overlapping relationships where the new one began before the old one had ended or fizzled out? That's what some might call a giant warning about someone's ability to be faithful and committed to one person. But not to me! I should have probably avoided that guy altogether but I didn't because I was sure he was going to be "The One" and I could change that about him. Surely "Happily Ever After" was just around the corner or some corner if I could just find a freakin' corner to look around. Shelf-Life: 6 months, Real Time Spent: 4½ years. Gasp! Well at least I'm still pretty young and I've got a couple years before I'm 30 so I'll be fine. Besides I learn from my mistakes ... Oh wait, not when there's best guy friend who's been nothing but supportive during my last breakup that I just adore who one night after too many beers drunkenly proclaimed his love for me. How could I not give it a try? I do love him, well maybe not like that, but we're such great friends, what could go wrong? Hmmm. I mean I really wanted it to work because he was so great and it would have been perfect because we were such good friends ... but it wasn't great. In fact it wasn't even great adjacent, it was only mistake adjacent and completely friendship ruining. Shelf-Life: 15 (drunken) Minutes, Real Time Spent: 1½ years. Holy Mother of

Pearl! What is wrong with me? At that point I really had to sit my own 30-year-old ass down and say, "What the f*#k?" When was I going to realize that sometimes lemons are just lemons? You don't have to try to make lemonade out of all of them. There are varying degrees of love and varying degrees of compatibility. Not every guy you like, love or lust after is worth giving up years of your life for, just like not every friend you've ever had will be someone you grow old with. Hell I couldn't pick my best friend from childhood out of a line up of three people unless the other two were my children. Same goes for my "soul mate" from college and my cousin Tim. It only took me fourteen years of dating to figure that one out because as we all know, you don't get to be an authority on anything without some serious schooling.

THOUGHTS FROM MAN CITY

We've all been there. You are seeing someone new, it's exciting, there are so many unspoken possibilities in the first few weeks. Everything's going great and then out of the blue they just up and do it ... They say something that implies a solidifying of the relationship. Like dropping the "I can't wait for my parents to meet my new boyfriend" bomb. Or they start a sentence with, "When we have our own place ..." or "What boys' names do you like? I think Justin is played." And you think to yourself "Awwwwwwwww why you gotta do that now? We were having so much fun NOT defining it." There is a time and a place for everything and, you know me, I have always been the advocate of ask for what you want in a relationship, but ladies, please! I know that men are guilty of the same thing so you know how it makes you feel when the shoe is on the other foot. The person you're casually dating and just getting to know suddenly becomes needy and it freaks you out. Trying to nail down a more defined relationship is not meant to scare guys away and you'd think we'd be flattered by it, but instead we withdraw because we are not emotionally ready to be there. Everyone comes along at their own speed and you have to consider that your new person may not be there yet. So when in doubt, wait. You'll know when it's time.

 DATING FORTUNE COOKIE

A race is something you try to finish fast. A relationship is something you try to make last.

WORST DATE EVER

Loris and I met at a convention and hit it off immediately. We hung out for the whole weekend and went to every discussion, event and dinner together. It's like we bonded out of boredom because, let's face it, conventions are D-U-L-L! So at the end of the weekend we exchanged information and decided to stay in touch. She only lived

35 miles away so I called her the week after the convention and asked her to dinner because we'd had so much fun together. I picked her up at her house and we went to dinner. During dinner she gave me a photo album that she had taken during the convention with a photo of the two of us on the front. She told me that she had looked into transferring to a branch closer to where I lived so it'd be easier for us to hang out. I started to panic but decided to calm down and give her the benefit of the doubt. A few minutes later she got a call on her mobile and she told whoever was on the other end of the call that she was at dinner with her boyfriend. When she hung up the phone I told her that we weren't boyfriend/girlfriend and that I considered this to be our first official date. I didn't want to embarrass her but, c'mon—hanging out at a convention for three days because you're trapped. She burst into tears, slapped me across the face and yelled that she didn't want to "trap" me any longer. Right in the middle of her air quotes and tears our meals came and I didn't know what to do so we ate in silence then I took her home. The thing that sucked is that I liked her and we might have actually gone on to be boyfriend/girlfriend if she had just been on a date with me instead of trying to lock it down.

IT'S JUST A F*#KING DATE PT.2

The journey has to start somewhere. We suggest a date. What's the worst that could happen? At the very least you left the house and went into the world, which is how every great adventure starts. Now, that doesn't mean every time you go on a date you are going to start a great adventure or even a good one. However, if you go in with an open mind, if you go in not wanting to bail or figure out where the two of you are going to honeymoon, if you go in knowing that any time spent with you is magical, then you might just have a great time.

The Original World Famous Winner Dater's Workbook

It's time for a personal inventory! Hooray! This is when you take a long look at all your past relationships and identify why you got into them in the first place, how you got into them and why they weren't the right fit. It's important for you to be able to identify any patterns you have with rushing into relationships, compromising who you are to be in them or bending and reshaping yourself to be what someone else wants you to be. It's this type of self-examination that helps you gain the ability to stop repeating patterns and mistakes when entertaining the idea of a relationship. So next time you find yourself rushing into a relationship and trying to define it quickly you'll be more able to think about what you're doing. Ask yourself why you want to be in a relationship so badly? Why are you in such a hurry to lock this thing down? Why are you more concerned with having any relationship instead of being sure it's a good relationship?

Ready ... GO!

part two

carpe datem— seize the date!

! WARNING!

The date you are about go on probably won't work out.
Most of them don't, that's just life. But if used properly
dates can be one hell of a way to spend an evening and
meet another person who, like you, has the hope of
someday meeting someone great, so at least you have
that in common.

**Dating combined with excessive alcohol intake could
prove harmful. Use only as directed.

As your dating "Doctors" we prescribe that you date as
much as possible to alleviate the pressure that comes with
only going on one date a year.

the essence of keeping it cool

Or Zen And The Art Of Carpe Datem

Welcome to the second part of the *It's Just A Date!* experience. This is where you learn how to take all your past mistakes, mis-steps and misconceptions and ignite them in a fiery mass and burn them in a bonfire of "who gives a shit?" because they are the past and you are the future.

You are now officially a dater. You are not a hooker-upper or a hanger-outer, you are a person who lives and dates at a higher level. When someone is trying to kick down the big steel doors to your prized heart they will have to make an effort deserving of your exclusive company.

By now you have read and are on your way to mastering the Super Extraordinary Principles For Ultra-Successful Winner Dating. You now know there are a lot of factors that influence any dating situation, from how you approach dating (does it give you hives and arrhythmia, give you verbal diarrhea?), how you prepare yourself (do you need a shot of whiskey before you open the front door?) to how to behave (ladylike always trumps hi-fives and beer farts) and what to wear on the date (panties yes, Crocs no!). What exactly are permissible topics on a first date (stay away from bodily functions, family dysfunction and ex-boyfriends)? Should you worry about waxing and lingerie? (Always, because you never know when you're going to be in a car accident and they're going to be seen. But it's *your* little secret.) What's he thinking when he does X, Y & Z? (Who f*#king cares? What are YOU thinking when he does X,Y & Z?) This next part of our excellent tome is dedicated to how to get dates and how to go on them.

Dating is like going on Space Mountain for the first time. Once you commit to doing it and strap yourself in you have no idea what's going to happen. Scary, right? Sure, but the other thing it can be is a blast or even a scary blast. Dating is supposed to be fun, or at least relatively painless, but somehow we've made dating the villain or the enemy in the quest to find love.

Yes, there can be a degree of fear, dread even when you're faced with the prospect of finding someone worthy of dating in the first place (which isn't the easiest thing to do), then pile on the factors of getting them to notice you back, going out on a date, playing your cards right, not having sex too soon or freaking each other out, not future projecting your wedding plans or reacting to scenarios that haven't and may not ever happen. Then there's the rejection, ohhhh the unrelenting sting of the rejection that tortures you while it dissolves your self-esteem like butter on hot toast. It's a complete maelstrom! A whirlpool of emotion and confusion that stays messes with your head indefinitely. Then why do you put up with it? Why should you put up with it? The maelstrom only happens because you do it to yourself. When you put that kind of pressure on anything, dating included, it's not going to be fun. How could it be when it's just a f*#king date? Why not take each challenge as it presents itself instead of trying to figure them all out before you've left the house? Heck, why even view it as a challenge instead of an opportunity? Dating is an opportunity to get to know another human being for all their quirks and shining glory. How is that not a good time? Even a shitty date makes for a good story the next day over coffee with your posse.

We know that it's easier said than done ... or is it? Here's a preview of what lies ahead to guide you on your quest for getting dates, going on dates and not blowing it.

The 6 Essences of dating success:

✓ **Essence #1 There is no one place to meet guys**
Where the boys are

✓ **Essence #2 The power of suggestion**
How to get asked out

✓ **Bonus section! Internet date-tacular!**
Tickling the mouse pad

✓ **Essence #3 It's just a f*#king first date!**
How to be a great first date and how to have one

✓ **Essence #4 First date follow up**
Communication and the RIGHT next move

✓ **Essence #5 2nd date and beyond**
Pacing your dates and the formula for success

✓ **Essence #6 Sexclusivity**
Getting it on and locking it down

Not to put too fine a point on it but dating is all we have for the next hundred years until we're all assigned a bar-code on our silver jumpsuits that correlates with our pre-selected mate. By the way, in the future we all live on the space station but at least we get to wear silver jumpsuits. Like we've mentioned before, most dates you go on won't work out just like most relationships won't work out ... UNTIL THE ONE THAT DOES. But that's the one that everyone is searching for and if you didn't know in your heart that when you find your person, your "one" that every single thing you've gone through and endured would be worth it you'd have given up already. Finding the one is worth it every day of the week and twice on Sunday.

That's why we say CARPE DATEM! SEIZE THE DATE!

11

essence #1: there is no one place to meet guys

Where The Boys Are

"There's no one out there to date" and "_____ (insert your town's name, your state's name, country, school or continent) is the worst place to date." Those are the two most common complaints that we've heard from all the Singles we've encountered since we first started writing relationship books. So either dating on the other planets is a piece of cake or finding someone to date is a universal problem. (We're betting our chips on the latter.) Here's the good and bad news: There Is No **One** Good Place To Meet Someone. Everywhere there are people is a good place to meet a potential date. Seriously, even the morgue could be a good place if the forensics guy was hot and you caught each other's eye. It isn't about where you go because there are men everywhere you go and look ... except at women-only venues like the ladies room and La

Leche League and who wants to date the guy at the breastfeeding meetings? These guys you see nearly everywhere you go in life, they're looking to meet you too. Besides, it's less about "where" than you think.

Maybe if you've been paying attention you know that making a connection or having an impact is more about *who* you are when you're there then *where* you are. Who you are pulls the focus of others and either keeps it or dismisses it. Our motto is why be dull or drab when you could be sparkly?

Let's expand on that concept because it draws upon a number of the Principal Principles of Ultra-Successful Winner Dating. Who you are when you go anywhere in the world (meaning what you project to others) will determine what types of people you will attract and how people respond to you. The goal is to have people respond to you, be drawn to you, be curious about you. So once you've put all the Principles of Ultra-Successful Winner Dating in effect you will start attracting new people. If you like yourself and know you're worthy you'll carry yourself with an air of confidence, which is sparkly. If you have a life that is buoyant, fulfilling and interesting you'll exude that kind of energy, an energy that reads as sparkly. When you've taken the time to look really good from your head to your toes and in between you'll radiate the magnetism of a woman completely self-possessed who has some serious standards and is, you guessed it, sparkly. Let's be real, you don't want to meet just *anyone* because just anyone won't do, otherwise you would have settled for the guy that threw up on you at the fair in high school. You want to meet someone that values himself as much as you value yourself (another Ultra-Successful Winner Dater type of guy if you will) that you might have something in common or share an interest with, right?

Now that you know *who* you need to be when you go (a radiant and together super hot lady who likes herself, knows her worth, lives a life that rocks even when she's just home hanging out) we need to get back to the *where* you should be going. If you want to meet someone that you share an interest with you have to narrow down, out of all the places available to you to meet the male of the species, where the best places for you to meet potential suitors would be. There are the obvious ideas like to go to the park or join a hiking group if you love the outdoors and want to meet a fellow outdoorsman. Or hit the galleries and museums if you want to find another art lover like yourself. Sure they are valid (if not predictable) suggestions but we think you should **get specific with who you are and where you will shine the brightest when deciding where to go to meet a great guy**. When you're somewhere that you truly are excited about being or that you connect with on a *deeper* level you are more likely to be comfortable, confident and magnetic. All of which are spectacularly winning assets when it comes to attracting future dates. So think about it, where do you love being? What do you love doing? Where are you the best version of you? (Beside at home where there aren't other potential human beings to date.) Those are the places that you are most likely to be a person that attracts and intrigues others and meet someone you will connect with. Do you get what we're talking about?

Do you love Coldplay? Does their music move you at the core of your being? Then go to Coldplay concerts where there will be other people that connect to their music and where you'll most certainly be looking foxy, exuding joy and being the most exotic and sparkly you that you are. If you happen to meet someone at the Coldplay show then you already know you have one thing in common that you can have a full conversation about. Or if you're a diehard supporter for the environment then get involved and *stay* involved with its causes, fundraisers or protests on a regular basis and go meet some other activists. Even if all the activists you meet that are appealing to you are women you still win because women sometimes have male friends and brothers as it turns out. If you like a woman, you'll probably like her male friends and siblings and you can ask her to hook you up.

Sure you can go to bars and nightclubs if that's where you feel great, but generally the people going to bars and nightclubs aren't there looking for long-term relationships as much as someone to hook up, hang out or have sex with. Not to mention that anywhere where drinking is the main activity that is offered is dangerous non-dating territory. C'mon people, we've discussed this already! The places you go, your venues, send a message to the people around you because they're probably at those same venues for similar reasons. A bar says "I like drinking and having some casual, letting-off-some-steam fun." A nightclub says "I like dancing, music, drinking and casual racy fun." Whole Foods says I'm serious about the planet and my body. I try to surround myself with the best options for me and I put a lot of thought into it … and I'm probably a yoga enthusiast. Jiffy Lube says I can handle my own affairs and am a self-sufficient woman who looks very cute in her casual weekend car-maintenance attire.

Alright, we know who you need to be when you're out in the world to attract guys, where you should go to narrow the field of guys, now it's up to you to meet them. Not every guy you want to approach you will. It's sad but true … mind control is still not perfected. So there are times when it's up to you to break the ice and pull the focus over to your "Sparklyness" or whatever you want to call your bad-ass self. Sure you can see a guy you want to meet and go over and introduce yourself and hope for conversation that makes him notice that there's something cool about you. But why not see a guy you want to meet and just be sparkly up front with the way you meet him?

Let us show you how it's done …

Setting: You're at a restaurant. He's cute but engaged in
  conversation with his buddies and doesn't notice you.

Possibly awkward introduction:

"Good burgers, huh? I'm Jen by the way."

(Now the reason this could be awkward is that he may
not want to be interrupted and be dismissive to you
as a result.)

Sparkly introduction:

"Can I borrow your ketchup?"

(Wait for ketchup)

"Can I borrow a French fry to go with it?"

(Wait for French fry and smile or laugh from cute guy
that appreciates how clever you are and is pleased to
be interrupted by such.)

"Thanks. You can put it on my tab, my name's Jen."

(Hello sparkly lady!)

The ketchup episode laid out for you above could be a
lady trying to pick up a guy OR it could just be a confident, flirty lady that wanted a French fry and can be
played off as either. There's always a way to stand out
without being too obvious and always a way to blend in
while still being sparkly. It takes work at first but once you
get the hang of it, it becomes second nature. Then it's like
bees to honey.

The other thing you need to know is that patience and
persistence are part of the equation to meeting quality
guys. Just because "he" wasn't at the place you went looking for him once doesn't mean he won't be there next

time. So be consistent about going to places that make it easy for you to be the best you. Find lots of places where you are the best, brightest and most confident you and get out often!

Then there's the Internet! Which is like a 24-hour international singles mixer where the possibilities for meeting people are right there if you have the patience to point and click your way through the room. There are specific dating sites, special interest sites, chat rooms and lifestyle sites all in an effort to connect people. If you put up a MySpace page or join a dating website it's hard *not* to meet people, but weeding through and nurturing cyber relationships takes a lot of attention. The time commitment alone can be the downside of looking solely to the Internet to meet people. But the upside is you can reach masses of people and the convenience of being able to window-shop for love in your pajamas. We advise that the Internet alone should not make up your social life or interactions.

SURROUNDED BY SINGLE MEN by Amiira

Another thing to think about when looking for potential dates is playing the odds. Where would you stand out? In addition to going to places where you shine because you are in your element, how about trying places where you will be exotic? I want to share the story of when I was asked out on the most dates in my life because I stood out and was exotic and sparkly. When I was single I decided to take golf lessons. I did not take golf lessons to meet men but rather that I wanted to learn how to play golf. Most of the men in my line of work played golf and had their business meetings over a round of golf, which seemed spectacular to me and I wanted to get in on that action. Getting to be outside playing a three- to six-hour round of golf instead of being in the office was very appealing to a girl like me who prefers basking in the sunlight instead of the fluorescents. Anyway I started taking golf lessons from a lovely old man named Ed that reminded me of my Granddaddy. I loved my golf lessons because Ed was both amusing and wise and for whatever reason, working on my golf swing was a very Zen experience that I came to crave. There was a stillness to the time during my golf lessons that was in complete contrast to every other aspect of my life. Basically my golf lessons were my time for me where everything else in my head disappeared and I was content and concentrating in the now. I was living in the moment with purpose. I didn't notice it at first because I was truly just working on my swing and learning the clubs and what I could do with them, but men would gather to watch my golf lesson. Or rather watch me take my lesson then wait for it to be over so they could chat me up. Ed noticed and would tell them to get lost, not to bother me because he was like my Granddaddy and he didn't need a bunch of lookie-loos interrupting our time together. The point I'm trying to make is that I stood out and was exotic and sparkly at the Golf club for a couple of reasons. Firstly, I was usually the only woman at the driving range or one of maybe three on a busy weekend compared to the nearly hundred men that would pass through during my hour there. Secondly, I had a purpose and wasn't easily distracted from it because I truly enjoyed what I was doing and had the desire and focus to get better at it. Thirdly, I wasn't trolling for dates which is by men's standards probably the same as playing hard to get, and since I was at a sporting venue you can imagine that there were men that like a challenge there and my disinterest was challenging to them. Needless to say, I have never been asked out on more dates in my entire life. Maybe it was because I had it going on, and maybe it was because I was the only girl there and guys couldn't believe their luck to find a girl that likes golf! Either way, I was exotic and sparkly and therefore brightened the place (which is quite an accomplishment for the outdoors) and everyone seemed to notice.

THE NEW LAW OF ATTRACTION by Greg

Here's what I know about attraction. It really isn't just about looks. Human beings give off a vibe when they are happy and they are, I believe, happiest when they are closest to the dream, whatever that may be for them. I know I'm a guy but let me share this with you and see if it resonates or at least makes sense. From the time I was old enough to know they existed I loved women. Almost every action I took from the age of four on was in an effort to get closer to them. Now I've always been a pretty good student of life but not a great student of me. Here's an example: When I was growing up and you wanted the girl you could do no better than play sports. Football especially was a really great way to get noticed so naturally I played football. I was horrible at it—I mean really bad. Needless to say I didn't do so well with the ladies. But I continued down this path because I didn't understand that it wasn't football that got the girls but how it made those who played it well feel and appear. The girls didn't just like Todd Leitz because he was dead sexy and played football, they liked him because he liked himself and loved being good at football. Joe Malatesta was great looking too but he couldn't catch a pass. No chicks for Joe. It wasn't until I took a theater class in college to fill an arts requirement that I began to understand this idea of who you are when you are closer to your dream. My mother always encouraged me to get involved in theater because she thought I was funny. I always thought that theater was weak and for pussies. Well, oddly enough I excelled at theatre and I'm not weak nor am I a pussy, and suddenly there were girls. I was at a place maybe for the first time in my life where I was comfortable in my skin and it showed. I didn't know it yet but I was getting closer to my dream. Later that year I was asked to join a band. More girls. Life was grand and I was more me than I'd ever been. Then tragedy struck. I graduated. Moved to San Francisco, no band, no acting, waiting tables. No girls. Then my mom calls and tells me about an audition for an improv group. I get asked to join and two weeks into it one of the other members of the group suggests I try standup. I do. I like it. Girls! Now when I say girls I'm not talking about just sex, I'm saying that is when I was the most attractive to them. When they would say yes to me asking them out and when I handled rejection better because I knew what they were missing out on when they said "No". Whatever my relationship with myself it was directly reflected in my relationships. And my relationship with myself corresponded with my proximity to my dream life. Now my dream was to be a great standup so it's no surprise I met my wife after taping my first HBO special. I'm not saying I'm a great standup, I'm saying I was in this world trying to accomplish what I think I was put here to do. That made me happy and so my sense of place and purpose made me attractive to the girl of my dreams. It really is a matter of sorting out what your dream is. It's there in your head, that thing that if you could wave a magic wand and do you would do in a heartbeat. *That's* the person you are waiting to become and that's the person you need to be or on the path to becoming to attract the right person to you. If you attract someone while *not* in pursuit of the dream and then you suddenly want to go get it they may not want to come with you or, worse, try and stop you. Go for the dream first.

LOVE IN THE BREAKROOM

"What if the place I am my best is at the office but interoffice dating is forbidden?" That's a good question and our answer may surprise you a bit. We just think it's a bad idea to rule any place out where a love connection could be made. (Okay, maybe prison.) Three of the happiest couples we know met at work, including Greg's parents. Now we don't want you to get fired or make foolish choices with your career just because the person in the next cubicle has a nice butt. However, we are loath to tell you to rule out the work environment as a place to find someone to date. Where else are you going to find someone with the same passion for blacksmithery than at your job at the blacksmith place where you do your blacksmithing? You get the point. When you meet through work there's already an ease and commonality because you have work and co-workers in common. You have the workplace to agree, disagree or argue about and you have the opportunity to spend a lot of time getting to know one another as friends and co-workers. While we think that the workplace is a good place to meet people, you have to understand what ultimately is at stake … your job. And how do you feel about the possibility of having to work with your ex? It's a slippery slope but it doesn't mean it's not worth trying it for the right person. It really comes down to what's more important: taking a chance that this might be your person (The One) or job stability.

Here are some tips to help you really decide if this guy or gal is worth risking your job and sanity over, as well as some suggestions about pursuing love in the workplace. These are offered in hopes that you won't be one of the many burned by a fiery office romance.

✓ Does your workplace have a policy against inter-office dating and what are the consequences? Is it frowned upon or will you be terminated? There is a sliding scale depending on your company as to what the feeling is about dating among the ranks, and probably another hurdle to get over which is how does your direct boss feel about it? Is it a respect killer? Meaning will they lose respect for you, treat you differently or ultimately make being at work a bummer?

✓ How important is your work or this job? Is this a career-making job for you, just a stepping-stone in the scheme of things or simply a place where you punch the clock? This evaluation plays a big part in your decision as well. If it's a career-maker you might want to hold off until he or she goes to another company. Perhaps you can even talk to your supervisor about it. Maybe you can transfer to the Starbucks across the street or maybe you'll never work for the company again and couldn't give a shit because this person is worth finding a new job for.

✓ Do you think this person is hot or is this THE person that you will always regret not having taken the chance for? Sometimes it's hard to really tell the difference because the office is like a suspended reality. Working together is almost like dating because you get to spend a ton of time together, talk constantly and really get to know each other within the confines of work. Certainly you can grow close to a workmate and the line can get blurry as to what you feel for them. When you are co-workers you create an intimacy, a bond, a relationship that has its own private jokes and shorthand. That in itself can feel really confusing and you may not be able to tell if you're having a crush or falling in love. And just because you work as work mates doesn't mean you'll work in the real world or under the pressure and scrutiny of your co-workers and bosses.

If you've decided to throw caution to the copier and go for it, here are some guidelines to consider.

✓ Be discreet and keep it on the DL (that's down-low for those of you untouched by popular culture). Respect each other's jobs and reputation. There is no need for Shari in the next cubicle to know what kind of boxers he sleeps in.

✓ Take it off campus. Keep the office a professional place and do your dating and heavy petting after hours.

✓ Get clarity from each other. Is this a fling or a relationship? Know what you're getting into because the fall-out is big when you have to see your ex every day and watch them date someone else.

✓ Ask yourself, is this exciting because it's forbidden or because you're crazy about this person? If you don't know the answer you're doing it for the wrong reasons.

THAT'S JUST YOU LOOKING FOR A LOOPHOLE

Why do I have to go out when I can shop online for men in my sweats? Because life is meant to be lived, besides since you are rocking it with so many men online going out should be even more fun. Besides who knows what awesome guy you'll attract when you are *not* looking for someone and are out of your sweats. We understand the appeal of not having to try or really put yourself out there because, damn it, that shit is hard! But take it from us when all is said and done you won't wish you'd spent more time sitting at home instead of being face to face with another human being. Most importantly, and here's the real truth, *you can't get to know a person until you are actually with them*. There is no better advertisement for you than the way you walk into a room or the sound of your laugh. Even the way you burp after you chug a beer is far more enticing than reading that you really wish you could meet Kelly Clarkson on your MySpace page. Not to mention that you'd have a better chance of doing that if you'd just leave the house.

Carpe Datem Rock'em Sock'em Superbook

It's time to figure out where you should be going to meet prospective dates. Hopefully you've been thinking about the things we've said along the chapter and doing some real searching about where you shine the brightest. Now we all know that you can find love in both the most random and predictable places and that ultimately it's not something you can control or will into being. But we also know that you can't lose by honoring yourself and being the best you by looking your best, then going to places where you project confidence and happiness. Let's figure out where that is.

List the five environments that you feel the best in. (Be specific. Is it walking down 5th Avenue in the bustling city at twilight? By the ocean on an absurdly hot day?)

1.

2.

3.

4.

5.

List the five places that you can go that you've always wanted to go. (This can be a restaurant, park, exhibit or an actual journey.)

1.
2.
3.
4.
5.

List the five places in your city that you love the most.

1.
2.
3.
4.
5.

List the five things you wished you had done that you haven't done yet. (Skydiving? Eating Sushi? Eating Sushi while skydiving?)

1.
2.
3.
4.
5.

Now get dolled up and go out and get 'em!

12

essence #2: the power of suggestion

How To Get Asked Out

While it would be great if there were no more hurdles, now that you've figured out *where* you should be going, *who* you should be when you get there and *how* to meet the right kind of guy, we're far from done. We don't know if you've noticed but guys aren't stampeding down the doors to ask ladies out on dates these days. Is it really that much easier to ask women to hang out or hook up than it is to ask them on a date? Apparently so. Muttering something along the lines of, "We're all going down to Fuzzy Jacks for some Spud Duds, Spicy Knuckles and Beer Biscuits" has a difficulty degree of negative 5 while mustering up the cahones to say, "How about having dinner with me this Friday?" is evidently a considerably more complicated challenge. As we explained in the very first chapter of this book, with an invitation to hang out or hook up the expectation on both sides is considerably lower because the subtext of a hang-out is "you can come or don't come … whatever." The other thing about hanging out or hooking up is that guys use it as an opportunity to sample your company to determine whether or not they like you enough to go out with you under more official circumstances. That means the guy feels like he's not totally putting himself out there, making himself vulnerable to rejection (even if his palms are sweating the whole time) PLUS the woman's expectation of what the actual get-together means are much lower. Less threat, less commitment, vague definition—it's a completely winning formula for a guy. Why is it not then winning for the lady as well? Because women like definition, they like to know what the game is, what's going on, who the players are and where they stand. That's why women who want to *date* need to not only stop accepting casual suggestions of hanging out and hooking up, but then need to make dating an easier prospect for men to get their head around. It's up to you to embody the **It's Just A Date!** philosophy (letting go of the whole process but not letting go of you) and remove the pressure and expectation from the situation so that guys can look at dating as a good thing instead of with trepidation. Otherwise, men will continue to NOT ask women out and women will continue to do the heavy lifting or, even worse, settling for quasi-dating on a man's terms.

Look, not every guy you want to ask you out will. Some won't be interested, some will be too shy, some would rather not date you because of a mild allergy to even *that* small form of commitment. That goes for when you're standing in the same room and when you're online. Then what? Should you give him your phone number? Hand him your business card? Write down your email or MySpace page? The goal is to make him ask for those things. Therefore it's up to you to **Give The Right Signals** and make asking you out easy and inviting when you find yourself in a situation where the guy you want is not making the move. As we talked about in the last chapter you can meet whoever you want once you're engaged in some level of conversation or short-distance flirting but you may have to create the opportunities. When necessary, you need to present the idea of going on a date with you as an incredibly enticing opportunity, that he wouldn't want to pass up. How do you accomplish that? By being confident, sparkly and *possibly* willing to find a place in your schedule for him.

Let us show you how it's done

Example: Say a guy is hinting around the idea that you should hang out sometime but not asking you out. Instead of agreeing to an undefined possible future get together, you give him specific choices.

> *"Ohhh, sorry. I'm booked through the next millennium for hang-outs but I'd be available for a date either Thursday for dinner or brunch on Saturday. After that I*

may be going out of town on a top secret assignment so those are really my only free days."

If he's hesitant to nail down a date then either he's actually propositioning you for the possibility of sex or not that interested and using the "hang out" idea as a way to wrap up the conversation so he can move on.

Example: You're at a party and he's across the room occasionally glancing your way. If he doesn't ever come over to you, even after you've shot him a number of smiles and flirty glances, you wave him over (as in "come here.") If he doesn't come then you have your answer; if he does make the journey across the room you offer something along the lines of ...

"Hey handsome, I couldn't tell if you were looking over here because you wanted to talk to me or because there's a clock somewhere behind me. So I thought I'd give you the opportunity to either ask me out or get a better look at the time."

He'll either be relieved at your humor or totally freaked out. Both give you an equally good reason to giggle with sparkly confidence.

Example: You're talking to a bunch of guys, all of whom you're having fun with, but none of whom is asking you out.

> *"It's too bad that all of you are cute and funny but none*
> *of you have asked me out because I have an extra ticket*
> *to the Lakers game that I'll have to waste on someone*
> *else."*

By the way, having tickets to a sporting event is an easy way to get asked out. Hell, it'd be worth you investing in season tickets with a girlfriend. You could go together because it's fun (plus there's always single guys there), give some tickets away and use the tickets to the really good games to get dates!

Example: You're anywhere with a guy who you want to ask you out.

> *"You know what I think? I think you should ask me on*
> *a date to go see Spider Man 7 (or whatever the hot*
> *movie that's opening that week is) Saturday night."*

Sometimes the power of suggestion isn't subtle, but what we're looking for is getting asked out in advance on an actual date.

Example: You're online dating and you see a guy whose profile you like because he's also a huge U2 fan and whose photo you REALLY like but he hasn't winked or emailed you. So you email him.

"Hey there. How do I know you? Were you the guy in the 14th row of the U2 show at the Forum that switched seats with me so I wasn't behind the tall guy or did we go to high school together? (If it's the latter, are you still friends with Steve?)"

Now clearly this is a load of crap but you're looking for a response in a wasteland of unanswered emails and this will peak his interest for two reasons. First, that you were at U2 and had great seats so you're clearly hooked up and secondly, everyone went to school with a Steve so he'll think it's possible. Once he emails back you can discover that he's not the same guy you met/went to high school with but by then hopefully you'll have struck up a correspondence. Sorry ladies, we don't mean to encourage dishonesty but sometimes fishing is fishing and there's got to be bait.

These are a few examples of ways to make asking you out easy for a guy and certainly some guys will bite at the opportunity and others will pass. SO WHAT! The guys that pass aren't right for you anyway and the ones that bite might not be either. Dating is a numbers game and you have to go out with a number of frogs before you find a prince.

THE PLAYS

There are only a few options available to you if a guy doesn't ask you out. You can:

- ✓ **Figure he's not interested and move on with your life.** Which by all means is a fine option to go with because who wants to be with a guy that doesn't even have enough balls to ask a girl out? If you've made eye contact, smiled in his general direction or undressed him with your eyes and he's not coming over he's either got a girlfriend, might be gay or is just lazy. None of which are good enough for you!

- ✓ **Ask him out on a date.** To that Amiira says, "Hell no you don't!" Just because you're an independent woman that can take charge of a situation and go for what you want doesn't mean that you can change the fact that men like to do the chasing and when women take that away from them by being the aggressor, they lose interest quickly. So you may get your date but you probably won't get your man.

- ✓ **Make him a one-time-only offer.** This is the great dating loophole that we've come up with that allows women to participate in their dating lives without having to do the asking. It goes like this: say there's a guy that you're hot for that's not making the moves on you. You saunter up to him, give him a tap on the shoulder and with a coy yet confident delivery let him know that you have a one-time-only offer for him. Tell him, "There's a five-minute window of opportunity that's opening right now for you to ask me out. After that I can't guarantee that it will ever come around again." This flirty offer delivers the same message as asking a guy out on a date because it lets him know that you'd like to go out with him but makes you seem more confident and intriguing.

✓ **Don't take it all so seriously**. It's just a f*#king date and if he doesn't ask you out then you're probably not missing much and he's not the guy for you.

ASKING MEN OUT by Greg

Can women ask men out? I have been asked this question since the first hour *He's Just Not That Into You* came out. The reason being is that in that book I asserted that if a guy is into you he will ask you out. That's what *I* believe. *I* was raised to ask women out, my friends were raised to ask women out. The powers that be, science or otherwise made you pretty so we'd chase you around. In fact I can't imagine any dad in this or any country sitting in their young son's bedroom saying, "Just look pretty the next time you see her at the library and maybe she'll ask you out." Now, that being said, I'm also not saying it's right. It just is. And I understand how infuriating this all is but I didn't set it up, we are all doing battle with history and gender roles. We'd love for the shoe to be on the other foot. Asking girls out is f*#king terrifying! But since women have periods and give birth maybe we should have the responsibility of doing one thing that's hard. Does all this mean women shouldn't ask men out? No. That's ridiculous. Women have minds of their own. But it does mean that *MEN KNOW THAT THEY ARE SUP-POSED TO ASK YOU OUT* and that *I* think they (men) are better or more invested when they are in pursuit. That was the truth for me. However, I would hate to encourage someone not to participate in his or her own life or be a victim of their circumstance. If you think asking a man out will make your life better than how could I possibly tell you not to? But if you were my sister I'd strongly encourage you to flirt heavily first, nudge him a bit and if he doesn't take the bait he's just not that …

THE RIGHT SIGNALS by Amiira

Clearly when you're out in the world meeting these guys that haven't got the ability to string together an invitation to dinner there's a part you play in the equation. The part is roadblock or doorway. The roadblock shuts down the possibilities for the approach whereas the doorway opens to it. Now, being approachable doesn't mean you're easy, it just means that you're receptive. Sending the right signals to let a guy know that approaching you is a winning idea is all about finesse.

Looks

Obviously it helps to look good and be your sparkly yummy self because we now accept that men are visual creatures and as such they respond to visual cues. That means a hint of skin be it *slight* cleavage, legs, feet (sorry flat-lovers, but men respond to a strappy heel even if you're tall), tattooed shoulder, back, neck … just something that reminds them that you're a woman. Also, gloss those lips, do something with your hair and wear something that alludes to the shape of your body, don't hide it in the equivalent of a giant sack. Even if you're a bigger lady, wearing big clothes makes you look bigger it doesn't hide you—and stop hiding anyway! In this day and age there are flattering, affordable clothes for every body out there, but you have to go find them. The idea is to subtly provoke a sexual response from men—and when I say response I'm talking about a flicker of thought not an erection.

Make Eye Contact

If there's a guy you fancy, look him in the eye. Make eye contact and hold eye contact for moment or two before looking away. Don't have a staring match but don't avoid holding his gaze. The frequency and duration of your glances in his direction, your actual eye contact and your holding his gaze is like a conversation the two of you are having with your eyes. This eye conversation (sometimes referred to as eye-f*#king) can determine whether he ultimately asks you out on a date or tries to get you in the coat closet so be careful with those laser beams 'cause they can get you into real trouble! I like playing it kind of cool and trying to draw out the eye conversation because it's a great flirting device and speaks volumes without having to say a word. Try something like … glance, look away (to the side not down), glance back, catch his eyes— hold for two seconds then smile, look away, catch his eyes, hold for four seconds with lips pursed in a slight grin but not smiling, pull shoulders down and back slightly to emphasize your assets and lower head deliberately for a moment then return to his gaze. Be small yet deliberate with your movements so you appear to be completely confident and controlled yet intrigued, not giggly like you can't believe he's actually looking at you. Repeat as necessary until he engages further.

Flirting

What's more fun than flirting? Almost nothing. While flirting comes naturally to some it is a skill that must be developed by many. The point of flirting is to connect with him in a playful way that creates a sense of familiarity and makes him want to spend more time with you. Flirting is not only a huge aphrodisiac but it's almost addictive. The positive attention of flirting feels awesome and makes you want more. Flirting is making eye contact as described above, it's being playful and suggestive without being too sexual, it's teasing and good-hearted kidding, it's using touch in an intimate way to emphasize your interest. Flirting is hard to describe, so for reference think Drew Barrymore whenever she's on David Letterman.

Body Language

Be open ... literally. Don't hunch down or over, instead throw your shoulders back, chin up and put a pleased look on your face. Be open and receptive to the approach. Be the bright spot in any room and the most inviting person to talk to. Use your hands to gesticulate, entice and emphasize, but don't overdo it. You want to invite interest without seeming like you're seeking attention. A person's body language is a representation of how they feel and who they are. If you want to be approached then make sure your body language says that it's safe to engage. That goes for you too, Goth girl!

Engaging Him

Be interested and interesting. Draw him in with the attention you give him and how well you listen. Ask questions about his life, work, interests, the political climate, the movie of the year, the difference between geckos and iguanas. Whatever! Just be able to talk and don't be a bore. Again this is all about your energy and connecting in an intriguing yet familiar way. Have something to talk about in case he (or you) isn't the best conversationalist. Is there a funny thing that happened to you, a bet you're trying to settle that he can weigh in on or a new CD that you think everyone in the world should hear? Trying to find something in common besides sexual attraction is the difference between being a girl he wants to make out with and being a girl he asks out on a date. If you're having trouble engaging him then maybe you don't want to go out with him anyway. Besides, what would you talk about for an hour over dinner if you can't get a conversation off the ground now?

What To Say

Now all you need to know is how to close the deal and how to decline an unwanted invitation with the finesse of an Ultra-Successful Winner Dater. Here are a few of my favorite phrases to encourage a guy to ask you out if he's not taking the initiative. For me it's the preferred method to doing the asking yourself because it basically sends the same message while making yourself seem smart, confident, flirty and most importantly—*still a challenge*. You will have better success if you're able to deliver these lines in a confident yet flirty way.

✓ "I only ever get asked out by funny guys but never funny **and** handsome ones like you."

✓ "Did you want to ask me something? It seems like
   you were thinking about asking me something like if
   I liked Chinese food and was available for dinner on
   Friday?"

✓ "As much as I'd like to hang out with you, hanging
   out is for amateurs and I've already turned pro. I can
   only go on dates now but you know where to find
   me if you ever get decide to turn pro too."

✓ "I'm going to be over here with my friends in case
   you wanted to come over and ask me out."

✓ "I don't care how charming you are, I'm not going to
   go out with you so don't even try to persuade me."

How to decline a date

There are going to be guys that ask you out that you don't
want to go out with. It just happens and it sucks to have
to reject another human being. So before you do you
should ask yourself why you don't want to go out with
them because part of Ultra-Successful Winner Dating is
not type-casting people and narrowing your field.

✓ "You seem like a very cool guy but I can't date
   anyone that I feel brotherly towards. But I love my
   brother very much so please take that as a
   compliment."

✓ "That's so funny that you asked me out because I was just thinking that I'd like to set you up with one of my friends. If you like me you'll really like her."

✓ "I can't go out with nice guys until I stop my 'dating assholes' phase."

✓ "I'd be doing a disservice to the next spectacular lady you ask out by wasting your time now when I'm still a bit messed up from my last go 'round."

✓ "I'm dying."

Remember, giving the right signals is a key component to getting asked out on a date. The sooner you master how to send them, the sooner you can reap the rewards—so get busy!

THE NEW LAWS OF ATTRACTION by Greg

Give us an opening.

If you are a guy and you are not on fire or Orlando Bloom, most women won't look at you. They just don't. Or if you women do, it's so subtle that we're quite sure it was a mistake. I've even talked to my best-looking guy friends about this so I knew it wasn't just me and they all agree it's very hard to tell if you are interested in us. Which makes it even more difficult to ask you out. We have the same self-confidence issues you have; we are only flesh and beer so it would be great to know you've noticed us. If you don't smile at us how are we supposed to know it's okay to talk to you or that you are not on your way to see your boyfriend? This probably hasn't kept some of us from coming up to you at the bar, Starbucks, or laundromat, and bugging the shit out of you and maybe that's the problem ... some creepy, persistent dude wrecked it for the rest of us. But all I keep hearing is no one is asking you out. So help us out, ladies. Throw a smile at a guy you think you'd like to talk to. Let's all agree on this rule: **Eye contact coupled with a smile means this cab is empty if you'd like to flag it down.** Don't just do the quick eye contact thing that just reads like you think we are coming for your purse. Most men are hesitant to strike up a conversation with a new lady so we need the encouragement. I know you think you smile at guys all the time but you don't and it doesn't count if you do it to the backs of our heads. Even if we are married, gay or otherwise, at the very least you've made our day by throwing us one of the delicious smiles we crave. Hell, while you're at it why don't you say "Now would be a great time to ask me out you big sissy." Okay, maybe just the smile for now.

THAT'S JUST YOU LOOKING FOR A LOOPHOLE

I know what you are thinking ... If a guy doesn't ask you out but still wants to go hang out, that's probably as good as a date to him, right? WRONG! We can't stress this enough, guys *know* that they're supposed to ask girls out. Otherwise there wouldn't be four to eight years of proms, homecoming dances and formal functions that require a verbal invitation, the rental of a tuxedo and the purchase of a corsage. (Most) men aren't daft—they're just as ambiguous as women let them be, which actually makes them kind of cunning. If hanging out and hooking up was working for you then you'd be in an awesome relationship, but clearly it's not so here we are. Look, you have to at some point define what it is you deserve in life and then be willing to go and get it. If it's dates you want then it's dates you will have, but not by compromising what you know feels right to you. A date isn't a marriage proposal for God's sake—it's a reasonable thing for an awesome chick like you to want. But if you don't put out the vibe that going on actual dates are how someone gets the keys to your kingdom, then dudes are going to keep trying to jump the fence. (Man, we are on a metaphor roll on this book!) For more on first dates proceed to the next chapter ... after you've done the workbook.

Carpe Datem Rock'em Sock'em Superbook

We realize that the idea of having to coerce a guy to ask you out doesn't sit well with everyone and doesn't seem fair. So don't look at it that way. Look at it as you taking control of your life and giving people who obviously don't know what they're missing a fighting chance. Even if it makes you uncomfortable to be so bold or embarrassed to show your cards without seeing theirs, it's the way for you to stack the odds in your favor so that you get asked out more often.

Okay look, you are only ever going to feel comfortable with the words that YOU are comfortable and capable of saying. So here's your assignment ...

Make a list of phrases you can say with the right amount of confidence and flirtation to give a guy the opening to asking you out. We'll start you off with a couple examples of fun and unexpected ways to alert a guy to the awesome opportunity that is you. After that, it's up to you to craft a few gems of your own.

1. "Besides asking me out what else are you up to this weekend?"
2. "You should ask me out so you at least can tell people you went out with me once."
3. "My friends all said you wouldn't ask me out but I told them you weren't a pussy."
4.
5.
6.

You get the idea. This is a good exercise whether you use these phrases or not because it forces you to tap into the creative, flirtatious and self-possessed sides of your personality. And how is that bad? Oh, it's not.

Thank you guys.

You are welcome.

bonus section: internet date-tacular!

Tickling The Mousepad

Most single people we know have at least dabbled in online dating, if not dedicated many of their after-hours to the incessant scrolling, clicking and scanning of profiles. If we've been asked it once we've been asked almost three times, what are the rules for dating a guy online? Our answer is it's no different than any other kind of dating. You have to have the same standards for online as you do in real life. So if in real life you wouldn't lift your shirt and show everyone your knockers at the bar, then certainly the same should apply online. However, if that is how you roll then click, click, upload, you Wonder-bra-wearing superstar! No wonder you have so many "Friends."

HOW TO WRITE A GREAT PROFILE

Like it's not hard enough to answer the three hundred questions and write the sixteen essays that each dating website requires you to complete in order for them to play Cupid and match you up with other people that *also* like to watch TV. You also have to post multiple pictures of yourself so that people can judge how you look at your birthday dinner with friends, what you'd wear hiking with your dog, what you look like on spring break and that time you met Pete Sampras at an airport. People look at your pictures just like you look at theirs, and make fun of what you're wearing, check out your body or possibly that other thing that some do when alone and looking at sexy photos. Yes, that's the thing we were talking about and, c'mon, you can't be surprised. We are of the belief that if your profile is specific and creative (creative as in clever not creative as in totally lying) you'll have a better shot at attracting the kind of person that you could seriously date. Here are our suggestions for making a winning profile.

The Photos

Everyone looks at your photo first, so let's start with that. We all have that one picture where we photographed better than we ever have in our whole lives. We call that the Cameron Diaz picture. So, your first photo, the one that lures the Internet daters to your profile, should be your

Cameron Diaz photo. Your Cameron Diaz photo must be current (within the last 2–3 years), must be close to your current weight and must somewhat resemble you.

The next photo you put up needs to be a personality photo. You playing guitar, you at the beach, you dancing, you doing something that shows what kind of life you live.

Third photo should be your favorite photo of yourself, the one that makes you really happy when you look at it, the one that makes you think all good things about yourself. For instance you with your family, or you passed out on the floor of the ladies room at T.G.I. Fridays. (Mini Workbook Pop Quiz: Which of these is a bad choice?)

Fourth should be a three-quarter to full body shot because even if you want to hide behind your computer, the goal is to meet in person eventually so they're going to see it anyway. It's better to be upfront with who you are than to go on a date and suffer through the nightmare of some idiot being disappointed by what you look like. (Like he should judge!)

IMPORTANT NOTE: Look, most people don't like looking at pictures of themselves, but we all recognize when we take a good photo. If that isn't happening for you and you find that when you look at pictures of yourself you're saying, "I don't like my hair," "I'm too pale," "I need to lose some weight," seize this opportunity to see what you're putting out into the world and think, "What could I be doing better?" and then start doing something about it. Also make sure you know what's in the background. How you would react if you saw you in a photo wearing a sack dress standing in front of an open can of beans, your Smurf collection or a week's worth of laundry? No bueno!

Ticking the boxes

Most of filling out a dating profile is ticking boxes or clicking a pull-down menu to choose one of the offered selected answers. There's not much we can do for you there except suggest you not be so stringent with your height requirements. Love knows no height so stop being such a sissy about it. If there's a question that you feel uncomfortable answering then don't answer it, or if that's not an option then pick the pre-selected answer that makes you laugh the most. It's Just A F*#king Date so screw them if they can't take a joke! Most of the box-ticking categories are pretty easy to navigate but there's always the one tricky one—the "Turn-ons and Turn-offs" one or whatever variation of that your site of choice offers. This is where you can attract the creeps, pervs and booty call solicitors. There are always some dumb-ass options like "Erotica" and "Skinny-dipping" that, ensure once ticked you will receive a bombardment of winks and emails from people just looking to get cyber-laid. "But what if I love Erotica and Skinny-dipping?" That's great for you, and you can let your potential suitors know that delicious little tidbit of information about you *LATER ON* after they already like you for all the other great things about you. Erotica, Skinny-dipping, photos of you in a bathing suit or anything vaguely naked or sexual will bite you in the ass every time on the Internet. Because regardless of what you think you're there for, once that card is played the sexual curiosity of others will trump their desire for dating. Now instead of people responding to your profile and asking you questions about your favorite movies or your work they want to know where you like to skinny-dip or what you're wearing when reading erotica, watching erotica or getting erotica.

The Headline

Most dating sites give you an opportunity to create a headline that goes with your photo to really sell you to window shoppers. You get about a hundred to a hundred fifty characters to do this in. Don't use them all. Don't be generic. Do incorporate one specific like or thing that would draw out a person that would connect with you.

Example:

Bad Headline: "Outdoor-loving mid-western girl looking for someone to share walks on the beach"

Why it's bad: Well, hopefully by your photo they can already tell that you're a girl and everyone from the nicest person in the world to a serial killer likes the beach.

Outdoors again is pretty general and there's really only a few choices; outdoors, indoors, outer space and underwater so you're not really narrowing the field by this headline.

Good Headline: "Environmentally conscious and seriously into the *Daily Show*, Cadbury Creme Eggs and Eskimo kisses."

Why it's good: Environmentally conscious tells lookers that you recycle, like organic foods and products, might even drive a hybrid vehicle and are a socially aware if not active. It also weeds out those that drive Hummers. Seriously into the *Daily Show* reveals that you are probably left of centre and appreciate satire, enjoy comedy and keep up on what's happening in the world though you may not read the newspaper. Cadbury Creme Eggs shows the guy that you have a discerning sweet tooth and you like looking forward to things that come only once a year. Eskimo kisses is the flirtatious part of the headline that is playful but not too sexy. It says that I'll get close enough to nuzzle the right person but I'm not here looking for a booty call.

The Essays

This is the fun part. This is where you show off your personality, wit and affinities. The fill-in-the-blank questions are usually "Describe yourself and your perfect date,"

"What do you do for fun?" "Favorite things?" "Celebrity you most look like." Never answer that last question (or other equally daft ones) it's a no-win question and your picture is already on your profile so they know what you look like. Now about the ones that you *should* answer, here's what we think. Irony and sarcasm, while very charming (we think), often doesn't read that way and you can come off as pompous or insane when you over-use them in your essays. Don't be afraid to tell people what you are really like because if you are lucky enough to hit it off with someone they are going to find out in the long run. You don't want to be going, "Did you think I was serious when I said I liked listening to Clay Aiken in my underwear while doing Jell-o shots and preparing my taxes? We're going to have to call the wedding off." You get it? Ironically, by telling everyone who you are not you're missing the opportunity to tell people who you really are, unless you are a tax-paying, Clay Aiken-loving boozebag. In which case, continue rocking, American Idol. This doesn't mean you can't be funny, just make sure we get some insight as to who you are and what you want. Another popular trick is to act above the dating site like "I don't usually do things like this." First off, yes you do, we all do. We all seek to meet people and get their approval and there is no shame in it. Meeting online is just as viable as meeting at Skybark (a club in L.A. that is a dog park on the roof of a fancy hotel for people and their pets to meet.) Be proud of what you are doing and why you are doing it. Don't act like you've bottomed out and this is your last chance. Don't sound bitter. Yes, dating is hard. Yes, the club scene sucks. And yes, there are a lot of losers out there. But you don't have to remind the people looking at your page, 'cause guess what? They are there too and they don't want to be called losers. Everyone is there because it's a cool new way to find folks to date. That's it. Not necessarily to marry or life partner with, but just to f*#king date.

Again, like in your headline, it will benefit you to write about things that are specific to you, not about generalizations that are also specific to you.

Example: "Tell us about you."
Bad Answer: "What can I say? I'm a laid-back and easy-going type of person. My friends and family are super important to me and I'd do anything for them. I'm as loyal as they come. I love to laugh and goof around and never take myself too seriously …"

Why It's Bad: This is just information that is way too general because nearly every person on the planet likes to laugh, fancies themselves easy-going, and is close to their friends and family.

Good Answer: "I'm a sunshine girl to say the least. I was born and raised in California so if it dips below 72 it's sweater weather. Out-of-towners will fight me but the locals are with me on this one. I have a strong set of beliefs. I believe that *Late Night With David Letterman* is better over coffee (thanks TiVo), the Hybrid SUV is an oxymoron but I drive one anyway and love it, there is nothing better than the sound of the ocean, powerful shower pressure (don't be dirty! I'm talking about the importance of a good shower here) and a good cup of coffee is imperative to having a good day. I prefer Coffee Bean to Starbucks and I'm not afraid to say it even if it means being stoned to death one coffee bean at a time. I'm allergic to cats or I just don't like them—I can't remember which one. I like days better than nights, light better than dark, sunny better than overcast BUT there are few things in this world more magnificent than a really great thunder and lightning storm that kills the power and rocks the house. Mother nature is a badass! I love a good TV show to rip at the old heartstrings or tickle the funny bone. Current faves are *Grey's Anatomy*, *Friday Night Lights*, *The Office*, *Lost* and *Project Runway* (I love watching talented people pursue their dreams). I am music obsessed and while U2, REM, The Replacements, The Clash and The Pretenders have my teenaged heart, I am currently being rocked by Snow Patrol, Band Of Horses, Buddy, Dashboard Confessional and the soundtrack to *Once*. I love a good movie score and think Carter Burwell, Danny Elfman and Ennio Morricone are masterful, you should check them out if you haven't yet ..."

Why It's Good: This essay not only gives you specific information about the things that "speak" to this person but also a sense of their personality. You could more easily sense whether you would be compatible or interested in this profile versus the "bad" one written earlier.

These are our ideas about how to engage the right type of guy online, we hope they're helpful. *However,* we must implore you to try to get in person as soon as possible if you think this thing might have any potential. Even if you're having the loveliest of e-mail relationships, if you finally meet and there's no spark, no chemistry, no physical attraction it's not going to work no matter how great an e-mail writer you or they are. So if you're really cooking by message, take the leap to the phone and then the leap to in person sooner rather than later. It's especially important to meet each other in person before things start going too far to the place of sexual innuendo and suggestion. Why? Because a lot of times once the sexual barrier has been crossed (even if it's only cyber) a few things can go wrong. There's the person that was just looking for a cyber sexual relationship and once they've gotten it they move on to another. You've got the person that once they've gotten too sexual or too open online they're too embarrassed to meet you in person. And of course the person that thinks that now that you're having cyber sex that when they meet you in person it will be to have actual sex. That's the super weird thing about Internet Dating, it can go really fast and get really intimate but then when you finally are with each other in person you don't know if you're on a first date or already a couple, if you're supposed to have your first kiss or already be sleeping together. It's confusing so be clear and keep it above the waist until you are actually sitting across from each other for conversation.

14

essence #3: it's just a f*#king first date!

How To Be A Great First Date And How To Have One

A good date is better than good sex. It lasts longer and you can't just have it with anyone. How's that for motivation to go on dates? Seriously, how great is that?

If used correctly a first date can prove to be an awesome way to get to know a new person, eat some food, take in some art, see a new part of town and live life like it was supposed to be lived by saying "What the f*#k!" and having some fun. Do you see what a great opportunity that is? You can put on an outfit that makes you feel great, spend quality time one on one with someone that you have some degree of interest in and share an experience. IT'S AWESOME … except when it's not. The cold hard truth of the matter is that you're not always going to connect with the person sitting across from you even if you do have *everything* in the world in common. That's why you have to *go and keeping going* on dates. There are millions of people out there and you've got to sort through them somehow to find your match so why not do it face to face over Mexican food?

There's no one right way to go on a first date but if you go with the spirit of It's Just A F*#king Date in your heart and mind, though you might not win you're 100% less likely to lose. How do you do that? Just let everything go. Let go of all of your past dating experiences, future hopes, expectations and just be.

So let's examine the first date and what it means now to you the Ultra-Successful Winner Dater type of gal. You shouldn't be overly invested in the guy at this point because after all, you've probably either just met or have a limited knowledge of each other and therefore should have limited or even no expectations. Going into a date without expectations not only lessens the disappointment if it doesn't go well but more importantly it increases the possibility for being pleasantly surprised. That's just smart living right there.

So there you are without any expectations getting ready to go on a first date. It's Just A F*#king Date prescribes that you play to win and that means that even though a first date isn't a big deal you should still be on your game and try. When you honor yourself and the occasion it not only shows in your appearance but it will radiate out your eyeballs with self-assurance. Imagine the difference you will feel when you begin a first date with the lightness of no expectations, the certainty of his intent and a shiny new outlook on dating.

What else works on a first date? Be easy-going but don't be easy. Let us not even align ourselves with easy because we always want to be a challenge. **Easy-going** doesn't mind if we're going for Italian or Chinese. **Easy** doesn't mind if we just stay in and kick it here in your bed.

When in doubt, we're here with a few first date Dos and Don'ts to get you off on the right stiletto.

Definitely Dos

✓ **Do be ready on time!** Being late is a great way to tell people that their time isn't as valuable as yours. That doesn't mean you need to be sitting outside the front door waiting for him but it also doesn't mean he gets to spend 40 minutes with your roommate Marla.

✓ **Do flirt!** Look, if you like a guy then flirt a little and let him know you're having a good time. Flirting comes in a variety of packages. Everything from good-natured ribbing about his basketball team to opening the restaurant door for him. Any version of actions and words that convey the message, "I'm a playful person with a sense of humor and I'm liking you" will do.

✓ **Do eat an actual meal!** Be on the date. He picked the restaurant because he likes the food. See if he's got good taste. Hell, if it doesn't work out at least you know another great place to eat with your next date. C'mon, you know you're hungry.

✓ **Do compliment him on his choice of restaurant, shirt or good sense to ask you out.** Give the kid props. Planning a date is stressful. Plus there are a lot of guys that don't like to date but this guy should be applauded for at the very least knowing you were worth asking out.

✓ **DO LET HIM KNOW THAT YOU HAD A GREAT TIME (especially if you want him to ask you out again!)** "I had a really good time" is fine. "Those were really good cheeseburgers" is not. "That was fun, we should do this again" is great.

Seriously Don't's

✗ **Don't drink too much.** If we have to explain this one to you then perhaps you might be looking for a different book.

✗ **Don't talk about your exes too much.** Yes, it's fun to crucify old lovers but not tonight. Let him find out why people have wanted to date you in the first place (because you're awesome) not why you spent a

night in jail (you set your ex's clothes on fire
when you caught him making out with your
roommate Marla. See why you never keep a man
waiting?)

✗ **Don't ask inappropriate questions**. How much
money do you make? Have you ever slept with a
man? How many women have you had sex with? Zip
It Miss Nosey Pants! It's none of your business and
won't be for some time.

✗ **Don't go back to their place**. I'm sure the movie
Knocked Up looks amazing in HD but tell him you'd
like to see a movie in a theatre first before checking
out the wide screen.

✗ **Don't have sex or get past first base**. Do we have to
go over this? Most guys who like a girl are only
hoping for a kiss. They'll take more if you offer it, but
a kiss will do.

FIRST DATE FODDER by Amiira

Here are the top five questions our babysitters ask me.

✓ **What should I order? Is it okay to order an appetizer
and a main course or is that too much?** If he picked
the restaurant then he's aware of the prices and the

menu and has most likely come prepared. Don't go buffet style hogwild but order what you will eat and don't sweat it. You can always ask what he's thinking about ordering to see if he's going to rock an appetizer then make the call. Or ask if he'd share a dessert with you later if you skip a salad up front.

✓ **Who Pays?** He does. He asked so he pays. Should you reach for your wallet and pretend to pay? Not on the first date. The only exception is if he's really sweating over the bill you can offer to split it but only if you think he's in over his head. You don't want to embarrass him.

✓ **Should I meet him there?** Only if you don't want him to know where you live or are unsure of your ability to leave him *outside* the front door instead of *inside* your bedroom at the end of the evening. Know your boundaries and play it safe.

✓ **How do I recover from an embarrassing moment on the date?** It's all about having a sense of humor and maintaining your confidence. Spill wine down your dress? Offer him the choice of switching outfits or swinging by your house so you can change before the next event. Did you get to the bathroom and realize you had black pepper in your teeth for the entire meal? March back out and throw your napkin playfully at him and tell him that he better beware because you're going get even with him for not being a friend and telling you. Everyone has embarrassing moments but how you deal with them determines their severity and his impression. If you let them go and find the humor in them instead of letting them be your downfall, it'll be another thing he likes about you.

✓ **How physical do you have to get on the first date to get asked on a second date?** Anything more than a hug and a kiss on the cheek is a bonus. Anything more than a upright make-out session and it can get wonky; too much too soon makes it less valuable. Gauge what you think you want to do and reel it back a step. Guys are hoping for a kiss goodnight. Truly. On a hangout they're hoping for sex, but on a proper date they're hoping you leave them wanting more. Anticipation rules, so don't wreck the opportunity to let him think about you.

TOO MUCH INFORMATION

There's "getting to know you" conversation and there's "please make it stop" conversation. It's important to be able to tell the difference.

Greg's First-hand Account:

There was this girl named Julie who I met while doing standup. She had rocking short dark hair and a great laugh. I asked her out and took her to a really cool old-school Mexican restaurant. I noticed right off the bat that she was a little nervous because she talked incessantly which was kind of cute at first. But then she crossed into no man's land when she proceeded to give the details of her sister's recent labor and childbirth which included graphic descriptions of her kin's swollen vagina and pooping on the table which is apparently a common side-effect of childbirth. Now, childbirth is sort of a dicey first date topic anyway, but pooping is a straight-up "NO THANK YOU," at least before the entrée. But more than the content of the story was the complete disregard for the listener. She wasn't noticing, or perhaps didn't care about, my reaction and the more she talked about her family the more enraged she became and by the end of the date I wanted nothing to do with her or her family. Even if she had just given the details of the childbirth she should have said something along the lines of "This is kind of gross, do you want to hear it before eating?" OR "I have a great story to tell you ten dates from now when I know you better and oh, by the way, you should know I hate my family." Think about the kind of images you are putting into your date's head and decide what effect it might have on his chorizo quesadilla, would be the moral there.

LEAVE THE ROOM EARLY

Leaving the room early is the term we use for leaving him still wanting more instead of satisfied or sick of you. We've been to a lot of concerts and rarely have they ended too early but man have some of them gone on too long. Some of them even forced us to go home early and reconsider our relationship with the band.

The philosophy of leaving the room early means when things are going their best, get out. The best way to ensure a second date is leaving a first one on a high note. So if dinner's been a blast, the show was even better and you're headed home and he asks if you want to stop for coffee the answer is NO. Even if it's really yes on the inside, NO says I've got things to do in the morning because my life doesn't stop for just anyone. NO says, even though you want to spend more time with me, you'll have to wait. NO says, he's going to be thinking about you because he didn't get enough.

DATING ALERT!

You have to get rid of the old feelings you have about first dates:

The majority of people hate first dates for two reasons. One, because they've been on bad ones and every bad or uncomfortable memory resurfaces every time you're about to give someone else a shot with a first date. Two, because they put too much pressure on the situation instead of just going on it with the attitude of It's Just A Date! and see what happens. The first date nerves seem to make you momentarily forget that the person they're going out with isn't any of your exes or past bad dates, yet you dump all of your baggage on them before they've even rung the doorbell. Surely they're thinking the same thing about you too, that you're just like their ex-psycho girlfriend or will suffer from at least one, if not all, bad characteristics that belong to her or the last total first-date disaster they went on. You have to let it all go, every past dating nightmare and disappointment and try to recognize that this is a new person that deserves a clean slate and a chance. If you're lucky they'll be smart enough to grant you the same luxury.

The problem with first dates isn't generally the dates themselves but actually all of the shit we pile on top of them. We have all of our past dating disappointments, our nervous energy, the expectations that it's going to suck, the expectations that you're going to marry this person, the pressure of any of those expectations on both you and them, your insecurities, those head trips we play on ourselves and all the unknown "what ifs" that are enough to sabotage any budding interest. It's crazy what we do to ourselves when it comes to dating, then on top of all that you've got "the sexes" at work on a date where the male is sizing up his sexual attraction (When will we have sex? Will it be good? Can I be attracted to this one woman the rest of my life?). Meanwhile the female is seeing if there's long-term potential to be found. (Could I marry this guy? Does he want children? Does he have his shit together?). That's not to say that every woman going on a date is looking to get married and every guy is just looking to get laid, it's just saying that the sexes have their own inner wirings that massage them in these directions.

But the point of it is that no one is on a date when they're sizing up what's yet to come. You're in the lab trying to predict what the future will be instead of "in the field" on a fact-finding mission or discovery voyage, which is what a first date is supposed to be. The short of it is you are so preoccupied that YOU ARE NOT ON A DATE EVEN WHEN YOU ARE ON A DATE! You can't possibly be if you are focusing on the "what ifs" and hypothetical situations and not on your reactions to each other, your compatibility, your chemistry, your value systems, beliefs, morals, taste in music, films and TV shows, political leanings, religion, favorite foods, sports franchises, hobbies, family values, future plans, so on and so forth.

A first date will either be every bad thing you think, a surprisingly good time or, most likely—something in the middle. And so what to all of it! Now that you are no longer heading up the Hanging Out and Hooking Up Society, all dates are good dates in one way or another. Every date is an opportunity to practice *going* on a date so that when you meet the right person for you, you won't blow it by being a terrible date. It's great to go through the exercise even if it's just so you know that you liked what you were wearing, hated that restaurant, discovered that Indian food comes back up and that the story about your uncle still wanting to play hide and seek with you even though you're well into your twenties is better to be debuted at a later date. It's all just practice so that you can be firing on all cylinders when the time comes.

So let it all go. Start fresh and Carpe Datem.

THE NEW LAWS OF ATTRACTION by Greg

Not having an expectation is the new black, not to be confused with not caring. You must care that you are on a date, but you must not care where it's all going. And that will read loud and clear and we'll be psyched. Let me let you in on a little secret. Most guys who ask you out will be nervous about it and at some point in the day consider calling the whole thing off. I know I felt like that about almost every date I ever initiated. Putting yourself out there with a complete stranger can be a stomach-churning experience. So knowing that your potential suitor feels that way should put you not only at ease but also at an advantage. You can set the tone by letting him know that tonight you are in his hands and whatever he has planned will be great. That may not be the case but you have a better shot at having a great time by putting the dude at ease. Don't have an expectation and if he says he's nervous you can remind him that *It's Just A Date!* In fact, if you both know that going in you may have the best date ever.

THAT'S JUST YOU LOOKING FOR A LOOPHOLE

Sorry, kitten, but there is no loophole here. You are going on a first date and that's it! Someone has asked for the pleasure of your company and by God they are going to have it. You will not bail on this at the last-minute resort to old patterns or set yourself up for disappointment. In fact you will suit up, show up and be sparkly and exotic because that's what you should do all the time in every aspect of life. You know what else? You will, against all odds, have a great time because, as you know, wherever you go is going to be great because you are there! The road to greatness starts on the first date. Got it?

Carpe Datem Rock'em Sock'em Superbook

When a first date comes your way, you need to be ready for it. Whether you do the asking or get asked, it will behoove you to have some solid 'go tos' in place so that you're ready for a rocking date.

First Date Go Tos
Put together an outfit for each occasion that makes you FEEL attractive and confident. List the pieces from head to toe.

1. Going for a walk/hike.
2. Having brunch/coffee at a hip café.
3. Going out to a casual dinner and the movies.
4. Going to an expensive dinner.
5. Day at the beach.
6. Fancy event for work.
7. Fancy event for fun.
8. Game night at their friend's.

Make a list of restaurants, places you'd like to go or things you'd like to do on a first date that fall within the budgets below.

1. Costs less than £10.
2. Costs less than £50.
3. Costs less than £100.
4. Is free.

essence #4: first date follow up

Communication And The Next Right Move

The first date is either a beginning or an ending, but what happens next? Unless you drank too much you can usually tell while you're still on the date how it went, right? Wrong. You only know how it felt for you and how it went for you. What happened on their end, and their impression of the same event might be totally different from yours. It happens all the time. This is where much of the frustration of dating lies. Two people on the same date with completely different stories—one of them thinks it was great, you totally clicked and can't wait to do it again, the other thinks it was okay but is on the fence as to whether or not they want to see the sequel. Even if you kissed you never really know how it went, but the thing is that you want to know! That's what this chapter is all about. In the absence of information, what is the next right move?

You are going to hate this, but the next right move is to remain completely still. Not actually still, that would be weird—especially if you have a roommate. They won't understand why you are standing frozen stiff in the kitchen. Even though surely you followed thru with our **First Date "Definitely Dos"** from the previous chapter which included letting your date know what a really good time you had, you will have the urge to call him and reiterate what a great time you had or some version of that. While that's a nice idea, let's be real … you aren't doing it to show him how well versed in the rules of etiquette you are, you just want to find out if he felt the same way. Hate to break it to you, Peaches, but that's a classic form of rushing him into a response. So put down the phone, get your hands off the instant messenger, blackberry, iPhone or whatever and just savor the date for a while and let him do the same. There is something kind of magical in those first 24 hours following a great date where you get to relive moments of it in your head, so enjoy them. In fact, go the opposite direction with your energy. Call your buddies and have a brunch, go for a run to remind yourself that no matter how your heart feels or how your stomach is filled with bees, you are still you and as such you must take care of you. Don't wait by that phone—in fact if you can leave yours at home when you go out, then do. Chances are if he had as good a time as you did he's wondering what to do next. Let's let him wonder!

Most guys aren't expecting you to make the next move, and often when you do it backfires. One of the things we have noticed in our culture is an inability to really seduce one another. In our Burger King drive-thru society we like to get to the meal before we get home, barely remembering afterwards what the food tasted like. That's because we know we'll eat again. But if we ate every meal like it was our last, we'd spend more time savoring the flavors. That's all we're asking you to do: slow the process down, enjoy it while it's happening and let it unfold the way it naturally wants to.

If the first date was totally a non-event, you didn't connect, had nothing to talk about and no chemistry, then it's pretty clear that not only won't there be a repeat performance but that it's likely curtains for any further contact. But if there was a spark, an attraction or a connection then you're now in the waiting purgatory. Was it good for him? Does he like me? Is he going to call? When will he call? How many days is an okay amount of days? How many is too many days? Do I have any messages? Is my phone working? Maybe I should check my email?

Look, a guy knows before the end of the first date with you whether or not he wants to go out with you again. How he plays it if he does want to date you again is what you're waiting to find out. Is he a wait-three-day caller? A next-day texter? Or a disappear-off-the-face-of-the-earth guy? You'll find out soon enough.

Even though you approached your date with a Zen mindset and the It's Just A Date! attitude, it's not always the easiest thing to carry over after actually having a *good* date. So don't let your mind run away with you now. Take a moment to recognize that yes, it would be great if he called, but if he doesn't then it's no biggie. If he wasn't down with the Sparkly and Exotic program that is you for date number two, then he certainly wasn't Mr. Right, Mr. Right Now or Mr. Knock Your Socks Off In Bed. It's no one's loss but his. Deep breath in, exhale out. Let it go. Okay, good. Now anytime you feel yourself getting fixated or anxious about the post-first date contact void, just repeat the mantra "It's just a date, so let it go." Then take a moment to remember that there are great things in store for all of us and they are all beyond our control. We can't make things happen but we can certainly stop them from happening by screwing things up.

WHAT DOES IT MEAN & WHAT DO YOU DO?

While your obsessing over his contact, lack of contact or methods of contact, we thought we'd help you decipher what is more than likely happening over at Dude Head Quarters and what your response to it should be. While our gut reaction is, "Who cares what's going on over there, you're where the action is" here are some popular scenarios …

What does it mean when ... He doesn't call the next day?

It probably doesn't mean anything. He's probably trying to figure out what his next move is and taking some space to think about you, whether he likes you "that way" and giving you space to do the same.

What do you do?

Barely notice because you have plans and aren't expecting to hear from him yet anyway.

What does it mean when ... He doesn't call after two days?

He's doing the regular guy stuff that he usually does and is either considering when is the right time to call or has decided not to call.

What do you do?

Continue having your life and don't call him, text him or email him.

What does it mean when ... He doesn't call within the first week?

It's not good news. If he definitely likes you and wants to date you again there will be contact within the first week ... barring his deployment to Iraq, his sudden slip into a coma or the spotty mobile service atop Mt. Everest.

What do you do?

If you like him then you can be sad for a moment, maybe even call a friend to commiserate, then you let it go. It was just a date. Move on to the next one.

What does it mean when ... He doesn't call within the first week but texts or emails "What have you been up to?"

That means he almost wants to date you and would be open to a booty call.

What do you do?

Don't respond. If he decides he wants to see you again he knows where to call you.

What does it mean when ... He doesn't call within the first week but texts or emails "Had a great time. Been thinking about you. You free on Friday night?"

That means he almost wants to date you.

What do you do?

Feel free to wait a while to get back to him, then text him that he'll have to call you for the answer.

What does it mean when ... He doesn't call for three weeks then texts or emails "What have you been up to?"

That means he's looking for a booty call and hoping you weren't crushed enough by him blowing you off to put out.

What do you do?

Wait a while to text back then shoot him a "Just dating losers like you."

What does it mean when ... He doesn't call for three weeks then texts or emails "Been out of town and thinking about you. You free on Friday night?"

The other girl I was dating didn't pan out so I'm willing to give it another try with you. Also, that he didn't miss you enough to call you.

What do you do?

Wait a while and text or email him back, "You must have the wrong number. My name is Mike but I'm free Friday night."

CONVERTING THE TEXT By Amiira

Boys will be boys and therefore they will often try to get away with the least amount of effort, commitment or communication possible. In our society the norms are that guys are bad communicators and women expect too much from them in this area. Now because of this stigma guys think that any form of communication is good and should count, and we agree with that to a point. Yes, there's a convenience of text messaging and there's something sexy about it when you get a "I'm in a meeting but I'm thinking about you. Talk to you later." Sure. But that's because there's a "talk to you later" chaser at the end. When you're in the stages of Post-First Date Meltdown and the phone isn't ringing, texting ain't gonna cut it. Texting says "I'm kind of into you" but calling says "I want to hear your voice." Someone who only text-messages you is just keeping you on the line in case he doesn't find someone he's more attracted to by the time he wants to get laid. If a guy's really interested in getting to know you then contacting you via text, email, IM, MySpace comment or whatever other modern and impersonal way they develop next would be secondary to talking to or seeing you in person. HOWEVER he still might see if he can get away with "shortcut dating" by way of technology in the beginning. It's up to you to be clear that getting to know the glory of you takes place on the phone or in person. The more you engage in impersonal communication, the more you're going to get it. The more casual ways of communicating are fine to supplement the already existing relationship, but to build one from scratch requires more time than it takes to type Prince-style short-hand into your mobile phone (U R so funny C U L 8 R).

How do you convert a texter or an emailer into a caller? Simple. Don't accept the idea that his chosen form of communication is enough. When he texts or emails you instead of calling you, then you simply reply any version of the following:

"Email system is being shut down. Call me in 5 minutes."

"Can't talk now. Call me at 7 p.m. Lots to tell you."

"Getting carpal tunnel from texting. Call me on my mobile."

"I'm better on the phone. Call me later."

"Typing is my day job. Give me a call."

"I can't remember what your voice sounds like."

You get the picture. Then when he calls, let him know that you're not much of an emailer or texter but are awesome on the phone. Basically if you don't engage in texting and emailing instead of talking to each other, he'll have only two choices: to call you or find someone willing to settle for less. For my money there's nothing like that good-night call at the end of the day from the new person you like. A text just isn't the same.

THE NEW LAWS OF ATTRACTION by Greg

Let him call you after the first date.

Just let it lay. Wouldn't you want your date to stand as the last good thing in his mind? Rather than a series of "Uh, Hi. I can't remember if I was supposed to call you or were you supposed to call me. Anyhoooozle, I just wanted to tell you I had a great time ... again. Okay bye." "Oh hey, it's me, my phone cut out I think. I just wanted to say um ... had a great time. Okay, bye for now." "Hey, it's me again, Janet … from Friday. I forgot to leave my number it's …" You get the point. If you went out and gave him the best version of you, that's really all you can do. He's had a taste of your delicious company, don't pour mustard on it. Look, sometimes a dude needs to take a moment to think about what's happened. A guy can like you and want to go out with you again, but may want to wait a few days to call you. That's the space he wants to think about you, enjoy thinking about the date, talk to his friends about it and give you plenty of time to do the same while hoping he's going to call. The immediate space is good. It can be delicate, too. If you crowd a guy with too many texts, emails, messages or whatever it can actually make us like you less. It goes back to rushing people into doing something they weren't going to do yet and freaking people out with your need to know what they're thinking. Rarely do you know after a first date that it's going to be true love, so we're sitting on a fence after date number one. The fence itself is *liking you* and on one side is *I really like her/could love her in the future* and the other side is *NOPE!* You can actually swing us over to the wrong side.

THAT'S JUST YOU LOOKING FOR A LOOPHOLE

We hear it all the time, it's been two days since your date and you haven't heard from him but there's been some glitch in your email, voicemail, mobile phone, SIM card or whatever. So you think you should use that as the excuse to make contact. Look, headstrong lady, you can do what you want but before you do, think about this. If you wanted to reach someone and their gadget had a glitch that disabled it from taking your message, would you stop trying to reach them or would you find another way? You'd find another way. Now, is this guy who hasn't called you yet a moron? Then let him figure it out. You're worth tracking down.

Carpe Datem Rock'em Sock'em Superbook

Okay, you are going to hate this, but let us tell you why it's a good idea before you shut us down. We think you should keep a dating journal. "You guys you have to be kidding me." No we are not. Look, you are now a person who goes on dates. How hard would it be to jot down a couple of notes about the date to remind yourself of who you dated, what you wore, where you went and what the highlights were? But, more importantly, what you did or said that was great, what you did or said that was stupid, did you get kissed, drink too much, etc. ... That way you can go back and see that 'Oh man, I loved that blue dress but I hated Crabs A Lot Seafood Playroom.' Below is a sample of the kinds of things that are good to remember.

1. Who did you go out with?
2. Did you like him?
3. Do you want to see him again?
4. Did you make plans to do so or at least tell him "I had a really good time"?
5. Did you like what you wore?
6. Did you like what he wore?
7. Did you like what you talked about?
8. Did you like what he talked about?

9. Were you sexually attracted to him?
10. Did he try and kiss you?
11. How did the date end?
12. What could you have done better?
13. What was your best moment?

16

essence #5: 2nd date and beyond

Pacing Your Dates and The Formula For Success

So, he ended the suspense and called for a second date because he obviously has great taste and appreciates the finer things in life like you. *So when is it okay to go on the second date?* We think the second date should take place within one week of the post-first date phone call unless your schedule doesn't allow it or one of you is out of town. Then it should be as soon as you can schedule it for the next possible opening. *How many days in advance should he ask?* We're not sticklers about this, but you don't want to appear too available so we'd say two days in advance at least. *How long should there be between the first and second date?* Here's where we stand—there should be **at least** two days between the first and second dates so that you can build some anticipation about seeing each other and hopefully have another phone call in between to continue getting to know each other. But anything past two weeks from the first date and you run the risk of losing momentum and forgetting what you liked about each other on the first date. The re-entry to a second date should be smooth and effortless, that's why you want to try keep the distance between dates limited. Otherwise it's like having a first date again.

The second date is where things really gel and impressions get cemented. Where the first date is a feeling it out discovery mission, the second date is where you really click or don't. This is a very important date because it's the date that things start happening on the inside, and either you start getting attached to the person or realize that they might not be for you. Though it's important there should actually be less pressure on it. It should feel a bit easier because there is already some level of familiarity and hopefully there's even been some communication between dates. It's also the date that can be less date-like (not to be confused with *overly* casual). Generally your date has done his homework on the first date and has some understanding of who it is that you are, so he'll probably ask you on a date relating to some facet of your personality. Like if you mentioned hiking, then that's a possibility and a totally acceptable second date. If you mentioned you liked the work of Michael Bay (*Die Hard* among others) he may ask you to a movie, also a totally acceptable second date. HOWEVER, if he asks if you want to rent a movie and order in pizza at his pad ... NOT an acceptable second date. Second date is not the date to get that *casual* yet! Trust us, if this thing is going to go the distance, there will plenty of time later to kick it couch style with a movie. Hey Hot Pants, let us not go anyplace—yours nor his—with an adjacent bedroom. It's just not time yet. This is still a very crucial point in developing what could be a relationship, and it's imperative that on date two you leave the room early.

Here is a quick list of acceptable and unacceptable second dates.

Acceptable:
✓ Dinner out again, your choice but it doesn't have to be
✓ A movie (it's a classic)
✓ Bowling or Mini Golf
✓ Dancing
✓ Concert
✓ Hike, bike ride or any outdoor activity
✓ Art Museums (cultural and romantic!)
✓ Coffee

Not Acceptable:
✗ Lunch (too early, feels like a downgrade)
✗ Breakfast (late night after a movie or concert's okay, otherwise same as above)
✗ His place for a movie
✗ Your place for sex

✗ Drinks (not time to meet for drinks just yet)

✗ The cafeteria at your dorm (even if he doesn't have any money, he can take you to a coffee shop for tea. Everyone can get five dollars.)

What about getting frisky? The second date is a fine time to get your smooch on, but that's it. Again, we're not saying that sex is anything less than stellar or that you shouldn't get to have it, but WAIT!!! You can't lose by parceling out the good stuff, and believe us your kisses are like Superbowl tickets—hard to come by and f*#king awesome! Let the little things speak of what the future might hold instead of showing him what's behind door number 1 before he's even taken a stab at solving the puzzle. Remember, teaser, trailer, THEN movie!

DATING ALERT!

While dating someone is great, dating more than one someone is even better. What better way to determine how deep your feelings are for someone than by having something to compare it to? We believe that it's good to date in the classic sense. Look, in the old days, before the advent of the Girls Gone Wild generation, people used to date more than one person. See, back then before premarital sex, you dated a bunch of people and then decided whom you wanted to get it on with for the rest of your life and hopefully it worked out.

It's easy to date lots of people when you are not having sex but it's hard to marry someone these days and not have had sex since premarital sex is so widely practiced and enjoyed. So why not date lots people then find the one you want to have sex with, then use *that* as an indicator that this is the person you are serious about? Another huge upside to dating more than one person is that it takes the pressure off of hoping that this one person will work out and it keeps you busy so you don't go too fast. The reason more people don't actively date more than one person is because they get into relationships so quickly. There seems to be a "sex on the third date" model that people are following. Then because the intimacy of having sex often implies more than "just dating", the next thing they know, date three has become an instant relationship. Unless of course you've both agreed to dating and sleeping with other people as well, which most people don't have the foresight to do before having a naked party. Or maybe you've agreed to sleeping with other people because you're a time traveler who lives in the 1970s. "But do I have to tell my date that I'm dating other people?" Not unless he asks, and all you have to tell him is "I'm dating." For some reason people feel the need to self-disclose everything right away. Keep some mystery. You don't owe anyone any explanation of how you live your life, especially on a first or second date. Trust us, the more you date the easier it will be to find the one you like. It's just good math.

Dating is the best system of eliminating people that aren't right for you and finding the one that is. It's the smartest way to move into the land of a serious relationship because then what you have is built on a mutual attraction (both physical and psychological), emotional attachment and respect for each other. It's a formula that worked for generations and hence is a classic. Get it? Old ideas, along with new ideologies about sex, we like to think of as a Custom Classic for today's Sparkly Super Dater. Now, if you're experiencing a dating drought (quite common in this part of the world) and you can't find anyone else to date that's of any interest to you, then still take it slow and really evaluate how you feel about this person instead of how you *want* to feel about someone.

After the second date, assuming it went as well as we think it probably did, we loosen up a bit and are less stringent about you calling him. That's not to say that you should do it a lot. The goal is to still leave him wanting more, and when he wants more he is still in pursuit, and that's a good thing. When timing out when to go on dates three, four and five, they can get closer together like going out every two days or so, though we still advise to space them *at least* one whole day apart. That means from dinner to dinner the next night, not dinner to breakfast the next morning! No same-day dating until date number seven. By date six we're not against you moving the date to your place or his for a home-cooked meal or a takeaway and a movie, but keep your clothes on and be clear and flirty about it. "I'm inviting you over for a meal. So don't bring pyjamas or anything." But keep dating other people until you know for sure that you've found the guy that you want to date exclusively … then you can cut the other fellas from your dating line-up one by one until the genius figures out that you're the one for him too!

THE NEW LAWS OF ATTRACTION by Greg

Let him ask you on that second date, after that it's up to you to do what feels right for yourself. If you want to ask him out for date number three, who's to stop you, but let him chase you down again first. If things went the way you hoped he's going to be chomping at the bit to get to see you again. And he should be because you kick ass. Look, the first date sets the tone for who you are and how you like to be treated, the second date reaffirms that by continuing with the same standards and mindset. He should be hustling to figure out what happens next. It's important to put some space between the first and second date just to continue to build the anticipation so no same-day ask-outs. "But Greg I was free, really." Hopefully you won't be free because of your super busy life *but also because it's not time to show him how easy it is to hook up with you*. That way when you eventually do break plans for him further into the relationship, it's a big deal. Right now you are a rare and awesome chick and people are going to have to climb a few mountains of disappointment to see you.

(Notable exception. If your first date was Dec. 30th and he wants to take you out for New Year's that's okay, but you should have plans, or if he's got No Doubt reunion tickets because they can't wait for you. We asked.)

THAT'S JUST YOU LOOKING FOR A LOOPHOLE

But what if I'm not sure if I like him? Do I have to go out with him? Yes, you should. Sometimes we don't click with someone because they just plain aren't a match for us but sometimes we don't click with someone because they are not what we are used to dating which is a totally different thing. Love, just like life, comes in a different package than you expect it to, so give the guy a second shot if you're on the fence. What's another couple of hours with someone who obviously thinks you're great going to hurt? At the very least it will be good for your self-esteem and at the very best it could also be the date that changes everything. If the guy was a good enough guy and seemed to really put in an effort, despite how nervous he may have been, give the guy a second chance. Why, you ask? Because that's the kind of ultra-successful winner dater you are. In case we haven't told you, one of us wasn't sure if we liked the other, but we went out on a second date anyway to find out and look where we ended up ... getting to write a dating book for you!

Carpe Datem Rock'em Sock'em Superbook

Second date assessment quiz. Not sure if you want to go out on that second date? Here's a quick quiz to put you on one side of the fence or the other.

Question		Point Value
Did he show up on time?	Yes	+ 2
	No	- 1
Did you like what he was wearing?	Yes	+1
	No	- 1
Did you think he was handsome?	Yes	+ 2
	No	+ 1

(That's right, give his looks another chance because people can become more attractive as you get to know them)

Was the conversation easy to make?	Yes	+ 2
	No	- 1
Was the conversation interesting?	Yes	+2
	No	- 1

| Did he have a good sense of humor? | Yes | +3 |
| | No | - 3 |

| Did he get your sense of humor? | Yes | +3 |
| | No | - 3 |

| Were you attracted to him? | Yes | + 2 |
| | No | - 1 |

(That can change on date #2)

| Did he have good manners? | Yes | +2 |
| | No | - 2 |

| Was he affectionate? | Yes | +1 |
| | No | - 1 |

| Was he too grabby? | Yes | - 3 |
| | No | +1 |

(We shouldn't have to reward him for not being a creep)

| Were you more impressed by him than you expected? | Yes | +2 |
| | No | +1 |

(No points off for being what you expected him to be)

| Did he have a plan for the date? | Yes | +2 |
| | No | - 2 |

| Did you like what he had planned? | Yes | +2 |
| | No | +1 |

(At least he planned something!)

| Did you want him to call after the first date? | Yes | +2 |
| | No | - 1 |

| Did you think about him the next day? | Yes | +2 |
| | No | - 1 |

Let's add them up and see how our guy did! If he scored anything above a 20 then by God you're going on that second date. If he scored between14–20 then you should still go and give it another shot. Anything below 14 and you should pretend he's got the wrong number when he calls.

essence #6: sexclusivity

Getting It On And Locking It Down

If you read just one chapter of this book let it be this one because it's about sex and when to have it. As stated earlier in this book we love sex and like to hear that people are having it. We also think that if you really like someone you should wait to have it. We are not advising you wait for some chaste or moral reasons but rather because *you have a much better chance of becoming a couple* if you do. Exclusivity and sex are meant to go together but one (Sex) is not a means to the other (Exclusivity).

Sex has a very prominent place in a good relationship but, like any good thing, people have managed to kind of f*#k it up. People use sex as a reward or as a bribe, they use withholding sex as a punishment because, as we have figured out—SEX IS GREAT AND PEOPLE WANT LOTS OF IT! Which is why many use sex as a device to persuade people into rushing relationships that they're not completely ready to commit to. It's certainly a tactic that can work in the short term but it's a long-term crap-shoot at best. Remember what we told you about coming along at your own pace? That goes both ways if you want to have a *great* relationship—the other person has to arrive at their own feelings uncompromised, just as do you, otherwise you have a relationship based on the desire to have sex for the first time. Let's be honest about it, the desire to have sex with someone is a little more common and a lot less lasting than you think. It can compel you to get there, but it can't keep you there.

Just like we encourage you to value yourself, not be too available and slow down when you date, we have to stress that those ideals apply tenfold to having sex. Having sex changes things and puts the relationship on a different trajectory. It can rocket you into the exclusivity of couple-dom or it can shake you out of any assurance you had about the connection with another person. If one of you had unspoken expectations tied to having sex and the other didn't, you're in trouble. Or if one of you gets freaked out because of what sex means to them, for them or what they think *you think* it means, you're in trouble. In short, if you're both not equally invested in the out-come of having sex you can get spanked by it … but not in a hot sexy way.

We've heard friends say when dating someone new that they "just wanted to get it out of the way". What? Just get sex, yummy sex, something that we should be anticipating, looking forward to, thinking about and wanting sex, you mean that sex? That's the one we should just get out of the way? Would you eat a bowl of cake batter for dessert instead of letting the cake bake, frosting that sucker and relishing every bite of it? Not that a stomachache doesn't sound better than delicious cake.

Getting it out of the way is a horrible way to look at the first time you have sex with someone new. As though it's a chore like doing the dishes, rather than what it should be—which is the ultimate way of sharing yourself with someone and rocking their (and your) world. There really isn't any greater way other than a mix tape, CD, playlist for your iPod to share your love than sex ... except for having sex while listening to the mix tape then having a cake encore. Sex should matter, so make having sex matter otherwise it's of no value to either of you.

It's our position that you shouldn't be having sex with everyone that you're dating *if* you want a *committed* relationship. Sex should signify that you're serious about *a* person. It should have some value, some significance and, if you bestow it with that value and significance, it can be the thing that sets you apart from all the other girls he's dated. It's a traditional idea, but if you want to have a boyfriend you shouldn't have sex with anyone until that status has been cemented. No exceptions. And sex shouldn't be the carrot you dangle to get the commitment, it should just be the thing that you only have while in a committed and exclusive relationship. That should be the standard that you live by. That tells the guy you're dating that sex with you is special and that you don't just hand it out as a party favor for any schmo who takes you out on the town.

So then how do you get to be boyfriend/girlfriend without having sex and without using sex as a motivation? Look, sex is always going to be an incentive but you don't want to be the kind of girl that positions it that way because that's lame and completely beneath an Ultra-Successful Winner Dater like yourself who has standards, a life, self-worth and is picky about whom they choose to spend their valuable time with. Well, under the assumption that you are actively dating *(which for the sake of this we'll define as seeing each other at least once a week and talking on the phone three days a week if not more—plus* **NOT instead of** *any extra-curricular emails, text messages or IM-ing if you partake in such activities)* then it's up to you to first decide *IF* this is the guy for you. Really think about it, how do you feel about only being with him? How do you feel about not being with him? If *YOU'VE* decided that he's the one for you then it's up to you to let him know that you are beginning to feel strongly for him (without having sex with him). You can let him know that you're "thinking" about letting go of the other guys you've been dating and gauge his reaction. He may just tell you right then that he's ready to make things exclusive. If he doesn't jump at the opportunity then he's probably still on the fence about doing the same; that's good information to have *before* you have a naked party. You don't want to be sharing a guy sexually because that's *the* most direct route to insecurity and low self-esteem you can find. So it's simple to say "Look I only have sex with people that I'm seeing exclusively. I'm not trying to define this as much as I'm doing what's healthy and smart for me. If this doesn't work for you than that's okay but these are the standards by which I live my life." Our guess is that he'd be psyched to be included in such a program. It's pretty safe to say that if you are sleeping together and are not seeing others then you are on your way to becoming boyfriend and girlfriend. Obviously, your sexual compatibility will determine if you want to proceed further.

Okay Hot Shots, what do we do and how long do we have to wait? We say 10 dates or a minimum of three weeks to four weeks of dating. That's right we've added seven dates, one whole week's worth, to the three-date rule and we really feel that it's a reasonable amount of time to wait. Considering that people used to wait until they were married, which is like an eternity compared to 10 dates or 3 or 4 weeks. Seriously, it's a blip in the scheme of things and in the end you've honored yourself and each other. Even if it doesn't work out you can at least say you gave it your best shot and not be wondering if you had it too soon.

If you've paced yourself, built a relationship based on an emotional investment, mutual respect and a healthy dose of anticipation, then sex is going to be even better and more exciting. Why is that? Because there will be an understanding that doing the deed is something that is reserved only for the elite.

Why does sex have to be such a big deal? *Because it just plain is.* And answer us this: why shouldn't it be? Why would they make sex feel so good if it wasn't supposed to be a big deal? What is the value in downgrading its worth or the power it has not only to give you pleasure but to elevate the relationship and make the connection you have more profound? Making sex matter with the person you love is a great thing because there is no more intimate way of sharing yourself. So why not make that a momentous occasion? One that has been planned out, thought about and has been worked for. Why not make it mean something? Why not give it value? After all, this guy isn't just having sex with anyone **he's having sex with you and that's a big deal!**

We never said don't be sexual or sexy, and again this is not a moral mandate. This is just a suggested way of getting the best out of your relationship. It is also about drawing out the good stuff, making all the moments count and building to something memorable. So if you aren't supposed to have sex for 10 dates or 3 to 4 weeks, what can you do and what counts as sex? Climaxing by either of you counts as sex and therefore should not be done. That means whenever things get steamy YOU STOP! Oral sex counts as sex and should not be done because it also generally leads to climaxing. Heavy petting is okay as you approach the goal line but not before. Keep your clothes on, keep your pants up and enjoy the glory of the journey because it's one of the best ones we get in this lifetime.

We've mapped out a timeline so you can know where to draw the lines.

Date 1: At the very least if you like this guy a peck on the cheek and a hug. If it was a particularly good date *ONE* good passionate kiss. We really don't care who initiates. If you are feeling it go for it. *But just one.* A sampler. Don't turn it into a make-out session. Especially if it feels like it could go there. Trust us he'll be thinking about that kiss all the next day wondering if he'll get more or why he didn't.

Date 2: Well, sister, it appears he enjoyed your ONE kiss last date. Tonight what's it going to hurt to make out a bit? Really enjoy the kissing, because sadly in relationships making out is the thing that goes first, which is so sad because it is so awesome. So rock a make-out party. What about his hands? Keep them above the clothes and off the juicy bits. That goes for your hands, too. Really concentrate on the kissing.

Dates 3,4,5: We are aware that in many modern relationships that these are the dates where people "get sex out of the way." It's almost an industry standard so it's probably time, if you haven't already, to start having conversations about sex. These conversations can almost be as exciting as the act it self. Acknowledge that you like sex and that it is something that is important to you but you don't just have it with anyone, especially if you are dating other people. You don't have to tell him how many dates you are waiting or what your time frame is, just that it's not time. Keep him on the make-out party plan. If he wants to know what's under that shirt of yours that's up to you but KEEP YOUR PANTS ON ... for now.

Dates 6,7: Here's something we know for sure. Men love great underwear. Perhaps it's time for an underwear make-out party with above-the-waist action. Know when to stop because it's not time for the "Happy Ending" if you know what we mean. That's not until game day!

Dates 8, 9: Bring on the heavy petting and NO SEX SLEEPOVER party. While you can pet away there should be *NO CLIMAXING!!* Mouth can do some exploring and pleasure-seeking but it stays above the belt. The mouth counts as sex and climaxing messes with guys' heads and therefore is considered SEX SEX, not messing around sexy foreplay.

Date 10: Ta Da! You have waited for the big event and worked each other up into a frothy lather so tonight should be memorable to say the least. Be safe, use protection and have fun!

CASUAL SEX CLAUSE by Greg

I worked on *Sex and The City* for three years so I am more than aware that women, like men, like to have sex for sport and trust me we are all for it. Just as long as that's *really* what you want. No doubt there are days where you just want to get laid. And why not? Sex is a great part of life. But make sure you're being honest with yourself about why you are doing it. Don't lie to yourself that you are okay with something casual if in fact you want something more serious. It's okay to want more, just don't try and come in through the back door and gamble that he'll develop the feelings you want him to. More often than not one of the two people having a casual sex relationship develops deeper feelings and attachments and the other doesn't. Have casual sexual relationships turned into something more? I'm sure it's happened, but more often than not we are asked, "How can I turn my booty call into a boyfriend?" and to that we usually throw our hands up and say, "turn back time and don't be a booty call in the first place." When I was dating there were girls I went out with and girls I called at 4 a.m. ... and they just weren't the same girl. I also had a crush on a girl who only wanted sex. I kept hoping I could turn it into a relationship but I never did. So make sure you are honest with yourself and the person you are having sex with about what it is. They may want more from the situation than you do, in which case full disclosure is a must to avoid hurt feelings. Be safe and rock the sheets and when you're ready to settle down, close up shop until you find the right customer.

THE NEW LAWS OF ATTRACTION by Greg

You are worth the wait. How many more ways can I say it? I took an informal poll off my MySpace page and here is what I found out. 97.9% of the men surveyed said that if they were dating Jessica Biel they would gladly wait 10 dates to have sex with her. I know what you are saying: "Well I'm not Jessica Biel." Okay fair enough but that's not the point. The point is that if Jessica Biel held herself to a ten-date policy these men would respect that. It's about a value system. Amiira and I waited. She is my Jessica Biel. If I like you enough to respect you, I'll wait because you have told me by virtue of the way you carry yourself that you are worth the wait. *People don't respond to what you tell them, they respond to what you show them.* It's all about your actions. If you are a strong independent woman you don't have to tell people that, nor will you feel the need to because it will show in your actions, and by virtue of that men will come to understand how to treat you. So if you know that waiting to have sex with you is worth it, men will too. Besides why would you want to date any guy that didn't like you as much as Jessica Biel?

THAT'S JUST YOU LOOKING FOR A LOOPHOLE

Won't having sex make him want to be with me more? It might ... but it could also repel him. Sex changes things, it just does as we've said before. Sure he might want to see you all the time if you're having sex but it's not enough to make a relationship last. A quality relationship needs a foundation of love, trust, respect, a burning desire to be with that person through thick and thin and sex. Sex itself isn't enough and doesn't always spawn the love, trust, respect and burning desire. It's a gamble and not a strong hand to play. People don't always know what they want after three dates so why risk it when you don't have to? There are a lot of arguments against having sex too soon but we can't really think of any for waiting a couple of weeks ... well, let's see, hmmmmmm ... nope not one. Good sex is more common and less lasting than you think.

THE TIME WAITING TO HAVE SEX PAID OFF FOR ME by Amiira

It was about six months after my marriage ended, I was getting a divorce, which was certainly depressing to say the least, and it had been years since I had dated anyone other than my soon to be ex-husband. There was this guy who worked for a different branch of my company so we

saw each other every month and a half for business meetings, but because we worked on projects together we
spoke daily. After a while it became clear that he was coming to our office more frequently and working out of my
office specifically instead of the conference room that he
normally used. Then one day he called me and asked if he
flew into town would I have dinner with him? I was certainly flattered that he thought a date with me was worth
the hassle of air travel, and we did get along really well, so
I agreed and up to New York he flew. We had a great date,
flirted shamelessly, shared some kisses and agreed that we
should do it again. So the next week he flew up, we had a
great date with flirting and kissing and started talking
every day on the phone. Same thing for week three—flew
up, dinner, flirting, making out (this time IN my apartment not at the front door) then off he went and we
talked every night on the phone before we went to sleep.
By week four and our fourth official date I was feeling
pretty excited about this guy and hopeful again about the
possibility of getting back on the horse so quickly in a
world where all my friends had told me that dating sucks.
(Not for me pal!) Our situation seemed almost perfect so
far. We had known each other for a couple of years,
worked together well, had been kind of dating for a
month, were definitely attracted to each other and he
made a huge effort to see me because flying to New York
every week cost time and money. Not to mention that I
wasn't really ready for a full-time relationship yet so his

living in another city was good for now. So we're on the fourth date and I'm seriously considering having sex with this guy tonight. It's been a month that we've been dating, it seems like we're going somewhere with this thing and I think I'm ready.

So we have "THE CONVERSATION". You know the one. The "are you sleeping with anyone else?" conversation that you always have before you jump in the sack with someone that you're considering getting into a relationship with. That one went pretty well. Neither of us were currently sleeping with anyone else. Then we had "THE OTHER CONVERSATION". Which in my book always follows the first CONVERSATION and starts with, "how many people have you slept with?" He said, "You first." To which I smugly replied, "Six." I'm not going to lie I was feeling pretty proud of how low my number was. Sure I had been in a relationship for the last five years so obviously I had been out of the game and resting on my Six for a while. "What about you?" I asked the new dreamy guy that I was making future sex plans with in my head. And I kid you not, this is verbatim what he said to me, "Including my brother's wife or not?" Now it took me a second to digest the information in his words because he asked it so matter-of-factly as though he had said, "Is it Tuesday or Wednesday?" And he definitely was NOT kidding! So I smiled and tried to keep my expression from showing any alarm or judgment and asked him, "Well, why wouldn't you count her?" And again, I kid you not this is what he said, "Because I didn't come." Needless to say I didn't have sex with this person nor did I ever go out with him again but we did continue to work together which was a little weird because I knew he had sex with his brother's wife. But had I already had sex with him before having this mind-blowing character-defining piece of information, I would have been throwing up in my mouth at the dinner table. Waiting to have sex paid off big for me and I'm grateful that I had the sense to take it slow, because otherwise I'd probably still feel yucky about sleeping with "that" guy.

Carpe Datem Rock'em Sock'em Superbook

For those of you who will have a hard time waiting to have sex it's time for the great ways to postpone sex workbook exercise. Come up with ten ways to keep having sex at bay. We'll start you off with a couple but it's up to you to not only think of more but to actually do them and keep your knickers on!

Ways To Postpone Sex by (insert your name here)
1. Don't go to their house or your own for dates.
2. Strip your bed before he comes over and throw your sheets in the washing machine so that they're wet and the bed isn't inviting.
3. Paint a bedroom wall so that the fumes keep the bedroom off limits.
4.
5.
6.
7.
8.
9.
10.

closing words

Dearest You,

We have great hope for you finding happiness. Let us leave you with a couple more thoughts before you head out into the world as a Super Extraordinary Ultra-Successful Winner Dater.

YOU BOYZ N' BOOZE!

You won't get a lecture from us on the evils of drinking and dating, we are sure you know the score on that one. We just have one simple rule. **Don't drink anything, smoke anything or take anything that makes you a different person, or makes you make different decisions than you would were you sober.** Look you've spent all this time becoming an even better you, so don't ruin all that hard work by becoming "boozy forgets her standards" if that's what too many Guava Gin Tumblers does to you. Pace yourself because in the end it's *you* he wants to know, not the girl that lifts her skirt over her head. (Sure he'll have sex with the girl who pulls her skirt over her head but he won't take her home to mom.)

EAGER IS FOR BEAVERS

Here's another gem of wisdom for you … Don't make yourself too available or be too eager. Do not stop your already fulfilling life at the drop of the hat. When you bail on your life and friends for a new person the message you're sending that new person is "my life isn't that great and I'm going to be needy because I'm putting all my eggs in your basket." It's the honest to God truth. For every action there is a consequence, and even the ones you think aren't a big deal can have seismic repercussions.

You being so excited that you spend every second with
    them = *You being too available.*

You being too available
    = *them feeling too responsible for you.*

Them feeling too responsible for you
    = *you being needy.*

Even if you didn't mean for your actions to provoke that train of thought it most likely will because it's hard to manage feelings and expectations on both ends.

ZIP IT!

Our feeling when you're dating someone new is that a little goes a long way. Don't reveal everything too fast. Parcel out the good stuff and let them relish all the interesting bits, pieces and facets of the superstar you are. Keep some thoughts to yourself *(for the time being)* and let him think and wonder about you. People should earn the things you share with them based on their interest and emotional investment in you. You don't need to give your biography on the first date and you don't have to solve the "what kind of underwear is she wearing?" mystery either. No one needs to know everything about you or *gets* to know everything about you. If you're dating a quality person and the opportunity exists for a future with him, then you'll have plenty of time to compare every experience, heartbreak or desire you've had in life as well as favorite sexual positions. Hell, we've been together for nearly a decade and we still learn new things about each other. So zip it why don'tcha!

Carpe Datem!

Love,
Greg & Amiira

The
Weekend
Warriors

The
Weekend
Warriors

James W. Burke Jr

iUniverse LLC
Bloomington

The Weekend Warriors

iUniverse books may be ordered through booksellers or by contacting:

iUniverse LLC
1663 Liberty Drive
Bloomington, IN 47403
www.iuniverse.com
1-800-Authors (1-800-288-4677)

ISBN: 978-1-4917-1276-4 (sc)
ISBN: 978-1-4917-1277-1 (e)

Library of Congress Control Number: 2013918987

Printed in the United States of America

iUniverse rev. date: 11/18/2013

To all the soldiers, Regular, Reserve, and National Guard, it has been my privilege and honor to serve with, particularly Vincent B. Lee, 2LT, USMCR (1945-1969), and John L. Burke, COL, USAR (RET) (1932-1989). In addition, most particularly, James W. Burke, LTC USAR (RET) (1924-1999), and Charles A. Bauer, LTCDR, USNR (RET) (1914-1989).

"All that I am and all I ever shall be, I owe to my first detail New Cadet Barracks squad leader, who wishes to remain anonymous for reasons that are intuitively obvious to the casual observer."

(Fourth Class Knowledge, New Cadet Barracks, West Point, 1968)

Prologue

Okecie International Airport
Warsaw, Poland

The Polish premier sat in the rear cabin of the Polish Air Force executive jet carrying him back to Warsaw, meditating over his private meeting with the chairman of the USSR. Perestroika and glasnost notwithstanding, the Russian bear still had claws and was not averse to showing them in private.

"We are walking on the edge of a razor blade," the premier said to his private secretary in a tone of weary resignation.

"You know that our political movement has split into two camps. The moderates in our party, like us, want only gradual change. We are willing to accommodate the Russians as long as they stay in their barracks, allow Poland to be Poland, and pay for their presence. Most of all, these soldiers provide a counterweight to Germany. And the radicals, the hawks look back on the days when Poland was completely free from foreign domination. They remember that Polish soldiers drove the Bolshevik legions of Trotsky from the walls of Warsaw and even conquered part of the Ukraine. They will accept no accommodations with the Russians and their commonwealth. They want them out now and will use force to remove them if necessary."

He sighed mournfully. "They don't understand that the West will not help us against them, except with words. If the Russian tanks roll today, we will receive many fine words but no help. Moreover, if our bank payments are late, we may not even receive the words. The world has not changed that much since 1939."

The private secretary was used to these monologues by the premier and continued studying the documents he held in his lap.

"An added factor in the equation that the radicals fail to consider is Poland's burden of debt to the West." The premier sprawled in the aisle seat opposite his private secretary and began filling his pipe, a well-worn, blackened, hunk of briarroot.

"Money from the West for our economic reconstruction has been only slowly forthcoming. Western banks and governments, regardless of our economic situation, will demand repayment. The Russians and Ukrainians are being openhanded in supplying oil and natural gas to us. They ask only a secret mutual defense pact in return. In addition, they will provide us with fuel and food in payment for the military bases. Can't these fools see that we can live with Russian bases but we are slowly bleeding to death trying to repay the West and their bankers? Our harvests are bad, and the bankers say only that the interest will increase if we miss payments."

Ten thousand feet below and ten miles away from the jet, a nondescript van stopped on a dirt road just outside the boundary fence of Okecie International Airport. Four men got out and removed a battered wooden shipping crate. One of the four pulled open the crate and removed a long, slender tube wrapped in canvas with a bulbous protrusion on one end. As he removed the wrappings, the shape of a Stinger surface-to-air missile launcher became visible.

The American hefted the missile to his shoulder and began the pre-operation checks. The three Poles watched with great interest.

The leader stood to one side. "Are you certain you can do what we require of you? You will have only one chance."

"Shit, man. I spent six years working with Stingers and qualified for distinguished gunner four times."

One member of the group pointed to the east. The small jetliner was visible as a rapidly growing speck, a black mote against the sky. The gunner shouldered his launcher and began the acquisition sequence. The missile's infrared seeker picked up the aircraft's exhaust, and a tone sounded in the gunner's ear. He set the aircraft in the reticule pattern and listened as the growl grew in intensity.

"I have a good lock," he told the others. "Stand clear of the back blast area. I'm firing on three." The gunner counted to three and squeezed his trigger, and the rocket motor ignited with a roar.

The missile leaped from the launcher and seemed to waver until the sustainer motors kicked in. Then it arced upward toward the engines of the jet, leaving behind a slight trail of brown smoke.

In the cockpit, the copilot was going over the landing checklist when something caught his eye. There, off to the right, on the ground, he saw a flash and a climbing smoke trail heading for the aircraft.

"Fuck my mother!" he screamed in the intercom at the pilot. "Stinger! Stinger!"

He had flown fighter-bombers in Afghanistan and knew what the flash meant and what was now climbing toward them. The pilot threw the aircraft into a violent diving turn, trying to break the missile seeker's lock on his engines.

He called the control tower. "I am being shot at! A missile is coming at me! A missile is coming at me!"

The beauty of the Stinger is that it can outturn any aircraft it is aimed at, and only expensive, highly complex countermeasure systems, which the small passenger jet lacked, could foil its seeker. The pilot's violent evasive maneuvers spilled some of the passengers out of their seats. The premier was thrown against the rear bulkhead, breaking his arm, while his private secretary was knocked unconscious. Slumped against the cabin wall, the premier reached for the badge of the Black Virgin of Czestochowa he wore on the lapel of his navy suit. But his arm wouldn't work.

Another violent corkscrew turn threw him the length of the cabin as he began to pray in a weak voice, "Hail, holy queen, mother of mercy . . . ."

Not that any of this mattered. The engines were mounted on the tail above the passenger cabin, and when the missile's proximity fuse detonated, the fragments killed the passengers before the exploding fuel consumed their bodies. The pilot and copilot, pinned in their seats by centrifugal force, lived a little longer until the flaming remnants of the jet met the ground at six hundred knots.

The pilot's message stunned the control tower operators into silence.

"Poland One, say again your transmission. What do you mean you have a missile coming toward you?" the senior controller finally responded after seconds of delay.

His answer was the hiss of the carrier wave.

"Poland One, what is your status? What is going on up there? The flight from Moscow just disappeared from our screens. Can you see anything? What is happening up there?"

The telephone from the ground control radar rang. By now, a column of black smoke was visible in the distance.

Once the missile was on its way, the gunner threw the launcher back into the shipping crate. One man went to start the van while the leader and the third man helped the gunner rewrap the launcher, load it into the crate, and shove the container back into the van. The co-driver produced a bottle of vodka for toasts of celebration as the van passed the outlying suburbs of Warsaw.

At an intersection, the driver ran a stop sign. A column of Russian BTR-80 eight-wheeled armored personnel carriers, returning from a live fire exercise, was entering the intersection on the priority road. The driver of the lead carrier slammed on his brakes but still clipped the front of the van, knocking it off the road and onto the shoulder. The APC skidded through the intersection and halted about twenty meters from the van, broadside to it.

What would have been a minor traffic accident resulting in disciplinary action for all Russian soldiers involved became tragedy. As the sergeant commanding the lead carrier dismounted to examine the damage, one of the Poles in the van panicked. He produced a pistol from under his seat and opened fire at the soldier. The Russian dropped with a bullet in his head. The troops in the first carrier immediately opened fire on the van with their rifles and the carrier's heavy machine gun and killed all four occupants.

The firing stopped when the soldiers ran out of ammunition. The company commander ran forward to examine the riddled van with his second-in-command. Both were contemplating long terms in Siberia for the problems this incident would create with the authorities, both civilian and military. The commander waved some soldiers out to pick up the body of the dead soldier and to begin blocking traffic through the intersection.

His second-in-command looked inside the van. The senior lieutenant swallowed convulsively several times as he pulled open the side door and two bodies rolled out onto the road. He noticed the wooden crate and pulled it open. He expected some form of black market goods and was not surprised to see a weapon in the crate. Some soldiers were selling arms and equipment for vodka and blue jeans.

"Comrade Captain!" he shouted to his commander. "These guys have a Strela in their van."

The commander walked over to look at what his lieutenant found. He first glanced at the crate uninterestedly and then did a startled double take. "Shit! That's not a Strela. That's a Stinger launcher. No wonder they started shooting. Put a guard on this box and the van. Then get the spooks out here. If these guys had an American SAM in their hands, we may be off the hook."

A Polish police car responding to the aircraft crash stopped when they saw the bullet-riddled van and dead Russian soldier in the road. The senior police officer talked to the Russian officers and called his superiors. Polish and Russian security officers descended on the site like a dark cloud. A gray Mercedes with tinted windows arrived on the scene. A flock of gray men in gray overcoats flowed out of the car.

One approached the company commander. "Pay book and name, Comrade Captain."

"Razov, Pieter Mikhailovich. Captain, 237th Motorized Rifles."

The gray man rifled through the pay book, noting the three tours in Afghanistan. "Do you know what happened here?"

"There's an empty Stinger launcher in the van and a column of smoke over there," Razov said with a wave of a hand.

"Someone shot a plane down. Your presence says it was an important aircraft. If I listen to American shortwave radio tonight, I will most likely learn what you're not going to tell me after you remind me of my socialist duty."

"Will your soldiers talk about what happened here? Have they listened to any of the conversations going on?"

"They are Uzbeks and Kazaks, Comrade. They barely understand enough Russian to obey orders. You think they understand Polish?"

"Do not speak of this to anyone, Comrade Captain, and ensure your soldiers do not as well.

"We have long ears and even longer memories. You are dismissed. Return with your men to your barracks."

The security teams moved the Stinger launcher and the four bodies to a heavily guarded storage building near the Russian embassy in Warsaw.

Chapter 1

The Kind Of War On Which They Are Embarking

The first, the supreme, the most far-reaching act of judgment that the statesman and commander have to make is to establish . . . the kind of war on which they are embarking.
—Karl von Clausewitz

Greenland-Iceland-United Kingdom Gap
North Atlantic

When the Russian BEAR-H maritime reconnaissance aircraft left its base in the Kola Peninsula, the crew expected the usual dull flight out over the Atlantic, around Iceland, and down the Canadian and US coasts to Cuba.

"I know twelve hours in our beloved BEAR is boring," the aircraft commander said to his crew as the bomber climbed to its cruise altitude. "Our friends in Iceland have returned to full strength and are sending out F-15s to keep us company. Keep a watch out for them. It's about time for the new edition of *Playboy* to appear."

"Even then," the electronic warfare officer told the tail gunner, a new recruit making his first flight, "if you've seen one F-15, you've seen them all."

As the bomber crossed the Barents Sea and rounded the North Cape, just south of Jan Mayen Island, the pilot descended to a hundred feet above sea level and turned off all electronic emitters.

"I will remind those of you who slept through my briefing before takeoff," the aircraft commander announced over the intercom. "We will fly a simulated attack profile against Iceland with a low approach, a pop up to cruise altitude to simulate a missile launch, and break back to sea level for our escape. Our goal is testing the NATO radar on Iceland to see how close to the island our BEAR can come before the radar finds us and scrambles the F-15s at Keflavik Air Station. So, tail gunner, stay alert back there, and keep a watch for the Americans."

An American E-3 AWACS, call sign REDCAP, picked up the BEAR three hundred miles away. REDCAP requested the alert patrol at Keflavik, two F-15s with call signs GRAYBACK 01 and 02, to intercept the intruder. The Russian EWO detected the E-3 as its radar painted the BEAR and could tell that the American aircraft was sending messages somewhere. Once the AWACS found them, the pilot climbed to launch altitude with a warning to the crew, particularly the tail gunner, to watch for the Americans.

REDCAP steered the F-15s to a position within visual range above and behind the Russian bomber. GRAYBACK 02 spotted the Russian first and waggled his wings to attract the leader's attention. Once 01 saw the target, he placed himself directly behind and three hundred feet above the bomber. Then he rolled into a dive, pushing his throttles to full military power. A half-mile from the BEAR, he turned on all his radars.

Pandemonium reigned aboard the BEAR. Threat warning receivers warbled and wailed as the EWO shouted, "They've found us! They've found us! An F-15 is out there, and he's got a good lock!"

GRAYBACK 01 roared by the BEAR at a distance of less than a hundred feet at twice the speed of sound. The F-15 was a gray blur that flashed over the cockpit of the bomber, shaking the giant four-engine BEAR as a terrier shakes a rat. As he flew over the Russian, 01 broke into a violent dive across the nose of the BEAR. The Russian pilots reflexively pulled up into an abrupt steep climb to avoid a collision.

As the sudden loss of airspeed caused the BEAR to wallow and stall, the copilot swore. "Goddamned cowboy! That fucking American is going to kill us!"

"Where did he go? Mother of God, he will kill us if he is not stopped. Can you see him, gunner? Can you track him?" the pilot shouted.

"He's painting us!" the EWO cried. "His fire control radar is on! Watch him!"

The tail gunner was on his first mission. The sudden appearance of the American fighter from nowhere badly frightened him. Isolated in his tail turret, the gunner could hear only excited voices over the intercom. The gunner reached to his control panel and turned on his fire control radars. As he did, his eyes caught the rapidly approaching blur of GRAYBACK 02, and he froze. Frightened, he did not call a warning of the new fighter. When 02 turned on his radar, it caused a second shock to the flight deck crew.

GRAYBACK 02 flashed over the right side of the BEAR as its tail guns swiveled in response to the radar controls. The F-15's own Radar Warning Receiver warbled when the Russian's fire control radar painted the American.

As the BEAR bounced in the turbulence of his passage, GRAYBACK 02 broke radio silence. "Lead, this is Two. BEAR has uncaged his guns and turned on his fire control radar. We've got him good enough. Let's quit now."

GRAYBACK 01 completed a circle behind the BEAR, ready for a second pass. The startled faces of the flight deck crew made the first pass fun. He was ready for one more before he stopped.

"Two, Lead. Negative. I'm going back in. He won't do anything."

REDCAP, watching the action on his radar and listening to the conversation, broke in. "GRAYBACK 01, REDCAP. Do not. I say again. Do not approach BEAR again. Take up position above and in front of BEAR, and escort him from the area into international air space."

GRAYBACK 01 already began his second run on the Russian, and he was too close to break off, so he ignored REDCAP. GRAYBACK was at the same altitude as the Russian aircraft, and the tail gunner saw only a rapidly growing F-15 heading directly at him. He could hear the wail of the RWRs in his earphones. As the copilot shouted that the Americans were out to kill them all, the gunner squeezed his triggers.

Two streams of green tracers blossomed from the tail of the BEAR and converged on the F-15. As GRAYBACK saw the muzzles of the twin cannons begin to sparkle, he jerked his control stick back to climb out of the path of the guns. The cannon fire caught the underside of his aircraft and shredded the right wing and engine.

As his F-15 shuddered under the impact of the cannon fire, the pilot shouted into his radio, "GRAYBACK 01 is taking fire! Mayday! Mayday! I'm hit! I'm hit! I've lost one engine! Mayday!"

REDCAP screamed, "GRAYBACK, get the fuck out of there! Do not. Repeat. Do not return fire! 01, where are you? 02, where are you? Can you see 01? What is his status?"

On board the BEAR, the cannons' blast brought everyone to startled speechlessness.

Then the pilot roared. "Gunner, what are you firing at? What are you doing? Who shot at us? Navigator! Flight engineer! Get back there and stop him before the fool gets us all killed!"

Tensions tightened another notch. The Russians accepted American assurances that GRAYBACK 01, who survived his bailout and raft trip in the North Atlantic with minor injuries, acted on his own in violation of regulations and policies and would be disciplined, but they did not believe them.

The Americans, for their part, publicly accepted the Russian story of the berserk airman who had panicked and fired on the F-15 but privately discounted it. It was common knowledge that Russian service members did nothing without orders and close supervision from their superiors, so obviously the whole mission was a setup to shoot down an American fighter plane.

Incidents between Germany and Poland began flaring up. A German fishing trawler wandered into the Polish twelve-mile limit in the Baltic and loaded its nets with illegal herring. When a Polish coast guard vessel challenged it, the German trawler attempted to run for open seas. The Polish vessel fired a warning shot across the bow of the German ship, who ignored it. The Polish cutter then fired on the trawler and sank it, drowning two crewmembers. The Poles rescued the survivors and charged them with violating Polish fishing laws. The Polish government ignored German protests and sentenced the fishermen to three months in jail. After this incident, German naval vessels with orders to shoot to protect their charges escorted German trawlers in the eastern Baltic.

When a Polish patrol boat tried to halt a German trawler escorted by the German frigate, *FGS Neckar*, the situation blew up, in all senses of the word. The Polish patrol boat fired across the fishing boat's bow with its 40 mm cannon. The *Neckar* responded with its 76 mm main gun and blew the patrol boat out of the water. When Warsaw denounced the *Neckar*'s action, the German government produced records and charts showing the incident had taken place in international waters and stated that the *Neckar*'s actions were reasonable and prudent. The *Neckar* was only protecting herself and an innocent fishing trawler against an unprovoked assault.

Supreme High Command Presentation to the
Warsaw Pact Council of Ministers

Our unanimous assessment is that NATO is in disarray and incapable of decisive unified action at this time and for the foreseeable future. Following the debacle of the Iranian Revolution, the former American president won election on building up the American military and made some small progress to that end. However, his disastrous interventions in Central and South American destroyed his regime and led the American public to totally repudiate his administration and party. Over the past five years, the current administration has turned its attention to domestic affairs and increasingly pulled back from international commitments. In the process, they have eliminated whatever improvements had been made to their armed forces and reduced the remainder to a shell. This gives us a window of opportunity to strike Western Europe, defeat our NATO adversaries, and secure unfettered access to the economic resources we need to provide for our own future.

Our analysis is that a major offensive launched into Western Europe with all available Pact forces will result in the rapid seizure of West Germany to the Rhine River, as well as the Netherlands, Austria, and Denmark.

Our success in Western Europe will give us leverage in the Mediterranean and allow us to move against Iran when we choose to seize their oil fields. Success will also destroy the spirit of the populations and governments of the surviving NATO nations. The loss of West Germany as a forward base will allow us to consolidate our hold swiftly without interference.

We propose mobilizing all available forces under the guise of a major military exercise celebrating the forty-fifth anniversary of our victory in the Great Patriotic War. We anticipate the mobilization and deployment will take thirty-five days to move all forces to their start positions. The announced start date of the exercise, five days later, will actually launch our offensive.

Our general plan of attack will be two thrusts. The major effort will be across the North German Plain along the Hamburg-Bremen-Rotterdam general line. The second supporting thrust will be through the Fulda Gap along the Fulda-Frankfurt-Wiesbaden line. The primary purpose of this thrust will be to pin the American forces in place and prevent their movement north to reinforce NATO's Northern Army Group on the North German Plain.

When we have secured our objectives, we shall pause and present our terms to the surviving Western European governments. The destruction of their militaries will force these governments to accept whatever terms we present. With Western Europe neutralized and their premier military force destroyed, the United States will have no other option than to accept our terms.

Washington, DC

The voice of the television anchor was solemn. "Ladies and gentlemen, the president of the United States is speaking to the nation in a special broadcast. The White House requested this broadcast with little advance notice and no explanation. And now, the president."

Tension exaggerated the New England accent as the president began. "Good evening. I am speaking to you this evening to discuss the current situation in Europe. Despite repeated appeals by me and the leaders of Western

Europe, Russia and its Warsaw Pact allies have continued to mobilize their forces and deploy them closer to the borders of Germany. Our repeated efforts to defuse the tense situation in Central Europe and to gain a fair settlement of the problems existing there have failed. The response of the Russians and their allies has been intransigent hostility and ever-increasing levels of military threat.

"In view of this, and at the recommendation of my military advisors and the leaders of Congress, I have this day called up two hundred thousand members of the Armed Forces Reserves and National Guard for a minimum of one-year active service. Those members affected are being notified now. I have further directed that the Return of Forces to Germany, or REFORGER, start within the next thirty-six hours. All noncombatants will be evacuated from West Germany beginning twelve hours from now. To expedite this movement, I have directed the Secretary of Defense to activate the Civil Reserve Air Fleet as of midnight tonight. I have briefed leaders of Congress of both parties extensively and continuously on the situation developing in Europe. It is our earnest hope and prayer that this situation can be resolved peacefully. I will keep you apprised of all developments. Thank you and good night."

Radio Moscow News Broadcast

"The peoples and governments of the Warsaw Pact categorically reject the demands made by the president of the United States and call upon him to cease his aggressive and provocative actions in support of the resurgent neo-Nazi and criminal regime of Germany. The government of the Warsaw Pact further asserts that all actions taken by itself and its allies are for their defense. Should the United States and the other nations of the NATO alliance stop this madness of war preparation and force the criminal terrorists in Bonn to be responsible for their reprehensible actions, peace can be kept. If this is not what happens, then the Warsaw Pact will take whatever steps are necessary to achieve a just peace and gain justice for the peoples of the world."

Chapter 2

Planning and Preparing

In preparing for battle I have always found that plans are useless, but planning is indispensable.

—Dwight D. Eisenhower

*Webster-Franklin Defense Electronics Systems
Ground Combat Directorate
Nashua, New Hampshire*

"Hey Mike! Have you seen what the fucking Russians are doing now? They're calling us warmongers and threatening to attack us because we're provoking them! Goddamn commies ought to have their asses kicked from here to Siberia." The middle-aged, rotund speaker with sandy hair wore a prominent NRA belt buckle and tie tack marring his Brooks Brothers suit. He proceeded into the cubicle, waving a copy of the day's *Boston Globe*. "Anyhow, Moscow's claiming that we're supporting a plot by German right=wing extremists to overthrow the Federal Union government as well as invade Poland to pay off our bankers in the West and that the CIA and the Pentagon sanctioned the assassination of the foreign minister. Of course, the warmongers in the military—industrial complex are manipulating the president, who really loves peace and knows nothing about the plot. And the Reserve call-up is just another part of the conspiracy by the people who want to destroy the peace-loving Russian Republic." He snorted loudly. "As if those weekend warriors in the Reserves are a threat to anyone."

A ringing telephone cut the visitor's tirade short. His unwilling listener, an athletically built, brown-haired man in his late thirties, picked it up. "Systems Engineering. Fitzmaurice."

"Major Fitzmaurice, this is Specialist Lebreque at the Reserve Center." The voice was young and nervous. "Sir, I have a bold carbine message."

Mike Fitzmaurice swore to himself. *Someone is off to kick some Russian ass, and it looks like I get to be part of it.*

"Okay, Lebreque. Go ahead."

"Sir, this is a bold carbine message, effective 140001 Zulu July. M-hour is 140100 Zulu July. Reporting time is M plus twelve at Site Bravo."

Mike scribbled on his desk pad and grunted. "Right, M hour is 140100 Zulu July. Reporting time at Site Bravo is M plus twelve. Anything else?"

"No, sir. Not now. Have a good day."

Mike hung up and gazed distractedly at his notes while rubbing his mustache. Zulu time is Greenwich Mean Time, five hours ahead of Eastern Standard (Daylight Savings) Time. M-hour was eight in the evening local time, which meant he had to be at Site B, or Fort Devens, Massachusetts, at eight in the morning tomorrow.

All at once, the meaning of the message hit him. Michael Patrick Fitzmaurice, Major, Infantry, United States Army Reserve, was going to war. The clock was ticking. The visitor rocked back and forth while Mike took the telephone call. He shifted his morning paper from hand to hand and fiddled with the rack of pipes on Mike's desk.

And when Mike hung up, he spoke impatiently, "Mike, what the hell was that all about? What's a Site Bravo? Are you weekend warriors playing some kind of spy game?" He waved the paper in Mike's face. "This stuff is important.

Those goddamn Russians need their asses kicked . . . if we only had the balls to do it."

Fitzmaurice looked at his visitor. Randy Parks was an electrical engineer who proudly waved the flag at any opportunity. He firmly believed in the supremacy of the American way of life, subscribed to *Soldier of Fortune* magazine, and kept a candle burning in front of his autographed picture of Oliver North. More than ready to call for the destruction of the bloodthirsty, godless commies, he never quite managed to get into the Armed Forces because it was "too much bullshit." Mike once remarked to his wife Elizabeth that people like Randy get people like Mike killed. That thought ran through his mind now.

"Randy," he said slowly and distinctly, "someone is going to get to kick some Russian ass, and a lot of them will be the weekend warriors you keep joking about. I only wish that you had balls enough to take part. Now get out of here because I am royally pissed off and have a lot to do in the next couple of hours." He stood up behind his desk.

At one hundred and ninety pounds, Mike was only five pounds heavier than when he played linebacker for the West Point football team. He still played rugby on the weekends, and now he faced Randy as though he were getting ready for the scrum. Randy left the cubicle hastily, muttering about an overdue report he had to work on.

The day passed in a whirl of phone calls and meetings. One advantage of working for a defense contractor was that many of the managers were retired military and understood, to a degree, what Fitzmaurice and others like him were going through.

At one point, Mike called Beacon Hill Orthopedic Associates in Boston and asked to speak to Doctor McCann.

When the doctor picked up the telephone, he began without preamble. "Hi, it's me. I just got a call from the unit, and I have to be at the center at eight tomorrow morning. I guess you're going to be a single parent for a while."

Doctor Elizabeth McCann had married Mike four years before, after he had left the active army, and therefore had missed the experience of being an army wife and facing the prospect of watching her husband leave for long periods to remote places.

Her immediate reaction was a soft whisper. "Oh, God. No."

"Hey, listen, we may not go anywhere. There has been nothing in the news about reservists going overseas or the support group's area. Everything's in Europe. So this may well be just a demonstration to impress the other side with how serious we are. The diplomats will probably all sort it out in the next couple of weeks."

They both knew he was whistling in the dark. For the past two months, there had been staff meetings two or three times a week at the reserve center. Moreover, Mike had spent the past weekend repacking his duffle bags with uniforms and clothing.

Two weeks ago, there had been a special assembly billed as a "family day." The families of unit members received a series of briefings on the benefits available to families of reservists and the mission of the support group. The briefing included scenic pictures of the unit's trips to their deployment sites in Guam and Okinawa.

Mike came to regret this slideshow. The slides of their training on Guam three years ago included some shots of Elizabeth taking scuba lessons wearing a most un-doctor like French bikini. Everyone else was amused. Elizabeth was not.

The assembly's central focus was long sessions with army lawyers who assisted each family in updating wills and powers of attorney and personnel clerks who made sure all insurance and survivor benefit forms were current and correct and all family members who were eligible for identification cards received them. Those half-dozen soldiers who were single parents updated their childcare plans in the presence of the company commander and group personnel section.

"No," she said. "This is serious. Some of our associates are in the Navy Reserve, and they are being called up as well. In fact, I may have to cover in surgery for two of them on Friday. When are you going home?"

"Well, I'm almost done here. Just one more meeting with the program office, and that shouldn't take long. Probably about three-thirty or four o'clock."

"Okay, I'll get out of here in time for the 5:10 train. I will see you at the train station about six. Then we can go get the kids at the sitter's."

As Elizabeth hung up, she realized the sheer banality of the conversation she had just had with her husband. He was going off to war, and they acted as though it was an extended business trip.

The secretary looked up at Elizabeth as she left her office. "Is there something wrong, Doctor?"

In a departure from her usual routine, Elizabeth rushed through her four o'clock patient and was now getting ready to leave for her train.

"I don't think so," Elizabeth answered. "At least not yet. My husband's Army Reserve unit has been alerted, and he has to report to Fort Devens tomorrow." She shook her red hair loose and let it fall over her shoulders. She had the classic Irish face: pale skin, large green eyes, reddish-gold hair, and a dusting of freckles from the summer sun. Her navy suit set off her slender figure. She was a long-distance runner so her five-foot-three frame did not reflect her love for Italian food.

The secretary nodded solemnly and looked at a picture of a young man in a sailor's uniform on her desk. "I'm sure glad that my fiancé is in the navy and his ship is in the Pacific. If anything happens in Germany, it won't affect him."

Elizabeth left her office feeling empty and angry with Mike for being mobilized. She had married Mike fully aware of his involvement in the Army Reserve and accepted the difficulties the Reserves caused in their lives somewhat grudgingly. Now she realized deep down inside that she always thought his service in the Reserves was a hobby. Other husbands were football fanatics or spent their weekends playing golf. Her husband spent his dressed up in funny suits. But it was just a hobby, an outside interest. It should not result in his going off to war.

Her walk to North Station and the train ride home reinforced the feeling that all was normal in the world, that today was another business-as-usual day. Everything proceeded as usual. The Boston traffic moved in its usual, maniacal, inconsiderate fashion, making the walk to North Station a game of chicken between motorist and pedestrian. The train to West Concord was overcrowded and late as usual.

Mike waited at the station as the train pulled in, the way he always did unless he was traveling. He had the two dogs along with him, standing at the foot of the platform. Bridget, the Soft Coated Wheaten Terrier, caught sight of Elizabeth first and exploded into wiggles as only a Wheatie can. Laddie, the four-month-old black Labrador Retriever, was more interested in the aromas floating from the small coffee shop in the old depot building and noticed Elizabeth only when Bridget went crazy. The combination of a forty-pound Wheatie and an eighty-pound Lab almost knocked her off her feet, but Mike pulled the dogs up short and reached for her briefcase.

"What's up, Doc?"

The demure peck on the cheek they normally exchanged became a tight, passionate embrace that drew stares from passing commuters. They unwrapped themselves from each other and the dogs' leashes and walked arm-in-arm over to where Mike had parked his Land Rover. Elizabeth almost convinced herself this was a normal day, just like any other, until she saw the two duffle bags and aviator's kit bag strapped in the back of the truck.

Mike caught her glance. "I thought I would load everything now and not have to hassle with it in the morning. I'm going to leave about five so I can get in early and check on how the assembly is going for everyone. How was your day?"

As they arrived at the car, Laddie jumped onto the backseat and flopped there bonelessly with his head resting on the window's edge. Bridget planted herself with hindquarters on the backseat and front paws and head between the front seats, resting on the console.

When Mike pulled out of the parking lot, Elizabeth reached for his right hand on the gearshift lever. "Mike, what's going to happen? Are you going overseas?"

"Your guess is as good as mine, hon. The problem seems to be in Europe. I don't know about us deploying to Guam. It doesn't appear there's any need. Nor does it make a whole lot of sense. I think somebody in the Pentagon hit a button on their computer that said 'Give us two hundred thousand reservists and guardsmen.'"

"Why call up the Reserves then?"

"One of the big mistakes in Vietnam, according to many historians, was not making a general call-up of the Reserves and Guard, as was done in Korea. It might not have changed the outcome of the war, but it probably would have shortened it because people would have been more aware of what was happening a lot sooner."

Later that evening, after they put the children to bed, Elizabeth walked up behind Mike and wrapped her arms around him.

She rested her head against his shoulders and asked softly, "Do you really have to go? Is there a way that you can get out of the mobilization? Do you have to go? Aren't you essential to the defense industry or something?"

He sighed and turned around to face her. "Not really, Beth. I'm not in a category that the company has defined as essential. Besides, I owe it to the troops in the unit. And I still have an obligation to the army—"

"But you've done enough, haven't you?" she interrupted him. "What about the Dominican Republic? You were there and you were wounded. Isn't it time for someone else to go off to war?"

"It's not a question of doing enough, Beth. It's a question of an obligation that I have because I have stayed in the Reserves and taken my paycheck for the past ten years. The Dominican Republic doesn't matter. At the time, that was part of my job. But now—"

"But now, you have other obligations. You have the twins and me. What about us? Don't we count?"

"More than you could ever know. More than you could ever know." He pulled her to him in a tight embrace and murmured into her hair. "If there were a way that I could get out of this, I would. But I don't see any way I can and still be the man you married. I have to do this, darling."

"I know." She sighed. "I was hoping I would hear you say something different, but I didn't expect you to." She pushed back from him a little and looked up into his face. "I'm not going to be the Spartan wife," she said in a fierce voice, "and tell you to return with your shield or on it. Just return to us."

Chapter 3

Morning Colors

Up in the morning at the break of day
Working so hard we never play
Running through the boonies where the sun
don't shine
All I do is double time

—Army PT Training

Bennington Gate
Fort Devens, Massachusetts

Headquarters and Headquarters Company, 805th Corps Support Group, were located in the area of Fort Devens known as "west post," about a twenty-five-minute drive from the Fitzmaurice-McCann household in Concord. When Mike turned off Route 2 at the Bennington Gate exit a Massachusetts state trooper, whose cruiser blocked the exit ramp, stopped him.

"Good morning, sir," the trooper said as he walked up to Mike's Land Rover. "May I see some identification and ask what your business is here?"

Mike fumbled out his military ID card without spilling coffee on his battle dress uniform. "I'm reporting in to my unit. We're part of the call-up. What are you guys doing out here?"

"There's been attempts to block military bases and armories to prevent the reservists and guardsmen from reporting in." He handed the ID card back to Mike and waved him through.

"Go ahead, Major. Once I get off shift, I'll probably be right behind you. I'm in the Guard myself, and I'm just waiting for the call."

Mike shook his head as he put the truck in gear. "Well, good luck. Maybe it's all just a drill."

He drove on, returning the trooper's salute absently, and headed for the reserve center. The group commander called late the night before, calling a special staff meeting at six in the morning. As the group security, plans, and operations officer, Mike had to be in by five.

"Why is it," he had asked Elizabeth, "that wars can never start at a decent hour, like ten or eleven in the morning?"

As Mike parked in front of the center and began unloading his bags, the group adjutant, Sally Grant, pulled up next to him. A tall, slender woman, she wore her shoulder-length black hair pulled back in a French braid when she was in uniform. Her pale skin appeared even ghostlier in the early morning half-light.

When she greeted Mike this morning, she sounded as dragged out and depressed as he was. "I guess I wasn't the only one to get a call from the good colonel last night. What did you think of yours? Nothing that starts at five in the morning can be good. Did the old man say anything to you other than 'Be here or else'?"

"No, he just said he wanted all principal staff here by 0500 for a meeting. I hope to God it's not about the goddamn mobe books again." Part of Mike's responsibilities included planning for the unit's mobilization. "I am so bloody tired of explaining load cards."

Conversation cut off as they reached the main door of the headquarters building, already redolent with the smell of freshly brewed coffee. A hand-lettered sign directed all staff officers to the conference room, which had large "Secret Meeting in Progress" signs on both doors. An armed sentry stood outside the conference room doors, checking ID cards as the staff entered. As Mike signed in, the assistant plans officer, Captain Ed Chambers, met him with a handful of manila folders. Chambers was a reservist assigned on a full-time basis.

Ed looked like a recruiting poster for the Ranger Regiment. He carried 205 pounds on his six-foot six-inch frame, but with his weightlifting, it was all muscle and not an ounce of fat. He had attended Texas A&M on a football scholarship but passed up the pro football draft to accept a Regular Army commission as a distinguished military graduate. Life in the Rangers had been fun, and he enjoyed the physical and mental challenges. However, the constant temporary duty travel took him away from his wife Barbara and their two children too frequently, so he left the active army and entered the Reserves.

"Morning, boss," Ed greeted Mike.

"Do you know what's going on? The colonel had me in here at four in the morning, calling around to find map sheets of Germany. He just put on that wise smile of his and said that all would become clear."

"Oh, yeah. The 2750th Trans called from Brookline. Someone broke into their motor pool and slashed a bunch of tires and brake lines. Captain White says six trucks are down right now, but she will have them back up by about 0900. Nothing else is happening now. Want some coffee?"

"Yeah, decaf with cream and sugar if it's handy. How are the people in the section coming along? Any problem with any of them making it in here this morning? I'm heading to the old man's office to find out what's up. I'll let you know what I can as soon as I can."

"No problems. They're all coming in about 0730. I figured I would get them started on packing us up for the upload." Ed handed Fitzmaurice a mug of coffee.

"Dumont called to say she may be a little late. She has to pick up Kevin Long in Hooksett, the opposite direction from here, and bring him in with her. Perhaps we should move him over from the S-1 shop so the two lovebirds can nest together if we deploy."

"Her father and his mother would combine to crucify us, Ed, if we let those two get together more easily," Mike answered as he took his coffee cup. "We'll keep Dumont with us and let Major Grant and Sergeant Lovall take care of Lothario. In any case, Dumont is the best of the two of them."

Starting on his coffee, Mike walked down the hallway to the colonel's office. A muffled grunt answered his knock, and he entered to find the group commander, Colonel John Hancock Warren, bent over his desk. The chief of Readiness Group-Devens, an active-duty full colonel, and Lieutenant Colonel Peter Rogers, the support group's executive officer, stood together on one side of the commander's desk. An unfamiliar major in a rumpled travel uniform stood opposite them, discussing a stack of documents strewn about the desk.

"Mike," the colonel said as he looked up when Fitzmaurice entered, "this is Major Thomas from Department of the Army. He is a member of the Deputy Chief of Staff for Operations staff. He is here as a direct representative of DCSOPS." Mike could almost see the sarcasm dripping off the colonel's words as he spoke. The visitor apparently had played his connections to higher headquarters a little too heavily, without knowing Warren was a poker-playing buddy of the current Army Chief of Staff. "He has a slight change in plans for us. Remember that change to the CAPSTONE mission we talked about last month?"

Oh, shit, Mike thought. *The support group was CAPSTONE'ed to US Army Pacific with the mission of providing logistics support to forces in Japan and Korea.*

"Yes, sir. The mission to XXVI Corps. I thought that was still up in the air."

The commander handed him a folder with a red cover sheet prominently stamped "SECRET/NO FORN" on the top and bottom.

"Not any longer, Mike," the colonel said. "Read this."

The folder contained a message assigning the 805th Support Group to the Corps Support Command, XXVI (US) Corps, effective midnight, 15 July. The commander of the 805th Support Group was appointed acting commander, XXVI COSCOM, until further notice. A second message from the Supreme Commander (SACEUR), directed that XXVI Corps begin deploying its combat support and combat service support elements to Europe, via sea and air, not later than A+10, or ten days after mobilization. A ten-day shift in the movement window would mean a lot of rewriting of everybody's plans for movement and pre-deployment training.

The chief of Readiness Group-Devens was responsible for overseeing the training and operations of all Reserve Component units in New England. He handed Mike a standard-issue three-ring binder with a large "SECRET/NO FORN" stenciled on the cover.

"This may ease your mind, Fitzmaurice," he said. "One or two shortcuts are contained in here."

"What you have in your hands, Major, is the battle book for Headquarters and Headquarters Company, 247th Corps Support Group. They were the original headquarters of one of the support groups tasked to XXVI COSCOM. They had an ARTEP in June while at annual training and did not perform satisfactorily." Major Thomas turned to face Mike and gestured to the binder in Mike's hands.

"Before you get too upset," Major Thomas read Mike's mind. "The 247th might not have been able to perform, but they could plan. These battle books contain all their mobilization and deployment plans and first seven days of operations after the unit arrives in-country."

Colonel Warren interrupted.

"One other way they are going to help us out is to fill our vacancies with people from the 247th. Getting the 247th into halfway decent shape for the Far East mission may take a while. On the other hand, we will need the extra help because we are deploying for Germany seven days from today."

"Seven days! They're out of their tiny fucking minds!" Mike said, exploding. "We've based all our plans on a fifteen—to twenty-day stage-out time. We have to absorb new people, draw new equipment, process everyone for overseas movement, load out vehicles, which we don't have—"

"Consider it a challenge, Mike," the colonel said in a tone that brooked no argument. "One week from today, we will be leaving Boston, bound for Ramstein, Germany."

"Ah, sir." Major Thomas broke in, glad someone else was drawing the colonel's fire. "Most of XXVI Corps' equipment is prepositioned in Europe. The 247th had all their organizational equipment and vehicles in the war reserve stocks around Kaiserslautern."

Lieutenant Colonel Rogers interrupted in his high-pitched voice. "Where is this place Kaiserslautern? Why should it help us?"

Thomas turned to face the executive officer. "Sir, as part of the drawdown in Europe, all the equipment for XXVI Corps is stored in a depot outside Kaiserslautern, Germany. The depot is about an hour's drive east of Ramstein Air Base, where you will be flying into." He turned back to Colonel Warren. "All the 805th has to bring is their individual equipment and any records, manuals, and so on that is necessary to function in the field."

"Thank you, Major. My plans officer, Major Fitzmaurice, sometimes lacks faith in higher-level staffs. He has a somewhat jaundiced view of their planning ability and how well they relate to the real world. Now that I've given you a preview, Mike, let's go tell the rest of the staff how they will be spending the next few days." Colonel Warren closed his copy of the battle book and led the group out of his office to the conference room where the rest of the staff waited.

The colonel began his presentation to the rest of the staff in much the same way he told Mike of the change in mission. And he received much the same reaction. Major Thomas could brief very well once he got started. He had studied the plans from the 247th thoroughly and walked the staff through them in a clear and concise forty-five-minute discourse.

When Thomas finished his presentation, Colonel Warren gave further guidance for the staff to do their planning. "The advance party will be leaving for Germany the day after tomorrow. Lieutenant Colonel Rogers will be in charge and act for me upon arrival in Europe. Finally, we may be going into a shooting war shortly after we arrive. Our soldiers are trained as well as they can be and will do their best to carry out their missions. What they need from us, and what it is our responsibility to provide them, is the best leadership we can give them.

"Go out and brief your sections as completely as you can before the muster formation. One problem that we will face very soon is the rumor mill. The more factual information we can supply the soldiers, the better this whole operation will run. Any questions? If not, let's get started."

As the meeting started to break up, the headquarters company commander, Captain Bill Sherwood, announced, "There will be a muster in front of the building in ten minutes. The supply room is open now, so you all can draw your field gear right after formation."

Captain Sherwood completed the muster by saying

"Those people scheduled to be billeted on post according to the mobilization plan will get one night home in the next five days. Those people who live within thirty miles of the post and will be staying at home should understand that the duty day begins daily at 0600 and continues until the work is finished. The duty uniform starting at noon today will be full field, less weapons.

"Now, the group commander has some words for us, so listen up."

Colonel Warren called the troops to fall out around the front steps of the headquarters. As they moved into place and slowly stopped shuffling, he began: "Soldiers, we are being mobilized and deployed to Europe, perhaps to a shooting war. Some of you are no doubt thinking, 'This is not what I signed up for when I joined the Reserves.' You are wrong. We all swore the same oath when we joined the Army. The first part of that oath was to defend and uphold the Constitution of the United States against all enemies, foreign and domestic. The second part was to obey the orders of the president and those appointed by him.

"When we joined, we signed a check payable to the United States of America, up to and including our lives. Today, the United States cashed our checks as well as the checks of two hundred thousand of our fellow soldiers. Remember that we are a team and we depend on each other. We are mobilizing and deploying as a team, one that has trained, worked, and lived together for the past three years. Our conduct and performance over those three years led to our selection for this mission. Our skills and professionalism will ensure our success in accomplishing our new mission.

"Over the next ten days, we will train hard. As First Sergeant Bellotti likes to remind us, a pint of American blood is worth a gallon of American sweat. Keep that in mind as we push ourselves in our training both here at Devens and at our operational site in Germany. I do not know what may happen when we arrive in Germany. I am certain we shall all perform to the best of our abilities. I will brief you all as our plans become more detailed. If you have questions, do not hesitate to bring them to your leaders. Finally, I am proud to lead you all into whatever the future holds."

Chapter 4

And We're Saying
Good-Bye to Them All

And we're saying good-bye to them all
As back up the gangways we crawl
There'll be no ice cream or cookies for
flat-footed rookies
So cheer up my lads, bless 'em all
　　　　—World War Two Troopship Song

After Mike left for Fort Devens, Elizabeth was unable to get back to sleep. She finally got up and began puttering around the kitchen, fending off the cats that returned for breakfast, even though Mike had fed them. The two dogs were out in the backyard, roughhousing as usual. She would have liked to take them on her morning run, as she did every day, in a futile attempt to burn off some of their energy. Her morning run with the dogs was a daily ritual, and routine was what she needed right now to help her cope with what was happening to her and Mike. But it hit her like a baseball bat that routine would not be the same for a long while without Mike around to play his many parts—like watching over the sleeping twins while she had her morning run with the dogs—like fixing the twins' lunches while Elizabeth woke and dressed them for "school," the daycare center.

Mike and Elizabeth had talked about the childcare problem if he were mobilized, but they never reached a firm decision. Now they would have to address the problem. As she dressed the children and fed them breakfast, she thought of her niece Margaret, a sophomore at Boston College. Aunt Maggie always hit it off with the children and enjoyed being around them. Though she shared an apartment with five other women in Chestnut Hill, she spent a lot of her time in Concord with Elizabeth and Mike. Perhaps Aunt Maggie would like to become a part-time nanny. After she dropped off the children at the daycare center and got to her office on Beacon Hill, she would call Maggie and ask.

As she drove along Route 2 into Boston, Elizabeth noticed many military vehicles traveling toward Fort Devens, both singly and in convoys. Approaching the city, as Storrow Drive passed the National Guard Armory facing Commonwealth Avenue, a police barricade restricted traffic to one lane. The barricade blocked off a large hole cut in the fence surrounding the armory's motor pool. A quick glance showed her some trucks splashed with red paint and others with broken windshields or slashed covers. On the far side of the fence, a young guardsman in full field gear stood holding her M-16 at port arms, looking very lost and forlorn.

Elizabeth's first thought was of how young and scared the soldier looked. Her second thought recalled Mike's sardonic comment of "the greatest killer on the battlefield," referring to his operations clerk, a woman as young as the sentry.

BLDG T-5701
Fort Devens, Massachusetts

The second day of mobilization began for the company with an 0600 reveille formation. Everyone was on time and present. There were none of the late arrivals that normally occurred every drill weekend.

Mike had not left the center until midnight. He was back in at five in the morning, making telephone calls to the new units he and the colonel would be visiting over the next three days. When Major Thomas returned to the Pentagon yesterday morning, he had promised whatever help he could provide in getting the support group ready to go overseas.

After the formation, Mike headed back to his office. His first order of business was a meeting with Master Sergeant Lehigh. Sally caught Mike yesterday and told him about Lehigh's request for deferral. She kicked the paperwork back to Lehigh for Mike's signature and action. Mike felt irritation rather than surprise at Lehigh's request, frustration that he had to take time to deal with Lehigh that he could better spend on other matters.

The sergeant was sitting at his desk when Mike entered the operations room. Mike walked directly to his office, waving Lehigh after him. He hung his web gear and protective mask on the back of his chair, put his helmet on a wall hook, and then sat down.

"I understand you have some paperwork for me. Let's see it." He held out his hand for the manila folder Lehigh clutched in his left hand.

"Yes, sir. It is all here. I'm expecting my twenty-year letter this month . . . ," Lehigh started to explain as he passed the folder to Mike.

"Right. Major Grant told me that yesterday." Mike flipped through the paperwork.

Michael Fitzmaurice Senior had retired as a first sergeant after thirty-one years and three tours in Vietnam in the army. He had taught his son that soldiering was a noble profession and that the higher an individual moved up the ladder of rank, the greater the obligation to serve the nation and the soldiers under him became. Mike's four years at West Point had only deepened that belief. Even the disillusionment with what he called "ticket punching" and careerism that led him to leave active duty nine years before had not dampened this belief.

He set the folder down on his desk and reached for his pen. "You want to quit?" he said to Lehigh in a flat voice. "Fuck you. Quit. Approved." He scribbled his signature in the appropriate place. "Report to Captain Sherwood for whatever he may need you for. On your way out, tell Sergeant O'Brian, Captain Wilson, and Captain Chambers that I need to see them now. That's all." He handed the folder back to Lehigh.

Sergeant Lehigh stood in front of Mike's desk and looked at him uncertainly. "What about finishing the section upload? I've got to make sure that the people going on the advanced party have—"

"You don't have anything to do in this section. The operations sergeant will handle the upload and preparing the advance party."

"But I am the operations sergeant."

"Not any longer. You are now a detail soldier for the company commander. Dismissed."

Mike looked back down at his notebook and dismissed Lehigh from his thoughts. The sergeant stood still in shocked silence for another few seconds and then turned and slowly walked out of the office.

When Ed, Bob Wilson, and Sergeant First Class O'Brian entered his office, Mike began going over the movement plan for the support group. Chambers was leaving at 2300 the next day as part of the advance party. They would begin drawing the company's equipment from the prepositioned stocks and conduct a fast reconnaissance of the town of Altendorf. This was Mike's last chance to talk to Chambers and pass onto him items of particular interest to himself, the commander, and the other staff officers. He then told Sergeant First Class O'Brian that he was now the operations sergeant, replacing Lehigh. Wilson would be the acting operations officer while Mike was traveling with Colonel Warren, so Mike gave him their itinerary.

As he was going over the movement schedule with Chambers, Wilson, and O'Brian, Specialist Ann-Marie Dumont, the operations clerk, stuck her head into his office. "Major, Captain Sherwood just sent over a runner. You and the colonel have to go over to Central Issue Facility at 0800 to draw your new field gear before you leave this afternoon. I've got a Blazer outside to take you over there. Captain Chambers and I are coming along too because we're both on the advance party. And Major Grant said to remind you about Sergeant Lehigh's Senior Enlisted Evaluation Report. She's sending over a draft for you to take on your trip."

"Okay, thanks, Specialist Dumont. We'll be out in a couple of minutes."

The Central Issue Facility, a former mess hall, was set up with aisles of bins containing items of clothing and equipment. The building smelled overpoweringly of mothballs and echoed with a popular morning radio show as the two disc jockeys tried to finagle tickets to a Red Sox game.

The four soldiers lined up by rank and received two new duffle bags each to begin drawing their new equipment. Mike began filling his with a Kevlar armored vest—"Personnel Armor System for Ground Troops," by its official name, or "flak jacket," as the troops called it; a new Kevlar helmet and camouflage cover to replace his old steel helmet; a set of Gore-Tex foul weather jacket and pants; and other items of equipment that he had only read about for the past few years. The facility's civilian manager said these items were from mobilization stocks. The rest of the company would receive their equipment later in the week as part of their overseas processing. The last item he was handed was a green cardboard box labeled "Ballistic and Laser Protective lenses, tinted."

Ed saw him looking at the box. "Open it, boss. It'll blow your mind. This army thinks of everything."

Mike opened the box and found a set of gray lenses wrapped around polycarbonate sunglasses with a crushproof, camouflaged carrying case. He held up the glasses and said wonderingly, "What the hell?"

The civilian manager said a trifle defensively, "These are to protect you from lasers or other directed-energy weapons. They will also stop fragments up to .22 caliber. We just got them in last week and can only issue them for mobilization."

Only in the American army, Mike thought. *Only in the American army would we go to war wearing surfer sunglasses.*

Mike returned to his office and started assembling his new equipment. As he was putting the Kevlar helmet together, Sally Grant appeared at the door to his office and knocked hesitantly. "Mike, are you busy? I have to talk to you about your childcare plan," she said from the doorway.

Mike immediately dropped the camouflage cover he was trying to put on the helmet and looked at her. An old friend of Elizabeth's who had introduced her to Mike, Sally normally was not hesitant about interrupting him.

"No, come on in, Sally," he answered. "I'm just fiddling with this stuff, but it can wait. What is this about a childcare plan? I'm not a single parent."

The woman walked in and sat down in the chair opposite Mike's desk, holding a stack of manila folders in front of her. "We were going through the packets, and I started to wonder what you and Beth were planning to do with childcare. I guess she's going to be pretty busy with all the medical professionals around here mobilizing. Are you going to do anything different?"

"Funny you should ask. We talked about this last night. Beth is going to be on call at St. Brendan's a lot more than normal. She said that her sister Maggie out at BC will be moving in with us as a part-time nanny. The kids go to school during the day, so the job is mainly getting them ready for school and picking them up at the end of the day. Maggie can still go to classes."

Sally was silent for a few minutes and then asked in an elaborately casual voice, "How is Beth taking your call-up? Is she giving you any grief about having stayed in the Reserves? Or how you're abandoning the family when they really need you?"

Mike laughed. "She's bullshit at the Russians for forcing a call-up, but she pretty much accepts that I have to go. She'd like it better if they mobilized me to count paper clips at Fort Swampy, but she knows and accepts how I feel about my obligation. We're both worried about the kids, but this deal with Maggie will be one load off our backs. Tom Bradley said he'll be in touch to see if Beth needs anything, so that's a help."

"Tell Maggie that Bradley will be around the house, and I guarantee she'll agree to move to Concord," Sally snorted. "Beth isn't giving you a hard time about this?"

"She knew I was in the Reserves when she married me. We talked about mobilization, and we both recognized that it could happen. She's not exactly overjoyed with the idea that I'm off to Europe and stand an excellent chance of being shot at. But she knows that if I didn't go, I wouldn't be the man she married." Mike paused and gazed at Sally closely.

She sat slumped in the chair, staring unseeingly at the folders in her hands. He got up from behind his desk and closed the door to his office.

"Sally, are you trying to tell me something? Is there something wrong? Is Mark really upset about this?"

"No." She suddenly sprang erect from the chair. "There's nothing wrong. Mark is being a good husband and is behind me, like always." She brushed the front of her jacket with the folders, still looking at the floor. "Well, I've got to get back to work. I was just wondering about how you people were going to handle taking care of your kids. I'll see you when you get back from your trip with the old man. Oh, by the way . . ." She handed Mike a folder. "This is a draft SEER for Lehigh. If you can fill it out and fax it to me, it will help expedite his transfer to the garrison here at Devens. He and all the other non-deployables are attached to the garrison until someone decides what to do with them." She pushed past Mike, pulled open the office door, and left without looking at him.

Flughafen Frankfurt
Frankfurt am Main, FRG

Ed Chambers stepped off the chartered Boeing 747 and gazed at the international arrival area of Frankfurt International Airport. Because the aircraft was a charter flight and would evacuate a load of American nationals to the United States, it arrived at the civilian international terminal, across the runway from Rhein Main Air Force Base. Ground transportation was to meet the advance party in front of the terminal building and take them to the equipment storage site. Ed had never expected to see Germany, particularly under the current conditions. His four years of active duty had been in one of the battalions of the Ranger regiment. In four years, he had made three trips to Egypt and more trips than he cared to think about to Honduras and Panama.

Germany looked different, he thought as he eyed a group of Lufthansa flight attendants walking through the terminal. *Very different.*

"Well, Chambers." A high-pitched voice grated in his ear as a fog of Old Spice aftershave enveloped him. "Let's get moving. You go track down those sergeants and enlisted personnel. Someone told me they sell beer here, and you know we cannot trust the enlisted people around bars. I'll get the rest of the officers and look for our escort."

Lieutenant Colonel Rogers was the senior officer in the advance party. Ed was the next senior so Rogers immediately dumped most of the work on him. There were two other officers in the party, both first lieutenants, Vicki Baxter, the property book officer from the S-4 section, and Colin Jones, the assistant maintenance officer from logistics operations. Rogers was concerned about Vicki, not Colin, because Vicki was one of those rare individuals who made the battle dress uniform look flattering on her. Turning to look for the rest of the party, Ed shook his ahead again in despair at the thought of dealing with the exec up close and personal on a continuing basis for the next week.

He did not have far to look. Vicki met the NCO In Charge, and had the other sixteen soldiers formed in two ranks. Ed was not quite sure how to deal with Vicki. She was, like Mike Fitzmaurice, a West Point graduate and a complete professional soldier when in uniform. Her intensity and aggressiveness made him uncomfortable around her, something he only reluctantly admitted to himself. When he first met her, he thought she was boasting about her abilities. He became even more wary when Vicki proceeded to back up her words with actions. When the company took the annual physical training test, Vicki maxed it. She actually outran Ed in the two-mile run by four seconds. On the firing range for annual qualification, Vicki outshot everyone in the company (including Ed) with the M-16 and .45-caliber pistol, except Mike Fitzmaurice and Colonel Warren. The soldiers immediately nicknamed her "Jane Wayne." Ed viewed this as an act of sacrilege, bordering on the un-American. Even in her civilian life, Vicki pushed herself to the limit. She worked in an investment firm in Boston, and was rapidly climbing the corporate ladder. Fitzmaurice mentioned before the mobilization orders arrived that he recently heard a rumor that her firm was offering Vicki a partnership within the next six months.

"Good morning, Captain. Welcome to Germany. Lieutenant Jones went to find our escort and the checked bags. Have you seen the executive officer?"

"He went to look for you and Jonesy." Ed waved casually in the direction the exec had gone. He turned to Sergeant

34

Major Carter. "Sergeant Major, the executive officer tells me that the Germans have the balls to sell beer in their own airport terminal. He is concerned that the enlisted personnel may lose their heads and drink themselves into a stupor."

Sergeant Major Carter looked ready to spit. "These people are not about to run off to the local *gasthaus*, sir. They're scared shitless about going to war. In any case, even if one of them did get pie-eyed, knee-walking, commode-hugging drunk, he or she would still be twice the soldier the exec is."

"Actually," Ed said, "they'd be about four of five times the soldier, but he is still the colonel. Let's just keep an eye on everyone, regardless of rank, and make sure we keep our soldiers as well as our powder dry."

"Yes, sir," the sergeant major replied. "I saw a USO lounge across the terminal. How about if I take the people over there and get them some coffee or Cokes while we figure out what happens next?"

Ed nodded assent, and the sergeant major moved the soldiers off to the nearby lounge. Most of the young soldiers had never been to Europe before. Therefore, this was an adventure for them, an unusual and perhaps deadly one, but a journey nevertheless.

Jones, a tall, rangy black man, walked up to Ed and Vicki, accompanied by another first lieutenant, a short, paunchy, dark-complexioned man in baggy, wrinkled BDUs without nametag or shoulder patch, The newcomer was also desperately in need of a haircut, a fact that Lieutenant Colonel Rogers lost no time in pointing out as he returned to the group simultaneously.

"Jones, Baxter. Where have you two been? I've been looking for you both. Why didn't you wait here? Who are you? You're a disgrace! Why don't you have a haircut? When's the last time you shined those boots? That uniform is disgusting. Who are you?"

The newcomer looked calmly at the exec and waited for him to finish his tirade.

"The name's Celluci, Francis X. Celluci. Up until eight o'clock last night I was the Munich branch manager of New York Transatlantic Bank. Because I am also in the Individual Ready Reserves, I am now the commander of the 222nd Transportation Detachment. If you are the advance party of HHC, 805th Support Group, I am also your ride to the equipment storage site at Kaiserslautern. Barbershops in Germany don't open before nine in the morning. Local time, if you haven't noticed, is eight-thirty. I was issued the uniform and boots about two hours ago. The quartermaster doesn't provide a shoeshine service. Does this mean I can go home now?"

Rogers looked at Celluci in total shock. The response had taken him completely aback, and he had no idea how to answer it. He gasped for a few seconds like a landed fish and then turned on Ed to vent his discomfort.

Celluci led the group to an olive green army bus parked outside the front entrance of the terminal. Sergeant Major Carter met the bus driver by the baggage claim area and started his detail loading the bus as the remainder of the party arrived. After the people were counted twice, first by Ed and then by Rogers, the bus pulled out of the airport. The driver swung onto the autobahn, heading south to Kaiserslautern. The drive to the storage site was about an hour over autobahns, through open agricultural areas.

When the bus arrived, two German soldiers halted it about one hundred meters short of the gate. Two dump trucks parked across the road blocked the gate.

As the bus rolled to a stop, Celluci grunted. "I think the Germans will want to talk to the man in charge. At least, that is what normally happens with roadblocks run by the police.

I doubt the army will be much different, and the country is under semi-martial law.

Rogers, with a shooing motion of his hand, told Ed, "Handle it. Handle it."

As Ed got off the bus, one of the soldiers walked up to him and casually saluted. He said in passable English, "Good morning, Herr Hauptman. What are you doing here, please? You have papers? May I see them, please?"

The collar-length hair, beard, and overall scruffy appearance of the guard's uniform were, in Ed's eyes, far outweighed by the well-oiled and loaded Hessler and Koch submachine gun and the competent, businesslike way the guard held it. Ed noticed that the other guard stood off to the left front of the bus. He held his weapon casually at waist level so it covered Ed and the front of the bus without getting his partner in its field of fire. He silently acknowledged that these people probably knew their business as well as anyone, despite their personal appearance. In any case, he did not want to find out the hard way. He slowly and carefully drew out his ID card and a copy of his orders.

"I'm Captain Ed Chambers," he told the guard as he held out the two documents. "I've got the advance party of my unit here. We are supposed to draw our equipment from this site."

The guard took the orders and compared the standard name line on them to the name, rank, and social security number on Ed's ID card. He handed the card back to Ed. "I must call my officer, Herr Hauptmann. There have been problems. Please wait."

The guard walked back to a small hut set off to one side of the entrance road.

A few minutes later, a German lieutenant came up to Ed. "Welcome to Germany, Captain. The American MPs have cleared you and your party. Once my men and the MPs have completed inspecting your personnel and vehicle, you may proceed into the site. Please have your troops dismount."

"You fellows seem to be very serious about security," Ed said to the German officer as the rest of the Americans dismounted and straggled into two lines.

"There have been several attacks on NATO sites by people wearing NATO uniforms, carrying NATO equipment, and driving vehicles with authentic NATO markings. We Territorials are called up to augment German and American military police in securing critical sites."

As the guards completed the inspection of bus, passengers, and cargo and moved the dump trucks, the gate opened and an American Chevy Blazer pulled in front of the bus.

"I hope you enjoy your visit to Germany, Captain," the lieutenant said dryly. "And now your American guide is here."

A warrant officer introduced himself as the property book officer who would be working with the 805th as they drew their equipment.

"The officers and NCOs have a briefing in the camp theater in one hour," he announced from the front of the bus. "Breakfast is available in the mess hall, and showers in the billets. Enlisted personnel will be trained for their European driver's licenses and receive an Opposing Force orientation."

The storage site had a small officer's club, and the officers from the four advance parties drawing their equipment met there after supper. One drink had led to another, and Ed ended the evening by teaching everyone the "Body Bag Song."

"Got shot in the head with an M-16. Doo dah doo dah. Got shot in the head with an M-16 and blew his shit away. You take his watch. I'll take his ring. He'll go home in a body bag when they blow his shit away."

Ed finished a chorus of "Napalm Sticks to Kids" and found himself facing Vicki.

"That's really gross," she told him. "Are you trying to be particularly disgusting tonight?"

"Hey, lighten up, Vicki." Ed was on his fifth beer, and his speech slurred slightly. The club's German beer came in one-liter bottles, not the twelve-ounce glasses he was used to. "We're just having fun." He waved a hand at the crowded, smoky room.

"I don't find your songs funny."

"Like I said, loosen up." The beer had relaxed his self-control just enough to let his mouth run away. "You know what your problem is, Jane Wayne. You're not getting any regularly. If you were, you'd be in a better mood. What you need is a real man, like an Airborne Ranger. Not some wimpy business puke in pinstripe." Ed thumped his chest and tried to drape an arm around her shoulder.

Vicki's face paled. Her gray eyes went so cold that Ed felt a chill. He knew he had gone too far.

She put her drink down on the table between them. "The name is Lieutenant Baxter to you." She snapped in a harsh, low voice. "I've known Airborne Rangers. And I prefer my men mature and sober, Captain." She turned abruptly and stalked out of the bar.

At breakfast the following morning, Ed appeared in full field gear, the prescribed uniform of the day. Conversation in the small dining facility died away as people caught sight of him. Hanging from the left side of his pistol belt, below his arm, was a bowie knife about fourteen inches long and four inches wide. The handle was wrapped in olive drab parachute cord, and camouflaged nylon webbing covered the sheath. He studiously ignored the comments concerning his knife. He carried his tray to a table occupied by Vicki, Ann-Marie, Sergeant First Class Lovell, and a pudgy, baby-faced soldier with wiry black hair in a prominent cowlick and a cloud of freckles, Private First Class Kevin Long.

"Captain Chambers," Sergeant First Class Lovell said as Ed sat down. "Where did you find that pig sticker? What are you going to do with it? Fence with the Russians?"

"I had it custom made when I was in the Rangers, Herb," Ed replied. "We needed long knives in our mission. I used this whenever we deployed. The blade can cut through aircraft aluminum, and the handle can double as a hammer. I learned a long time ago that a good knife comes in handy in the field. Anyone who's had a lot of field experience can tell you that."

"That's right, sir," Ann-Marie said. "Major Fitzmaurice carries a Ka-Bar on his Load Bearing Equipment. When I asked him about it before we left, he said a good knife does come in handy." She paused. "He recommended I get a Swiss army knife. He said the Ka-Bar was good for killing people but not much else."

"Well, Major Fitzmaurice wasn't in the Rangers, just the Eighty-Second and some Mech outfit here in Germany. So he doesn't really know how useful this Bowie of mine can be."

Vicki put down her coffee cup and looked at Ed with a deadpan expression. Then she turned to Ann-Marie. "Besides, Ann-Marie, there's an ironclad rule about Rangers and their knives. I learned about it from my Ranger ex-husband."

"What's that, ma'am?" Ann-Marie asked.

Vicki stood up and picked up her tray. "The bigger a Ranger's knife," she answered, "the smaller his penis. Good morning, Captain."

Highway B-429
Vicinity Altendorf, FRG

Altendorf had a population of about six thousand people. It contained an inn dating back to the sixteenth century; two churches, Catholic and Protestant; a railroad station with a switching yard; and two bridges over the Nidda River, one highway and one rail, representing the only crossings over the river for thirty kilometers up or downstream. The town clustered around the intersection of Bundestrassen 429 and 380. Highway B-380 passed through the length of town from the northeast, the general direction of Lauterbach, and served as the main street. Highway B-480 entered town from the southeast and exited to the northwest in the general direction of Giessen. Altendorf lay in the valley of the Nidda River. The long axis of this valley ran roughly northeast-southwest, paralleling the E-4 autobahn to the north. High-speed movement along the valley was restricted to roads, particularly Bundestrasse 380.

Ed found himself in a Blazer with Lieutenant Colonel Rogers, Sergeant First Class Lovell, and Specialist Dumont, traveling from the storage site outside Kaiserslautern to Altendorf. They planned to reconnoiter both the convoy route and the locations of the buildings identified for the headquarters' use by the 246th's battle book. This was his second day in Germany, and Ed was still suffering the effects of jet lag and too much German beer the night before.

"Driver, watch your speed," Rogers rasped from the backseat. "I don't care what the signs say. I don't want to see you going a hundred miles an hour on these back roads."

The colonel had taken the warnings and stories of attacks on NATO personnel and facilities seriously. He sat huddled in the back seat of the Chevrolet truck, next to the radio, wearing Kevlar helmet and flak jacket, with a second flak jacket draped around the right side of his body.

"The speed limits are in kilometers, sir," Ed said as he snapped awake. "So a hundred kilometers per hour is sixty miles per hour."

"I know that," Rogers said, snapping peevishly. "I'm just warning the driver that I don't want her speeding. I'm watching to make sure that she doesn't."

"Sir, the company policy is forty-five miles per hour max on back roads," Ann-Marie said. "I'm doing thirty right now because Captain Chambers said that will be the convoy speed and he wants to time the trip for when we bring out the convoy."

Ed looked across at Ann-Marie. She was the operations section clerk, a nineteen-year-old woman who had joined the Army Reserves to save money for college. She was a shy, retiring person, so her retort to Rogers was out of character. Ed was an extremely outgoing, aggressive, self-confident young man who tended to judge other people by their appearances. Ann-Marie's appearance did not inspire faith and trust. She was almost a foot shorter than Ed's six-foot-six and tended toward overweight.

For his part, Ed was beginning to enjoy his situation. The Active Guard Reserve program was beginning to get very competitive, and any edge a person could find would help in the future. He had started working on a company defense plan, a project his background in the Rangers especially suited him for. Once he completed the plan, he would press Fitzmaurice and Colonel Warren to find him an assignment as a company commander in an infantry battalion. He wanted to smell gunpowder and see the elephant.

——°°°••°°°——

BLDG T-5701
Fort Devens, Massachusetts

When Mike returned to Fort Devens, he found Master Sergeant Lehigh waiting outside his office. Lehigh wore BDUs without the field gear all the other personnel were wearing in preparation for deployment. He held a manila folder in his hands.

"Major," the sergeant said. "If you've got a couple of minutes, I want to talk to you."

Mike groaned to himself. The last thing he wanted to do was to talk to Lehigh, but he had no real choice. "Okay, Sergeant, just let me get a cup of coffee and put these documents away. Then you can come in."

Lehigh closed the door to Mike's office. He stood in front of the desk and took a deep breath. "Sir, I've been thinking about what you said in my SEER. And I don't like it."

Mike filled out a draft SEER, on Lehigh and faxed it to Sally's S-1 section from Fort Bragg. Lehigh was being transferred from the company as a non-deployable and required a "change of rater" report. Mike could not remember what he had put in the report.

"What did I say that you don't like, Sergeant?"

"Your comments about professionalism and dedication only being average and specifically that my request for deferment was unprofessional."

"Oh. Those comments. I happen to believe that your conduct now is unprofessional for a senior NCO, especially one in a leadership position. Besides, if you're going to retire, what difference does it make to you what I put in the SEER?"

"I don't think you understand the situation. I've been in the Reserves for almost twenty years. It's not fair I get called up this close to retirement when there's other guys who haven't been in as long as I have who don't get called up. I spent my time, and it's only fair that I get what I deserve."

Mike sighed. "Look, I've been in the army almost as long as you have. I spent nine years on active duty and about eight in the Reserves. What's important here is that you and I are both in positions of responsibility. We have a responsibility to the soldiers under us and to the country, which has been paying and training us to carry out our jobs. We each have a lot of knowledge and experience that we can pass on to the younger men and women in the unit. More importantly, the soldiers in the company have learned to trust us, to rely on us."

"I don't have any responsibility like that," Lehigh said, breaking in harshly. "It's not my job to nursemaid these kids. You mean you're not going to change it?"

"No, I'm not," Mike said in a flat voice. "If I didn't believe it, I would not have made the comments. Now, you are dismissed. I've got real problems to deal with."

The day before the company's departure, the Secretary of Defense announced that certain Reserve units called up as part of the mobilization would be leaving the next day for Europe. He identified them, including Headquarters and Headquarters Company, 805th Support Group, stating they would be the first increment of the mobilized reservists and guardsmen deployed and called their departure a sign of the resolution and commitment of the United States. He promised further that the remainder of the two hundred thousand soldiers called up would soon follow.

"Let no one doubt," he said, concluding in ringing tones, "the willingness and ability of America's citizen soldiers to bear the burdens of defending freedom." His statement did not refer to the ongoing deployment of active component units.

When Colonel Warren learned of the secretary's announcement, he called a staff meeting to determine the status of the company's preparations. The consensus of the staff was that all had been done that could be and the unit was ready to go. The colonel agreed and released all personnel who were deploying until 0800 the next day.

"Remember," he said in closing, "there will be a muster formation at 0900. We will be leaving for Logan at 1030. Make sure your people know that they have to be back by 0800. Any one missing movement will be sent on to join us in Germany. They will not remain in the States. I can guarantee that. Missing movement may be a court martial offense. In this case, the punishment will be an Article Fifteen and no jail time. That's one lesson we learned from Vietnam. Nobody goes to jail to get out of going overseas."

Mike chased the members of the section out of the building and locked the offices behind him. He told the duty officer where he would be for the evening and headed home to Concord. He fed the dogs and cats, told Maggie that he and Elizabeth would be late coming home, changed into a blazer and slacks, and headed down Route 2 toward Boston. Going against rush-hour traffic, he made good time and pulled into the parking garage at Government Center about five o'clock. It was a fifteen-minute walk from the garage to Elizabeth's office. He arrived as her last patient was leaving.

"Hi, the old man let us go for the night, so I thought I'd spare you the train ride home," he said as they embraced in her office.

"Oh, bullshit," she said, elbowing him in the ribs. "What's really going on?" She stepped back and looked at him seriously. "There was something on the radio earlier today about reservists leaving for Europe tomorrow. Is that you?"

"Yes, that's us. Our departure date was classified, and we were supposed to be confined to the post tonight. The secretary gave away everything but the bloody flight number, so Colonel Warren gave us all overnight passes. We have to be back at 0800 tomorrow for a muster at 0900, and then we leave for the airport."

"Oh, so this is 'Kiss me tonight, fair maid, for I sail at dawn'?"

Mike picked up her jacket and purse. "Actually, the plane probably leaves closer to noon, but it's the same general idea. Come on. Let's go get some supper."

She planted herself in front of him with arms folded and glared up at him. "So you think you can just ply me with food and wine, have your way with me tonight, and slip off to Germany in the morning?"

Mike nodded. "Yeah, something like that. You have any better ideas?"

They left the building arm in arm and walked up the long hill of Cambridge Street toward Government Center. They crossed the street at City Hall Plaza and walked down the steps toward Quincy Market. The warm summer weather had filled the market with tourists and office workers on their way home. The food stalls flooded the air with a blend of smells from pizza to fried dough.

As they moved slowly with the crowd, Elizabeth tugged Mike's arm. "I know. Let's go over to the North End and get something at Mother Anna's. It's been a while since we've been there."

They continued their walk through the market and then, in true Boston fashion, jaywalked across Haymarket Square into the North End. Mother Anna's was Elizabeth's favorite Italian restaurant and one of her superstitions. During their courtship, she told Mike about it but never took him there until shortly before their wedding. She said in the past, whenever she had taken a date to Mother Anna's, the man stopped seeing her shortly afterwards.

"Now that I know you're going to be around," she told him that night, "I'm willing to go there with you."

This evening, they found a table as soon as they walked in. Their conversation was light, speaking of inconsequential matters that avoided the thought of tomorrow's separation. They both ordered the carbonara and had enough left over to take home. Mike told her to skip dessert. He had another place in mind. They walked silently back to the car, hand in hand.

Mike took a roundabout way home and stopped in Carlisle at Bates Farm, their favorite ice cream stand. He ordered the special, a dish of three kinds of ice cream and toppings five inches high topped with a three-inch mound of whipped cream. Elizabeth looked sideways at him and his ice cream, as she always did when he ordered it. He told her he needed all the real food he could get because he would be eating nothing but MREs and tray packs for the next several months.

After the ice cream, they went back home to Concord. Bridget and Laddie began barking a welcome as soon as they pulled into the driveway. The cats appeared at the front door so Mike could open it for them. Elizabeth called her answering service to tell them she was at home for the night.

Mike let the dogs in and gave them the "puppy ice cream" he had picked up at the ice cream stand.

They made love with a passion and intensity spurred by the impending separation. In the afterglow, they lay in each other's arms and drifted off to sleep.

Elizabeth woke up with a start, feeling as though she were being slowly crushed. She found Emily, the Maine Coon, curled up on her chest, purring in contentment. As she shoved twenty-two pounds of cat off her, she noticed Mike lying on his back and staring at the ceiling.

"What's wrong, hon? You haven't been awake all this time, have you?" she asked softly.

"I'm okay. I just can't relax tonight. I guess it's something to do with tomorrow."

She rolled over on her left side to face him and propped herself up on an elbow. "That's perfectly understandable," she said in what Mike called her "doctor voice." "A lot of uncertainty is in front of us. And you've been under a lot more stress than normal these past couple days. You're just worrying about what will happen in Germany."

"I am, but not in the way you think. I've spent my life getting ready for this, one way or another. I've told you before that I look at my Reserve pay as a retainer fee. Now they are calling in the markers. The taxpayers paid for my education, West Point and graduate school. Now they want to see what kind of return they are going to get on their investment. I'm worried I might screw up. What happens if I make a mistake that results in getting people killed? What kind of an officer will I be then?"

"You know what it will be like," Elizabeth said. "You've been in combat before in Santo Domingo. That was nothing like what your father saw in Vietnam, but it was still combat."

Mike grunted and rolled on his side to face her. "The Dominican Republic was a lot different from this. Then, it was just get on a C-130 and go. At my level, a machine gunner, there wasn't a whole lot of time to think about what was happening. Everything was immediate. We focused on the next couple of hours, worrying about getting everyone and everything loaded up right away. We measured the buildup for the Dominican Republic in hours, not weeks or months like this one. Besides, I had only been in the company for two months. I hardly knew most of my fellow soldiers. I've been with the headquarters for over two years, and I feel a lot closer to these people, like Ann-Marie and Sally. The Russians and other Warsaw Pact forces are probably going to be tougher opponents than Dominican rebels. And most of all, I didn't have you."

She reached over and hugged him tightly. "You keep telling me that all we can do is our best. That's all anyone has any right to expect from a person, that each gives the best effort that he or she can. I think you'll be fine. I've seen the unit at parties and when you leave and return from summer training. The soldiers respect and trust you. They know you will do the best job you can to take care of them. You'll be better than some officers that will be around."

He pulled her over on top of him and looked deeply into her eyes. "I love you, Doc. You are my best friend and the rock of my life." As they embraced, matters took their normal course. And Emily, the Maine Coon cat, was unceremoniously kicked off the bed.

BLDG T-5701
Fort Devens, Massachusetts

The company's departure became a media event. The senior senator from Massachusetts, as well as the Assistant Secretary of the Army, were on hand to bid farewell to Headquarters and Headquarters Company, 805th Support Group, the first contingent of Reservists to leave Fort Devens for Europe. A Massachusetts National Guard unit was also deploying, so the governor and leading members of the state's political establishment were on hand as well.

The 805th and the 334th Signal Company of the Massachusetts National Guard assembled in the parking lot in front of the group headquarters building. The support group wore full field uniform: battle dress with weapons, protective masks, LBE, flak jackets, and Kevlar helmets. Colonel Warren and First Sergeant Bellotti harkening back to their Vietnam days, directed that soldiers would carry their M-16s assault—rifle style, with the nylon sling fastened to the front sight post and the small of the stock just behind the charging handle. This way, the soldier slung the weapon over the shoulder or around the neck so it hung about waist level. The soldier could immediately reach the trigger with one hand and begin firing. While practical, the army did not recognize it as an accepted practice. The soldiers fell in with their rucksacks at their feet. The guardsmen, who were not leaving until 2330, assembled in the normal duty uniform of BDUs and soft caps. The contrast was stark and immediately noted by all present, including the state adjutant general. The sudden glare of publicity did not bode well for the company commander's future.

First Sergeant Bellotti finished the muster and reported to Captain Sherwood that all personnel were present or accounted for. Sherwood then turned and reported to Colonel Warren, and the two officers began a walkthrough of the company. As he moved through the silent ranks, Warren saw in his mind's eye the first platoon he commanded, long ago in the Central Highlands of Vietnam. As he spoke to each of his reservists, the faces of those twenty-three soldiers overlay the faces of the men and women in front of him, and he wondered how many would return to Fort Devens for deactivation.

The assistant secretary stepped forward and spoke of the commitment of the United States to NATO and Europe and how the soldiers in front of him represented the first increment in fulfilling that commitment. Mercifully, the speeches were brief. The commanders released their soldiers for one final farewell with their families before boarding the drab army buses that would be taking them to Logan and the DC-10 charter bound for Ramstein Air Force Base.

Elizabeth stood to one side of the speaker's stand with Sally's husband, Mark Cooper, and Colonel Warren's wife, Caroline. Cooper looked extremely upset with the proceedings. He did not approve of Sally's decision to stay in the Reserves and had only reluctantly supported her over the years that Elizabeth had known the couple. Now, as Mike and Sally walked up to their spouses, Sally shrank in on herself. Elizabeth greeted Sally with a hug, and the two women touched cheeks. Elizabeth's green eyes shone with unshed tears, but she made a determined effort to be cheerful.

As the two women embraced, Elizabeth caught the flash of something metallic from Sally's right foot.

"What do you have hanging off your leg, Sal?" she asked.

"A dog tag," Mike replied. "It's Top Bellotti's idea, a legacy of his Vietnam days. He had us all put one of our dog tags on a bootlace and the other on the neck chain. He says that, if you get your head blown off, you'll lose the neck chain as well. Without the dog tags, it's difficult to identify the body. It's unlikely that you'd lose both head and legs. If one dog tag is on a boot lace and the other is on a neck chain, identification will be easier."

"God, how morbid." Elizabeth shivered. Then she tried to brighten the conversation.

Mike nodded to Cooper. "How are you doing, Mark? The children okay?"

"How do you think I am?" Mark snapped in reply. "My wife is going off to a ridiculous war she has no business in. Well, I hope you and all the other West Pointers are happy. You have your war at last. It should be good for your career, and maybe you'll make general."

Before Mike could respond, Sally slipped away from Elizabeth and pulled her husband off to one side. She spoke rapidly in a low voice to him and drew him away from Mike and Elizabeth.

Mike shrugged and turned to his wife. "And a fine morning to you, too, Professor Cooper. He doesn't appreciate how hard I had to work to arrange this. It was really difficult trying to convince all those guys in Eastern Europe to go along with these plans just so I could get promoted."

"Mike, stop it. You're beginning to sound as bad as Mark." Elizabeth gazed after her friend in concern.

"It's easier for you, I suppose? After all, it's only your husband."

"In a way, yes." She assumed her "doctor's voice" again. "I hope there is nothing permanent there to hurt the two of them." She looked back at Sally and her husband.

Mike nodded. "Well, I'll try to keep an eye on her over there. Maybe someone should talk to the good professor and explain to him just how lucky he is to have a wife like Sally."

"I know what kind of an eye you'll keep on her. Just make sure that it's only your eye."

A cough brought them back to the ceremony. A middle-aged couple had come up to where Mike and Elizabeth stood.

The balding, slightly overweight man stood self-consciously next to Mike. "Excuse me, sir. My wife and I would like to ask something special of you." He spoke with a slight French accent, which helped Mike to place him immediately. He was Ann-Marie's father, Pierre Dumont. Dumont's wife gripped his right arm with white-knuckled tension. She looked like an older and heavier version of her daughter with white hair. Mike and Elizabeth could feel the tension in both of the Dumonts.

"Sir, I don't believe that you've met my wife," Mike said smoothly to try to set the couple at ease.

"Elizabeth, this is Pierre and Blanche Dumont, Specialist Dumont's parents. Specialist Dumont went on the advance party last week with Captain Chambers." He turned back to the Dumonts. "Thank you for coming down from Manchester to see us off."

Elizabeth held her hand out to Pierre Dumont, who shook it awkwardly.

"I'm glad to meet you." She smiled at the two of them. "I have met your daughter Ann-Marie several times. I have to tell you that I feel very secure knowing that she'll be around to take care of my husband."

Dumont blanched at Elizabeth's comment, and his wife sobbed suddenly.

"What I want to ask you, sir," the man said hoarsely to Mike, "is to please take care of my Ann-Marie and bring her home safely. She is all we have now."

Blanche Dumont let go of her husband's arm, buried her face in her hands, and began sobbing. Elizabeth immediately embraced the older woman and tried to comfort her.

"Her brother, he was a Marine," Pierre said. "He died in Vietnam when she was a baby."

Blanche broke away from Elizabeth's embrace and grabbed Mike's right hand. "Please, please. Keep her safe, and bring her home. My baby girl. My baby girl."

Mike laid his left hand over Blanche Dumont's hand and looked her husband in the eye. "I will do my best to bring her back to you," he said softly. "I promise I will do all I can to keep her alive, she and all the other soldiers in the company."

Another man closer to Mike's age but a younger version of Pierre joined the group and embraced the mother. "Hey, Mama, Annie will be alright. The major here, he is a good officer for a doggie." He was Ann-Marie's uncle, also a Marine veteran of Vietnam. Mike had met him at a company picnic the uncle had attended as Ann-Marie's guest.

"He will keep our little Annie safe." His eyes told Mike he knew all too well just how problematical that promise was. He broke his glance with Mike and turned to his brother. "Pierre, Blanche, let's get some cake and let the major say good-bye to his wife."

Blanche Dumont looked up at Mike through tear-stained eyes. "I will keep you in my prayers, sir. Watch over my little girl."

Mike and Elizabeth watched the Dumonts walk slowly toward the refreshment tent, both men comforting the sobbing woman. Mike felt humbled and awed by the trust in his powers displayed by the Dumonts. He clutched his wife tightly. For her part, Elizabeth felt part of the burden her husband bore and understood some of the pain he was feeling. She rested her head on his shoulder and blinked back tears that started to form behind her eyelids. Then she shook herself and stood away from him.

Reaching in her purse, Elizabeth held up a small, gift-wrapped box to Mike. "For you to use as needed."

Mike took the box and opened it. Inside was a Peterson briar pipe and a large bag of custom blended tobacco from David Ehrlich's, a pipe store on Tremont Street where Mike bought his tobacco. Elizabeth gave him a new pipe every year at their anniversary. There was a card in the box in Elizabeth's neat handwriting: "I told you when we got married that I'd put you through one pipe a year. Here is this year's installment. Come back to me, Major. Please."

Mike stared silently at the pipe and tobacco for a minute and then crushed Elizabeth to him wordlessly.

Chapter 5

Setting the Stage

No matter how enamored of his plans a commander becomes, he must at some point take the enemy into consideration.
—Winston Churchill

Excerpt, Annex B, Intelligence, XXVI (US) Corps OPLAN 1-5510

The terrain between Bad Hersfeld and Frankfurt is predominantly forested with a mixture of coniferous and deciduous trees with small urban buildup in the nonforested areas. The terrain generally appears to favor the defender, but the small number of north-south roads would hinder rapid lateral movement. The numerous small towns provide good covered and concealed fighting positions that may be readily occupied and hardened with minimum effort and resources. These small towns and villages are generally clusters of buildings, surrounded by hedges, trees, walls, and fences. Areas surrounding these towns are large, open cultivated fields, generally without cover or concealment, which will provide forces occupying these built-up areas with good to excellent fields of fire for direct-fire weapons in all directions, while providing excellent protection from air and ground observation as well as from direct and indirect fires. The forested high ground provides good observation and fields of fire as well as some concealment from ground observation and fires. Unimproved secondary roads and trails permit low-speed movement through the forested areas by tracked and wheeled vehicles, although inclement weather will limit this movement.

Occasional rainstorms during the evening and night characterize weather during the July-August time frame. Fog, particularly in low-lying areas, is common during the early morning hours but will generally burn off before midmorning. Temperatures are moderate with mild humidity.

Rolling terrain, thickly forested with some cleared areas, generally characterizes the Nidda valley. Open terrain approximately five hundred to one thousand meters wide surround Altendorf. There is a small knoll approximately two hundred meters northeast of the town, along Bundestrasse 380, that provides excellent observation up the valley but masks that part of the valley from observation in the town.

A ruined castle, Markehrensburg, is located on a large hill mass south of Altendorf, across the Nidda River. Markehrensburg provides excellent observation in all directions and dominates the southern half of the valley.

The slopes of the valley walls are heavily forested. The areas on both sides of the valley are *Staatforst* (national forests) and can be traversed by vehicles only by using the firebreaks and hiking trails. Although numerous, these firebreaks and hiking trails would not support heavy vehicle traffic during periods of inclement weather and would not allow high rates of movement at any time. The heavy growth of trees restricts vehicle movement to these trails and does not permit wide dispersion or off-road movement.

Stadtliches Kinderschule
Altendorf, FRG

According to the 247th's plan, the support group's headquarters would occupy the elementary school, a two-story building located just off the main street in Altendorf. When he completed this inspection, Mike met with Colonel Warren and the rest of the staff outside the school.

"We have to make some changes in the way we organize the operations here. The first, and most important, concerns the radio antennas," Mike said to the cluster of staff officers and NCOs. "We need the antennas remoted away from the school to lower our electronic signature. The Russians have radio direction finding equipment capable of locating a transmitter to within a hundred meters based on a ten-second transmission."

"We can park the communication trucks right out back in the schoolyard," Lieutenant Colonel Rogers interrupted Mike's presentation. "Why do you want to move them?"

"If the Russians DF us and do a traffic analysis, they'll identify us as a headquarters and drop a battalion's worth of artillery on where they identify our signals as coming from. We've got to remote the antennas as close to a thousand meters away as possible," Mike answered the XO.

"Okay, Mike," said Colonel Warren. "Have the commo officer get with Bob Sherwood and pick a location to set up the remotes."

"Sir, the second change I recommend is to move the war room and Lieutenant Colonel Michaud's logistics operations center to the basement instead the ground floor," Mike said. "The roof and upper floors provide standoff against incoming bombs, rockets, or artillery rounds by causing them to burst above the basement. The more we are shelled, the more rubble is added to the bursting layer protecting the basement. We also get away from all the large windows in the building. I also suggest we put the S-1 and S-4 sections somewhere else in town to provide an alternate command post if required. Our plans call for this dispersal. If the school gets clobbered, that takes everybody out."

"Sounds good, Mike," Warren replied. "Sally, you and Bob Roberts pick out a site for your shops." His gaze swept the rest of the staff. "I want the headquarters up and running by 1800. That gives you about six hours. Let's get moving."

As Mike watched his section set up the war room, someone tugged on his arm. He turned to see an irate Sally Grant standing beside him.

"May I speak with you outside, Major?" She pulled him out of the school building to a corner out of earshot of the work crews. "Do you want to do the rest of my job or just certain parts of it?" Sally growled at him in a low voice.

"What are you talking about, Sally?" Mike asked in surprise. "I'm not doing your job—"

"Bullshit. As the S-1, the layout of the headquarters is my responsibility. Rogers has already been talking about getting rid of the women officers and enlisted because we are in a combat environment and he does not think we can hack it. I don't need you helping him out."

"Wait a minute. Wait a minute." Mike held up his hands to stem Sally's tirade. "I haven't heard anything Rogers said, and I don't listen to him anyway. I just looked at the 247th's plans, and they sucked. They have everyone in the headquarters located in the same building, above ground in the classrooms. Look at the bloody windows in the building. The damn things are floor to ceiling glass. They will filet the people inside the first time a good-sized blast is nearby. I figured we first should remote the radios. Then, we split the S-1/S-4 from the war room and LOC into different buildings and put everyone in basements. I didn't think—"

"That's the whole goddamn problem. You didn't think. I read the plans, and I know they suck. I had the same goddamn ideas that you did." She pounded her index finger into Mike's chest. "By SOP, the internal organization of the headquarters is my responsibility. You pick the location, S-3, and I pick the layout. Let me do my fucking job. If I can't, the boss will decide, not the XO or the S-3." She stopped, out of breath, and stood in front of him with arms crossed and eyes glittering with anger.

"Okay, you're right. I was out of line. But it was not a reflection on you or how you're doing as S-1. For the love of God, Sally, I'd tell you face-to-face if I didn't think you were doing your job." Mike paused and looked at her. "From now on, I'll come to you if I think we need a change in the headquarters organization."

Sally nodded once, spun on her heel, and stalked away. Suddenly, she stopped and whirled around to face Mike again. "If you can find time to run your own section, Major, tell Dumont to get a haircut so she looks like a soldier and not some bimbo trolling for boys back in the mall." She continued down the street, her back rigid with anger.

Mike watched her walk away, toward the site of the S-1/S-4 section, a two-story apartment building a block down the street from the school. Her outburst surprised and shocked him. Normally, she would have treated Mike to a bitingly sarcastic lecture about staff functions. The scene between Sally and Mark as the unit left Fort Devens flashed in Mike's mind. There was more to her upset than an unintended power grab by another staff officer.

*Stadtliches Kinderschule
Altendorf, FRG*

The buildup of the Allied forces continued as units arrived in Europe, drew their equipment, and moved to occupy their general defense positions. Two days after the group headquarters had arrived and set up, Colonel Warren called Mike into his office.

"I've got two things I want you to look into, Mike," the colonel said. "The first is the question of refugee traffic. The general defense plans restrict our movements and main supply routes to the back roads on the assumption that refugees and evacuees will be moving on the autobahns. I'm not sure that is happening. Yesterday, when I drove down to Schotten, many civilians were on the road. They were primarily heading west, but they still created a lot of congestion."

"Sir, what you might have been seeing was some of the vehicles the Germans gave NATO. We're really short of trucks for line hauling so the German government handed over many commercial trucks. The ones I've seen so far are still in their normal markings. The only way that you can tell they're military is to look very closely at the drivers."

"The other matter is a family matter. The progress in organizing our defense is unsatisfactory. Bill Sherwood is not as aggressive as I want him to be about setting up our defenses and training our people in self-defense. He has the attitude that, because we're support troops, the combat units to our front will protect us. That's not going to happen; at least not in the way he and some others in the headquarters think it will. I want you to take over as an unofficial headquarters commandant and make Sherwood get his act together.

"We need a solid plan to defend Altendorf, one that ties all American units together and includes plans to train up with battle skills. The Germans have set up firing ranges for all types of weapons. I want our people to start using these ranges. I want our machine gun and automatic rifle crews trained to use their weapons effectively. I want hand grenade and claymore mine training, including live firings. I want people trained to use the AT-4 anti-tank rockets. You were my headquarters commander back in the 3rd Battalion. I want you to put together the same kind of plan that you developed for HHC, give it to Bob, and tell him to execute it." The colonel paused and looked at Mike. "How's your German?

The Germans are responsible for the overall defense of the town, and we will have to tie our plans in with theirs."

"Rusty, sir," Mike responded. "But it will improve with use or wine. I have some old plans from the days of the 3/487th in my file. I'll pull those out and get with Bill. Ed has some ideas about defending this place that he's been hashing over since he arrived last week. He's done some reconnaissance of the local area on his own and has started talking with the Germans. We both feel that this place is a bottleneck. Anyone trying to move southwest from Fulda or Lauterbach is probably going to run right into Altendorf."

"What do you think our biggest threat is?"

"Spetsnaz, for now," Mike replied. "Special operations forces running around, ambushing convoys, or raiding the various unit sites. They probably would be backed up by some airmobile forces to try grabbing the bridges and road junctions here in town." Mike stepped around the colonel's desk and traced a line on the map hanging on the rear wall of the office. "We're pretty close to the E-4 autobahn, and this river valley runs roughly parallel to it. I would say we are in a secondary avenue of approach right down here to the Hanau-Frankfurt area. If the Russians got lucky and split open the division in front of us, we could be looking at a fairly heavy ground attack coming right down the road from Lauterbach to Nidda and on to Hanau."

"Assume that happens, what do you think will result? How will it affect the group?"

Mike paused to collect his thoughts and studied the map. "We'd be forced to jump back toward Schotten, to the southwest here or northwest out along B-457. Depending on how much warning we have, it could be an easy move or a real goat rope. I am not sure how much planning has gone into selecting alternate locations for our units. And they probably didn't get around to performing route or site reconnaissance. The headquarters is only forty percent mobile with our own vehicles. We'd need a lot of support to move our equipment and personnel. I'd say that we could very well be out of action for up to eighteen hours, depending on where we move to."

Warren swiveled his chair around and gazed at the map. "Assume that jumping is not an option open to us. Assume we will have to stay here in town and act as a blocking force to reinforce the Germans."

"We have to start now preparing the town as a strong point. That means a lot of work in hardening the buildings and preparing obstacles. One of the first steps I would take is to lay a belt of concertina wire over the most likely routes of advance for armored vehicles. And then back that up with mines and fougasse, fifty-five-gallon drums filled with napalm and a shaped charge."

"Concertina wire? Against tanks? They'd simply drive through it."

"It works," Mike said defensively. "I used it when I was a company commander in my ARTEP at Hohenfels. You make the belt thick enough, the tank or APC will get the wire wrapped around his drive sprockets and lock up the track system. In any case, even if we don't stop them, we will slow them down and channel them into any kill zones you have picked out. Our anti-tank missile gunners will pick them off like birds on a wire.

"We also have to preposition ammunition in the buildings we occupy as fighting positions. We'll need grenades and anti-tank rockets stockpiled in each position as well. We should also begin collecting empty fuel and ammo cans we can make into flame mines. My tanker friends always told me that fire from Molotov cocktails was effective against tanks. If a tank catches fire, the crew likes to abandon it right away."

"I've seen Ed's plan for the defense of the town. It looks pretty good," Colonel Warren said. "It ties some of what you mentioned in it but not all of it, particularly the barrier plan. We will have to coordinate with the Germans, along with anything else that goes outside purely self-defense. I want you to call Corps G-3 and find out where we get our artillery support. Call the artillery and get a fire support coordination team over here so we can start planning defensive fires. I don't want to rely on what the 247th did because I think the situation has drastically changed from when they wrote their plans."

By this time, Mike had pulled out his notebook, and he was rapidly making notes of the conversation. "I have a call into Corps about the overall rear battle plan, sir. We're still acting as temporary COSCOM headquarters, and I want to find out from the Corps G-3 shop what they intend about the rear battle plan and who they thought was in charge of it."

Warren nodded and turned back to his desk. "Very well. Keep me informed of what you find out. When you talk to Sherwood, tell him that I want him to brief me daily on the status of training in battle craft and survival skills for the company."

Over the next few days, Mike began working closely with Bill Sherwood and Ed to set up and execute intensive training in combat skills for the soldiers. The Germans set up firing ranges immediately outside the town, and small groups of Americans went out daily to learn how to use each type of weapon available to them, from the American M-16 rifle to the German Carl Gustav 84 mm recoilless rifle. The training's high point was throwing live hand grenades and firing live AT-4 light anti-tank rockets.

Other aspects of the training were not as welcome. Mike set up training courses in patrolling for the company reaction team, a group of fifteen soldiers. The team conducted day and night patrols in the local area. Other soldiers began fortifying buildings within the town and erecting barriers around it. In coordination with the Germans, wire obstacles and anti-tank ditches blocked the most likely approaches into the town. The

German pioneers dug the ditches with their bulldozers, but the wire was laid by hand. Minefields were also set up, again by hand. Many of the soldiers grumbled they were support troops, not infantry. Support troops were not supposed to fill sandbags, dig foxholes, go on patrol, or man observation posts. Their complaints received little sympathy from the chain of command.

The responsibility for the actual conduct of the training devolved on First Sergeant Bellotti, under the supervision of Mike and Ed. The first sergeant was a short, stocky, balding Italian from the North End of Boston. He managed the local branch of the Bank of America, and was active in the social neighborhood activities. His cherubic nature hid the character of an iron-willed Harvard Business School graduate who demanded the utmost from those who worked for him. Mike discovered that it also hid a bloodthirsty mind that produced a stream of nasty ideas for defending their portion of the town. A teenaged rifleman in the 101st Airborne Division, Bellotti was one of several Vietnam veterans in the unit. The training time at Altendorf peeled his years away, refreshed his memories of combat, and he drove the soldiers mercilessly. To any complainers, he quoted General George S. Patton, "A pint of American blood is worth a gallon of American sweat."

"You know, Top," Ed said at the end of one of their planning sessions, "Back in the Ranger Regiment, we always talked about using Molotov Cocktails and Eagle Fireballs filled with napalm to use against tanks in built—up areas. Do you think we can use those kinds of things here?"

"Sure we can, sir," Bellotti responded. "We can scrounge empty bottles and small cans from the empty houses around town to make the stuff. Teaching the troops to use them will be easy and fun."

"How do we get napalm?" Mike asked. "I've already had Log Ops check with the ammo company. They don't stock it. Only the Air Force does, and only in bombs."

Top Bellotti looked up from tamping his pipe. "We can make it, Major."

The two officers looked at Bellotti as if he had just grown another head.

"How do you make napalm?" Mike asked.

"Napalm's easy to make here locally. It's just thickened fuel, and the thickener is just a glorified form of soap. We take some dishwashing liquid from the mess hall and mix it in with the diesel and oil. Stir it up, and we've got napalm." Bellotti leaned back and blew a vast cloud of grey smoke in the air.

"How do you know about this stuff?" Ed asked suspiciously. The first sergeant had played practical jokes on the young captain before.

"We used to make fougasse's for our base camps in Nam. We couldn't get either napalm or the thickener compound, so we used laundry detergent. The first week I was in country I spent mostly stirring soap flakes into gasoline to make napalm. It wasn't fun, but it was a hellava lot better than burning shithouses, the other detail that replacements got stuck with." He sat up in his chair and looked at Mike. "Can we get some sections of Bangalore torpedoes and some cratering charges?"

"Probably, Top, but what do we want them for? The Germans are cratering the roads or at least putting the charges in. And Bangalores are for cutting wire obstacles. We have to build the damn wire, not cut it."

"We can make some fougasses for the perimeter. Next, we dig a hole. Then we put a shaped charge in the hole, put the drum on top of that, and lay a roll of concertina wire on top of the drum. Wire the shaped charge up, and then just wait for the other person to try to come in. If you want to get fancy, we can aim the barrel by digging the hole in a particular direction. We can trip-wire the fougasse or leave it hooked up to a blasting machine. The Bangalores, we stand up on end wrap barbed wire around it for additional fragmentation and connect it to a trip wire. Now we have a claymore mine with a three hundred and sixty-degree field of fire. Speaking of claymores, I wonder if we can hang some of those on the sides of buildings."

"Why would we want to hang claymores on the sides of buildings?" Ed asked.

"A Vietnam story," Bellotti replied. "Charlie and the NVA used to hang them in trees over trails and roads. He would point the mines down onto the road and leave a trip wire that a radio antenna or the top of a truck would set off." He paused, looking back at memories he had buried for twenty-something years. "Think what the blast of a claymore would do to a tank or an APC with open hatches. You were Mech, Major. What do you think?"

Mike nodded slowly as the idea sank in on him. "You've got something, Top. Most times, the TC and driver would have at least their heads out to see where they're going. A claymore going off a couple feet above their heads would butcher them. It would also destroy everything on the top of the vehicle, like rangefinders, periscopes, and whatever. We'll stock up on claymores as well."

Mike stood up and nodded to Ed. "Okay, Top, this is sergeant's business, and we'll get out of your hair. Let me see your training schedule and equipment requirements tomorrow. If you need anything else, just tell me. Captain Chambers and I are also available for instructors."

Mike and First Sergeant Bellotti trained the tank-killer teams intensively in the use of demolitions, mines, and flame weapons against tanks and other armored vehicles. The training included each soldier sitting in a foxhole as a tank drove over it. This exercise was done several times, first with the soldier just sitting in the hole to show that the tank could not easily crush him. Once the soldier was accustomed to the noise and heat of a moving tank, the exercise stepped up to throwing simulated demolition charges and Molotov cocktails on the back of the tank after it had rolled over the soldier's position. The main weapons for the teams were the Eagle fireball and satchel charges.

"The Eagle fireball is a field expedient flame weapon for attacking armored vehicles," Mike said, beginning his first training session. "It consists of a container, in this example, a .50-caliber machine gun ammo box filled with napalm or a mixture of waste oil and diesel fuel. Once the can is filled, we strap a half-pound block of C-4 and a white phosphorus grenade to the outside and a couple of these homemade hooks. We fix the fuse to the C-4 with a nonelectric blasting cap. Before we throw it at the target, we pull the fuse lighter and the pin on the WP grenade."

"Major, is this shit really going to work? Where are all the fucking missiles and rockets we keep hearing about?"

Mike looked up to find the speaker, pausing in his work on the Eagle fireball in front of him. He never personally doubted the effectiveness of the expedient weapons. The tanks they would attack would be operating blind in a hostile environment, depending on infantry support that might be there or not. Now, he had to convince his soldiers.

"Okay, listen up, Gonzalez and the rest of you." He waited until he had their undivided attention. He spoke softly and determinedly, his intensity plain. "Yeah, this stuff is pretty basic, not like the high-tech stuff we're used to. But now, we're going to be in a pretty basic battle. We're not going to be shooting at black targets two or three hundred meters away. We will be toe-to-toe with the other guys. We will see his face and hear his voice. We might even smell him. And when we shoot him, we will see the bullet holes and the blood.

"Tanks are now in our world. In the close-up fight, MBT stands not for main battle tank but for mighty big target, a fifty-two-ton mobile crematorium for the crew. The tank's weapons are designed for long-range fights, not up close and personal. Most important, they can't see us if they button up, and if they don't, our job's easier because putting a grenade down a tank hatch is like shooting hoops back home. And finally, these weapons." He waved at the Eagle fireball and Molotov cocktail nearby. "They work. I know they do because I used the same things in Santo Domingo to blow up bunkers."

"So you really think they'll work?"

"Goddamn right," Mike said, snapping back. "And I will be in front of you showing you how it's done."

Stadtliches Kinderschule
Altendorf FRG

The TOC guard stuck his head in the war room. "Major Fitzmaurice, I got a call from the OP on the south road. There's a general on his way to see the colonel. He should be here in about five minutes."

Mike thanked him and went to get the colonel. Warren was listening to Lieutenant Colonel Michaud give a quick update on the corps' ammunition supply. Mike interrupted the colonels to deliver the guard's message.

"Shit," the colonel said, swearing softly. "Generals are never good news. I wonder what the devil they've thought up now."

Two Humvees pulled up in front of the headquarters building. As the engines died, a tall black officer climbed out of the second vehicle, put on his Kevlar helmet, and looked up at Colonel Warren.

"Tubby, you ol' sonofabitch!" he shouted. "How's it hanging?"

Colonel Warren's face lit up as he bounded down the stairs.

"Linc, it's good to see you. You cheap bastard, now you can pay me the Glenfiddich you owe me from the last Army-BC game."

Mike watched bemusedly as Colonel Warren and Major General Lincoln Barrett, deputy commander for Support, XXVI Corps, pounded each other on the back with the joy of long-lost brothers. He had heard the colonel called many names before, but never "Tubby."

"Colonel Warren," Barrett said, "this is Colonel Porter from the Corps G-3 shop. He came with us to give you the latest version of the corps operation plan."

Colonel Porter said, "I'll try to keep it simple for you reservists." The word "reservists" came out as almost a sneer. "You probably don't do things like this at summer camp."

The general grimaced. "Colonel Porter, this is Colonel Warren, the commander of the 805th Support Group, and his operations officer, Major Fitzmaurice."

Porter nodded to Colonel Warren and fixed Mike with a gimlet-eyed stare. "I guess you don't salute senior officers in the Reserves, Major."

Mike felt himself redden as he stared at Colonel Porter and then brought up his right hand in a perfect parade ground salute.

Before he could say anything, Colonel Warren said in a quiet voice, "We have a policy of not saluting in the field. It identifies your officers, and you don't know who might be watching. We have had several sniper attacks in the past few days."

Porter had not returned Mike's salute, forcing him to hold it while Colonel Warren spoke. He gave a casual wave of his right hand to Mike. "That's what I'd expect from a Reserve unit. Can we get on with the briefing? You do have a conference room, don't you?" Before anyone could answer, he turned his gaze back to Mike. "Your chinstrap's not fastened, is it? Now that I think about it, I've seen quite a few unfastened chinstraps here."

Colonel Warren said coldly, "My SOP states that chinstraps will not be fastened unless the soldier is involved in airmobile or airborne operations. Have you ever seen what concussion does to someone wearing a helmet with a fastened chinstrap?"

General Barrett interposed before Porter could respond. "John, your conference room or office, please." He turned to the aide, who was trying very hard to pretend nothing was going on between the two colonels. "Tom, why don't you and Major Fitzmaurice get a cup of coffee or something while your elders talk. Be back in about twenty minutes."

"Yes, sir. If Major Fitzmaurice will show me the mess hall, I'll also see about some breakfast for the escort and drivers."

"Sure, come on," Mike said to the aide as he extended his hand to the captain. "I'm certain Sergeant DiNapoli has some breakfast squirreled away. Besides, it's time to check the morning output from the bakery platoon. I'll have the runner bring something over to your office, sir," he said to Colonel Warren as he led the aide down the stairs of the command post and across the main street of Altendorf.

"Captain Tom Simons," the aide said gripping Mike's hand firmly. "I'd like a look around your set up."

The mess hall was in a *gasthaus* about a block down the street from the elementary school. As they walked toward it, Captain Simons noticed the buildings being prepared for defense. Groups of German and American soldiers boarded up doors and windows and covered them with chicken wire or netting. Other details carried sand bags into or stacked them in front of the buildings. More details boarded up the windows and doors of buildings that were not going to be occupied and blocked them with barbed wire. German territorials and American soldiers emplaced wire obstacles or created roadblocks with abandoned cars. They placed the cars in the street and then removed the wheels and filled them with earth. Once in position, the cars disrupted the flow of traffic and blocked access to and from side streets.

"You guys must be expecting trouble," Simons commented, gesturing at all the activity.

"This town sits on a major intersection that controls two major highways in a regimental-sized avenue of approach," Mike replied. "The Germans believe the intersection and bridge at the other end of town make Altendorf a key objective for the other guys. Since we moved all our support activities in here, the town's just increased in importance.

"The Old Man agrees with them. He also believes in digging fighting positions. He learned the hard way when he was a platoon leader in the Cav in 1971. He was at a firebase that almost was overrun because no one dug in. He got his Silver Star and second Purple Heart out of that episode. He vowed it would never happen again to any unit he was in. If you stop for more than an hour, you dig. And the longer you stay, the more you dig." Mike stopped and then said with a chuckle, "When he was a battalion commander, he bloody near got us banned from Fort Drum. We were digging too many foxholes for the garrison staff to accept, and they got really pissed off at us. We were known as Warren's Gophers, 3rd Battalion, 487th Infantry. I was his headquarters company commander then. Fortunately, the active army evaluators wrote glowing reports of our tactical skill, so the garrison people had to eat their complaints."

As they walked into the mess building, Simons nodded. "I guess he must be part of the old team. That's really going to frost Porter."

"What do you mean?"

"I forgot. You probably aren't plugged into army gossip channels. When the new chief of staff took over last year, he started making many surprise appointments, particularly as XXVI Corps evolved. The common thread to all these appointments was people who served with the chief in the First Cavalry Division in Vietnam, so they were dubbed the old team. Porter is not part of the old team. Since he's out to make general, he doesn't like people who are members, particularly when they are reservists in colonel command positions."

The mess sergeant saw Mike and Simons walk in and hurried over to the two officers. When Mike told him about the six soldiers in the general's escort, Staff Sergeant DiNapoli put together a light breakfast—scrambled eggs, bacon, home fries, reheated pancakes, toast, sweet rolls, coffee, and juice—in insulated containers and sent two KPs over to the vehicle park to feed the escorts. He sent another KP over to the colonel's office with a tray of sweet rolls and coffee cake.

Simons watched the whole process in silent amazement.

As he and Mike walked back to the command post, he said, "I don't believe this. We don't eat as well up at Corps Headquarters. How did you get fresh bread and rolls?"

"The bakery platoon from our supply and services company took over an abandoned German bakery about a half-block from here. That plus their own equipment gives them the ability to produce about three thousand rations a day. They also have some German territorials helping them. As far as the pastries go, Staff Sergeant DiNapoli makes his own right here. He runs a bakery and restaurant back home in Gloucester."

When Simons and Mike reentered the command post, the two colonels and General Barrett were still in conference so Mike gave Simons the fifty-cent tour of the headquarters. Then he gave Simons an overview of how the group was supporting the corps' forward divisions.

Stadtliches Kinderschule
Altendorf, FRG

The door to Colonel Warren's office opened, and Major General Barrett walked out into the briefing room with the two colonels following. Porter and Warren walked as stiff-legged as two strange dogs meeting in an alley. Their tight-lipped expressions made clear the meeting had not been a friendly one.

The general walked over to the situation map, where Mike and Simons stood. "Major Fitzmaurice, Colonel Warren said you could brief me on the current plan and status of the support group." Barrett pulled over a chair and seated himself in front of the map. "Dazzle me."

"Yes, sir." Mike stepped up to the map.

Captain Simons moved over behind Barrett, and Colonel Porter seated himself on the general's left. Mike began explaining the group's operational plans and pointing out the units and service locations. As he identified a particular facility, the general would fire a series of questions about its capabilities, current workload, and status. At the same time, Colonel Porter would ask questions about the group's rear battle plan and how it intended to perform the rear area security mission. In a letter that night, Mike would tell Elizabeth that this briefing was worse than anything he had experienced before, including the defense of his thesis in graduate school. The question and answers went on for forty-five minutes and might have continued longer.

A solemn-faced staff sergeant, Barrett's driver walked into the briefing room and handed a message to General Barrett "Sir, I just received this flash message for you from Corps headquarters. I knew you'd want to see it right away."

Barrett looked closely at the river as he took the message and then glanced down to read the paper in his hand.

He finished and looked over at Colonel Warren. "It's started, John." Then he read the message to the entire group:

From: CINCUSAREUR

To: All Commands

1. *Warsaw Pact forces crossed inner German border 020359Z August. German forces have engaged lead elements, results not known.*

2. *Per direction SACEUR, execute General Defense Plans 5500 series effective 020850Z August.*

   3.   Establish MOPP Level II and Air Defense Condition
       Yellow/Weapons Hold effective 020850Z August.
    4.   Authenticate Tango November.

"You're right, John. It has started. And God only knows where it will end," Barrett said softly into the silence that filled the room after Warren had read the message. He stood and turned to Porter and Simons. "We must be getting back to Corps, gentlemen. Major Fitzmaurice thanks for your briefing. It was most informative and well done. Colonel Warren will brief you on the new plan. It will entail some changes to what you have now."

The group came to attention as the general picked up his helmet and map case and went out the door of the briefing room. The contents of the message were beginning to spread throughout the headquarters, and conversation was dying. A heavy silence replaced the normal bustle of the headquarters as the soldiers absorbed the full meaning.

At the front door of the school building, Barrett turned to Warren and the two men gripped hands firmly.

"Stay out of trouble, John. I may not be around to bail you out this time, as I did at Romeo, and Caroline would never forgive me. Besides, I'd miss my lobster dinners," the general said.

"Linc, you just keep your head down and don't worry about bailing me out. I've learned to dig holes since Romeo," Warren replied.

Simons pulled Mike aside as they stood on the steps of the school. "You probably don't remember this, but I owe you. You were a firstie on regimental staff when I was a plebe, and I sat on your table for a month. You spent enough time and interest in me and the other two plebes that I decided not to quit and stuck it out."

Mike tried to picture Simons as an eighteen-year-old freshman sitting at his mess hall table back at West Point but failed. "I'm sorry. I don't remember, but what—"

"Part of the general's purpose in visiting here was to check you out. He has a green book, like George Marshall had a black book. Colonel Warren said your name should be in it so General Barrett came down to see if you should be or not. He puts a lot of faith in Warren's opinions. I don't know what the general's decision is. I just want to let you know he's watching and he may move you out of here if he thinks you could do a better job somewhere else."

"Okay, I don't know what that means, but thanks for telling me. And any time you want some coffee rolls, stop by."

"It's a deal. Good luck."

After the general and his party left to go back to corps headquarters, Colonel Warren called a staff meeting. He described the changes to the corps operations plans.

"The Germans shifted a number of their units north toward Northern Army Group. XXVI Corps extended its front to cover the positions formerly held by the Germans. What this means to us directly is that our own area of responsibility has just become larger." Colonel Warren continued to outline the changes that Colonel Porter had given him during their meeting in his office.

He finished presenting the new situation and his preliminary intentions to the staff by telling them that he wanted their staff estimates for the new plan by 1200. He directed Mike to publish a new fragmentary order by 1500. At 1500, he wanted a meeting of subordinate unit commanders where each staff officer would brief their portion of the frag order.

As the staff left to begin the estimate process, Warren called to the executive officer to wait. Rogers had accepted his deployment stoically and performed adequately. Warren spoke to Major General Barrett about moving Rogers to some other assignment once a suitable replacement was available.

When Rogers walked up, Warren said, "I remember our conversation back at Fort Devens. You have met your end of the agreement, and I'm trying to carry out mine. I should have some word in a day or so." He took Rogers over to the situation map. "I'm concerned about the possibility of our being forced to move the headquarters. Fitzmaurice and I have picked out three alternate sites. I want you to take Bill Sherwood and look at all three. Pick out the one that you think best suits our needs."

"Yes, sir," Rogers said as he studied the map. "I can't take Captain Sherwood though. He's working on the staff estimate." Rogers' face lit up like a klieg light. "I'll get Lieutenant Baxter. She's the company executive officer. And the S-4 won't need her for a while since he's got Fredricks, that new captain from the 247th who came in last week."

——∘∘❖∘∘——

Highway B-457
Vicinity Neider Stolzenwald, FRG

When Lieutenant Colonel Rogers was directed to find an alternate location for the group headquarters, he decided this required the Headquarters Company executive officer. So Vicki found herself in the back seat of a Blazer driving southeast toward Frankfurt while Rogers told her what he would do if he were the group commander. They visited one location Rogers felt was acceptable. En route to the second town, along a deserted stretch of road, Vicki decided she drank too much coffee and needed a break. She asked the colonel to pull over and make a rest stop.

"Sure, Vicki. Anything you want," Rogers said heartily. "Pull over up ahead, driver. You need some help, Vicki?"

As the truck pulled over and she scrambled out over the front seat, she replied, "No, sir. But thanks anyway."

Rogers gave her a hand getting out of the truck and held on to her arm a little longer than was necessary. He tried to brush the back of her jacket as she adjusted her web gear, but she twisted smartly and accidentally swung her M-16 into

75

him. She apologized and walked off into the wood line, going about fifty meters into the woods. Up a slight hill, she found a thick clump of pines that obscured the view from the road. She waited a few minutes to see if anyone had followed her. She wouldn't have been a bit surprised if Rogers had trailed her. He hung around continually and lacked only his tongue hanging out to complete the picture of being in heat.

She heard a vehicle pull up and the sound of people getting out and talking in German to Rogers. She could hear his high-pitched voice, grating like fingernails on a chalkboard, but could not understand what he said. She picked up her M-16 from the tree she had leaned it against and started back down the hill. She could see an Iltis, a German army jeep, pulled up behind the Blazer. Two German MPs were talking to Rogers and the driver. A third MP stood behind and to the left of the Americans. Vicki noticed something funny about his weapon. The barrel looked out of shape, somehow longer and thicker, than the barrels of the H&K submachine guns that the German MPs normally carried.

Suddenly, the third MP lifted his weapon and shot Rogers and the driver in the back of their heads. All she could hear was a "phhhht, phhhht" and realized the weapon had a silencer. She dropped to the ground and snuggled up to the base of a pine tree while chambering a round in her rifle and flipping off the safety. From where she lay, she could cover the Iltis and two of the three MPs. They were obviously Spetsnaz, Russian Special Forces, dressed as Germans to grab whatever intelligence they could. As one went through the truck, collecting documents, another cut open the protective suits of the two dead Americans, rifled their pockets, and cut the insignia off their battle dress. The gunner moved over to inspect his handiwork. He stepped back and surveyed the woods around him, as though looking for her. Vicki pressed herself closer to the forest floor and turned her head away. She remained there frozen until she heard voices again. She looked up to see the three bogus MPs drive off, following the road to the south.

She waited to make sure they left the area and then scrambled down to the road. Rogers and the driver sprawled lifelessly next to the Blazer, bright scarlet puddles growing about their heads. She steeled herself to touch each man's throat and be sure there was no pulse. Her hand came away clammy with clotting blood, and breakfast rose like a geyser in the back of her throat. When she checked Rogers' body, she saw that the company gossip was correct. He did wear a hairpiece. She caught the scent of his aftershave as she crouched over him. She would never again smell Old Spice without becoming nauseous.

As she bent over the driver's body, a German Iltis with MP markings came around the bend in the road, from where the other one had just disappeared. It seemed to pick up speed and head toward her. She scuttled back behind the front of the truck and leveled her M-16 at the approaching jeep. It stopped, and the passenger climbed out.

"*Hallo. Was ist heir los?*" he called. "Do you need help? Do you speak German? What has happened?"

"Stay where you are." She was proud that her voice did not crack. "One step closer and I'll shoot."

Out of the corner of her eye, she could see the ambushers had not destroyed the radio in the truck. If she could reach the handset, she could get help and capture the Spetsnaz in front of her.

"Please, what is wrong?" the German asked again and started to move toward her.

"One step closer, you sonofabitch, and I'll blow your fucking head off. God help me."

Her voice did crack then, but the German stopped. He turned to his partner and shouted something in German that Vicki did not catch. She could hear the whine of a radio cooling fan start up and the driver speaking into a handset. He paused and then shouted to his partner outside.

The first MP turned to Vicki. "We have asked for help with the American MPs. They will be here soon. Please be careful."

As he spoke, the warbling sound of an emergency siren split the air. It grew louder until a Humvee from the 577th MP Company sped around the corner and screeched to a halt next to the Iltis. When the passenger dismounted, Vicki had no doubt he was genuine. The American walked up to the German with all the strut and swagger of a Georgia state trooper catching a BMW with expired Massachusetts plates in his speed trap, something no Russian Special Forces soldier could ever imitate. As he spoke in low tones with the German, he took off his oversized mirrored sunglasses, folded them up, and hung them from the front pocket of his battle dress.

Finishing with the German, he turned in Vicki's direction and asked in a syrupy, butter-honey drawl so thick it could be spread on toast, "Are you all right? I'm Staff Sergeant McCraw, 577th MPs. The Germans said something about a shooting here."

She challenged him with the current password. When he responded with the correct countersign, she lowered her rifle and stepped away from the truck. The German exhaled audibly, and the two MPs came forward to where she slumped against the front bumper of the truck. She told her story, and within minutes, another MP vehicle from the 577th arrived. An ambulance that took away the remains of Rogers and his driver followed the MPs. She helped the MPs search the truck and confirmed that Rogers' maps and radio codebook were missing. The MPs immediately relayed this information to the group headquarters. The missing CEOI compromised all frequencies, call signs, and passwords for the next seventy-two hours.

After Major Fitzmaurice, the MP company commander, a major from Corps G-2, and the German liaison officer debriefed her, Vicki sat by herself in the group conference room. She stared unseeing at a cup of coffee in front of her and played the incident over in her mind. She did not like Rogers and did not know the driver, Sanchez, a replacement who arrived a few days before. But the manner of their deaths upset her. She could accept death in battle with equanimity, but this was cold-blooded murder. She could not express the difference, but there had to be one. As she sat, staring at her cold coffee, war became something personal for her, and the enemy crystallized into those three Russian soldiers. They became the personification of all Russians, and she resolved to give them the same chance they gave Rogers.

A voice intruded on her thoughts. "Are you okay?"

She looked up to find Ed Chambers standing across the table from her.

"Yeah, I'm all right. Just getting my thoughts together."

"Too bad about Rogers. Did you get a shot at the Gomers?" Ed had picked up the term "Gomers" referring to the Russians from the MP Company and used it frequently in his conversation. He considered that it made him sound like a veteran.

"No," Vicki replied. "I was too busy ducking and making sure they couldn't see me."

"Shit, I would have nailed the three of them if I were you," he said.

Once he was over the shock of the war message, Ed regained his enthusiasm about fighting. He campaigned for reassignment to a line battalion so he could get his Combat Infantryman's Badge and a decoration or two. The war message only increased his eagerness to get where the action would be.

Vicki slammed her coffee cup on the table. The picture of the bleeding, graceless bodies was still vivid in her mind, and she could taste the bile in her mouth.

"Go fuck yourself, buster. There are two dead men down in the hospital, and all you can think of is medals for your record. You're sick."

Ed stepped back, stung by the vehemence of her response. "Hey, they're dead. What can I do about that? Sure, I am thinking of my record. I need something out of this for my future. It's easy for you. You're going back to your business when this is all over. Not everyone is a big-time investment account manager, driving a Mercedes 450 and living in a condo on Commonwealth Avenue. Some of us are soldiers and have to worry about our records."

"Right. Well, if you got a real job in the real world, medals and Officer Efficiency Reports wouldn't be so fucking important." She pushed herself erect and walked out of the conference room. "And the Mercedes is secondhand, asshole," she said as a parting shot. She shoved the door open and literally bumped into Mike.

As she pulled away, he saw the tension and anger in her face. "What's up, Vicki? This afternoon still bothering you?"

"No. Yes. Shit. I don't know." She turned back to face Mike squarely. "Ed's in there, asking me how many of the Russians I killed. I just hid behind that pine tree, hoping they wouldn't see me. Ed thinks I screwed up and says, if he had been there, he would have killed all three and been a hero."

"Different people react different ways to getting shot at." Mike remembered his introduction to combat in the Dominican Republic as a brand-new machine gunner in the Eighty-Second Airborne Division. "The first time I heard live bullets coming in my direction, I was too busy trying to find my platoon sergeant and squad leader to worry about anything. I fired my machine gun, but I didn't hit anything except the island of Hispaniola or maybe the Caribbean. After everything calmed down, I got sick to my stomach and couldn't eat for the next two days. Don't worry about Ed's opinion. Do you think you could have done anything different that would have changed the outcome? Would Rogers and Sanchez still be alive if you had opened fire?"

"I don't know . . ."

"Then don't worry about it. It happened, and you can't change the past. Don't let it affect your job now and in the future. Ed's just jealous that you had the first taste of action. It offends his view of the world that he's been left out of the fighting so far. You know the old slogan, 'Danger's no stranger to an Airborne Ranger.' He believes it."

"Well, he's a perfect ranger. Nineteen-inch neck and six-inch head." Vicki was starting to regain her poise. "He is hung up on that CIB and a medal, though."

"Well, there's probably going to be enough of those going around." Mike started down the hallway toward the war room and then looked back at the young woman. "Vicki, if you need someone to talk to about this, I'm available." He went into the war room. "And Vicki, when the time comes, you'll do good," he said before he closed the door.

Vicki watched him enter the war room and thought, *No, you're not available, major. Doctor McCann has you sewn up tight. Why are all the good men either married or gay?*

2515 Acton Road
West Concord, Massachusetts

When Elizabeth returned from her run with the dogs, the red light on her answering machine was blinking merrily away. She dropped the dogs' leashes and leaped for the playback button, hoping the call was from Mike. The commercial telephone system was still operating, and he had called her from Germany before. Instead, she recognized Jack Adams, an acquaintance from the parish liturgy committee who worked in the city and sometimes rode the commuter train with her. He asked that she call him at home to discuss a medical matter, not an emergency, but a request for some information. Feeling tremendously let down, she fed the dogs and began making a salad for her supper. This was another reminder of Mike's absence. Part of the division of labor in the kitchen was that he made the salads for their meals.

She finished supper and dialed the Adams' number. Jack answered the telephone on the second ring.

When she identified herself, he said, "Elizabeth, I'm glad you called back. Susan and I have been worrying all day, and we need your help. It's really great of you to call back so soon."

"Well, Jack, what's wrong? Is the problem with you or Susan?" Elizabeth responded.

"No, it's not either of us. It's Jack Junior."

"I thought Jack Junior was still in school. Didn't classes just start? He's not home, is he? Did he get hurt in practice?"

"No, he's not home, and he hasn't been hurt. That's part of the problem, you see. The president reinstituted the draft when he announced all these war preparations. Jack just got a notice to report for a pre-induction physical next week. We want you to write a letter saying that he's unfit for service. Tell the army he's got some kind of bone problem that will make him fail the screening. Elizabeth, are you there? Did you hear me?"

She heard him, and the bluntness of the request shook her. "I'm sorry, Jack. Did you say you want me to write a letter saying that your son has a medical problem that prevents him from being drafted?"

His response was brisk and businesslike. "Right, just a short letter addressed to the draft board. I can get you the address—"

"I can't do that," Elizabeth interrupted him. "As far as I know, there is nothing wrong with your son that would prevent his serving in the military. I'm not your regular orthopedist, but if he can play football, there shouldn't be any problem with his pre-induction physical."

"What do you mean you can't write the letter for us?" Jack's voice had raised a few notes on the scale.

"It's not any big deal. It's just like something you do to an insurance company. I'll pay you your regular office fee. Jesus, my son is too smart to go in the army like some dumb street kid out of Southie. He's got his whole life ahead of him, and he can't have the army screw it up."

Thomas and Mary McCann moved to Southie (or South Boston, the traditional home of Irish immigrants) when they left County Clare forty years ago and raised their seven children there. The comments about the army and the dig about Southie heightened Elizabeth's anger another notch.

"Mr. Adams," Elizabeth said, snapping into the telephone "Unlike bankers, doctors have a code of ethics. I will not lend my name to an attempt to deceive anyone, whether it is an insurance company or the United States government. Your son will have to take his chances with the pre-induction physical like everyone else. And judging from the soldiers who are serving in Germany with my husband, your son isn't good enough to be considered in the same breath as them."

She slammed down the telephone, almost cracking the receiver. Laddie, the Black Lab, heard the anger in her voice and scuttled for the basement, some ancient guilt pricking at his conscience. As she stood next to the desk and tried to calm herself, the telephone rang again. She thought it was Adams calling back.

She snatched the receiver off the hook and barked, "I won't write your letter, and if you call me one more time, I will report you to the draft board myself and ask that they expedite your case."

"Oh, really," a mature, cultured female voice said. "Can I count on that? It would be one way to see John again," said Caroline Warren. "If this is a bad time, Doctor, I can call back."

"Mrs. Warren," Elizabeth said, stammering sheepishly. "I just had a disagreement with a neighbor and thought he was calling back. I apologize—"

"That's all right. I've had some of those telephone calls myself. Are you busy now, or should I call back later?"

"No, it's quite all right now. What can I do for you?"

Elizabeth was never quite sure how to deal with Caroline. Mike had served with the colonel for several years, and his active duty training transferred some of the respect due a senior officer to his wife. Caroline was impressive in her own right, though. Her family was old-line Boston Brahmin. She was a product of Smith and Harvard Business School, and she was a senior partner in one of the larger investment firms in Boston. When the headquarters was first alerted for deployment, Caroline had begun putting together a support network for the families of the soldiers and asked Elizabeth to act as her assistant.

"I just got a call from the casualty office at Fort Devens. Peter Rogers has been killed, along with his driver, a soldier named Sanchez. The casualty notification officer has been to see Betty. I am going over and would appreciate very much if you would come with me. I know it's a terrible imposition, but I need the support. Betty and I haven't been close, but I have to see her now."

Elizabeth went cold inside. She did not like either Lieutenant Colonel Rogers or his wife. She was certain the feeling was mutual. Hearing that her husband was dead changed the situation. Whether she liked Betty or not, she had to at least offer what comfort she could.

"Certainly I'll go with you. What about the other man's family? Are we going to see them as well?"

"No, he was not from this area. According to what the people at Devens could tell me, he joined the company in Germany and was only there for a couple days. His home is in Texas." Caroline paused. "It's quarter of seven now. Could I pick you up in a half hour? We can go over to Medford and see Betty tonight."

Elizabeth showered and found a plain black suit to wear. One aspect of her heritage was knowledge of mourning clothes and what to wear to a wake. Funerals, wakes, and all their accouterments were important to the Irish.

Caroline arrived promptly at seven thirty, and the two women set off for Medford in her dark blue Mercedes 430 SLE sedan. Caroline drove down Route 128 with the unconscious élan of the veteran Bay State driver that reduced Elizabeth to a white-knuckled, catatonic state. Slipping between two eighteen-wheelers, the car slid around the exit ramp and onto the local street leading to the Rogers' home. As they pulled up, Elizabeth could see the green military sedan that showed the casualty assistance officer was still present. A distraught captain in dress greens answered their knock on the door and told them that Mrs. Rogers was not accepting visitors.

"She will probably see us," Caroline told the young officer and stepped by him into the house.

They found Betty in the living room, sprawled in an overstuffed chair with a half-filled bottle of scotch on the coffee table in front of her. From her greeting, she clearly had been working on emptying the bottle most of the afternoon.

"Well, if it isn't the lady of the manor and her maid of honor." Betty's slurred voice was almost incomprehensible. "Why are you here? Have you come to gloat? Your husband succeeded. He finally got my Peter killed. I hope you're happy."

"Betty," Caroline said, ignoring the other woman's remarks. "I just heard about Peter's death. Elizabeth and I came to extend our sympathy and ask if there is anything that we can do to help you."

"Yeah, there's something you can do." She shoved herself out of her chair and tried to stand erect. "Get your rich bitch ass out of my house. I don't need your sympathy. Your husband killed my husband. There was no need for him to go to Germany. He had an important job that should have kept him here. But your husband, the big-shot lawyer and war hero, had to drag him over there just to prove how powerful

Colonel John Hancock Warren was." Betty stood away from her chair, weaving slightly, and moved toward Caroline. "I hope he gets killed, just like my poor Peter. I hope you have to go through what I'm going through." She hurled the contents of her highball glass into Caroline's face. "Just get out of my house and my life!" she screamed. "Just go away and leave me alone, and take that toy soldier with you. I don't need anything from you or the goddamned army."

Abruptly, like a puppet with its strings cut, she collapsed in a heap on the floor.

Altendorf, FRG

The opening of hostilities concentrated on the British, Dutch and German forces in Northern Germany and had no immediate direct effect on the rest of NATO. There were no massive missile strikes and no clouds of attack aircraft skimming treetops looking for lucrative targets. There were none of the opening moves that NATO planners had envisioned for the past forty years. The AWACS and Joint STARS aircraft on patrol had some feel for the battle because their radars picked up the opening air strikes, and one or two of the aircraft had to dodge enemy fighters. But the American ground forces were left out of the war.

In fact, the only action against non-German forces in the first twenty-four hours of the war was the ambush of Lieutenant Colonel Rogers and his driver. That attack proved Spetsnaz teams were operating in the Allied rear areas, but the expected wave of Spetsnaz strikes against command and control facilities and logistics operations did not occur. Gradually, the edge began to wear off the Allied soldiers in Southern Germany, particularly within units like the 805th Support Group. It was not that people forgot the threat. It was just that it was so far away as to be almost irrelevant.

Since the end of the Vietnam War and the reorientation of army thought and doctrine toward war in Europe, the Russian Spetsnaz soldier had loomed over support units like a dark, brooding nemesis. In the opening hours of the war, Spetsnaz was coming to get the rear area. His abilities to disguise himself as soldier or civilian, to speak English like your next-door neighbor, and to hide behind a single blade of grass were going to spread panic and devastation throughout the rear areas. For the first twenty-four hours of the war, nothing happened, except the ambush of Rogers and his driver. Everyone said they never really believed all those stories about the Russian commandos who were a cross between Zorro, Batman, and the Scarlet Pimpernel.

One of the few dissenting voices was Colonel Warren. He believed the rear area battle was only being delayed, not forgotten, and he strove to keep the support group at a high level of readiness. He visited commanders daily, stressing the need for alertness and security precautions. One commander told Warren that his battalion was too busy to play grunt. His soldiers were too tired to train in battle skills, so he was cancelling any activities not directly related to the combat service support mission. In any case, if he needed protection, many combat units could protect his activities. Warren treated the staff members present to an awesome display of his temper.

"Colonel," Warren said in a soft, cold voice. "I don't think you get the picture. We are the targets the other side is after. And there is not any guaranteed protection except what we can provide for ourselves. We cannot perform our support mission if we're being overrun or ambushed. Your people may be tired now, but if they don't learn the basics of combat, they're going to be dead. That would be a bad loss. But even worse, if they're dead, their jobs won't get done, and other soldiers will die because of that." Warren paused. "If you have trouble accepting my philosophy, there are ways to soothe your mind. Where's your XO?"

The battalion commander acknowledged Warren's point, and training continued. Warren pushed his staff to visit their counterparts in the subordinate units and emphasize the same message, that teams of Spetsnaz were watching and reconnoitering the unit areas and preparing for attacks. To many members of the group, including some of his own staff, Warren was the little boy who cried wolf. Just how wrong they were became clear, tragically clear, on the morning of August 4, the third day of the war.

The Corps G-1 called a conference to discuss reconstituting units as they pulled out of combat. Sally took Herb Lovell and the assistant S-1, Captain Dave Ouellette, and drove out of town in their pickup truck about ten minutes ahead of Mike, who had a meeting with Colonel Porter. Mike sat in the front seat of his Blazer and tried writing a note to Elizabeth as Ann-Marie drove toward Corps Headquarters.

A loud bang, like a peal of thunder, came from the road to their front. Over the tops of the trees, a ball of black smoke rolled skyward.

Mike threw his note pad into the backseat and said to Ann-Marie, "Get up there fast." He turned to Sergeant First Class O'Brian. "Get on the horn, Top, and tell Net Control Station we have contact with someone or something. Have them send some MPs out here."

As O'Brian began trying to raise the Net Control Station, Ann-Marie floored the accelerator and raced around the bend in the road. As soon as she rounded the curve, she had to slam on her brakes to avoid plowing into the wreckage of a pickup truck sprawled on its roof next to a large crater in the road. "Dumont, you stay with the truck while O'Brian and I secure the area. Top, you go left about fifty meters out, I'll go right. Meet me on the other side of the crater." The engine compartment was missing, cleanly sheared off as though by a knife. All the windows were blown out, and two bundles of limp MOPP suits lay on the ground on the right side of the truck.

As soon as the Blazer stopped, Mike threw open his door and jumped out. He found Ouellette first, spread-eagle on his face, a pool of blood collecting under him. When Mike rolled him over, the man's head lolled limply. Then Mike saw the wound that exposed lungs and intestines.

"Major!" Dumont shouted. "Over here, sir. It's Major Grant."

Mike ran over to where the young woman crouched over an unconscious Sally Grant about six feet from Ouellette's body. Ann-Marie had pulled Sally's field dressing from its pouch on her LBE harness and was trying to apply it over a hole in the officer's face.

"She's bleeding from here and her chest. It's all torn open. I don't think she can breathe."

Mike pulled out his Ka-Bar knife and cut away the front of Sally's MOPP and BDU jackets and T-shirt. A small blue-edged hole below her right breast bubbled blood as the unconscious woman breathed shallowly.

"Shit. It's a sucking chest wound. Shit."

Mike fumbled with his own field dressing, trying desperately to remember the first aid steps. He had to seal the wound from both sides so air would not leak from the lungs.

"If you've got that bandage on her face done, help me lift her up," he said to Ann-Marie. "We have to check and see if there's an exit wound."

Ann-Marie heaved the woman halfway erect and pulled off the remnants of her jackets. She found the exit hole, about the size of a dime, and showed it to Mike. He slit open the plastic pouch containing the dressing and slapped the foil liner across the exit hole.

"Hold this while I cover the front, and then we can get the dressing tied around her."

Ann-Marie nodded and took the bandage from Mike. She was pale and grimacing as she held up Sally and helped Mike tie off the dressing.

She laid the wounded officer down as they finished and then gasped. "My God. Her foot. It's gone."

Dumont lunged across Sally's body and grabbed the calf of Grant's right leg. The leg ended there. Instead of a foot, there was a bloody mass of muscle, bone, and flesh. Blood pulsed brightly in the sun as the arteries pumped in time with the labored beating of Sally's heart. Ann-Marie pulled up the leg to a vertical position while Mike fumbled under his own jacket and pulled off his belt. He wrapped the belt around Sally's leg and slowly tightened it until the flow of blood subsided. Ann-Marie took her own field dressing and wrapped it around the stump.

"I got a medevac on the way, sir!" O'Brian shouted. "And there's two MP patrols around the corner and should be here in five minutes."

In the background, Mike could hear the sirens start their warbling cry. He shook himself and stood erect. As close as he felt to Sally, he had other responsibilities.

"Okay, Dumont, thanks. Go back to the vehicle and keep a watch off toward that wood line across the fields. I'll take a look around here and see if I can find anything else."

Ann-Marie stood up. "Sergeant Lovell was the driver, sir. I want to look for him."

She turned and walked toward the ruined truck. She found Lovell, still in the cab of the truck, dead. A dust-off helicopter darted over the treetops as O'Brian ran out into the clover field next to the road and threw a red smoke grenade about ten meters in front of the trucks. The UH 1 Huey fluttered down, and the medic ran over to where Mike stood.

"What do you have, Major?" the medic asked Mike.

"I've got one wounded, with a traumatic amputation of the lower right leg, a sucking chest wound, and a face wound," he replied, handing the medic a printed casualty tag for Sally Grant."

"Your radio message said three . . ."

"The other two are dead. Just get this one to the hospital."

O'Brian and the helicopter's crew chief followed with a stretcher. The four men rolled Sally on the litter and carried her back to the helicopter. The aircrew strapped the litter in place, and the medic began inserting IV tubes as the pilots wound the engine up for takeoff.

Ann-Marie had followed them out to the helicopter and watched as the wounded officer was loaded on the aircraft. As the dust-off helicopter completed its takeoff, she started walking back toward the trucks and stumbled over something lying in the road. She bent over to pick it up and began retching violently. When Mike ran over to her, she turned and wordlessly handed him a leather and nylon jungle boot, with a foot still in it. A dog tag dangled from one of the laces, Sally's.

337 Cambridge Street
Boston, Massachusetts

Elizabeth sat at her desk going through the normal routine paperwork—case notes, consultation sheets, and insurance reports—when her beeper sounded. When she picked up the little box to turn it off, she saw the call was from St. Brendan's Trauma Center. She reached over and punched a button on her telephone.

"Doctor McCann here. I'm on my way over. What's going on?"

"A load of wounded from Europe is arriving at Logan, Doctor. There are seventy wounded on the aircraft, and we are going to get twenty-five of them."

Elizabeth hung up the telephone and felt her insides knot up in a ball. She had not heard from Mike since the war started five days ago. She realized now that no news might be good news in peacetime, but in wartime, when your husband was somewhere close to the front lines, no news was terrifying.

She caught a cab for the four-block drive to the hospital. A large yellow ribbon waved from the antenna. Inside the cab, the driver had hung a small American flag from his rearview mirror. She half-listened as the cab driver complained about the Red Sox and the summer weather in Boston. She found herself wondering why the driver was in Boston and her husband was in Germany. It just was not fair.

The cab finally pulled up near the emergency room entrance. Elizabeth looked at the meter, thankful to be getting away from the driver's drone of comments, and fumbled in her wallet for the fare.

"You work here? You a doctor or a nurse?" the driver asked, turning to face her.

"I'm an orthopedist on the trauma team," Elizabeth said.

"You guys are getting the wounded from Germany, ain't ya?"

"Yes, we are. In fact, some are due in now. That's why I'm here."

"My kid's over there, in Germany. He's a sergeant, a tank commander. All of twenty years old. Take care of him and his buddies, Doc." The driver reached over and blanked out the meter. "This ride's on me."

Operating Theater 3, St. Brendan's Hospital
Boston, Massachusetts

Elizabeth was scrubbed up and gowned as the first ambulances pulled up. The triage team began sorting out the wounded and directing them to the appropriate operating rooms. The orderlies pushed one bandaged and blanketed form into Elizabeth's theater and gently swung the patient onto the operating table. Elizabeth waved her team into action and reached for the casualty tag hanging from the patient's stretcher. The face was heavily bandaged with only the nose and mouth exposed. Long blonde hair, matted with dirt and dried blood, showed that this soldier was a woman.

Elizabeth's first thought was an involuntary, *oh, thank God it's not Mike.*

She thrust that thought away angrily and absently scanned the patient identification data and felt her world lurch to a halt. The devastated body on the table in front of her was her oldest, dearest friend. Her relief at finding a woman patient and not her husband vanished like rainwater in an Arizona summer.

How could this happen? How could Sally—so alive, so vigorous, so Sally—be this broken bleeding piece of flesh on my table?

NAME: Grant, Sarah K
RANK/SSAN: MAJOR/143-50-7843
BRANCH/MOS: AVN/41A05
BLD TYP/REL: A+/Prot

WOUND: Traumatic amputation, (R) foot; fragment wound (R) chest, broken clavicle; fragment wound, face; broken jaw; Tracheotomy performed 040746 Aug, qtr grain morphine 040746 Aug, 3 units whole blood, 1 unit albumin.

"Oh, goddamn them all. Just goddamn them all."

Her operating team froze. Dr. McCann never showed emotion in the operating theater.

"Goddamn the Russians and all their works."

The war was now something very personal.

Doctor's Lounge
St. Brendan's Hospital, Boston, Massachusetts

Elizabeth left the operating theater drained physically and emotionally and went to the doctor's lounge. She had worked on four patients after Sally. None was as critical as Sally, but late twentieth-century high-tech weaponry is not respectful of the human body, so repairing the damage is closely akin to trying to put Humpty Dumpty together again. She dropped her cap and mask in a wastebasket and shook her hair free while she made a cup of herbal tea. She collapsed in an easy chair and stared into the teacup, trying to lose herself and her thoughts in the brewing mixture.

"Doctor McCann." An orderly stuck his head into the lounge. "There's a man out here who wants to talk to you. Shall I tell him that you're busy?"

"No, I'll be right there." She heaved herself out of the chair and chugged her tea as she walked to the door. The orderly pointed silently to a middle-aged man, dressed in an L.L. Bean windbreaker, chinos, and deck shoes, seated on a couch in the hallway. His salt-and-pepper beard stood out starkly against his pallid face. It was Sally's husband, Mark Cooper.

Elizabeth sat down on the couch and hugged him. She could see his eyes were red from crying.

"How is she? Elizabeth, they won't let me see her. All the army or the hospital will tell me is that she's been wounded severely enough to be brought here, but no one will say how she is. The hospital said she's in the ICU, but no one can see her."

"Sally is alive and should recover," Elizabeth said. "Here, sit down. Sally has lost her right foot and has been wounded in the chest and face, but there's no permanent damage there."

"Her foot? Lost what?"

"It's what we call a traumatic amputation, probably from some kind of an explosion. I think a bomb or a land mine, particularly with the other wounds."

"How do you know what happened to her?"

"Because she was my first patient this morning. I read the casualty tag that the field hospital in Germany had put on her. Right now, she's in the ICU because she's in critical condition, but that's normal for someone with her injuries. There are no signs of any other complications." Elizabeth stood up and pulled on his arm. "Come on. I'll find out what the story is in ICU, and maybe I can sneak you in."

Mark stayed seated, in a daze as if someone had beaten him over the head with a baseball bat. "Lost her foot?" he said groggily. "What do I tell the kids? Their mother's lost a foot? She's going to be a cripple for the rest of her life. She'll live in a wheelchair?"

Elizabeth's frustration and tension boiled up and out. "You can tell them that she is alive and should recover completely." Her voice hardened as it did when she got angry. "Yes, she's badly wounded, but she's alive. That's more than some parents will be telling their children. Betty Rogers would be more than happy to tell her children that their father lost a foot, but she can't. She has to tell them he's dead. Sally is going to need support from all of us to help her pull through. It won't be easy for anyone. But she is alive."

Chapter 6

Nothing So Exhilarating

Nothing in life is so exhilarating as to be shot at without result.

—Winston Churchill
Highway B-455
Vicinity Heidenkopf, FRG

Ed Chambers was beginning to feel left out. So far, the war had been going on for five days, and the only people in the headquarters to see any action were his boss and two women. He had finished his plan for the defense of the company's sector of the town and given it to Bill Sherwood, who gladly accepted it. Colonel Warren had expressed satisfaction with His plan, but when Ed sought a transfer to a real unit, Warren had not been encouraging.

Now, he and Fitzmaurice were returning to Altendorf from a meeting at the headquarters of the Division Support Command of the 16th Mechanized Division. The Sixteenth was the division in front of the support group, and questions about boundaries and other coordination matters had become rather acrimonious in the past few days.

The unseasonal torrential rain that arrived two days before made the trip a slow and depressing drive. Halfway to Lauterbach, the truck coughed twice and stuttered to a stop in the middle of the road. When Mike tried to start it, nothing happened. The starter wouldn't even turn over. Ed reached in back for the radio handset. When he tried to call the Net Control Station, he couldn't even get the hiss of the carrier wave.

"Fucking truck is completely dead." Mike smashed his fist against the steering wheel. "I think the electrical system shit the bed."

"I saw a farmhouse off the road, about a hundred meters back up the road, boss," Ed told him. "I could see the lights anyway. How about if I go back there and ask to use their phone to call the company and get a wrecker out here?"

"Okay, you take a run back there. I'll look under the hood and see if I figure out what happened to this truck." As Ed started to get out of the truck, he said, "Take your weapon with you."

"Right, boss. I know. We're in Indian country," Ed said, barely muffling the exasperation in his voice.

Ever since Major Grant's ambush, Fitzmaurice had become a fanatic about preparing for an enemy attack. In Ed's mind, any Russian special operations teams were well out of the area, if not phantoms of the major's imagining. Ed tolerated the emphasis on increased alertness but personally considered the likelihood of attack very low.

The farmhouse was a cold and wet ten-minute walk from where the truck had broken down. As Ed approached the house, he could see lights on in all the windows but no other sign of life. He went up to the front door, slung his M-16 over his right shoulder, and knocked on the door. When there was no answer, he knocked again, hard enough to jar the door open. He could hear a radio playing rock music and smell burnt chicken.

He called out "*Hallo, Sind jemann zu haus?*" in badly fractured German.

There was no reply. He pushed the door open further and looked around. He couldn't see anyone, but the house did not look abandoned. He stepped into the front hallway. The living room opened off to his left, and he saw a couch, two overstuffed chairs, and a television visible through the entranceway. The television was on, showing a German translation of an American adventure show. To the right was the dining room, the table set for supper. Something caused the small hairs on the back of his neck to stand erect, and he swung his rifle off his shoulder to port arms. He chambered a round and flipped off the safety.

He began moving down the hallway to his front, sidling along with his back to the wall. When he came to a door, he pushed it open with the muzzle of his rifle, took a deep breath, and spun into the room in a crouch. It was the master bedroom and empty of occupants. He saw a telephone on a nightstand and slowly tiptoed over to pick it up. There was no dial tone, and when he looked down, he could see where the wire had been cut at the wall plug. He continued to check the rooms, finding no trace of the homeowners. He found one other telephone, its wire was also cut. When he entered the kitchen, a fine haze over the stove showed the supper meal of chicken slowly charring to waste. He stepped in to turn the stove off and noticed a scattering of small, brown specks leading to a door. Pulling the door open, Ed discovered it led to the basement. There he found the family that had lived in the house. A man and woman in their mid-fifties, a woman in her twenties, two teenaged boys, and a ten-year-old girl lay piled in the corner of the basement. Each one was bound, gagged, and shot once in the back of the neck.

He never remembered anything about the run back to the truck until he threw himself in the passenger seat next to Mike.

"Christ, boss, they're all dead. Every one of them."

"Ed, what's wrong? Who's dead? Did you find a telephone?" Mike asked. "What the hell happened to you?"

"The family in the farmhouse. They're all dead. They're tied up in the cellar, and everyone is shot in the back of the head. Somebody fucking executed them. And the bodies are still warm, so whoever did it is still around here."

"Fuck me. Okay, let's get away from the truck for the time being. The electrical system is dead, so we can't use the radio. I thought I saw a clump of trees up ahead. Get the maps and notebooks. We'll move up there and wait for someone to come by. The MPs should be running some kind of road patrols."

"Okay, I've got everything," Chambers answered. "You go first, and I'll cover you from here."

Mike ran up the side of the road to the clump of trees he had seen earlier. As Ed joined him, he found that the trees surrounded a weathered roadside shrine. Age had worn smooth the features on the crucifix, and the pedestal was split in several places from exposure to decades of German weather. The shrine itself sat in a half-moon-shaped pit, the open end facing the road with a semicircular berm about four feet high enclosing the rest of the area. The Americans threw themselves on the ground beside the pedestal, Ed watching the open field to their rear and Mike watching the road and the field across the way. The rain continued to fall in intermittent squalls, cutting their sight to less than ten meters during the downpours and then letting up and allowing them to see out to the wood lines on either side of their position.

Mike paused and stiffened as he saw something move across the road near the abandoned truck. "Ed," he whispered. "Do you see anything out behind us? I think I picked up some movement by the Blazer."

Ed peered out across the open pasture behind the shrine. "No, I don't see anything out here. When the rain lets up, I can see about fifty meters, and that's out to the wood line. Maybe it was just one of those wild boars you're always talking about."

"Not unless boars have started walking on their hind legs. Goddamn this rain. I can't see shit."

"Boss, I hear something that sounds like splashing. Sounds as though something is moving across the field over here," Ed whispered.

Suddenly, a brilliant orange flash split the night as the truck blew up. The concussion knocked branches down on them, and the glare momentarily blinded Mike.

As he shook his head, trying to clear the lights dancing in his eyes, Ed kicked frantically at his legs and whispered hoarsely, "I see one. I see one. He's over by the wood line. Looks like he's got some kind of rocket launcher."

Ed's M-16 shattered the night a second time as he fired at the black blob he had detected. Before he could tell whether he had hit his target, two rifles opened up on him from the wood line.

"I guess they aren't wild boar after all." Ed grunted as he switched magazines on his rifle.

Bullets chipped the stone crucifix and spanged wildly off into the darkness. Ed rolled about six feet to his left and fired again, this time in tightly controlled bursts of three or four rounds rather than the magazine emptying full automatic of his first salvo. Mike slid around to the left side of the monument and started firing at one set of muzzle flashes. The afterimages from the explosion of the Blazer had disappeared, and he could again see clearly.

"It looks like there are three of them. At least there are three muzzle flashes. Maybe we found our Spetsnaz team after all," Mike said. As quickly as it began, the firing died out. "Are you okay, Ed?"

"Fine. They were shooting high and didn't even come close."

"Don't get smug. We probably shot just as high and just as wide. I think what hit the truck was a rocket-propelled grenade. If it was, we had better move away from here before they try a second round at us."

As Mike spoke, almost as if someone had heard him, a red flower blossomed in the wood line, and a ball of flame arced out toward the monument where the two men lay. The rocket-propelled grenade struck the crucifix halfway up the column and severed the shaft. Fragments of stone and hot metal rained down on the two Americans huddled in the floor of the pit. The top part of the monument toppled over and fell to the ground in front of the pedestal.

Before the two Americans could lift their heads, a hail of machine gun fire swept the top of the berm they sheltered behind. Some of the rounds tore into the berm itself; others passed over and struck the shattered pedestal, bouncing crazily into the air. Mike and Ed automatically curled into balls as a cloud of granite chips enveloped them. Through the whines and cracks of the ricochets, Ed could hear Mike reciting an ancient mantra of combat soldiers through the ages.

"I don't believe this shit. I just fucking don't believe this shit."

The machine gun paused, and Ed slowly peeked over the berm. A black shape suddenly erupted in front of him, about ten meters away. It ran toward the Americans, firing an automatic weapon from the hip in short bursts of three or four rounds that clipped branches from the bushes the Americans hid beneath. The shock of this apparition springing from the ground momentarily froze Chambers. Ed couldn't react to the speed at which death was closing in on him.

"Motherfucker!" Mike roared as he caught sight of the Russian in the corner of his eye. "You bastard cocksucker!" he shouted as he rolled over and sprayed the onrushing enemy soldier with a long burst from his own rifle that died abruptly.

The impact of the 5.56 mm rounds at less than ten feet threw the Russian backward and knocked the rifle from his hands. A second Russian stuck his rifle over the lip of the berm separating the two sides and started shooting blindly into the pit. Mike dropped his useless M-16, grabbed the barrel of the other weapon, and yanked it toward him. The Russian pulled back, and the two men settled into a deadly game of tug-of-war.

"Shoot the son of a bitch, Ed!" Mike yelled as he pulled on the rifle. "Shoot the son of a bitch!"

Ed snapped out of his shock, crawled forward, and fired into the darkness. A choking cry indicated that he scored some kind of a hit. He pulled the trigger three more times, and the cry cut off abruptly. Mike fell back into the pit, holding the other weapon by the barrel. He looked at it, shook his head, and threw it to one side.

"Fucking thing didn't jam, the magazine spring gave out, and the fucking magazine fell out. Beautiful. Just fucking beautiful. We're in the middle of a goddamned firefight, and my rifle quits on me." Slamming another magazine into the M-16, he slid up the berm beside Ed. "Can you see anything out there? Any sign of movement?"

"No, nothing. Where did those two come from? How did they get so close?"

Ed was panting with excitement. His mouth felt as though it was full of cotton balls, and he had an overwhelming desire to urinate. He glanced over at Mike, who was coolly watching his side of the field. The near brush with death appeared to have left the major unruffled, and Ed hated him for it in a momentary, blinding flash of loathing.

"Who knows?" Mike answered curtly. "Maybe they snuck up during the rain. Just keep watching and make sure their buddies don't repeat the trick."

Something crashed into the branches above their heads. Mike yelled, "Grenade! Get out!" And he rolled over the top of the berm.

Ed followed suit, only to find himself sliding through a puddle of slimy liquid. He put his hands out to stop his fall and touched the body of the first enemy soldier they had killed. Ed's hands were in the wound torn into the man's torso by the bullets that killed him. Ed was wrist-deep in entrails and vomited violently. After what seemed to be several eternities, Mike stirred, crawled to the lip of the gully, and slowly looked around their field.

He slid to where Ed lay and whispered, "I think they're gone. Move out directly backward toward the road. When you get there, let me know, and I'll join you. I'll cover you from here."

Ed wormed his way about ten meters backward and slipped up the shoulder of the road. "Okay, boss, I'm here."

A faint rustle of sodden grass and standing rainwater told him that Mike was moving toward his new position. As the two men crouched there, deciding what to do next, they heard the chugging of an approaching diesel engine.

A Humvee with its service drive headlights on came around a bend in the road about sixty meters from them. A gunner manning the rooftop M-60 machine gun was faintly visible against the night sky. When the Humvee caught sight of the burning truck in the road, it slammed to a stop, and the headlights went out as the engine idled. Ed and Mike could hear the machine gunner nervously charge his weapon and begin swinging it to either side of the road. They could also hear the rushing hiss of a radio transmission begin. The engine changed pitch as the Humvee backed up and pulled off the road into a defilade position with just the machine gun exposed.

"Okay, Ranger," Mike said to Ed. "What do we do now?"

"Well, if they're MPs, we'll get them to call the company and report that we're okay and get us a ride back to Altendorf."

"How do we know that they're really MPs and not friends of the guys who just played grenade tag with us?" Ed whispered.

"There's only one way to find out," Mike answered.

"Do you know today's challenge and countersign? I forgot the goddamned thing."

"Yeah, it's gateway platters."

"Right. Cover me while I find out whether these guys are legit or not." Mike began to crawl down the shoulder toward the parked vehicle. When he came opposite it, he called out softly, "Any of you guys know where the gateway is?"

Mike could hear muffled voices from the other side of the road. From the sounds, at least two people had dismounted from the Humvee and positioned themselves about ten meters up and down the road from it. He could see the machine gunner swing his weapon to cover where the voice had come from, and he could hear M-16 bolts clicking as rounds were chambered.

After several sweat-soaked, stomach-churning minutes, a voice came from across the road, "No, but I got some platters over here if you want them."

"Two friendlies coming in!" Mike shouted as he stood up and rushed across the road.

Ed joined him at the MP vehicle. After a few tense moments presenting cards to verify identities, Mike got on the radio and reported the ambush to the group headquarters. The MPs reported the incident to their command post and asked for backup. Within fifteen minutes, four more MP patrols arrived on the scene.

A helicopter swept the wood lines on either side of the road with its night vision devices but found nothing. The only solid traces of the ambush team were the two bodies, dressed in *Bundeswehr* uniforms, by the roadside crucifix. These were wrapped in body bags by a graves registration team that arrived shortly after the last MP patrol who took them to the morgue at the 302nd Combat Support Hospital in Schotten.

As the graves registration team was preparing to move the bodies, Mike sat in the back door of an ambulance having his hands treated. In the fight, when he had grabbed the barrel of the AK-74, he had burned both hands, as well as torn his left hand on the front sight of the Russian rifle.

"Well, boss, we won. We showed those guys not to fuck with the 805th," Ed said as he walked up. "I guess we should get something out of this. After all, we did stop one Spetsnaz team all by ourselves. That should be worth at least a Bronze Star."

Mike watched silently as the graves registration team wrapped the last body in a body bag and laid it on a stretcher. If he had delayed a split second during the firefight, he would have been the one they were bagging and tagging. What Ed said finally sank into his consciousness.

He looked up at his companion. "We got something out of this already, Ed, and it's all we really need."

"Yeah, what's that?"

"Our lives." He stood aside, and the graves registration team loaded the bodies of the dead Russians on their truck.

Evergreen Cemetery
Medford, Massachusetts

Caroline kept an eye on the obituaries and called Elizabeth the evening before Rogers' funeral and burial. They both felt obligated to attend the funeral to show Betty that they were with her in her grief.

Betty refused to allow her husband to be interred in the Cape Cod National Cemetery, so the burial took place in a local cemetery in Medford. She fought with her children, but she eventually gave in over the trappings of a military ceremony. The solemn presence of uniformed pallbearers, firing squad, and flag-draped coffin mocked the beautiful summer's day. Betty was heavily draped in black dress and veil and clung like a barnacle to her oldest son's right arm. She sat rigidly throughout the church service and graveside rites. She did not flinch when the three volleys were fired and the plaintive notes of "Taps" sounded through the graveyard.

The commander of the honor guard, a lieutenant colonel preparing to take his battalion overseas, accepted the folded flag from the pallbearers, knelt in front of the family, and held it out to Betty.

"Ma'am," he said in a loud but solemn voice. "On behalf of the president of the United States and the people of a grateful nation, may I present this flag as a token of appreciation for the honorable and faithful service your loved one rendered this nation."

"I don't want your flag. Just go away and leave me alone." Betty jerked erect and knocked the flag from the officer's hands. She abruptly subsided into great, body-wracking sobs.

As the startled officer stepped back, unsure whether to try to comfort the widow or retrieve the flag, her oldest son stepped to his mother's side and took her into his arms. As he murmured comfortingly to her, his sister faced the crowd and thanked them for coming. She asked that they leave quietly and allow the family to be alone. Betty walked woodenly to a waiting car surrounded by her children and relatives.

Chapter 7

Paying the Price—First Installment

Blood is the price of victory.
—Karl von Clausewitz

Intensive Care Unit
St. Brendan's Hospital, Boston, Massachusetts

Elizabeth returned to the ICU the day after Sally's admission. The head nurse told her that Sally was awake but not aware of her situation.

"She's depressed, Doctor." The nurse finished her report. "She's upset about something and won't talk about it to anyone. She just lies in bed and stares into space."

Elizabeth read the charts at the nurse's station and went to see her friend. She found Sally dozing, surrounded by the IV tubes and monitors common to all ICU patients. The curtains on the windows were half-opened. If she strained her neck, Elizabeth could see the sailboats on the Charles. Instinctively, she reached in the pocket of her white lab coat for her stethoscope as she approached Sally. She caught herself and instead moved to close the curtains and block the sunlight that flowed into the room.

"It's okay," a weak, tired voice said. "I'm awake, nurse. Please leave them open." The voice was distorted as though it were coming between clenched teeth. Sally's jaws had been wired together.

Elizabeth turned to the bed and leaned over the recumbent figure on it. "Hi, Sally," she said softly. "How do you feel this morning?"

"Beth? Is that you? Are you here?" At the sound of a familiar voice, Sally tried to sit up. She struggled to pick her head up a few inches from the pillows and then fell back down.

"Take it easy," Elizabeth told her. She put one hand on Sally's chest and reached for her right hand to take the other woman's pulse. "You need your rest for now." The pulse was weak but regular. "I came by to check on how you're doing and talk to the staff here."

As Elizabeth took her pulse, Sally gripped the other woman's hand with both of hers in a viselike grip. "Beth? Beth?" she said in a weak voice. "Is it really you? Where am I?"

Elizabeth patted her friend's hand. "Easy, Sally. Easy. You're safe in Boston now."

"What happened to me? All I remember is a loud bang and a lot of lights."

"Your truck was destroyed when it ran over a land mine. That was three days ago. We've kept you sedated until now."

"Do you know what happened to Herb and Dave? They were with me. We were going to a G-1 meeting. Are they all right?" In her agitation, Sally tried again weakly to sit up.

"You're the only person from the group that I've seen here at St Brendan's," she answered. "I don't know if anyone else was sent to another hospital."

Sally's grip relaxed, and she sank back on her pillow. Elizabeth quickly scanned the monitors grouped about the head of her bed and saw all were in the normal range.

"You're doing well, Sal. In fact, you're doing a little better than we expected. If you're up to it, I'll change my instructions to the staff to allow visitors. I'm sure Mark is waiting to see you. I told him that I would call him as soon as you were able to have visitors."

Sally's grip on Elizabeth's hand tightened. "I don't want to see him. Don't let him in. I don't want to see him." Sally repeated herself. "Please don't let him in." Elizabeth saw that Sally's heartbeat was picking up and her body was stiffening as well. Something about the thought of meeting her husband was upsetting her.

"Well, okay. If that's what you want, I won't change anything right now. We can talk about this later when I come back to see you." Elizabeth tucked Sally's hands under the bed sheet and turned to leave. "I have to complete my rounds, but I'll come back before I leave the hospital."

The ICU supervisor told Elizabeth that she had a visitor in the waiting room. Elizabeth walked over to the waiting room, expecting to see Mark Cooper and wondering how to explain Sally's request.

Her visitor was a young man dressed in a blue pinstripe suit, blue oxford shirt, and red foulard tie.

He stood up as Elizabeth entered. "Are you Doctor Elizabeth McCann?"

"Yes, I am. Can I help you?"

He produced a business card and held it out to her. "My name is Peter Lawrence. I am a junior partner at Warren, Warren, and Hill. We are representing Major Grant," he said in a deep, grave voice. "Major Grant's commander has retained the firm to represent her in divorce proceedings."

"Divorce? Sally? Are you serious?"

"Quite serious, Elizabeth," a voice said behind her. She turned to find Caroline entering the room. "John called me this morning before he talked to his brother Bill. When they inventoried Sally's personal effects, they found a letter from

Mark. It said he had decided to ask for a divorce because she chose the army over him and the children."

"Caroline, I don't believe this. Who said they found such a letter?"

"John wanted me to be here when Peter asked you about seeing Sally because we know how close you two are. As far as the letter goes, Mike found it when he was inventorying Sally's effects yesterday. Mark is asking for custody of the children because Sally showed herself to be a poor mother by not resigning from the army when she had the chance. John decided to have the firm act for Sally."

As Elizabeth entered the ICU following her morning rounds, she found three men in uniform in the hospital waiting area. One was Tom Bradley, Mike's West Point roommate. The second was a white-haired man in his mid-sixties, still vigorous looking and wearing the silver eagles of an army full colonel on his green uniform. The third man was also in his mid-sixties, and he wore sergeant major chevrons on his uniform. He held a leather briefcase in his lap as he read a two-week-old copy of *People* magazine.

Tom saw Elizabeth enter the room and stood up to introduce her to his companions. "Good morning, Dr. McCann. I'd like you to meet Colonel Carter and Sergeant Major Woodhouse. Colonel, Sergeant Major, Dr. McCann. She is Major Grant's physician, running partner, and best friend."

The colonel sprang up and took Elizabeth's hand in a surprisingly strong grip. She saw that he had an impressive amount of ribbons on the blouse of his army greens, framed top and bottom by a CIB and Airborne wings. On the right shoulder of his blouse, he wore a patch Elizabeth recognized as the First Cavalry Division. John Warren wore the same patch on his right shoulder, a sign that both men had served with that unit in combat.

"Dr. McCann," the colonel said, "I'm very glad to meet you. Lieutenant Colonel Bradley has been telling us quite a bit about you on our ride in from Fort Devens. I must admit that you don't appear quite as ferocious as he described. Do you really devour army officers for breakfast?" Tom had the good grace to blush at this remark. The colonel spoke more. "Sergeant Major Woodhouse and I are here representing the Commanding General, First US Army. We are both recalled retirees. We have some awards to present to Major Grant, if you approve and she can have visitors."

"Please, Colonel, Sergeant Major, sit down." The two retired soldiers reminded her of her father-in-law. She wondered briefly if he had been recalled to duty. "I'm sure that Lieutenant Colonel Bradley exaggerated his description. What awards are you talking about?"

"A Purple Heart for one, Doctor, and some others that the unit put her in for after she left. She probably doesn't know about them," the sergeant major answered.

The sergeant major was a portly, bald man whose greens fit rather snugly. He lacked the CIB, Airborne wings, and Ranger tab the general wore, but he too wore a patch on the right shoulder of his blouse. Both men might be balding, somewhat overweight recalled retirees now, but in their younger days, they had been warriors.

"The colonel and I have been recalled to do administrative work with the survivor assistance office at Fort Devens. Part of it is visiting wounded and their families to present them with awards. We also check into their situations and see if there are any problems that the army may be able to help solve. That's where we work closely with Lieutenant Colonel Bradley and his IG shop."

"Sally does have a problem in addition to her wounds," Elizabeth said. "Let me check on her. If she is up to having visitors and is willing to see you, I'll come back and get you."

Elizabeth found Sally half-reclining in her bed. Sally had talked the nursing staff into elevating the top end of her bed so she could watch television and look out the window of her room. The cable news report caught her attention, and she didn't notice Elizabeth until the doctor stood over the foot of her bed.

"Good morning, and how are we doing this morning?" Elizabeth asked in a burlesque of the nurse's greeting as she picked up Sally's chart. "We seem to be doing fine today."

"Beth, it's you." Sally was more alert today. "And my foot that isn't there itches like mad."

Elizabeth took Sally's wrist to check her pulse. "The itching is a normal symptom of the amputation. It will subside in a few days." Both women had decided that they would not sugarcoat Sally's wounds.

Elizabeth dropped Sally's wrist and picked up her chart again to make a note. According to the night nurse's report, the stump of Sally's leg was healing well. There were no signs of infection in the leg, chest, or jaw wounds.

"I'm planning to move you out of the ICU in four or five days if you continue to heal as well as you have been. Now, are you up for visitors? Medically, you are and can see people for short periods. But you have to decide if you want to let them in. Tom Bradley has a colonel and a sergeant major outside in the waiting room. They are here to give you some awards. If you want to see them, I'll bring them in."

Sally nodded and said quietly, "Okay, you can bring them in."

Elizabeth led the three soldiers to Sally's bedside. Tom Bradley inhaled sharply when he saw Sally's injuries, then quickly controlled himself. Sergeant Major Woodhouse set his briefcase on the table next to Sally's bed and handed Colonel Carter a green vinyl folder embossed with the Department of the Army seal.

"Attention to orders," Colonel Carter said as he opened the folder. "The following award is announced. The Bronze

Star Medal for meritorious service is awarded to Major Sarah K. Grant, US Army Aviation, Headquarters and Headquarters Company, 805th Support Group."

The citation described Sally's key role in preparing the unit for mobilization and deployment from Fort Devens to Germany and her part in establishing the smooth operation of the entire five thousand-person support group in country. When he finished reading the citation, Sergeant Major Woodhouse handed him a second folder.

"The Purple Heart medal is awarded to Major Sarah K. Grant for wounds received as a direct result of hostile action."

As Carter read the citations, Sally's left hand began to curl and twitch. Elizabeth reached out and grasped it tightly in her own.

Carter pulled a separate sheet from inside the folder. "Major Grant is also awarded the European Campaign Medal with one battle star and the National Defense Service Medal."

The sergeant major produced a black velvet pillow with the four medals pinned to it. Colonel Carter removed each and stepped up to pin them on the pillow next to Sally's head. Sergeant Major Woodhouse replaced the velvet pillow in his briefcase as Colonel Carter closed the two binders and set them on the night table next to Sally's bed. Then, all three soldiers came to attention and saluted her. They held their salutes for a count of ten and dropped them. As the three men saluted her, Sally closed her eyes and nodded. Elizabeth could see tears forming on her eyelids.

Elizabeth leaned over Sally and whispered softly, "Are you all right, Sal?"

The other woman nodded silently with her eyes still closed. Then she opened them to look at the four medals pinned to her pillow. She gently touched each and then began to stroke the Purple Heart slowly.

Chapter 8

Just Before the Battle

Just before the battle, mother, I am thinking most of you,
While upon the field we're watching, With the enemy in view.
Comrades brave are 'round me lying, Filled with thoughts of home and God
For well they know that on the morrow, Some will sleep beneath the sod.

—Just Before the Battle, Mother
(American Civil War)

Pickup Zone Borodino
VIC Dermbach DDR

The Russian 875th Air Assault Battalion considered itself the division's elite. The soldiers trained long and hard for their role in leading the division's attack. Now their moment had arrived, and they loaded their MI-17 helicopters with eagerness and anticipation. The battalion lifted off on schedule heading for their objective, a town called Altendorf, a key road junction located in the Americans' rear area and the division's final objective for the first day's attack.

The battalion would seize and hold the town and its bridges until one of the two first echelon tank regiments linked up with them. The town's garrison, American support troops, and German territorials would be no match for the air assault soldiers. The battalion commander sat in the lead helicopter as it skimmed the treetops, with the rest of the thirteen helicopters carrying his battalion trailing in groups of threes. He was confident that he had solved all possible problems during the training period and he could count on the aircrews to deliver the battalion to the landing zones outside Altendorf successfully.

The planning and training had covered everything—except high-tension lines strung across the valley the battalion was using as its final approach into Altendorf. The cables were not marked on anyone's maps and were invisible in the pre-dawn darkness until the lead helicopter flew into them. The pilot had time to curse into the intercom as the cables wrapped themselves around the rotor mast and tore the blades from his aircraft. At sixty feet above the ground, there was no time to recover, and the fireball marking the graves of the aircrew and soldiers lit the valley. The two trailing aircraft immediately broke up and down to clear the wire hazard. Number two dropped below the wires and found a "widowmaker," the only pine tree in the area that was a hundred feet tall. The impact of the helicopter into the tree split the nose of the aircraft and spilled its load of troops over the forest floor. The wreckage of number two joined the remains of the lead in a funeral pyre that rapidly spread through the dry forest floor. The fire served one positive purpose. It illuminated a second bank of wires strung slightly higher than the first. The pilot of the third MI-17 had just enough time to recognize the new wire hazard as he flew into it and it tore him from the sky, adding another beacon to light the morning sky.

The second, third, and fourth chalks of aircraft trailed the lead by enough distance to be able to react by raising their altitude to above one hundred and fifty feet. The rapid climb caused many of the soldiers in their troop bays to become violently ill. The fourth chalk climbed above the rim of the valley and right into the beam of an air defense radar system. The American operator broadcast a warning to all his fire units, and a dozen gunners began looking for targets. The Chaparral air defense systems picked up the helicopters' heat signatures, and a half-dozen missiles roared off their launchers. Bradley gunners used the thermal sights on their cannon to follow the Chaparral trails, orange streaks against the lightening dawn sky, and picked out the helicopters. The Chaparrals caught two helicopters and the six Bradleys' 25 mm chain guns chewed the third into scrap.

The surviving helicopters stayed below the valley's rim out of the radar beams. The highly trained pilots were veterans of Afghanistan who knew how to use the terrain to mask them from the air defenses in the area. They hugged the trees and slid into the field outside Altendorf marked as the battalion's landing zone. Instead of a full battalion of highly trained, aggressive air assault soldiers, the six remaining helicopters deposited roughly two companies of shaken and disorganized men who took almost a half hour to consolidate and reorganize themselves to seize Altendorf. All NATO forces in the area were alerted to their presence. As they began moving toward Altendorf, patrols of MPs and cavalrymen were beginning to prowl throughout the support area, looking for the Russian helicopters and troops.

The support group watch officer woke up Mike and Colonel Warren when the first alert of the helicopter flight came over the command radio net. By the time Mike arrived in the operations center, the duty officer had flashed a red alert message over the command net, and the base clusters were reporting their status. The liaison officer from the German territorial battalion was posting the operations map with new data as he received updated reports. Colonel Warren was already standing in front of the situation map in deep thought.

As Mike walked over to stand beside the colonel, the command radio squeaked twice, and a deep, rich, Southern drawl announced, "Kilo six hotel two niner. This is Quebec four lima zero five. Permission to enter net. Over."

"Quebec four lima zero five. This is kilo six hotel two niner. Authenticate golf juliet. Over."

"I authenticate sierra." The reply came after a few seconds of delay.

"This is Lima zero five. One of our patrols reports helicopter activity vicinity Tango Romeo Papa three five zero. If you have no friendly activity in the area, we're going to shoot that sucker up. Over."

Mike looked at Colonel Warren. As the support group commander, he was in charge of the rear battle in the support group's area of responsibility. Any decision to fire on suspected enemy forces using artillery or aviation was his to make.

"Do we have people in that area, Mike? If not, I am going to let the Cav shoot that mission."

Mike checked the map. "We don't show any friendly forces around Target Reference Point 350. If any are there, they shouldn't be."

Warren turned to the radio operator. "Tell Lima zero five to go ahead and shoot. We show no friendly forces around TRP 350. Tell him to let us know what the results are."

"Lima zero five, this is hotel two niner. Hotel six five says there are no friendlies in that area. Go ahead and shoot. Let us know what happens. Over."

"Lima zero five, wilco. Over."

Lima zero five's own 155 mm howitzer battery and a 155 mm howitzer battalion from Corps artillery answered the fire mission. The howitzers fired dual-purpose improved conventional munitions—ICM-DPs—the field artillery's version of cluster bombs. The last six helicopters were, as pilots say, "light on the skids" as the first salvos landed. A direct hit obliterated one MI-17. The airbursts of the ICM-DPs caught two more helicopters as they pulled away from the landing zone and converted the aircraft to scrap metal. The three surviving helicopters, leaking hydraulic fluid, fuel, and blood, crept away off to the east and sanctuary. The artillery fired four more salvos into the landing zone, scattering the burning wreckage of the helicopters around the German countryside and catching the remnants of the Russian battalion as they tried to rally themselves and move out.

The Second Company commander was the senior surviving officer, one of three surviving officers and a veteran of Afghanistan used to operations turning into shambles. He organized what was left of the battalion into one composite company and moved out toward Altendorf, still confident of completing his mission. But fate was not through playing with the 875th. The long-range reconnaissance patrol that marked the landing zone tangled earlier in the night with a patrol from the 577th MP Company. The Russians had killed or driven off the MPs. The Russian patrol leader died in the firefight, though, and the Americans recovered his body. On it, the surviving MPs found a map marked with routes into and out of Altendorf. The MPs passed the map to their company headquarters, which in turn passed the information to the S-3 of the Second Squadron, Eleventh Armored Cavalry Regiment, Lima zero five. Two-Eleven was refitting and reorganizing after the covering force battle. The cavalrymen were survivors of thirty-six hours of combat that cost them 40 percent of their unit. Now, they were hungry for payback, and the 875th walked right into them. As the Russians moved out, they ran into Echo and Golf troops who had set up a massive horseshoe-shaped ambush with their tanks and cavalry-fighting vehicles.

Afghanistan prepared the Second Company commander for operations that fell apart and had to be extemporized. It had not prepared him for the massed firepower of two armored cavalry troops at point-blank range. In a blizzard of fire from tank main guns, automatic cannons, heavy machine guns, mortars, and a few automatic grenade launchers from some of the 577th's MPs who attached themselves to Echo troop, the 875th died. Some two dozen dazed and bleeding soldiers did make it to the objective of Altendorf, but they made it as prisoners of war.

Lima zero five reported that he had destroyed three helicopters, killed between seventy-five and ninety soldiers, and captured twenty-six, all of whom were wounded. As Echo and Golf troops policed the battlefield, they found several copies of maps and operations orders that intelligence personnel eagerly examined. The MPs took the prisoners to the 302nd Combat Support Hospital for treatment before evacuating them to POW pens closer to Frankfurt.

As the last of the air assault forces were being mopped up, the secure telephone from Corps Headquarters rang. When Mike picked it up, the voice on the other end said that Major General Barrett was calling for Colonel Warren.

"Sir, it's Major General Barrett for you." Mike turned to Colonel Warren and handed him the handset.

Warren stepped back from the map board, took the telephone handset, and spoke into it. He listened for a few seconds. "Wait one I'm going to put this on the speakerphone. It may save a little time in telling the story."

He punched the speaker button, and Barrett's voice filled the war room.

"John, we've just received word that a division-sized operational maneuver group has broken through the Sixteenth Mech between Lauterbach and Fulda. One of the lead regiments is heading south along the Lauter and Nidda Rivers in your direction, probably trying to get to Schotten so they can control the north-south road network and block any shift of our forces in sector. I'm trying to put together a counterpunch, but I need some time. You are going to have to hold Altendorf for me. I can't let you jump back."

"Roger," Warren said in a flat voice.

"The attack has badly ruptured the Sixteenth. Some of their units are still trying to delay the main attack. It looks as though the air assault that you just took care of was supposed to seize the road junctions and town and the OMG was going to link up with them. I'm putting you in command of all US forces in the area. Have your people start collecting anyone from the Sixteenth that drifts through. I am chopping Two Eleven ACR to you, and I am putting a field artillery brigade in direct support. I'll try to get some TAC air and attack helicopters up to you as well."

Barrett paused.

"Roger," Warren answered firmly.

"I need at least eight hours from you. The French committed part of their corps to reinforce us, but they are coming from the Darmstadt area. If 52nd Armored can continue to hold, the 287th Armored Brigade will switch over to cover the Sixteenth's sector, but they have to move cross-country, and it will take some time to get there. Seventh Army may be able to break part of VII Corps reserve loose sooner, but not before daybreak. The travel time will depend on how much CAP the air force can provide. Any questions?"

"Not now, but I will be calling you back later. Have you told the Germans about this? I'll have to coordinate the defenses with them because the town is their responsibility."

"Roger, they've been told. They're going to try to move a tank battalion up to the west of the town."

"Okay, I guess that is it for now. I'd better get started." The colonel cut the connection and turned to Mike. "Get the commander of the 577th MPs and the Cav squadron over here, as well as the principal staff officers. Have the German liaison officer contact his headquarters and let them know the new mission we have. I also want Sherwood in here to review the company's plans for the defense of our slice of the town perimeter.

"Set up a conference call with the other commanders and make sure that all our efforts are tied together and we do not have any holes in the perimeter. Also, put everyone in MOPP 2, even if the Russians haven't used chemicals yet. I don't want to take any chances." Warren paused and then said in a lower voice, "Mike, I want you to check out Sherwood's plans carefully. Make sure they are airtight and he executes them completely. I want to make sure that he ties in with the Germans and the 152nd S and S. All we need is one penetration of our perimeter and the Russians will eat us up in house-to-house fighting."

"Yes, sir. I had already planned to sit on him. Ed is in command of the reaction force, and I've told him to stay close to Bill."

"You and Ed are the only two other infantry officers on the staff. This is going to become an infantryman's battle shortly, and our support mission is going to go by the boards for a while."

Intersection Highway 246 and 459
Vicinity Altendorf, FRG

The Russian tank regiment moved in a column, led by its recon company and motorized rifle battalion. The past week's heavy rains restricted movement to the highway itself. The rain-soaked trails and unimproved secondary roads would not support the rapid movement of large numbers of tracked vehicles, and speed was key to the success of the attack. This same demand for speed meant the lead elements ignored the numerous small ambushes from either flank of the column. While these ambushes, just one or two anti-tank missiles fired at long ranges, did not pose a serious threat to the movement of the column or the main battle tanks that made up most of the regiment's fighting strength, they did erode the infantry battalion. BMP armored personnel carriers were good targets for the TOW and Milan anti tank guided missiles fired from the flanking wood lines. Each exploding missile meant another infantry squad wiped out before the column reached Altendorf. Another waste of his fighting power not immediately clear to the regimental commander was in his special purpose vehicles, tanks with mine-clearing plows and flails. If the ambushers could not get a clear shot at a BMP, they fired at the mine-clearing tanks and combat engineer and anti-aircraft vehicles. Even if these weren't destroyed, they were disabled badly enough to stop them from continuing to Altendorf. The drain in the fighting power of his infantry battalion did not greatly concern the tank regiment commander because the Allied garrison at Altendorf was composed of support troops who were no match for his tankers. In any case, if he needed infantry support, the airmobile battalion was already there.

The commander's plan was to encircle Altendorf. If he could cut off the town and its garrison from reinforcement, it should fall into his lap like a ripe apple off a tree. Accordingly, he sent one of his depleted motorized rifle companies off to skirt the town to the west, along a trail through the woods crowning the ridge overlooking Altendorf. In theory, the plan was a good one. In practice, it bogged down literally in the rain-sodden fields and forest trails.

Team Charlie lurched out of Lauterbach as the Russians caught their breath and prepared to launch their second echelon units into the breach in American lines. Charlie Six watched the survivors grudgingly withdraw to their next battle position. Then he looked back at the five smoke plumes marking three of his Bradleys and two of his attached Abrams tanks.

As Team Charlie arrived at its new position on a hill overlooking about five or six hundred meters of open ground sloping down to a shallow stream and then up to another wood line, each track dispersed to its defensive position, and the crews began to dig in. They had barely started when a listening post reported track noises approaching through the far woods. With that word, Team Charlie stopped digging and settled behind their weapons, sights glued on the wood line opposite where a sodden forest trail emerged into the shallow valley.

A single BMP emerged along the trail and rolled hesitantly into the open meadow. Trailing him by about fifty to seventy-five meters came a clump of three BMPs. These vehicles started to spread off the trail to either side and succeeded only in bogging down. Two more poked their noses out of the wood line and paused as though considering their next moves.

Using their thermal sights, Charlie's gunner detected more heat signatures in the woods. Charlie Six quickly assigned the targets in the wood line to his tanks and the vehicles in the open to his TOW anti-tank guided missiles. The team drew in a collective breath and waited. Charlie Six said "Kill," and the gunners squeezed their triggers. The three Abrams belched reddish balls of fire as their tracers flew into the far trees where bright silver flashes marked the destruction of their targets. TOW missiles flew into the meadow as the four BMPs scrambled to escape. One BMP dissolved in a fireball, spewing wreckage of vehicle and crew in a large circle. The lead vehicle sped up toward the Americans in a desperate attempt to escape the cloud of missiles. A blizzard of machine gun and auto cannon fire reduced it to a colander leaking fuel and blood. The other two armored personnel carriers simply vanished under the hail of guided missiles.

Charlie Six smiled grimly in satisfaction as seven funeral pyres announced the back door to Altendorf was closed.

Hill 287
Vicinity Altendorf, FRG

Ann-Marie shook herself awake and grimaced in greeting to the morning. A little over six weeks ago, she had been a bank teller. Now, she crouched in a hole on a small hill in Germany, in charge of a listening post and three other soldiers. She felt something kick against her boots.

Kevin's voice hissed in her ear, "Annie. Stand-to. Wake up."

In response, she pulled herself fully erect and propped her M-16 against the berm of the observation post. Stand-to was part of the company's battle drill. For thirty minutes before and after sunrise and sunset, all personnel manned their fighting positions with all weapons locked and loaded. As the NCO in charge of the outpost, she had to set the example.

The war started three days ago. The only physical evidence of fighting was the damaged vehicles and weary soldiers of the covering force filtering back through Altendorf. To be sure, that traffic had picked up in the past few hours. But except for some sniping attacks, small ambushes, and road mining, the past three days had been a letdown for the troops of the support group.

Now, the situation was getting livelier. Almost two days ago, the corps-covering force, a reinforced armored cavalry regiment, had moved to the border. For the past day and a half, a distant muttering, like summer thunder, announced that the covering force met the advancing Warsaw Pact forces. Yesterday afternoon, Ann-Marie and the other soldiers in Altendorf watched the cavalrymen pull back to recover from their battle. The battle-weary vehicles and men told the support group that war was coming.

Then, the company was called to full alert about 0130 because of an expected air assault. The cavalry and MP reaction forces destroyed the attackers before they could get organized and conduct their attack. Ann-Marie and her team had heard the firefights, off to the west on the other side of town from their position. Now, they could hear something that sounded like vehicles moving off to the north and west of the town. Sometimes, they could see flashes of light, like fireflies or flash bulbs, as well.

Ann-Marie and the other three soldiers watched to their front without speaking. She was cold, tired, and hungry and only wanted a hot meal, a warm shower, and a change of clothes. Her teeth felt cloaked in wool, and her mouth tasted sour. August nights in Germany were chilly, and even the chemical protective suits and overboots did not keep the cold and damp completely out. As dawn neared, the typical chilly, clingy morning fog began to roll up out of the bottom of the valley and blocked her view. The only positive to the morning was that the heavy rain of the past week had stopped.

Thirty minutes after Ann-Marie woke up, the TA-1 sound-powered telephone buzzed. Kevin answered and passed it to Ann-Marie, who was in charge of the listening post.

"Sergeant Dumont, this is Captain Sherwood. What's your situation up there? Any activity?"

The company commander sounds particularly cheerful and peppy, as befits someone who had slept in a warm, dry building, Ann-Marie thought bitterly.

"No, sir. It's real quiet. Nothing's stirring. We heard some noise out to the northeast last night, mostly artillery fire. About an hour or so ago, Kevin said he heard something off to the west and saw some flashes of light. There's been nothing else though. Our night vision goggles quit working about a half hour ago. I changed batteries, but they still don't work. Now that the fog's come up, we can't see a lot."

"Okay. Well, here's the situation. The Russians have broken through the Sixteenth Mech and have a column headed toward us. So we must keep the OP occupied all day. I'm going to try to get the Germans to send some people up to relieve you. Until I do, I want you to stay up there. Send someone back with the goggles, and I'll have him take back a pair of binoculars and some hot coffee. I'll also have Sergeant DiNapoli hold breakfast for the four of you. Keep an eye out to the northeast. Got that?"

"Yes, sir. Send the NVGs back, and keep a lookout to the northeast. What about the stuff Kevin heard out west of us?"

"Don't worry about that area. It belongs to the 156th and the Germans. Okay, that's all I've got. Sherwood out."

Ann-Marie set the telephone down on a shelf in the side of the position and faced the other three. "That was Captain Sherwood. He said we are to stay here until he can get some Germans up here to replace us." She pointed to one of the soldiers. "Ben, you take the night vision goggles back and give them to the CO. He's going to get a set of binoculars and some coffee for you to bring back up here. Kevin and Brenda will stay here with me. He said the Russians have broken through the Mech division northeast of us and may be moving toward us from the northeast, so we have to keep a watch in that direction." She nodded to the other woman soldier. "Brenda, you and I will take the first watch. Kevin can hang out for a while since he was on before stand-to."

Kevin asked, "Annie, what about breakfast? We haven't had anything to eat since supper."

"The CO said he'd hold breakfast for us. Anyway, you must have had at least one MRE last night while you were on watch judging from the trash around here. Besides . . ." She poked him in the stomach. "You could do with missing a meal. Here are the NVGs, Ben."

Ann-Marie handed the goggles to Private Bennett, who put them in their carrying case and scrambled out the back of the position. The observation post was a V-shaped trench dug along the boundary hedge of a clover field on the military crest of the hill. The apex pointed toward Altendorf, and the two legs ran along the base of the hedge. The hedge had been carefully thinned to allow observation to the front while maintaining concealment. Each leg was eight feet long, two feet wide, and four feet deep. The spoil from the holes had been piled in front to create a berm that added another two feet of protection and concealment. Viewports in the berm corresponded to those thinned out of the hedge.

As Bennett trotted down the hill, hampered by the clumsy rubber overboots of the MOPP suit, the two women took up their posts looking to the northeast. Kevin settled himself in one corner of the trench.

He produced an MRE from inside his MOPP suit. "Boy, corned beef hash. Just what I always wanted for breakfast. It'd be really nice if I had some fried eggs."

"How can you eat that stuff?" Brenda asked over her shoulder. "Besides, I thought you were worried about not getting any breakfast."

Kevin grunted as he began tearing the brown plastic envelope open. Before he could respond to Brenda, a banshee wail split the morning.

"What the hell is that?" Ann-Marie shouted as she pulled off her helmet and ripped her protective mask from its carrier. Masking was automatic for incoming artillery fire or air attack. As each person finished, they shouted "Gas! Gas!" She looked sheepishly at Kevin and Brenda as she pulled the heavy black butyl rubber gloves on to complete MOPP IV.

A thunderclap threw her to the floor of the fighting position. Artillery fire drummed around the position, hurling fragments of metal and bushes and clods of earth on top of her. Ann-Marie curled into a fetal position as the walls of the trench vibrated with each nearby shell burst. She could watch the shock waves bulge the trench wall out toward her, each time expecting the position to collapse on top of her. The sound of shell bursts became a solid roar, blotting out all other noises. Shrapnel, dirt clods, tree splinters, and other debris pelted down on her like a heavy hailstorm. Her uncle had been a Marine at Khe Sanh and talked about the artillery bombardments he had endured. Now she could relate to his memories. Now she understood trying to crawl up inside a steel helmet. The drumming crash of the artillery stopped suddenly. The lack of noise was as loud as the barrage, only the walls of the fighting position didn't tremble. Ann-Marie lay huddled on the floor of the hole with Kevin and Brenda, their bodies touching but each person separated by the cocoon of their protective mask, NBC suit, and flak jacket. Slowly, the three deafened and numbed soldiers raised their heads and looked over the front berm of the foxhole.

Their world ended about ten meters away. A solid cloak of oily, pearl-gray haze walled them into their position. They could see two large craters on either side, ugly, ragged pimples still smoking from the high explosives that created them and tore away the bushes from the front of the position. Beyond that, they could see nothing. For all the three of them could tell, they were alone in an alien, evil cloud.

Kevin reached for the field telephone and cranked it. Nothing happened. He cranked it again. No response. When he tried a third time with the same result, he tugged viciously at the field wires leading out of their position. The wires gave easily and fell to the bottom of the hole. The three looked at each other wordlessly. The artillery had cut the telephone wires somewhere between the OP and the town. They were isolated from the rest of the company. Two hundred meters seemed like two thousand miles.

"Let's get out of here," Brenda said, her voice distorted by panic and the protective mask. "We're cut off. The telephone's dead. Even if we could see anything, we can't tell anyone. We gotta go back to town. Back to the company. The Russians may be out there anywhere."

Kevin looked at her and then at Ann-Marie. "Ya, she's right, Annie. We can't do anything with the phone gone. Let's get outta here while we can." His voice went up an octave as he spoke.

Before Ann-Marie could respond, an ominous low throbbing, punctuated by squeals of metal on metal, filled the air. The noise reverberated around them, magnified by the smoke screen, getting louder as though it were moving toward them. As one, they turned to the front of the position and stared at the smoke in horrified anticipation.

As she watched, a squat, black shape started to grow in the haze. A massive gun tube suddenly broke out of the fog bank, jutting into her vision and swiveling from side to side as though scenting out its prey. Slowly and massively, the rest of the tank appeared, growing out of the smoke. Ann-Marie stared in frozen, terrified fascination as it crawled toward them. Even in her terror, a part of her mind coolly noted the long thermal-wrapped 125 mm gun tube, the squared-off turret splotched with the blocks of explosive reactive armor, the heavy anti-aircraft machine gun on the commander's hatch, and the infrared searchlight to the right of the main gun and classified it as a T-72 main battle tank.

At least, this part of her mind thought, *I know what's going to kill me*.

The tank stopped about twenty meters from them. The turret swiveled to the left and fired at some target known only to the crew. The main gun bucked and belched a bright orange fireball. The blast wave kicked up debris around the position and slapped the three Americans with a physical violence.

Brenda shrieked, "Oh God! We're gonna die!" and scrambled out of the OP running down the hill to Altendorf.

As she ran, stumbling in the NBC overboots, she dropped her M-16, hurled her helmet and protective mask away, and tried to shed her flak jacket and web gear. She had stumbled about ten meters to the edge of the smoke when the turret of the T-72 turned ponderously in her direction. The main gun wagged like a dog's snout, testing the breeze for scent. Then a stream of tracers from the coaxial machine gun reached out and casually flipped the running woman off her feet. A series of cones appeared in the earth around her. She danced briefly in a mad jig and then flopped to the ground, like a rag doll carelessly thrown away by an indifferent child. The main gun tube dropped until it pointed directly at Ann-Marie and Kevin. The gunner fired a burst from the coax machine gun at them. The tank was too close to depress the gun enough, and the rounds passed harmlessly over their heads. The driver gunned his engine and swung the tank toward the two Americans.

Kevin and Ann-Marie screamed in raw terror and threw themselves to the floor of their position. Her world turned black, and the walls of the hole shook as the tank rolled forward and over the trench. The right track passed over the hole, dropped into it, and seemed to press down on her with a tangible force. She rolled onto her stomach, screaming in terror, and scrabbled at the ground with her fingers. The engine roared as the driver gunned it and pivoted the tank left and right, back and forth over her. The earth crumbled and shook, raining large clods of dirt down on her. The roar of the diesel and squeals of the tracks drowned out her screams and sobs.

Ann-Marie could not hear her own screams, even locked in her protective mask. The noise of the tank penetrated her whole body and was a solid pressure on her. She felt wetness on her thighs as her bladder emptied. Suddenly, the noise stopped again as the tank ceased moving. A blast of concussion slapped her as the Russian fired his main gun. A cloud of dust floated down on her, and it was sucked back up as the tank fired again. Each time the gun fired, the tank rocked on its tracks and shook more dirt loose from the walls. The engine roared again, and the tracks pivoted as the tank rolled in reverse off their hole and then rolled forward. The front of the track dipped down into the hole, aimed directly at her. She felt her bowels empty and sobbed in terror and self-disgust. The tank rolled forward off the position and down the hill toward Altendorf.

As she lay in the bottom, feeling fouled and shamed, her fear turned to hatred, her panic to rage. She wanted only to kill the men who degraded her. She slowly pulled herself erect and looked out. The smoke was starting to fade, and she could see the tank about fifty meters away. It was stopped with the main gun pointed in the general direction of Altendorf. As she watched, the commander's hatch opened, and a tanker stood up in the hatch. He saw Brenda's body off to the right of the tank, about twenty meters away. He casually swung the heavy anti-aircraft machine gun around and fired a long burst into the corpse. It jerked and twitched in a macabre dance as the heavy slugs tore into it. The tanker paused, aimed the gun again, and blew off Brenda's head in a fountain of red spray. He relocked the machine gun in its traveling position and dropped back down inside the turret, slamming the hatch behind him. Something inside Ann-Marie snapped.

She dropped and shook Kevin by the shoulder. He still lay huddled in the floor of the OP.

"Come on. We can get that cocksucker. He's stopped out in front of the town, right behind us. We can nail his ass now."

The protective mask distorted her voice, and she panted with a mixture of fear and adrenaline, but Kevin understood her. The two of them fumbled in the bottom of the fighting position and found the six AT-4 anti-tank weapons they had stored there the day before, an eternity ago. They each armed three of the throwaway rockets and laid them on the back berm of the position.

"We'll fire salvos of two together as fast as we can. Aim for the engine grill," she told Kevin. They each picked up the first two rockets.

"Ready. Aim. Fire." Two AT-4s streaked out to the T-72. One burst short of the tank, the other hit the right track and severed it, immobilizing the tank.

"Fire." The second pair hit the engine grill, the weakest point of the tank. One smashed into the radiator fan. The other severed a fuel line and started a small fire.

The turret was swiveling around to deal with them when the Americans fired their third salvo. One rocket hit the engine block again, starting another fire. The last rocket missed the engine compartment. It skimmed over the top and smashed into the turret ring. Its explosion jammed the turret with the main gun locked in the three o'clock position. The two small fires fed on spilled diesel and leaking oil to become one big fire. As they did, the hatches on the turret popped open, and the gunner and commander began scrambling out. No tanker likes being in a vehicle on fire.

Ann-Marie and Kevin were ready for them. The two crewmen fell to a hail of M-16 fire, their bodies draped half in and half out of the hatches. The third tanker, the driver, appeared from in front of the vehicle with his hands in the air, shouting something in Russian as he ran blindly toward them.

Ann-Marie let the man get within three meters of her, close enough to see his unshaven, acne-pocked face and oil-stained coveralls. She would wonder later what he was shouting as he waved his arms at her. Now, she coolly and deliberately shot him three times in the head.

Haupstrasse 84
Altendorf, FRG

The field telephone buzzed, and one of the clerks picked it up. "S-4, Private First Class Green, sir," he shouted into the mouthpiece.

The shelling had deafened everyone, and the protective masks only added to the sense of isolation. "Roger, wait a minute. She's right here, sir. I'll get her." He turned and looked at Vicki. "It's for you, ma'am. Major Fitzmaurice." He handed her the handset.

"Lieutenant Baxter, sir."

"This is Major Fitzmaurice. The company command post took a direct hit. Sherwood is dead, along with people who worked in the orderly room. You're now the company commander. Tell Roberts what happened and get over to the operations room right away. The Germans are reporting tank noises up the valley, masked by all this smoke. First Sergeant Bellotti is out checking the line now and trying to get the hot loop reestablished. I think life is going to get interesting in a while."

"Roger, I'm on my way." She put down the phone and turned to Major Roberts. "Sir, the Three says I'm now the company commander and I've got to get over to the operations room."

"What happened to Bill Sherwood, Vicki?" Roberts asked.

Vicki relayed Mike's message as she reached for her weapon and Kevlar.

Roberts nodded solemnly. "Yeah, thirty fucking minutes of artillery preparation probably means an attack. Good luck." He held out his hand, still encased in the butyl rubber NBC glove.

As she left the cellar the S-4 shop occupied, she found herself in the midst of desolation. Most of the buildings along the street were in ruins. The town was silent, except for the crackle of fires and the crash of collapsing masonry as a damaged building gave up the ghost.

She could see the bank that had been the company's command post a few doors up the street. It was now a mass of smoking rubble, its shattered bricks flowing out into the street like a frozen wave. Obviously, no one inside had survived. It was also apparent why Mike had been so adamant about occupying basements of buildings. She wended her way up the street to the school building that housed the operations center and saw the artillery barrage also had badly beaten it up. The incoming fire had smashed the roof in and shattered the full-length glass windows on the two upper stories. The front of the house across the street was demolished, leaving the interior of the two-story building exposed as though it were a museum display. Two rounds had struck the road immediately in front of the main entrance. The craters blocked the street to road traffic beyond the school as effectively as the roadblocks erected so laboriously and carefully before the war began. Pockmarks from shrapnel pimpled the façade of the school itself. Rubble from the house and the upper stories of the school forced her to go around to the back entrance of the school.

Chapter 9

The Success of His Fighting

Every soldier must know, before he goes into battle, how the little battle he is to fight fits into the larger picture, and how the success of his fighting will influence the battle as a whole.

—Bernard Law Montgomery

Stadtliches Kinderschule
Altendorf, FRG

When Vicki entered the war room, she found Mike talking with the group chemical officer about whether or not the Russians had mixed chemical rounds in their barrage. The NBC officer was saying that, because none of the automatic alarms had gone off, he thought there were no chemical agents in the area. All personnel were still in full MOPP 4 because no one had declared "all clear" yet.

"So you're telling me that it's clear and I can tell the old man we can go to MOPP 2, right?" Mike said when Davis finished.

"No, I don't know for sure if it's clear or not. The artillery might have knocked out the alarms, or they might have malfunctioned. Sherwood's got to get his survey and monitoring teams out, have them do their tests, and get the information back to me. He hasn't done that yet, so I don't know what their reports are."

"Well, get going. I need an answer right away. According to the Germans, half the bloody Russian army is coming up the valley toward us."

"Yes, sir. I'll tell the company commander to get the teams out right away," the chemical officer replied.

"The company CP has been knocked out," Mike told him. "You'll have to take the teams out yourself."

"It's not my job to run the company teams. I'm just supposed to collect their reports and consolidate them—"

"I know it's not your job. The company commander is fucking dead. You're the only one I've got to run those teams. Grab your sergeant, and the two of you collect the teams, get a survey, and get back here with the answers. If there's no need to wear these goddamned masks and gloves, I want them off everyone."

"Major, doctrine says I'm supposed to stay at the NBC control center, collect reports, and monitor the overall situation, not run survey teams—"

"Fuck doctrine." Mike leaned forward, almost touching the face piece of the other's mask with his own and said slowly and distinctly, "You go out and run that survey, or I'll fucking well check for gas right now by ripping off your fucking mask and watching if you fucking die or not. Am I making myself clear, Captain?"

"Yes, sir." The NBC officer turned to get his helmet, flak jacket, weapon, and web gear.

Mike watched him leave and turned to Vicki.

"What's the situation, sir?" she asked.

Mike turned and pointed to a one-to-fifty thousand-scale map of the town and outlying areas that showed the defensive positions. "The Germans' town commander reports his scouts are picking up tank noises out around here." He tapped a spot on the map about three kilometers northeast of the town. "The Germans still have a landline back to their brigade headquarters. Believe it or not, the commercial telephone lines are intact and still working."

"Can we use them to get artillery support of our own?" Vicki asked. "We've got some defensive fires plotted out there around the OP. And I'd like to get some FASCAM fields laid outside the wire as well."

"Ed tried a couple minutes ago. We don't have landline commo to the artillery, and we don't know if they're even near a commercial phone. I did reach Two Eleven Cavalry, and they'll give us what help they can, but it won't be much or for very long."

"Speaking of Ed, where is he? He's supposed to be leading the company reaction force."

"He's over at the German CP with the old man. He caught a piece of brick in the head when the building here got hit and can't do much. I'm going to be taking the reaction force. As soon as you can get the first sergeant to brief you on what our section of the perimeter looks like, let me know where you want me to be."

Vicki nodded grimly and left to find First Sergeant Bellotti. As she left the war room, Colonel Warren and Ed returned from their meeting with the German territorial commander.

"The Germans think the lead elements of the attacking regiment are about three klicks up the valley from us. Their scouts are retiring ahead of the Russians and have started firing the cratering charges and the demo charges for the two abatis around checkpoints twenty-five, thirty-nine, and forty-eight." Warren tapped the map symbols. "The obstacles and rainy past few days have slowed down the Russians somewhat."

Mike nodded in agreement.

"The rain's softened the ground so they can't really use the trails as much as they would like to in order to bypass our obstacles. If they get off the hard ball, they'll just chew those trails and back roads into soup after five or six tanks go by," he answered the colonel.

"Ed, get on the commercial phones and see if you can raise the artillery. Also, make sure that we have landline commo with the 156th," Warren continued. "Mike, I want you to get with Vicki Baxter and take charge of the reaction force. I am going to have Ed, once he gets off the phone, put together a reserve that we can use to shore up the line if we have to."

The adjutant, Major Paul Harrison, appeared in the war room. Harrison was Sally Grant's replacement, pulled from a replacement battalion in Frankfurt, and sent forward to the group. He was not happy with an assignment this close to the battle area, and to a Reserve unit at that.

"Colonel Warren," he shouted. "Sir, we have a serious problem that you must take care of right away. It needs your urgent attention."

"Tell me, Paul. What can be more urgent than a regiment of Russian tanks bearing down on us?" the colonel said calmly as he continued to contemplate the map board.

"Reporters, sir." Harrison was almost hyperventilating in his excitement. "There's a TV news crew from CNN in the town. Their escort was killed earlier, and they just escaped from Lauterbach with some soldiers from the infantry. When they arrived here in Altendorf, the infantry was sent out to the perimeter. The reporters now have no way to get back to Frankfurt. We have to find a way to get them out of here and back to where it's safe."

Warren shook his head. His experience with reporters in civilian life was that they would rather stay here in Altendorf, where the story was going to be, than be evacuated to safety.

"Paul," he said quietly, turning to face the agitated officer. "I have other things to worry about. We all have other things to worry about. Tell the news people to enjoy their stay here in Altendorf and to keep their heads down. I'm sure they can get lots of good footage. After we resolve the situation with the Russians, we can worry about the reporters."

"But they're civilians—"

"They take their chances here just like everyone else," Warren said in a tone that allowed no argument.

Ringstrasse 36
Altendorf, FRG

Vicki moved to the alternate command post, a two-story building on the northeast edge of town that overlooked the company's perimeter. She moved to the master bedroom and checked the telephone connection to the company switchboard. The room's large bay window provided excellent observation of the approaches to the town. In front of the window, the dining room table held a map board with a large perspective sketch of the company's defensive sector, portraying the terrain features and buildings around the town and in the town itself with all obstacles and artillery targets marked. The drawing highlighted the houses fortified as blocking positions showing their fields of fire. A commercial telephone rested on the table in front of the map board. Beside the telephone lay a laminated sheet listing call signs for all the units in the Altendorf Base Defensive Cluster. Vicki checked her call sign as company commander, scholar two six; pine tree three five oscar, the fire support officer of the National Guard artillery brigade located about fifteen kilometers from Altendorf; and plowman two, the base defense cluster's direct support artillery battalion. She picked up the phone, heard a buzzing dial tone, and returned the handset to the cradle. Immediately after she put down the telephone, it rang, and she picked it up.

"Scholar two six," she answered.

"Yo, Scholar. This is pine tree three five oscar. What's going on over there?" the voice on the other end of the telephone asked in a jovial tone. "We've been trying to call you on the fox mike for the past ten minutes," three five oscar said. "But you haven't been answering. You guys got some problems up there?"

"Roger. The artillery knocked out our radios temporarily. Do you have commo with plowman two foxtrot?" Vicki answered. "I want to get some targets fired as soon as possible."

The voice on the telephone changed. "This is pine tree three five." It was the fire support officer himself. "Send me your targets, and I'll pass them to Plowman. For now, we'll use this telephone line. I've passed your number to them, and they will be in contact with you directly. They are also going to send a fire support coordinator down to you. That should be there in about twenty minutes. Now, give me your targets."

Vicki looked at her map and the terrain sketch. "Roger. I need delta hotel 0012, 0019, and 0027. All are FASCAM."

Ringstrasse 65
Altendorf, FRG

Mike looked out from the second-floor bedroom window of the house his fire team occupied. The house was on the northeastern edge of town and looked up the valley. The smoke curtain that lay about a hundred meters to their front was beginning to thin, and Mike could see vague black, beetle-like shapes bouncing and jerking across the fields toward Altendorf.

Suddenly, two figures appeared out of the smoke clouds waving small orange survival panels and stumbling awkwardly in their MOPP suits toward a safe lane through the wire obstacles and minefields surrounding the town.

The machine gunner next to Mike nestled his M-60 into his shoulder and flipped off the safety. Mike slapped the barrel of the machine gun before the gunner could open fire.

"Don't shoot. They're friendlies," he said, snapping. "Keep watching the smoke, and worry about the fucking vehicles."

As he spoke, a Russian BMP-2 reconnaissance vehicle broke out of the smoke about a hundred meters from the town. It stopped, as if the appearance of the built-up area shocked it. The turret traversed right and then left, as though trying to make its mind up where to go. The BMP started up again with a belch of black diesel smoke spiraling from the exhaust and began rolling toward a gap in the wire barrier east of the house Mike occupied. The BMP gunner began firing his 30 mm cannon at the town, but the bucking vehicle prevented him from hitting any particular building. The armored vehicle rapidly built up speed and hit the wire fence. Its momentum carried it about halfway through the ten-meter-wide belt of concertina wire and jerked to a halt as the wire wrapped itself around the track sprockets. Furiously, the driver threw his vehicle into reverse and gunned his motor, but he succeeded only in wrapping the concertina more tightly around the sprockets. The revving engine reached a crescendo. The gunner fired more rapidly into the town, and, almost anticlimactically, a Milan anti-tank missile streaked out from a bunker built into the basement of a house and blew the BMP apart.

Immediately, two lines of green tracers erupted from the smoke bank and converged on the Milan bunker. The blocky shape of a T-72 emerged from the smoke screen, trailing a band of dirty gray smoke from its exhaust as the driver threw raw diesel on the manifold to create his own smoke cloud. The main gun bucked as it fired at the bunker, but before the tank could fire a second round, another Milan shot from a different bunker. The missile smashed into the flank of the tank but succeeded only in igniting the reactive armor blocks on the hull without stopping the tank's advance.

Behind it came more tanks and BMPs, each spewing smoke from its smoke generator and blasting the town with machine gun and cannon fire. A third Milan, fired from a third bunker, blasted the lead T-72 to a halt with a hit on its running gear. The attack continued to roll on toward the town until the lead tanks entangled themselves in the wire belt, momentarily checking their advance. The infantry carrying BMPs followed the tanks by about fifty meters. Sparkles crowned the BMPs as the infantry fired their weapons out the firing ports. Milans began leaping toward the stalled tanks, first stripping away the blocks of reactive armor, exposing the tanks to follow-on missiles, and causing several to erupt into balls of flame. Mike watched in awe as one T-72 exploded, and the turret catapulted fifty feet into the air. The turret flipped like a falling leaf and fluttered to the ground a good forty meters away, on top of a closely following BMP. Now vehicles were entering the minefields that lay under the concertina. More shuddered to a halt as the mines exploded underneath them, destroying suspensions or, in some cases, the entire vehicle.

The infantry dismounted from their carriers to begin firing blindly into the town, while combat engineers came forward to cut holes in the wire and clear paths through the minefield. As the Russians left the cover of their vehicles, machine guns and automatic cannon opened up from the defensive positions in the houses and buildings on the edge of Altendorf. The M-60 gunner next to Mike gritted his teeth and opened fire on a squad of Russian soldiers frantically scrambling out of their disabled carrier. His first burst was low and short, kicking up a cloud of dust about twenty meters in front of his targets.

Mike slapped him on the shoulder and screamed, "Up! Bring it up! Get the bastards!"

The gunner sent his second burst into the group, scattering them like a flock of pigeons who suddenly find a cat in their midst. Two or three flopped bonelessly to the ground, and the survivors dove for the protection of a burning tank hulk. The gunner shifted his fire to a group of four engineers gingerly probing their way through the minefield. He walked his fire over the men, throwing one ten feet away and onto a mine. The blast flipped the body into the air and left it dangling on the concertina like last week's dirty laundry. The other three lay still.

A personnel carrier backed frantically away from the wire, running over the squad that had just dismounted from it. It was smashed in turn by a T-72 scrambling for protection from the barrage of anti-tank missiles from the Allied positions. The tank rammed the APC broadside, locking tracks with the smaller vehicle in a tight embrace. A Milan struck the rear of the tank, igniting the fuel cells in a volcano of flame that enveloped both vehicles. The hatch of the tank opened, and the commander tried to scramble to safety. He was immediately wrapped in the geyser of flame marking the explosion of the main gun ammunition and sending the turret spinning through the air.

The attack faded back into the wood line, leaving behind burning hulks of tanks and APCs sending puffs of black, oily smoke skyward. The surviving dismounted troops scuttled after the retreating vehicles, trying to avoid the Allied fire that followed their every move. Mike kept pointing out targets to the machine gunner until all were motionless. The firing gradually died away, a heavy machine gun tapping out its last volley at an APC that jerkily started and stopped in a series of futile attempts to escape. The tracers from the .50-caliber machine gun walked up to the BMP and danced the length of the crew compartment. The armor-piercing rounds sparkled as they struck the vehicle. The BMP shuddered and then collapsed in on itself to lie inertly halfway between the wire belt and the haven of the far wood line.

In the silence that followed, Mike told the gunner to move to the alternate position prepared on the ground floor. As the gunner picked up his machine gun and tripod, the other two crewmembers grabbed extra ammunition cans, anti-tank rockets, and whatever else they could pick up. Then all four Americans stumbled out of the bedroom and down the staircase to the ground floor. The alternate position was in the living room of the house, now half-filled with sandbag revetments. The gunner positioned his weapon on a table placed just far enough back into the room to conceal it from outside observation, yet still provide a field of fire covering the approach into town. The window, like all the other windows in the house, was screened by a chicken wire frame, fastened on the top to the outside wall of the house. In theory, the chicken wire would prevent attackers from throwing hand grenades in through the window. Because the bottom was not fastened, the occupants of the room could throw hand grenades, or whatever was handy, on any attackers outside the building.

A heavy preparation from both artillery and tanks preceded the second attack. The artillery tried to clear paths through the mines and wire on the outskirts of town, while the tanks fired directly at the houses to destroy fighting positions detected during the first attack. As Mike and the machine gun crew moved to their new positions, a heavy crash and expanding fireball that flashed down the staircase announced they had left their old position just in time. Dust floated down from the ceiling as a second round smashed into the roof.

The gunner looked at Mike. "Jesus, sir, how did you know they'd do that? Shoot right at our window?"

"It's what I'd do in their place. Pepper every window that I saw someone shooting from with tank guns or missiles." He gestured to the sandbags piled against the outside wall. "Everyone get down against the wall. We're going to be catching shit for a while."

A salvo of 152 mm artillery rounds burst outside the house, as if in agreement. Shrapnel from the bursting rounds sliced through the chicken wire and thudded into the side of the house. A second salvo landed almost in the same place as the first. One round slammed into the roof, shaking the house and knocking part of the ceiling loose on top of the Americans. A ceiling beam fell into the room and ripped loose a shower of bricks. One of them spun down and slammed into Mike's helmet, knocking it off his head and driving him to the floor. As he picked himself up and reached for the helmet, he noticed drops of blood speckling his hands and the floor under him. A piece of brick had torn a long gash across his forehead.

He forgot about the cut as a second salvo smashed into the house. Fragments from the explosion cut one member of the machine crew in half against the front wall of the house. Dust and smoke clouded the room and hid any sign of the outside world from the soldiers inside. A round with a delayed-action fuse smashed through the house and burst in the basement. The ground floor buckled upward and settled down into a deep dish with a six-foot hole in the center marking the impact of the burst.

The next salvo landed beyond their house. In accord with their doctrine, the Russian gunners had determined the required number of rounds to destroy their target, gun positions in buildings, and fired them into the outer ring of houses. Now, they shifted to alternate targets, secure in the knowledge they had destroyed whatever obstacles had stopped the first assault. Mike sprang to the window and looked out to see more tanks and APCs emerging from the wood line and crawling toward town. As he watched, small puffs of gray smoke appeared above them. These were volleys of FASCAM, scatterable mines fired by American and German artillery pieces from behind Altendorf. Vicki or someone else had gotten through to the artillery support.

Mauerstrasse 24
Altendorf, FRG

Ann-Marie and Kevin stumbled over a safe lane through the minefields and wire belts surrounding Altendorf. They waved orange marker panels frantically as they emerged from the smoke cloud at the foot of the hill, praying the gunners watching would see the panels before they opened fire. Their breath came hard through the protective masks, and sweat from the run down the hill began to fog the eyepieces. As they came through the obstacle belt, a German combat engineer impatiently waved them further on and out of his way. His job was to close the safe lane and complete the minefield before the first Russian attackers arrived. The two frightened and exhausted Americans just barely made it to safety. A few minutes later, the gap would have been closed, and they would have been isolated on the enemy side of the barrier.

They shuffled raggedly by the pioneer without noticing that he was unmasked. At the first house they reached, they collapsed in exhaustion and tried to catch their breath. The idea that they were safe began to sink in on them.

Ann-Marie leaned back against the wall and exhaled heavily. She was alive. She, was off that goddammed hill and safe with her friends. As that feeling soaked through her body, she began to feel liberated. She had killed the Russians who tried to kill her. She had destroyed the goddammed tank, with Kevin's help of course. She had been terrified. She had the shit and piss actually scared out of her, but she hadn't lost her cool—well, maybe a little—but she hadn't run like poor god-forsaken Brenda. She'd kept Kevin alive and brought him back safely. What was it Major Fitzmaurice said once, "All men know fear, a brave man faces his fears and carries on despite them." Yeah, she had faced her fears and carried on. She was brave, braver than she ever thought.

"Annie, what now?" Kevin panted. "Where do we go from here?" He sat up and looked around, the destruction finally becoming clear to him. "The town . . . the company . . . my God. What happened here? Are they all dead?" His voice was beginning to rise in panic.

"Ah, there are two of my lost sheep." First Sergeant Bellotti's voice came from their left, out of the door of the house they slumped against. He walked out and stood in front of them. "It's all clear. You two can take your masks off. In your case, Long, the mask is probably an improvement." He tuned to face Ann-Marie and said brusquely, "Sergeant Dumont, the company commander needs your report on the LP and whether or not you saw any bad guys up there."

Bellotti remembered his own baptism of fire one humid summer day in the Au Shau Valley. His platoon sergeant had acted as though nothing unusual had taken place, and normalcy served to steady the nervous and shaken soldiers. Now, in Altendorf, Bellotti was trying the same approach to help his soldiers calm down.

"Where's Brenda?"

Ann-Marie pulled herself erect and began taking off her mask. The rim of the mask had left a deep red mark outlining her face. The shock of the past few hours had drained the blood from her face, making the red mark even more prominent.

"Brenda's dead, Top. The Russian tank got her right before it tried to run over our hole."

"A Russian tank tried to run over your hole?" Bellotti repeated. "What happened out there? Never mind. Let's go find the company commander, and you can tell us both the story. Come on, Kevin. You, too."

As the three soldiers began moving back up Ringstrasse, two new explosions jolted them. A house at the end of Ringstrasse, where the street stopped and farm fields began, puffed smoke from the front of its foundation and gracefully slid over the roadway. Its rubble lapped against the house opposite and effectively sealed the street against vehicles, unless the piled rubble was bulldozed aside.

"Shit, Top," Long exclaimed as he flinched from the explosion and looked for a safety hatch. "Are the Russians still shelling us? Aren't they ever going to stop?"

Bellotti chuckled and slapped the younger man on the shoulder. "Easy, Kevin. Easy. It's not the Russians. That's the Germans doing a little selective rubbling."

"What's that, Top?" Ann-Marie pushed Kevin on his way. "Let's get moving, Kev. The faster we get inside, the safer we'll be."

As they entered the alternate CP, Bellotti answered her question. "We identified buildings that we didn't want or couldn't occupy. The German pioneers rigged them with demolitions. Now they're blowing them up. They'll create roadblocks that will either slow down the Russians or force them to come the way we want them to. You two just became the company commander's messengers so come with me to the new command observation post."

"Before we go anywhere, Top," Ann-Marie answered the First Sergent. "Kevin and me have to make a stop in that alley over there." She led Long into the alley, where they pulled off their MOPP suit pants and disgustedly threw away their soiled underwear and BDU trousers. Donning the MOPP suit pants, they retrieved their rifles and helmets and stepped back on to the street.

"I'm ready now, Top," Ann-Marie told the first sergeant. "Let's go kill Russians."

The first sergeant led the two soldiers up to the second floor of the building just as the first salvos buried themselves in the buildings and erupted like hell's mushrooms, gray and black laden with death. They hurled themselves flat on the bedroom floor and curled into small balls of humanity.

Across the width of the room, Vicki crouched against the front wall of the house as the Russian artillery flowed like lava over the edge of town. As the house shook with concussion and shrapnel impact, Vicki trembled against the wall.

Her every instinct screamed, "Run! Run, you dumb bitch! Run and fuck everyone else!"

A round burst on the roof, splintering the ceiling and dumping years of family memories on the cowering Americans. A second round exploded on the front of the house, and a hand-sized fragment sliced through the wall, inches from her head.

"Now!" a voice roared in her mind. "What are you waiting for? Run!"

She found herself involuntarily gathering her legs into a sprinter's crouch. A single leap would have her out the door and on her way to the safety of the basement. Suddenly, a flash of Mike gripping her shoulder, saying, "When the time comes, you'll do good!" appeared in her mind.

A fist pounded her back, almost knocking her over and shaking her loose of her reveries.

First Sergeant Bellotti pulled her half around to face him. "You okay, el-tee?" Bellotti's punch was the punch of teammate to teammate just beating a power play or breaking the opponent's serve. "I generally don't disagree with General Patton, but right now, I really really would rather be shoveling shit in Louisiana!" he shouted over the incoming artillery. "How about you?"

The sheer mind-blowing incongruity of the question brought her up short. Without thinking, a laugh bobbled up, and she shook her head.

"I think I'm with you this time, Top, and not the general." She took a deep, cleansing breath and became a company commander again.

The second barrage fired into Altendorf drove the Americans from the building. The large window acted as a magnet and drew heavy attention from the Russian gunners parked in the wood line outside town. As she left the window, Vicki saw that some vehicles were going to penetrate the

Allied defenses. The battle was moving into a new and more dangerous phase.

Flushed from the alternate CP, Vicki now crouched beside Bellotti in the doorway of a shattered row house a few doors down the street and watched a BMP-2 slowly crawling toward them. The long barrel of its 30 mm auto cannon waved from side to side as though it could sniff out the danger the carrier rolled toward. Bellotti positioned his tank-killer team in the second story of the houses on either side of the street in a classic tank ambush. The soldiers lurked beside windows, each with three AT-4 anti-tank weapons that they could fire down onto the roof of any armored vehicle trapped in their kill zone. Bellotti positioned a daisy chain of anti-tank mines he would pull across the road in front of the target to blow off tracks and road wheels, leaving the tank or APC immobilized in the kill zone. The ambush team would then volley their rockets into the roof of the target and complete its destruction.

The carrier lurched to a halt as the mines exploded under it. Lost in the blast of the mines, six AT-4s smashed into the top of the BMP in small puffs of brown smoke and golden sparks. The driver's hatch popped open, and the driver scrambled out and down the front slope of his dying vehicle. He rolled to one side of the road and looked frantically for a safe place to hide. Vicki's world narrowed to the enemy soldier as she watched his frantic search for cover.

The memory of Rogers and Lopez flashed in her mind, and before she knew it, she called out in Russian, "Soldier. Quickly. Over here."

The tanker heard a voice offering him sanctuary and dashed toward the open doorway. Diving into the shelter, he looked up and saw two Americans watching him over the muzzles of their rifles. As he crouched there in shock and amazement, Vicki slowly and deliberately settled the stock of her M-16 in her shoulder, stopped breathing, and gently squeezed the trigger. The impact of the three-round burst threw the Russian soldier back out into the street, as dead as the APC he sprawled against.

She turned to Bellotti and said in a cold voice, "That's for Rogers, Top. He deserved that much."

"I didn't know you spoke Russian, Lieutenant," the first sergeant replied in a conversational tone as he turned from the dead tanker.

"I studied it at West Point," Vicki answered calmly as she switched magazines on her rifle. "Then my firm had vague plans of doing business in Eastern Europe so I brushed up on it." She refilled the magazine and slammed it into the weapon's receiver, a fresh round in the chamber.

Ringstrasse 65
Altendorf, FRG

About midmorning, Mike and his team were forced out of their house when the building on their left was overrun and the American garrison was killed. Mike contacted Plowman throughout the morning to call fire missions on the attacking Russians.

Now, as his team prepared to abandon their house, he dialed Plowman again.

"Plowman two five victor," a woman's voice answered after the third ring.

"Scholar zero niner. Fire Mission. Delta hotel 0037. Troops in open. Will adjust. Over."

"Plowman two five victor. Roger, delta hotel 0037. Troops in open." The operator repeated Mike's call for fire. She passed the request to the fire direction center and then called back. "Scholar zero niner, Plowman two five victor. On the way. Over."

Mike stepped up to the shattered window and peered around the sash, counting to himself.

From the first floor, a voice called, "They're getting pretty fucking close, Major. Anytime you're ready."

Two mushroom-shaped clouds appeared a hundred meters from the house, scattering a small group of infantrymen. Mike measured the distance between the impact point and their fighting position. From the corner of his eye, he saw a tongue of flame licking the house next door. The Russians moved a flamethrower team forward to clear out the Allied fighting positions. The bright flash of the flame sent a trickle of scared sweat down his spine.

"Fuck," Mike swore to himself. "I goddamn well didn't sign up for fucking flamethrowers."

"Right now would be a good time to leave, Major," the team leader shouted up the stairwell.

He had seen the flamethrower as well. The team's M-60 gunner fired a long burst toward the flamethrower and his support without noticeable effect.

"I really don't feel like being fried for their fucking lunch, Major"

"I'll be right there, Sergeant. Just give me a minute." As he dialed Plowman, he heard the sergeant's reply, "It ain't me hurrying you up. It's the fucking Russians. Fucking crazy officers—"

"Scholar zero niner. Drop one hundred. Fire for effect," he shouted in the phone as the machine gun opened up again.

"Drop one hundred?" Plowman repeated. "Are you sure, Scholar? That's your position."

"Where do you think the Russians are, Plowman? Fire the bloody mission." Mike threw the phone over his shoulder, dove out the bedroom door, and headed down the stairs to the front dining room.

The team leader waved his soldiers out the dining room window as he threw smoke grenades into the street to cover their movement.

"It's about fucking time, sir," he said, greeting Mike. "I thought you were going to introduce yourself to those guys." They each threw a fragmentation grenade into the hallway and climbed out the window.

Mike's fire mission landed on the house and the Russian flamethrower team just as the Americans made their escape. This bought them an extra five minutes to dash across the street into the next strong point and reinforce the crew.

As they settled in the new bunker, Vicki appeared with her radio operator trailing. When she saw Mike, she pushed her way over to him. "Major, can you get your tank hunter team together? Some tanks have managed to get into town and are roaming around, shooting up the place. So far, they don't have infantry support. Ed's gone over to the Cav to get some help from them, but I think we ought to start our own efforts instead of waiting."

Mike nodded, shouldered his M-16, and told the machine gun crew to take care of themselves. He followed Vicki out the back door of the building. They headed back toward the center of town, to an empty store that the Americans had taken over for use as a storage room. By the time the two officers arrived, First Sergeant Bellotti had assembled the two tank hunter teams Mike had trained earlier.

Each team consisted of six soldiers—one SAW gunner, two grenadiers, two riflemen, and the team leaders, Mike and First Sergeant Bellotti. Each team member carried two AT-4s and as many hand grenades, both smoke and fragmentation. They also carried as many extra magazines for their M-16s and SAWs as they could stuff in their pockets or hang on their LBE. Each team carried a PRC-77 backpack radio tied into the company command net to track the movement of attacking tanks. As Vicki showed Mike and Bellotti the situation, the teams put together their main weapons, the Eagle fireballs, and satchel charges. Now, the two teams were silently preparing to perform their drills for real.

Haupstrasse 85
Altendorf, FRG

Mike gathered his tank hunter team in the corner of a building on the main street. Over the crackle of small arms and burning buildings, they could hear the throb of diesel motors and the squeal of tank tracks. At least two tanks had broken into the town and now slowly moved down the main street, alternately firing their main guns into each house as they passed. There were no reports of Russian infantry passing over the wire belt so the tanks were on their own without infantry escort.

Jesus, Mary, and Joseph, Mike thought to himself as he watched the tanks waddle down the street. *Those fuckers are big. I'd forgotten how fucking big. Beth will fucking kill me if she ever finds out what I'm doing. I must be out of my fucking mind. But I can't let my men see that.* Mike swallowed his fears and turned back to his team, poker-faced.

"Okay, here's the plan." Mike wrapped detonating cord around a half-filled five-gallon fuel can. "We'll use the doorways to move up the street toward that tank and try to catch him while he's working on one of the houses." He paused, taped a white phosphorus grenade to the outside of the can, and looped some more det cord around the grenade. "When I give you the word, start throwing your smoke grenades between us and the tank. Each of you throw two grenades and then get ready to use your rifles. I'll move up and throw this thing on the rear deck, light the fuse, and get the fuck out of there. When the fireball detonates, we'll move back here as fast as we can." He pointed out an entrance staircase, six houses down the street. "We'll head for that entryway and use it for cover."

The Americans ran toward the doorway Mike pointed at and crouched as low as they could and still move. The lead

Russian tank slowly rolled toward them but buttoned up. The crew could not see the ambush team move into position. The tank stopped opposite the ambush site and swung its gun toward the house across the street from where the Americans had gathered. A machine gun was firing from the second floor of the house, pecking at the turret in a futile gesture of defiance. The tank's main gun elevated and fired, destroying the front of the house and the machine gun in a mushroom of fire and dust.

As the turret began to turn toward to the front, the six soldiers hurled their smoke grenades into the street. Some landed in the road, sputtering and fizzing. Others bounced onto the tank and began creating a bank of green, red, and purple smoke. Mike laid down his rifle, took a few deep gulps of breath, murmured a quick Hail Mary, picked up the gas can, and dashed through the smoke to the rear of the tank. He swung the can up onto the rear deck, pulled the grenade pin and the fuse lighter in one motion, and dashed back to the staircase. As he slid into the cover of the landing, the bomb detonated on the back of the tank and set off a secondary explosion from the tank's fuel cells. Hatches on the turret popped open, and the crew tried frantically to bail out of their burning vehicle. The SAW gunner hosed his fire over the turret and cut down the tankers.

"Let's go before his buddy shows up and tries to do the same to us," Mike said.

He led his team back toward the town square. Behind them, they could hear the diesel of the second T-72 rev as though in anger and frustration, as it slowly reversed to find a way around the wreck blocking the street in front of it.

Fuck, Mike thought silently. *If he pushes hard enough, he can go around the wreck, and we are royally and truly fucked.*

Ahead of them, from a side street, a group of Russian infantrymen spilled on to Haupstrasse. One saw the approaching Americans and began screaming a warning to his fellows. The SAW gunner in Mike's team flipped his weapon around to his front and opened fire, followed by the rest of the

Americans. Their rounds kicked up dust and stone fragments around the Russians who immediately returned fire. For an eternity, both squads stood almost face-to-face and sprayed each other with steel until everyone ran out of ammunition at the same time. At that instant, a Bradley fighting vehicle entered the street from the Markplatz. The Bradley began firing indiscriminately toward the two groups of foot soldiers. A 25 mm cannon shell blew the SAW gunner standing next to Mike in half and decapitated his RTO. The Americans scattered like pigeons for cover before the Bradley gunner could fire a second volley and pick up the targets he had missed.

The second burst of fire from the Bradley never arrived. The gunner saw the second T-72 moving around the burning hulk of its partner and switched his aim from the infantry to the greater threat of the tank. From where he crouched behind a pile of rubble, Mike watched the TOW launcher on the Bradley's turret swing up to the firing position and spit a missile toward the Russian tank. The T-72 caught sight of the American vehicle as it launched a TOW missile and fired back in desperation. The two projectiles passed in flight. The tank dissolved in a fireball as the ATGM passed over its turret, and the tandem warhead detonated down onto the tank's weakest part. The Bradley did not survive to celebrate its victory. The Russian gunner punched off an armor-piercing sabot round as his last act. The long rod penetrator skewered the Bradley like a Christmas turkey. Passing through the vehicle at twice the speed of sound, the penetrator ignited the fuel and ammunition load. The Bradley disintegrated in a golden fireball and a thunderous clap.

As the two armored vehicles subsided into their death throes, Mike rallied the surviving members of his team in a narrow alley off the street between two houses. "Okay." He grunted as they gathered around him. "Now we've seen Murphy's Law of War number twenty-two: Friendly fire isn't; and Murphy's Law number fifteen: Incoming fire has right of way in action. Anyone else hurt besides Little and Cagney?"

"Negative, Major. The rest of us are okay," one said. "But that fucker in the Bradley did a job on our radio." The man held up the PRC-77 he had just removed from the RTO's body. A large hole in the middle of the chassis dripped circuit cards and ribbon cables. "This thing is for sure deadlined."

"Just like Little's been deadlined," another said with a voice sliding into hysteria.

"At least he won't have to worry about his complexion problem anymore." Little was notorious in the unit for a severe case of acne so bad that he had medical permission not to shave.

Mike let the laughter flow for a few minutes to relieve the tension and then snapped. "Right, now knock off the bullshit and get serious. Did anyone see where those Russian grunts went? They might be a little pissed off that we blew up a couple of their tanks and tried our best to blow them away."

The consensus was that the Russians disappeared when the Bradley opened fire. Mike cautioned his troops to keep alert and led them back toward the company command post. He wanted at least one replacement for the wounded and dead solders and a new radio. He also wanted to find out what the general situation was and whether there had been another breakthrough on the town perimeter.

On his way back to the company CP, a runner met him with a report of an emergency at the group's headquarters building. A Russian tank and two accompanying APCs were attacking it with direct fire. The first sergeant's tank killing team was trying to destroy the enemy vehicles and needed help. Mike and his team broke into a double time, actually more of a fast shuffle, toward the building. As they moved closer, they could hear a tank main gun firing into the buildings around the school. They stopped in a cross street two houses down from the schoolyard to take stock of their situation.

As Mike went forward to see what was happening, Ann-Marie and Kevin appeared loaded down with demolitions and fuel cans. They arrived in time to resupply his team so they could attack the Russian vehicles menacing the group's command post.

When Mike returned from his scouting trip, Kevin was taping a white phosphorous grenade to the outside det cord-wrapped fuel can. Mike began preparing the second can as he briefed the team on attacking the tank. He would carry one bomb and throw it on the tank while the team concentrated on suppressing the accompanying infantry.

Kevin stood up and took the SAW from the soldier who had taken it from the dead gunner. "I always wanted to carry one of these suckers. I fired expert back at Devens before we deployed." He slung the carrying sling around his neck. He draped extra ammunition belts Rambo-style around his neck.

"But you were wearing your glasses then, Kev," Ann-Marie replied. "You better get close now so you can see what you're shooting at and not hit any of us by mistake."

Mike looked up at the sound of Ann-Marie's voice. She never would have made such a remark before. He thought briefly that something had happened to her and changed her. *After the battle*, was his next thought. He would worry about it then. Everyone was changing.

"What are you two doing here, Dumont? I thought you were on the OP/LP."

"We got evicted, sir. The Russians wanted it more than we did. The old man told us to find you with this resupply and then stick with your team if you needed any help." Dumont looked around at the rest of the team. "I'd say you need two bodies for now. Anyway, we can't get back into the CP until those goddamned Russians outside get killed." The tone of her voice was hard, and the profanity was something she rarely used before.

Mike moved around to the front of the school, where the Russian tank squatted in the street, firing its main gun into the building. The artillery had badly battered the two-story row house next to the school. Its roof was smashed in, and the top floor was collapsed inward. The front of the building had been split open, and rubble from the interior spilled like entrails out onto Hauptstrasse. This provided a covered way for the Americans to approach the tank and set themselves up for the assault. In an inexplicable blunder, the accompanying Russian infantry had not secured this pile of wreckage. Mike made great use of their failure.

As the team took up its positions, a figure appeared in one of the shattered windows on the second floor of the school. It was Major Harrison, the new adjutant. He carried one AT-4 anti-tank launcher ready to fire with another slung over his left shoulder.

Mike watched in stunned amazement as Harrison stepped into view. *What in God's name is he trying to do*, Mike thought. *He can't possibly be thinking of shooting at the fucking tank! I don't think he knows which end of the bloody rocket points where.*

Harrison stepped up in the open frame, sighted his missile, and fired at the turret of the T-72. The missile's back blast blew debris past him as he swung the second round from his shoulder and began arming it. His first shot struck the gun tube just where it joined the breach. Before the tank crew could react, Harrison fired his second rocket. It struck the trunnion of the main gun, freezing it in position. With two rockets and a great deal of luck, Harrison had disabled the tank's main gun and transformed the T-72 from a deadly main battle tank to a diesel-powered, 45.7-ton portable radio. Harrison did not live to enjoy his success. A machine gun opened fire and smashed him back into the empty room.

"Fuck," a rifleman next to Mike swore. "Dude had balls the size of watermelons. Not that it did him a whole fucking lot of good."

Mike folded Harrison's' bravery in a corner of his mind to be reflected on later. Now, he had to kill Harrison's killers.

The tank crew began to react to their situation. The engine belched black smoke as the driver threw his transmission into reverse to begin his flight to safety. In their haste, they backed into one of the craters blocking the street. The driver tried to pivot out of the trap, but he only succeeded in snapping the left track and leaving the tank stuck like a beached whale. Without hesitating, Mike ordered his team to open fire and throw their smoke grenades. As the smoke clouds began to bloom and surround the tank, Mike slid over the shattered bricks and beams of his hiding place and ran toward the tank. The tank commander popped open his hatch and manned the heavy anti-aircraft machine gun. He caught sight of Mike as the American ran up to the rear deck of the vehicle and slung the firebomb onto the engine compartment. As the tanker frantically tugged to swing the gun to bear, Mike yanked the fuse lighter and dove back to cover. The Russian was swinging his gun around when the fireball ignited, and a burst of rifle fire hit him in the chest and head. He slumped and fell back into the turret. The tank stalled, and the driver threw open his hatch, scrambled out, and dove for safety on the side of the T-72 away from the Americans.

When Mike returned to the shelter of the rubble pile, he found Ann-Marie crouched in the lee of the pile, watching the burning tank.

"That tanker almost got you, sir," she said. "I managed to get him first. You ought to bring Kevin to cover you with his SAW next time." Her tone was conversational, as though she were discussing a trip to the shopping mall.

Mike leaned back against the bricks and caught his breath. He gripped his rifle with both hands to hide the shaking from Ann-Marie.

"Thanks for the help, Ann-Marie. Next time, I think I'll let someone else do the hard part." He noticed then that she had the second charge beside her. "What are you doing with that?"

"If you didn't make it, I was going out. After this morning, I think I don't like Russians," she said flatly. She kept her back to the major so he wouldn't see how white her face was.

"Next time, let someone who's been trained with those things be the backup." He paused and tried to take the sting out of his words. "I'll write your parents and tell them you're trying to get a medal out of this and not listening to me. They want me to keep you out of trouble."

"If you do that, sir, I'll tell Dr. McCann that you're doing a sergeant's job," Ann-Marie said, snapping back. "She wants me to keep you out of trouble."

The Russian infantry finally realized their mistake in not securing the area across the street from their positions and began to move against the Americans. Before Ann-Marie and Mike could complete their retreat, a volley of Russian grenades fell around them. Most hit the lip of the pile of rubble and bounced away, but one rolled to the bottom and detonated as it tumbled under a slab of concrete. Ann-Marie was sheltered from the blast, but Mike caught the edges of it. The concussion slammed into him like a baseball bat, snapping his head back against a broken cinder block and knocking off his helmet. He felt something pluck at his right arm and something else slam into his flak jacket. He toppled forward, dazed.

Ann-Marie grabbed him by the LBE and jerked him up. "Come on, sir." She grunted. "They'll be coming in person next."

She pulled the groggy man erect and shoved his helmet on his head with one hand as she held him up with the other. A slithering of rocks proved she was correct. She looked over her shoulder in time to see the top of a Russian helmet appear at the edge of the rubble pile. She dropped Mike, swung up her M-16, and pulled the trigger. She had locked her weapon on full automatic, and the thirty-round magazine emptied in one long burst.

As she fumbled with the magazine release, Mike came out of his daze. "Let's go, Ann-Marie." He shook his head to clear the cobwebs. "You get moving. I'll cover you."

The two scuttled back to where the rest of the team lay, pouring fire into the Russian position to shield their retreat. Two machine guns and then a third began to fire on the Americans. One of the Russian gunners rapidly found the range. His fire swept over the Americans and forced them to hug the ground. One of the team stuck his head over the top of the rubble to spot where this gun's fire was coming from.

He toppled back with the top of his head shot off. As Mike and the rest of the soldiers huddled behind the broken concrete and cinder blocks, a diesel engine roared as one of the BMPs began to edge its way around the burning carcass of the T-72. The BMP gunner sprayed the buildings on either side of the street liberally with his auto cannon as the vehicle slowly advanced. He spread his fire so freely that he silenced the Russian machine gun team pinning the Americans down. The surviving members of the tank-killer team ran back down the alley away from Haupstrasse.

They moved back to the abandoned shop the Americans were using as a staging area and began to resupply themselves with grenades, C-4, det cord, and AT-4s. Ann-Marie dragged Mike over to where a medic from a forward detachment of the 302nd Combat Support Hospital was treating other wounded soldiers.

"Doc," she said, snapping as she jerked the man around to face her. "My major's been hit in the arm. Take a look at him."

As the young woman spoke, Mike looked at his arm and saw a long tear across the right sleeve of his MOPP suit. The medic cut away the MOPP suit and BDU jacket to reveal a jagged tear in the right bicep that slowly oozed blood along its six-inch length. The medic wrapped a field dressing around Mike's arm and then saw the cut on his forehead.

"These both need sutures, sir," he told Mike. "I don't have time to do them now, but you're not real bad. I'll just fill out this evac tag and send you down to the aid station where the PA can take care of you." He put a small square of gauze on Mike's forehead and taped it in place. Then he pulled out a field evacuation tag and started to fill it out.

"Take that goddamned label and paste it on a bottle." Mike tore the document from the young man's hands. "I'm not going anywhere except back out with my troops."

Markplatz
Altendorf, FRG

In the final throes of the fight, Mike was separated from his teammates and found himself on a side street leading to the Markplatz. Lumps of camouflaged fabric marked the course of the battle, green woodland for Americans, leopard spots for Germans, and light green leaf pattern for Russians. Debris spilled out of damaged and destroyed buildings, family treasures mixed with shell casings, bloody uniform scraps, twisted and burned vehicles, and odd bits of personal equipment.

Through a ragged hole in one two-story building, he saw two Americans hunched in death over their machine gun. Below them and to his front, a squad of Russian infantry poured over the ramp of their BMP, frozen for eternity in their battle drill. The BMP's cannon pointed upward in a pose of retaliation, slightly masked by fire and smoke from the anti-tank rockets that killed it.

Mike walked wearily across the town square, carrying his M-16 in his left hand by the pistol grip. He detoured around a solitary T-72 that had penetrated the defenses this far, only to be stopped by a Mercedes sedan parked across the street. The driver had tried to run his tank over the car and exposed the belly of the tank to an ambush of AT-4s and Carl Gustav recoilless rifles as he tried to climb the obstacle. Now, the dead hulk of the tank squatted half on the car and half off with its gun canted skyward. A thin column of black smoke spiraled from the commander's hatch, sprung open by the blast that killed tank and crew. Behind the T-72, a volley of AT-4s fired from the second and third stories of the buildings on either side of the street had hammered a BMP-2 into a pile of spare parts. It burned now in a low fire as its load of small arms ammunition cooked off like popcorn.

Mike stopped and looked at the body of a Russian infantryman, sprawled in the gutter at the edge of the square. The Russian lay on his back with his eyes closed and his mouth open in a silent scream. He clutched his AK-74 in one hand and a pink teddy bear in the other. The incongruity of the two made this corpse stand out from all the others.

"Jesus Christ. I wonder what he was going to do with that." Vicki walked up behind Mike and saw what he was staring at.

"God only knows." Mike stretched his back and shook his head. "What's the situation now?"

"Our sector is quiet. They have pulled back beyond Hill 287, and the counterattack by 287th Armored and the French has moved right on by us. The Germans are getting ready to follow out after them."

Mike shifted his M-16 and draped the sling over his shoulder. He walked over to a pile of rubble and sat down, removing his helmet. The part of his mind keeping him sane and functioning overlaid the square with a scene of Waterloo and a quote from the Duke of Wellington. "Nothing except a battle lost can be half as melancholy as a battle won."

He rubbed his face, pulling open the cut above his right eye. The wound in his right arm was beginning to sting again. He could feel the wetness spread as the blood slowly soaked through the field dressing.

Vicki slung her own M-16 over her shoulder and sat down beside him. She stretched out her legs and then laid the rifle across her lap. "What's that god-awful stink?" she asked, almost rhetorically.

An atmosphere of burnt rubber, diesel fumes, and charred pork hung over the square.

Mike waved absently at the burning vehicles. "The crews, fuel and ammo. Dulce et decorum est pro patria mori, Lieutenant Baxter. One of history's balder-faced lies." He put his helmet back on. "You know that the old man's been medevac'd. He caught a round in the shoulder."

"Yeah, Dumont told me a couple minutes ago that she helped put him on the dust-off. She said he was kicking and fighting all the way about leaving us in the middle of the fight. I guess that makes you the acting group commander for the moment. Lieutenant Colonel Michaud's dead, so's Harrison, the S-1, and Baker from Log Ops. The only other O-4 left is Major Roberts, and you're senior to him. I don't know if we have commo to any of the battalions or even which battalion commander is senior. If you don't want the job, I suppose we could elect Lieutenant Colonel Morris over in the 152nd S and S because he's right here in town."

"Shit. Shit. What's the rest of the butcher's bill, Vicki?" Mike stood up in agitation. "Who did we lose? Has Top Belloti got a count yet?"

"No," Vicki said in a dead voice from where she sat. "Top's dead. O'Brian is now acting field first. Right now it looks like twenty-three dead, seventeen seriously wounded and another thirty slightly wounded, and six missing. The company's been wiped out." She stopped and looked up at Mike. "Have you had your arm looked at? You're bleeding like a stuck pig."

Mike looked down at his right arm. The medic had cut away the jacket sleeves earlier, and now the field dressing had slipped off his bicep down to the elbow. Blood slowly oozed in a spiral down his arm and dripped from his hand to form a puddle in the brick dust in the street. He was suddenly aware of a burning sensation, as though someone was slowly driving a red-hot nail through the muscles of his upper arm.

"It's not as bad as it looks. Let's start getting the company reorganized."

"Why don't you get over to the aid station at the Catholic church and get your arm looked at," Vicki said. "I'll get with Major Roberts, Ed, and O'Brian. Among the three of us, we'll take care of the company. You can also tell Lieutenant Colonel Morris that he's the acting group commander for the time being." She put her helmet back on and stood up.

"No, we'll go back over to the TOC first. I have to put together an updated SITREP for Corps. Then we have to make sure that we are being tied in with the 287th Armored as they pass through here. I'll get a medic there to take a look at this. Here, just give me a hand rewrapping this thing." Mike started to pull the dressing off his arm, but Vicki moved over and knocked his hands out of the way.

As she was retying the dressing over the wound, Ed appeared across the square. He was leading a file of six soldiers, festooned with bandoliers, smoke, and fragmentation grenades and anti-tank rockets. In contrast to the people behind him, Ed was bareheaded, a result of his earlier wound, and the dressing stood out like a khaki turban. He carried a SAW slung around his neck. The ammunition belt was draped over his shoulders like a stole. As he came closer, Mike could see that his face and hands, like everyone else's, bore the distinguishing marks of house-to-house combat—bruises, cuts, splinters, and burns. His flak jacket had a ragged tear down the right side. At least once during the day, combat had become literally hand-to-hand.

"Hey, boss," he called out when he saw Mike and Vicki. "I think we got them all." He led his team over to where the other two stood. "You know, Major," he said as he came up, "you look like shit. Know any good doctors?"

"A comedian," Mike said. "Just what we fucking need. A fucking comedian. What are you doing now, Ed, with your band of merry men?"

"We just mopped up the last two tanks in town. That is, we chased them into a kill zone for the Cav. Ever see what a 105 mm does at point-blank range. I think at least one round went right through the first guy they shot up," Ed answered in a cheery voice, as though he was describing the Monday night football game.

"Okay, but now it's time to get back to work. I want you and Vicki to start getting the headquarters reorganized. We'll need a count of dead, missing, wounded, and equipment losses. We also have to get the command net up and running again."

Mike started walking toward the Catholic Church where the aid station was set up. Ed and Vicki fell in beside him as he moved off.

"Vicki said Master Sergeant O'Brian is now acting as first sergeant, so we'll need a new operations sergeant. Vicki will continue as company commander—"

"Wait a minute. I'm senior to her," Ed said, exploding. "I should be the new commander. And besides, she's Quartermaster Corps—"

Mike swung around and grabbed Ed by the LBE with his good hand. "I don't give a flying fuck about seniority," he said, snarling in a low voice into Ed's face. "She fought the battle as the company commander, and she knows more about the situation than you do."

When he heard the anger in his own voice, he stopped and released Ed. He stepped back and shook himself as though emerging from a dark pit. "I want you to take over the Three shop while I get my arm looked at."

He turned in the direction of the aid station and started to walk down the rubble-strewn street. As he lifted his foot, everything went black, and his last sensation was falling down a long, dark cavern.

Chapter 10

Paying the Price—Second Installment

Blood is the price of victory
                    —Karl von Clausewitz

337 Cambridge Street
Boston, Massachusetts

Elizabeth sat at her desk, listening to her patient, Mrs. Antonia Portnova, describe in detail her aches and pains. Elizabeth listened with half her mind. Mrs. Portnova's biggest problems were her love affair with pasta and total aversion to exercise, a combination that led to a grossly overweight condition and the resultant sore hips and back. The part of her mind that wasn't listening to the catalog of aches and pains, all of which she had heard before on previous visits, concentrated on Mike and the lack of word on his condition. The news coverage of the clashes between Russian and American forces talked about the heavy fighting and severe losses but did not identify locations or units. As Mrs. Portnova droned on in a dull, dreary monotone, Elizabeth crossed her left leg over her right knee. Her concern was not modesty so much as a need to keep her feet still and not have them beat a tattoo on the carpet.

"Come on!" she screamed mentally at the older woman. "Come on. Finish up and get out of here. I want to call Maggie and find out if the mail has arrived yet."

"Well, Mrs. Portnova, I'm going to order some x-rays of your hips and back," she said aloud. "I can tell you now that the problem is your weight. You're just going to have to lose about forty pounds and start doing some exercise."

She reached for her prescription pad and began writing out instructions for her patient. What she really wanted to do was scream at Mrs. Portnova, "For the love of God, woman, get out of my office and leave me alone. Take your troubles elsewhere."

"Oh, Doctor, it's so hard for me to do anything. I work around the house and cook and clean, and by the end of the day, I'm just too tired to exercise. And my back hurts so much that I can barely work around the kitchen." The older woman moaned, as she did every visit. "Can't you just give me some medicine for this?"

Before Elizabeth could answer, her intercom buzzed. When she picked it up, the receptionist said, "Doctor, there's an army officer out here. He wants to talk to you as soon as you're available. He won't say what it's about."

Elizabeth's heart stopped. She recalled the visit she and Caroline made to Betty and the presence of the survivor assistance officer when they arrived.

Oh God, she prayed. *Not Mike.*

"I'll be right out." She put down the telephone. "Mrs. Portnova, I'll leave your paperwork with the receptionist, and you can pick it up later on. I have a visitor that I have to see right now." Elizabeth ushered the woman out the door of her office.

As she pulled the door open, a tall, leathery-faced man in army greens stepped into the office. Elizabeth recognized him as Tom Bradley, Mike's West Point roommate and the inspector general at Fort Devens. He drew Mrs. Portnova out by her elbow and firmly shoved her down the hallway toward the receptionist's desk.

"If you'll excuse me, ma'am," he said in a broad Texas drawl, "I've got some business with the good doctor."

"It's Mike," Elizabeth whispered. "Something's happened to him. Oh, God, Tom. Tell me he's all right."

Bradley led her back into the office, closing the door and sitting her down in one of the overstuffed chairs in front of her desk. His normally jovial face was strained, and his manner was unusually subdued. He sat down opposite her and pulled a message form from inside his uniform blouse.

"I just got this out of the communications center at Fort Devens about an hour ago. The center manager is keeping an eye out for traffic concerning my friends." He unfolded the paper and held it out to Elizabeth. "It says that Mike was wounded, but not seriously enough to be evacuated. She's sent an inquiry back to Europe for more details, but there was no response when I left to come see you. I thought I'd better get here before you saw the TV news."

Elizabeth looked at the document in her hands. It was a list of wounded, and Mike's name was highlighted. The wound category was "gunshot," and the disposition was "return to limited duty."

She looked up. "What does limited duty mean? And why are you worried about the TV news?"

"Do you have a TV here in the office?"

"Yes, there's one out in the reception area, but what—"

Tom stood up and looked at his watch. "Come on," he said. "We've got about five minutes if they're still running the same loop."

He opened the office door and strode down the hallway to the reception area. A television set stood in one corner, and a local talk show hostess was holding forth on the subject of extramarital affairs. Elizabeth caught up with Tom just in time to see him brusquely change channels to the cable news station and step back.

He folded his arms across his chest. "Watch this, please."

The half hour headline news began. The anchor immediately led into on-the-scene film of "a battle between US and Russian forces somewhere in Germany." The reporter described a Russian attack on a town held by US logistics troops trapped by the attacker's swift advance. As he spoke, the black shape of a Russian tank filled the camera lens. The tank stopped and began firing its main gun into a house on one side of the street.

The narration continued in a low, hushed voice. "The Russian tank is about fifty yards away from me, and I can feel the concussion from its gun as it fires. He is going from house to house and firing his cannon into the buildings to wipe out any resistance."

The camera swiveled to focus on a group of American soldiers, clustered around a pile of five-gallon fuel cans. One of the soldiers carried a radio on his back. Another had a machine gun with several belts of ammunition draped over his torso. A third knelt over one of the fuel cans, wrapping what appeared to be clothesline around the outside of the can.

"These soldiers are preparing to attack the tank with Eagle fireballs." The narrator picked up as the camera moved closer to the kneeling soldiers. "They will throw these napalm-filled gas cans on the tank in a last-ditch effort to destroy it by fire. Despite the odds against them, the soldiers are ready to try this desperate act."

At that point, the kneeling soldier looked up directly at the camera and said to the cameraman loudly and clearly, "Get the fuck out of the way, asshole."

The soldier was Mike.

Tom snorted loudly. "How eloquent. Can't you teach him manners?"

Elizabeth watched the rest of the clip in dry-mouthed silence. The six soldiers moved slowly down the street toward the tank, hugging the house fronts that lined the street. A short distance from the tank, behind the safety of a staircase, they stopped. Five of the soldiers began throwing smoke grenades around the vehicle. Mike, carrying the firebomb, crept slowly up to the back of the tank. He pulled the fuse on the fuel can and swung it onto the engine compartment. He scrambled back to the cover of the entranceway, and the film clip ended as an orange fireball consumed the tank.

"What's an Eagle fireball, Tom?" she asked quietly, trying to assimilate what she had just witnessed. "What was he doing?"

Bradley kept looking at the television screen, now showing a colored map of Germany with animated arrows and cartoon symbols of tanks, airplanes, and soldiers depicting the flow of battle.

"The Eagle fireball is a field expedient anti-tank weapon. It consists of a five-gallon can of napalm or a mixture of oil and diesel fuel. A two-pound block of TNT and a white phosphorus grenade are strapped on the outside." He spoke in dull, flat monotone, as though repeating a lesson. "Sometimes, barbed wire or grappling hooks are also attached, so the can will catch on the tank and be held in place. The device is delivered to the target, and the fuse ignited. The explosion will generally set off the tank's fuel cells and destroy the vehicle."

He turned to face Elizabeth. "What he did was just save a bunch of soldiers. That tank would have kept going down the street shooting into houses, either killing anybody in the building or causing it to collapse on them. It's a standard Russian tactic for fighting in cities, called 'more rubble, less trouble.'"

"How come Mike was doing it? He might have been killed."

Still looking at the television but not seeing anything, Tom replied, "Probably because there was no one else to do it. Someone had to show the other soldiers what to do. And, yes, he could have been killed. But sometimes, that is what being an officer all about. You lay your life on the line to show your troops what has to be done."

The anger and frustration that had been growing in Elizabeth for the past month exploded now at Tom. "Why does Mike have to lay his life on the line? Why does a reservist have to be the one to show other soldiers how to blow up tanks with firebombs? What happened to all the Regulars? All the career soldiers? Where are they? Why aren't you over there? You're the professional, not Mike. You're the one who stayed in for twenty years to get the retirement. So now why don't you earn the goddamned thing and let my husband come home safely where he belongs?"

Blinded by tears of rage against the army for sending her husband off to war and tears of fear for him, she turned and fled back to her office, slamming the door behind her.

For a moment, Tom stood and stared at the television. Every word Elizabeth said cut into him like a knife. He truly believed he should be in Germany because he was a Regular. Whatever she had said to him now, he had said many times before to himself. Ignoring the stares of the other people in the waiting room, he went over to the receptionist.

"I think you will probably want to cancel Dr. McCann's patients for the rest of the day," he said. "She really isn't in any shape to see them." He paused for a moment. "Tell her that I will be in touch with her as soon as I find out anything more about her husband. Here are my office and home telephone numbers. She can call me any time."

Headquarters, 16th Infantry Division (Mechanized)
Mainz-Gonsenheim, FRG

Casualties among the officers and soldiers of the Sixteenth Infantry Division were heavy. Not all were from enemy action. The division commander, Major General George R. Chandler, had relieved one of his ADCs thirty-six hours into the battle for what Chandler found to be gross incompetence and unsuitability.

After the relief was finalized, the deputy corps commander, Major General Barrett, visited the Sixteenth Mech. "General, I need a new ADC for support. Somebody who's hard-charging and fire-breathing and knows logistics," Chandler told Barrett over coffee in his office. "One of our major headaches is making sure that DISCOM puts out the bullets, beans, and fuel when and where the fighting soldiers need them. What I'd really like is a combat veteran who understands the stresses and pressures of combat and won't fall apart under them."

"George, I think I've got the man you're looking for. You heard about the fight at Altendorf, right?"

Chandler thought for a moment. "Yes, sir. One of my battalions, the one that got pushed out of Lauterbach, fell back on Altendorf. Before they could pass through the town, some support group commander grabbed them. He was putting together a blocking force to hold the town and delay the Russians. His people acted like a plug in a bottle and stopped a tank regiment. I have to tell you, General, there had been some heavy fighting there. Whoever put that force together knew his job."

"Well," said Barrett, "I think I might be able to help you out. The support group commander is an old infantryman. Why don't you have a talk with him and see if he's what you're looking for? He probably would make a better ADC than a support group commander."

"Okay, sir, I'll talk to him."

302nd Combat Support Hospital
Schotten, FRG

"Colonel Warren?" the officer asked. "Sir, I'm Captain Harding from the Sixteenth Mech. The chief of staff has instructed me to take you down to headquarters. Major

General Chandler would like to talk to you this morning." The captain paused and then pulled an envelope out of his BDU trouser pocket. "Sir, the chief told me to give you this letter when I found you. He said it would explain everything."

Warren took the envelope from the officer and opened it. When he unfolded the letter, he recognized Linc Barrett's scrawl.

Tubby, I have another job for you. George Chandler in the Sixteenth Mech needs a new ADC for support. I think it's time you moved on. You helped the 805th come over here, get set up, and go through its first fight. Now the Sixteenth needs you to help put it back together. Besides, there's a star in it for you. That means a promotion party and a chance for me to eat your lobsters and drink your single malt. I've already sent word to Caroline that you're in one piece. Linc.

Warren smiled grimly to himself, folded the letter, and put it in the chest pocket of his BDUs. He looked at the captain. "Captain Harding, I am yours to command. Let's go see what Major General Chandler has in mind."

The headquarters of the Sixteenth Infantry Division was an abandoned warehouse complex on the outskirts of Mainz near the Rhine River. Chandler's office was a bare, windowless concrete cubicle. The walls were empty of decoration, except a 1:150,000 scale topographic map showing the current disposition of the units of the division and corps. Chandler sat behind an old, battered wooden desk that appeared to have been salvaged from the local landfill.

Warren knocked on the doorframe. When Chandler said, "Come in," he walked to the front of the desk and saluted.

"Colonel Warren reports, sir," he said.

Chandler dropped the report he had been reading and returned Warren's salute. Then he jumped up from his seat and came around to the front of the desk to grasp Warren's hand firmly. Chandler was a short, bandy-legged man with a compact body. His black hair was cropped almost short enough to conceal his growing baldness.

"Colonel," he said, "I've heard a lot about you and your old unit, but I didn't make the connection right away. The 805th provided our general support when we were up forward on the line. I was very impressed with the support your soldiers gave us. Both my DISCOM commander and my G-4 tell me that it the best we ever received. What impressed me most about the group was the esprit and morale of the soldiers I met. That came from the leadership that they received, the guidance that you and the rest of your officers provided. That's what I'm looking for you to provide here at the Sixteenth. We took a licking last week, but it wasn't the soldiers' fault. We have to get their spirits back up and get them thinking that they can win again. I need someone who can think both tactics and logistics. I've got lots of fire-breathers, but they lose sight of the rest of the battle, the part about keeping the bullets and gas flowing. I've heard about Altendorf. You know how to fight. And you know logistics. I want you to be my ADC support. Are you interested?"

Warren had listened to the general in silence. The import of Barrett's note had not sunk in until then. "General," he said slowly, "I will do whatever is required of me. I have a young major, one of your fire-breathers, who used to have a line about our annual training. 'The army owns me for as long as I'm here, so they'll do with me what they want.' If you want me as your ADC, I'll do the best job I can. I have to admit that I'm not sure I'll live up to the advance billing."

Chandler leaned back against his desk. "Don't worry about the advance billing I received yesterday from a certain major general. I just made another connection that goes back a long time. Back to ancient history, in fact."

"What's that, sir?" Warren asked.

"About ten months after I was commissioned, I was assigned to Charlie Company, Fifth Battalion, Seventh Cavalry. We were outside Dak To at the time. The company commander was just getting ready to rotate home and get out of the army. He was going back to law school to join the family law firm."

Years fell away as John Warren listened. The office in Germany suddenly became a dusty landing zone in Vietnam. The stocky, balding major general became a short, skinny, sunburnt second lieutenant weighted down with rucksack, steel helmet, and M-16.

"Jesus," Warren burst out in amazement. "Bobby. Bobby Chandler. You took over second platoon about ten days before I went home."

"And started learning how to be a leader from you. I never got a chance to thank you before now." Chandler paused. "I want you to teach the same kinds of lessons. And do the same kinds of things you did back then for us now."

302nd Combat Support Hospital
Vicinity Schotten, FRG

Mike's arm wound required more extensive treatment than the aid station could provide, and the physician's assistant thought he detected traces of concussion. Mike tried to refuse evacuation and stay at the headquarters. Vicki, Ed, and Ann-Marie had bundled him on the ambulance, saying that, if they could medevac the colonel, they could medevac the major.

As the doors were being shut, Vicki stuck her head in the cabin. "I promise to keep the headquarters in one piece until you get back. We'll put the war on hold while you're gone."

Once the ambulance had started moving, the adrenaline gave out, and he lapsed into unconsciousness. He woke only briefly at the triage section of the hospital. The surgery on his arm was done under a local anesthetic, but it still put him out for most of a day. His diagnosis was a slight stress reaction as well as a minor concussion. He was confined to bed for twenty-four hours during which time he compared the bedside manner of the doctors in the combat support hospital to the bedside manner of a redheaded orthopedist in Boston. He decided he much preferred the latter.

Now he lay in a cot in the light surgical ward, half-asleep, trying to sort out the events of the past few days. Images of the battle flooded his mind. He replayed attacking the T-72s again and again, wondering if he were brave or stupid. He shuddered as he recalled leading his soldiers into the attack. Beth would kill him if she ever found out.

A shoulder patch thrown on his chest interrupted his thoughts. A battalion crest was pinned to the patch, the flying griffin of the Sixteenth Mechanized Division.

As he picked it up, a vaguely familiar voice said, "I've always known the hardest part of an Irishman is his head. That must be why the Russians went for the arm." Major General Barrett stood at the foot of Mike's cot, holding a sheaf of papers folded in one hand. "The doctors here tell me that you're about ready to do some honest soldiering. Them, I'll believe. My old Ranger buddy, and your former boss, says you can probably help me out. You, I'll give the benefit of the doubt to, considering he recommended you to me. And he also refuses to go without you."

Mike struggled to sit up. "Good morning, sir. What are you doing here? Have you seen Colonel Warren? How is he? When will we be getting back to the group?"

"Take it easy, Fitzmaurice." Barrett moved up alongside Mike's cot. "You two aren't going back to the group."

"What? Why not?" Mike exclaimed.

"For one thing, the group commander slot doesn't call for a BG. That's why Tubby isn't going back. If you look at the other item I gave you, it will help explain why you're not going back."

Mike picked up the shoulder patch and looked at the crest pinned on it. The crest was an infantry battalion's, but Mike couldn't recognize which one.

"I'm afraid I don't understand, sir. The patch is the Sixteenth Mech, but I don't recognize the crest. Maybe it's the drugs I've been taking, but I have no bloody idea what you're talking about."

"Well, football players always were kind of slow, even when I was a cadet. Must have been all the hits on the head. The Sixteenth got pretty badly chewed up. They lost a lot of officers, including an ADC. John Warren is going up as the ADC, which will get him the star he should have had a long time ago.

"The Second Battalion, Sixty-Sixth Infantry, needs a new executive officer. The new support group commander, my former G-3, Colonel Porter, has his own choice for group S-3, leaving you without a job. And Colonel (promotable) John H. Warren IV refuses to go without you. Once you get off your ass, Major, the job at 2/66 Mech is yours."

Mike changed into battle dress and went after Barrett. When he arrived at the break room, he found Barrett sitting alone with three cups of coffee and a plate of doughnuts in front of him. The cigar lay next to his helmet, extinguished.

"Sit down, Major, sit down. This is also a no-smoking area." He gestured at the unlit cigar. "At least the coffee and doughnuts are free."

Mike sat down opposite the general and pulled one of the cups over in front of him. "Sir, what's the situation outside now? I have been out of it for the past thirty-six hours. The last I knew, the counterattack through our position had started successfully."

Barrett took a long drink of his coffee and settled back in his chair, lacing his fingers in his lap. "The counterattack restored the front. We pushed the Russians back to the old border, and that's where it stands right now. The French Fourth Armored Division is manning the Sixteenth Mech's former sector now."

"The French came in?" Mike asked in surprise. "I thought they were sitting this out until they could pick a winner and get on that side."

"What the French government said at the start of the war was that they would honor their political commitments to NATO. They would not act as a military partner unless French interests were threatened. They were engaging in the old French custom of deliberation, examining their bread to see which side it was buttered on.

"About the time the Russians collided with our covering forces, one of their sub commanders earned himself an everlasting place in our naval pantheon by torpedoing the French carrier *Clemenceau*. To rub salt in the wounds, he didn't sink the damn thing. He only damaged it enough to dry-dock it for a month." Barrett paused and sat forward. "But he did supply a reason for them to enter the war as part of the NATO military structure. SACEUR put a French corps behind us and the VII Corps down south as a reserve. That's where most of the counterattack force came from. In any case, they are now holding the sector that belonged to the Sixteenth. The Sixteenth is being reconstituted now back around Mainz.

"The second of the Sixty-Sixth took a bad hit during the attack and lost about all their officers. That's why I'm sending you down as the battalion executive officer. The battalion commander is coming straight from CONUS. Three of the new company commanders are coming from outside the Sixteenth. There's a shortage of combat-experienced officers available to fill the units that were shot up during the past week. That's why I want you to get out of this place as fast as you can. 2/66 needs you. I imagine the grunts in 2/66 will be very happy to have an executive officer who blows up tanks single-handedly on national television and has a CIB already."

Mike had the grace to blush. "I didn't know those guys were running around when we were going after those tanks. And I sure didn't know they were filming everything."

"No matter," Barrett answered. "The film clip received good play both stateside and over here. The troops have seen it, and it gave them something to cheer about." He paused and then continued seriously, "If it creates a legend, that's good.

You have to provide inspiration to your soldiers, Fitzmaurice, and every little bit helps. You must know your job and care for your soldiers. Then you must show them that you are willing and able to share all the dangers that they face. Those were two lessons we forgot in Vietnam, and we can't overlook them now. The CIB on your chest gives the soldiers a warm and fuzzy feeling that you've been at the sharp end. Your episode with the tank and TV news crew shows that you're the kind of officer who goes up front with the grunts. Remember what I told you. The battalion needs you. Get well soon, and get out of here."

302nd CSH
Vicinity Schotten, FRG

The hospital had reported Mike's release to the support group, so when he finished checking out, he found Ann-Marie and Kevin waiting for him.

"Hey, Major," Ann-Marie Dumont called. "Over here. We're your ride back to the group." Once she had his attention, she hustled across the waiting room, deftly avoiding the other personnel waiting for transportation back to their units and smothered him in a bone—cracking bear hug. Her left hand was bandaged, and she had wedged it inside the harness of her LBE . . . "God, it's good to see you again, sir. We hadn't heard a word on you or the colonel until this morning, when the S-1 got your orders." She released him and Kevin Long gripped him by the forearms.

"Kevin, get the major's gear, then put it in the truck and come around front to the dismount point. We'll wait here until you do."

"I can't get his bag, Annie." Kevin sighed as he followed in her wake. "You're still in front of me."

Nonplussed, Mike mumbled something appropriate in reply. The breezy self-assurance was the most notable change in the young woman standing in front of him. As he tried to adjust to the new Ann-Marie, Kevin deftly slipped the plastic bag of extra dressings, medications, and Red Cross toilet supplies from Mike's left hand and started back out the door of the reception area. The last time Mike had seen the young soldier before the attack, Kevin shuffled rather than walked and tried to avoid eye contact with others. Now, he strutted like a conquering hero. Both the man and woman were more confident of themselves and their abilities. They had survived.

As Long collected Mike's bag, the young woman led them outside the building under a camouflage net.

"Word is you're leaving the group, sir. Is that true?" she asked without looking at Mike.

"I'm being reassigned to an infantry battalion in the Sixteenth Mech, as far as I know. I had a visit from a two—star archangel this morning. How's everything back in Altendorf?"

"Outside Altendorf, really, sir. The new group commander, your friend Colonel Potter, took over the day after you were evacuated, and his first move was out of the town and into the forest park southwest of town. Says it's more tactical. Ed's being transferred out, finally. He was the first one to hit Colonel Potter for a fighting slot as soon as Potter signed the change of command orders."

"You mean Captain Chambers—" . . ." Mike started to interrupt and Ann—Marie surprisingly cut him short.

"I mean Ed-where's-my-medal-I'm-the-company-commander-not-some—woman—lieutenant. That Captain Chambers. He said that I am to bring you straight to Colonel

Potter when we arrive, without any stops to visit before your meeting. So you better give me your rifle and take this."

She handed Mike a 9 mm pistol in a black leather holster. "Field—grade officers aren't authorized rifles, and rifles can't be carried assault style." Mike noticed both soldiers still carried their rifles assault style but withheld comment. "We're in the Real Army now and not at summer camp. Your helmet chin strap is already buckled, so no problem there, but roll your sleeves up once we get in the truck, and leave the flak jacket with me. New company uniform SOP." She surveyed him critically from head to foot. "At least you didn't gain any weight in the hospital. Height and weight standards are enforced strictly now."

With that comment, Mike noticed Ann-Marie wore the eagle pin of a specialist and not the sergeant stripes he'd pinned on her before the battle. She studiously ignored his questions about that.

Kevin turned his truck off the main road about three kilometers south of Altendorf and headed into the woods that surrounded the town. About fifty meters inside the woods, an MP stopped the truck. All three occupants had their ID cards checked before they could proceed. The dismount point was a short distance down the trail, and Ann-Marie led Mike into the barbed wire-surrounded CP.

His interview with Colonel Porter was brief and pointed. Porter had indeed brought along his own choice as S-3 and wanted Mike out of the area as rapidly as possible.

"I'm tightening up a real slack ship here," he told Mike. "And I don't want any reminders of the old regime around at all. If you were a real soldier, you would understand. Nothing personal, Major. Just get your gear together and move on."

"Yes, sir," Mike answered through gritted teeth. "Do you want me to brief the new operations officer on the status?"

"I really don't think you have anything to contribute," Porter said disdainfully. "The situation here has changed quite a lot since you left the other day, and you're probably not up to speed on it." Porter gave his attention back to the papers on his desk. "That's all." He didn't look up.

Mike walked out of Porter's office to look for the company orderly room, about a hundred meters from the CP. He asked for the company commander, and a bespectacled, short black officer holding a canteen cup of coffee, dressed in a T-shirt stenciled with name and rank and BDU trousers, appeared from around the hanging blanket that partitioned the tent.

"Can I help you?" he asked as he stared blankly at Mike.

"Yeah, I'm Major Fitzmaurice, the old S-3. I came back to get my personal gear. I'm being reassigned to the Sixteenth Mech."

The captain sniffed loudly. "I don't know anything about personal gear, Major. I just took over. You'd have to see the supply sergeant, who's not here right now. Or maybe Baxter would know. She inventoried all the personal belongings of the casualties. She's getting her stuff together before she leaves."

Mike went over to the S-4 area and found Vicki briefing a new staff sergeant on the headquarters' property book. When she saw Mike walk into the van, she excused herself and jumped up to greet him.

"I understand you're leaving. I thought you would have kept the company. What happened?" Mike asked as they shook hands.

She picked up her helmet and rifle and led him back into the supply tent. Once inside, she dropped helmet and rifle and swept him into a deep, passionate embrace. Momentarily stunned, Mike instinctively responded. The embrace became a long, savage kiss filled with heated, almost animal desire. Mike pushed Vicki's web gear off her shoulders as she fumbled with his BDU jacket.

"Sweet suffering Jesus, Vicki." Mike regained control of himself and pulled away from his friend. "I don't know what . . . please forgive me . . ." Despite his halting rambling words of embarrassed apology, he still held the young woman pressed tightly to him.

Vicki laid her head on his chest. "Mike, don't apologize." She didn't lift her head. "I almost died back there a few days ago. Worse, I nearly broke and ran. Your trust and my fear of letting you down kept me sane. Whatever I did was because of you. You saved my life. And if Beth weren't a good friend, I would give you a rodeo that would leave you with a smile the size of Texas."

She pulled his head down for a final savage, passionate kiss and then broke free and picked up her helmet and weapon.

"What happened," she said in a bitter voice, "is that Colonel Porter arrived with his new broom, like Christ cleaning the Temple. I am not eligible for command right now because I am still a first lieutenant. He also feels I lack sufficient experience for such a demanding job. My promotion is effective September fifteenth. He can't wait that long for a qualified company commander." She paused for breath and then continued in a flat voice. "You will also be interested in knowing that he has pulled back all recommendations for awards from the battle, particularly the ones you did on me and Dumont. He said reservists always exaggerate the situation and he had to review the documentation to be sure all were correct in fact as well as format. He also had to check that the recommendations were reasonable and appropriate. We don't want to inflate the award system.

"He was really bullshit when he found out that Dumont had been in charge of the OP/LP. Both the Germans and the Cav say she was responsible for knocking out a tank with some AT-4s from about fifty meters. He told me privately that women should never be allowed into combat zones, and he was not about to forward a recommendation for an award that would reflect poorly on a unit that he commanded. He also told me that Dumont is going to lose her acting sergeant stripes."

"What is all that supposed to mean?" Mike asked. "I started most of those recommendations from the hospital and sent them to Harrison to finish off. I didn't know about the tank for Dumont, but that should only increase the chance that she'll be decorated. And you. Christ, you're a big part of the reason he still has a headquarters to command." Mike slammed his helmet to the ground. "Fuck it. I'm going back in to see just what the fuck he thinks he's doing."

Vicki grabbed his sleeve as he stepped out of the tent. "Major, it's not worth it. Besides, you're no longer a member of this command, and the one thing Porter knows is protocol and turf rights. If you start anything, you'll only screw yourself. We're alive, and that's all that counts." She dropped her hand away and sighed. "In any case, Harrison's dead. I guess you didn't know that."

"Vicki, what did you just say about Dumont losing her stripes?" Mike asked as he digested all that Vicki had told him.

"Oh, Porter had the new S-1 do a personnel inventory. She found the flag in Dumont's records because she's overweight. If a soldier is flagged, there can be no favorable personnel actions. The promotion to acting sergeant is a favorable action so it had to be rescinded. The flag was also justification for pulling the award for Dumont's actions during the battle. We can't have fat heroines." She kicked at the leaf-covered ground where they were standing and then looked off into the distance. "I argued all this out with him when he first arrived. He told me I no longer had any voice over personnel actions. When I persisted, I was told to pack my bags and leave. My services as PBO for the support group were no longer required or desired.

"About an hour ago, he called me in and showed me the endorsement he is putting on my OER. It's an adverse report. I am argumentative and disrespectful to superior officers, and I have a lackadaisical approach to property accountability. He wasn't very happy with the Carl Gustavs that we borrowed from the Germans. I think I'm being reassigned to the 156th, but there's been no official word."

A tap on his shoulder stopped Mike from answering her. He turned to find a short, stocky man behind him. "Are you Major Fitzmaurice, the old S-3? I'm Calvin Woods, your replacement. If I can interrupt for a moment, I'd like to ask you to tell me what you can about the group's status when you left. I just arrived yesterday, and I need some background about what was going on here before the shit hit the fan last week."

"Sure, I can tell you what I know," Mike said. "But Colonel Porter already said that he saw no need—"

"We just won't tell the colonel, will we?" Woods answered. "He's got this thing about reservists, and he doubts their abilities. Me, I don't care what kind of job you did before the war. I want to know what was going on so I can start doing my own planning. Come over to the Three shop and have some coffee while you spill your guts."

Mike excused himself from Vicki and entered the operations van with Woods. After about an hour, he had brought the new man up to date on the status of the group before the battle of Altendorf. Woods thanked him heartily and then asked about his new assignment. Mike told him he was on his way to an infantry battalion south of Mainz. Woods said he would get a driver and vehicle from the headquarters to take Mike to his new home.

That evening, as Colonel Porter sat down to supper, the S-1 entered the mess tent with a full colonel that Porter vaguely recognized. The S-1 brought the visitor over to Porter's table and introduced him as Colonel Pickering, the chief of staff for the Corps Support Command.

Porter stood up, and the two colonels shook hands. The S-1 grabbed one of the KPs and asked the man to bring over some coffee and cups for the commander and his visitor. As they sat down, Pickering asked Porter if he were getting settled in yet.

"Trying to, Colonel. Trying to." Porter recognized the name and remembered that Pickering was several years senior to him. In fact, Pickering was supposed to be on the next list for brigadier general. "I've got a lot of new people on board. It's an effort meshing them with the old-timers that are still here. There are a few bad habits that still have to be broken in the headquarters, but I think I'm getting somewhere."

"Yes, the old-timers." Pickering opened his notebook and pulled out a piece of paper. "They're actually what I'm here about, Colonel. Specifically about four of them that you will be losing." He handed the paper to Porter. "The first two names on that list are being assigned to HHC, Sixteenth Mech. The last two are going to a rifle battalion in the Sixteenth."

Porter took the paper without looking at it and handed it to his S-1. "I'm afraid I don't see the need for your visit. A personnel action like this could be handled through S-1 channels—"

"There seems to be a problem with the S-1 channels from this headquarters to ours," Pickering interrupted.

"Problem?" Porter looked darkly at his S-1. "I'm not aware of any problem."

"Things get lost in the 805th, Colonel. Things like recommendations for awards."

"I don't understand."

"A number of awards were written up for the soldiers in this headquarters and subordinate units as a result of the fighting last week. They've never arrived at COSCOM." Pickering took a cup of coffee from the KP and thanked her. When she stepped out of earshot, he said, "The names on that list rang a few bells among the staff, and we began wondering where the paperwork for their awards was. Especially when the COSCOM commander got two telephone calls from the German Territorial Brigade and the commander of the Eleventh ACR. They wanted to add their endorsements to the awards for the first two people on that list I just gave you." Pickering stopped and stirred his coffee.

Porter reached for the paper from the S-1 and read it. He looked back at Pickering. "Oh those. Well, I reviewed the drafts and decided the recommendations were inappropriate. They had put in some women for awards. The women had been shot at, and the former commander and his staff let their sympathy run away with them. But you know how reservists are, no sense of judgment or fitness." He chuckled softly. "They wanted to give a Bronze Star to one enlisted woman who was flagged for weight control. That obviously was impossible, so I stopped all the other recommendations."

Pickering considered Porter's comments for a moment and then said softly, "The last I knew, Colonel, the approving authority for the Bronze Star is the COSCOM commander. What is embarrassing about this matter are your actions in holding up the paperwork. You can recommend downgrading or disapproval. The final decision is the CG's. And we do have an awards review board up here, Porter. So just give me the packet, and I'll take care of it for now." The last was delivered in a curt snap.

Without waiting for Porter's reply, the S-1 stood up and left for her office to retrieve the file. After the captain left the table, Pickering, a veteran of Panama and Grenada, looked pointedly at Porter's right sleeve, bare of any combat unit insignia.

"I've always felt that you should judge a soldier on performance, particularly in combat. Anyone, male or female, fat or skinny, who is willing to take on a main battle tank with a couple rockets from fifty meters away, deserves some kind of medal."

The two colonels sat without speaking until the S-1 returned with a thick manila envelope and handed it to Pickering.

As he took it, Pickering stood up and said to Porter, "I'd expedite those transfers, colonel, if I were you. Colonel Warren, the former support group commander, is now ADC-Support, Sixteenth Mech, and he needs an aide and driver. Those are the two soldiers he's chosen. Major General Barrett up at Corps mentioned that Warren's name is on the list that went to the Senate today for confirmation as brigadier general. A positive response is expected shortly. Thanks for the coffee, Colonel. No need to get up. I can find my way out. I trust there'll be no more lost paperwork from the 805th."

Chapter 11

Pause Between Battles

The secret of all victory lies in the organization of the non-obvious
—Marcus Aurelius

Command Post, 2nd Battalion (Mech), 66th Infantry
Vicinity Finthen, FRG

The Second Battalion, Sixty-Sixth Infantry, set up their headquarters in a *gasthaus* named "Zum Dicke Katz" (the Fat Cat) on the outskirts of the town of Finthen, where the battalion was being reconstituted. Mike climbed out of the truck that carried him from the support group and entered the building. Ann-Marie and Kevin, who had volunteered to drive him from Schotten to his new home, sat in the truck and waited for instructions.

"Pull the truck around in the shade, Ann-Marie, and wait there." Mike pointed to a parking place beside a Humvee. "I'll find out where the mess hall is so you and Kevin can get something to eat."

The young woman nodded in assent and started up the truck as Mike pushed the door open and entered. Inside, the dining room was now a large map room and work area. Several tables had been pushed together to create a larger table, and a half-dozen computers and typewriters were busily clicking away. Behind what had been the bar now hung several large white, unlined paper tablets that contained scrawled lists of personnel and equipment. A group of three officers stood in front of the bar and discussed the lists in low tones. No one noticed Mike's entrance. He walked up to the three officers and introduced himself.

They were the Battalion S-3, Major Paul White; the S-3 Air, Captain Wally Bauer; and the S-4, Captain John Dugan. They were discussing the proposed reorganization of the battalion and the best way to integrate the new replacements and equipment into the companies. Mike's arrival pleasantly surprised Major White. He needed someone to take control of the planning and management of the reconstitution process so he could get on with planning for future operations. He told Mike the battalion commander was at brigade headquarters and would not be back in Finthen until later in the afternoon. Dugan was happy to find someone with a background in logistics. Three days before, he had been a lieutenant leading a rifle platoon in Bravo Company. Now he was learning the S-4's job the hard way. When Mike asked about the mess hall, Dugan said he was going to lunch and would take Mike and his two soldiers with him.

Conversation in the mess hall, two GP medium tents erected end-to-end behind the *gasthaus*, died as Mike, Kevin, and Ann-Marie walked in with Dugan. Mike had forgotten how unusual the appearance of a woman in a line unit was. As Ann-Marie moved through the tent, chatter fell off as the diners caught sight of her. After she passed each table, the talk picked up again.

Suddenly, as she slid around a group of soldiers clustered at a table, a tall, pimply-faced young man pulled her to him in a tight embrace. "If you want a good time, Johnnie boy here can give you the best you ever had." Before Mike or anyone else could react, he squeezed her buttocks.

Ann-Marie's face turned a bright cherry red and then white. She swung her free hand around to catch the soldier on the left side of his face. She half-twisted in his grip and smashed a knee into his groin. Locked together, the two toppled to the floor of the tent as the man folded in on himself in agony.

Ann-Marie wrenched free. "Touch me again, you jerk, and I'll cut your throat." She spat at the groaning soldier. She kicked him in the ribs and glared at his friends. "I choose who touches me. You guys have any problem with that?"

A tall, gangly black soldier held his hands up in mock surrender. "Lady, you can do anything you want. We ain't gonna come near you at all."

"Ann-Marie," Mike said in a conversational tone of voice, "I think the young man wants to apologize for his actions once he gets his breath back. Why don't you and Kevin move along? I'll take of this."

At that point, the battalion command sergeant major appeared on the scene. "Is something wrong, Specialist?" he asked Ann-Marie in a booming voice that matched his large frame and red face.

He wore a waxed handlebar moustache that stood out from his cheeks like horns on a Brahma bull. Now it quivered with suppressed rage as he glared at Ann-Marie's assailant. Both young soldiers began to speak at once. The sergeant major cut off the man with a swipe of his hand and a snarled "I'll hear your story later."

He turned to Mike. "If the major wouldn't mind, I'll handle things now."

The black soldier took a closer look at the patch on Dumont's left shoulder, the insignia of the 106th ARCOM, a mailed fist holding a battle axe.

"Shit," he exclaimed. "I know you guys. You're from that support outfit in Altendorf." He turned to the other soldiers grouped around him. "I was up there with these guys last week. We and them kicked us some royal Russian ass and made up for getting chased out of Lauterbach." He turned back and squinted in Ann-Marie's face. "There was a woman buck sergeant that got herself a T-72 tank. Then she followed that crazy-assed major around that was hunting tanks and got himself on television." His voice trailed off as he gazed between Ann-Marie, Mike, and Kevin. "Shit, it's you guys. You're the ones I been telling all these funugies about." He held out his hand. "Sarge, I want to shake your hand. You and your bro back there behind the major. I saw him doing some bad shit with that SAW of his the other day."

Flustered, Ann-Marie shook his hand. The other soldiers, veterans of the fighting in Altendorf, then surrounded her and Kevin, anxious to swap stories.

Mike nodded to the sergeant major and stepped away from the crowd. "I'm Major Fitzmaurice, the new battalion executive officer. Specialist Dumont and Private First Class Long drove me down from Altendorf. Once they get some chow and I unload my gear, they'll be heading back north," he told the NCO.

"Command Sergeant Major Taylor, sir. I recognized you as you came in. I'll take care of your soldiers, not that they need it now. The troops who were in Altendorf have quite a lot of respect for you," Command Sergeant Major Taylor answered as the two men shook hands. "Some of them refuse to believe that you're really reservists." His glance caught the man who had mauled Ann-Marie. He was now staggering upright as the other soldiers ignored him. "I'll also take care of that scumbag. No one assaults another soldier in my battalion area." He nodded to Mike, stepped over, grabbed the man, and led him out of the mess tent.

Command Post, 2/66 INF
Vicinity Finthen, FRG

The battalion commander of 2/66 sat behind his desk as Mike entered the office. Lieutenant Colonel Brian Carswell was a short, stout man in his late thirties with thinning black hair combed straight back over his head. As he reported, Carswell impatiently tapped a piece of stationery with the index finger of his left hand.

"So you're the famous Fitzmaurice," he said in a high-pitched voice. "Tell off the press and get your picture on the television, and you're a big hero."

Shit, Mike thought. *That goddamned television clip is going to follow me around forever.*

"Major Fitzmaurice reports, sir," he answered, holding his salute.

The commander finally returned it, and Mike dropped his arm to his side. It was still tender from the sutures. Irrationally, he thought that if Elizabeth had sewn him up, it wouldn't hurt at all.

"I suppose," Carswell said, "that we in the Second battalion, Sixty Sixth Infantry should be honored to have a real hero assigned to us. Now that you have your medals, are you coming down to slum with the grunts? Is this going to be the next ticket you punch? Ranger, Airborne, and now a star on your CIB? You must have some real pull. It's not every major that a two-star shoves down a battalion commander's throat." He made a show of studying the documents in front of him. "Ah, I see. The WPPA strikes again. That's why you're here."

The WPPA, Mike thought to himself incredulously. *The West Point Protective Association. I haven't heard that since I left the Eighty-Second Airborne ten years ago.*

"Colonel," Mike said aloud, "I'm not sure what this is all about. I've been assigned here as your exec because I'm a qualified infantry officer and because the battalion took such heavy casualties outside Lauterbach. If you have another choice for the position, I'm sure the G-1 would listen favorably to your request."

Carswell closed the file and looked up at Mike, who was still standing at attention. "Oh, the G-1 will listen favorably to my request all right. He just will listen to the request of the deputy corps commander more favorably. You must really have some kind of pull. Are they going to make a big hero out of you? Are you coming down to redeem us for our failures? I know all about you, Fitzmaurice, and all the others like you. You think everything has to go your way just because you went to the Point. Yes indeed, I know all about you. Now that you're back in the army, you think you can get away with using your pull to get ahead and make up for lost time. Well, I don't care who your friends are. I don't like reservists. Particularly those who think they can pull strings to get their own way just because they went to West Point. You're in my battalion now, and I'll fix you the first time you look cross-eyed. Understand?"

Welcome to the USS Caine, Major Fitzmaurice, Mike thought to himself.

Hiding his thoughts, he replied, "Yes, sir. Perfectly. While I am here, I will do the best job I can. I didn't ask to be your XO, but being the executive officer of a Mech battalion has been a goal of mine for a long time. I'm looking forward to the assignment."

Carswell snorted and dismissed Mike with a wave of his hand. As he headed for the door, Carswell called to him, "In the active army and in this battalion, Fitzmaurice, we don't address junior enlisted personnel by their first names, particularly women. Or is your relationship with that woman something other than purely military?"

Mike spun around on the colonel and snapped. "That was uncalled for. Goddammit, you have no right making comments about soldiers you don't know. For your information, Colonel, Specialist Dumont saved my life twice in Altendorf. Not only that, she and Private First Class Long killed a T-72 tank at about fifty meters range with a couple of AT-4s. Anyone who suggests she is not a good soldier had better have the same or better qualifications, whatever his rank."

He had heard that Carswell had just arrived in country from CONUS and had no combat experience. "Our relationship," he said in a low, angry voice, "is one of soldiers who have been shot at together. You'll get a chance to understand what that is in a few days."

He walked out of the office, feeling he had won a battle but probably lost the war.

Headquarters, 16th Infantry Division (Mechanized)
Mainz-Gonsenheim, FRG

The gossip in Headquarters, Sixteenth Mech, began working overtime when the new Assistant Division Commander announced that his aide and driver were two women soldiers from his former command. When the aide arrived, the gossipmongers nodded knowingly. The new ADC had his priorities straight and an excellent taste in partners. The driver was a little mousy, shy woman, but everyone knows those kinds get excited when they get turned on.

The company fell out for an awards ceremony in the morning. The new aide and driver stood among the soldiers who were to receive awards. Ribald comments flowed through the formation describing how the two women had earned their awards. The snickers died as the citations were read.

"The Bronze Star medal with Vee for valor is awarded to Specialist Ann-Marie G. Dumont, 125-42-4318, HHC, 805th Support Group, for heroism in action against hostile forces, Altendorf, FRG, August fourteenth. Despite being overrun by elements of an armored reconnaissance patrol, Specialist Dumont rallied a fellow soldier to attack and destroy a T-72 tank at point-blank range using AT-4 anti-tank weapons. Returning to friendly lines, she joined a tank hunter-killer team and assisted in the destruction of six other enemy armored vehicles during the fighting in Altendorf. While participating in this action and disregarding her own injuries, Specialist Dumont exposed herself to enemy fire to rescue friendly wounded on three separate occasions. The Purple Heart Medal is awarded to Specialist Ann-Marie G. Dumont, 125-42-4318, HHC, 805th Support Group, for wounds received in action against hostile forces, Altendorf, FRG, August fourteenth."

"The Army Commendation Medal with Vee for Valor is awarded to First Lieutenant Victoria L. Baxter, 213-70-8932, HHC, 805th Support Group, for gallantry in action against hostile forces, Altendorf, FRG, August fourteenth. Assuming command of HHC, 805th Support Group, after the death of the company commander, First Lieutenant Baxter rallied members of the company to repel and defeat repeated attacks by enemy infantry and armor forces. First Lieutenant Baxter's skillful use of supporting fires greatly aided the successful resistance of Allied forces holding Altendorf and played a key part in preventing the enemy's capture of the town."

Command Post, 2/66 INF
Vicinity, Finthen, FRG

After supper, Mike returned to his office and began wading through the pile of paperwork accumulated before his arrival. His immediate task was reviewing the Field and TAC SOPs. One purpose was an introduction to how the battalion planned to operate in field and garrison. He also was making a study of changes required to meet the new situation of wartime Europe. His meeting with Carswell ate into his mind like a slowly spreading pool of acid. One of his goals in the Reserves was to become an infantry battalion XO and then a battalion commander. When Major General Barrett visited him in the hospital at Schotten and announced his new assignment, Mike had been elated. But Carswell had successfully rained all over that parade. Instead of elation, Mike felt a nagging foreboding. Carswell was out to make a record and a name for himself. He would do whatever it took to look good to his superiors. And God have mercy on the person who slipped and caused him to look less than outstanding. Carswell wouldn't.

The same rampant careerism and ticket punching that drove Mike to resign his Regular Army commission and leave active duty nine years before was still alive and well. He shook his head with a sigh of resignation and reached for his copy of the battalion's field SOP. He would do his best. As Elizabeth had told him the night before he shipped overseas, that was all anyone could reasonably expect of him. If it weren't good enough for Carswell, then fuck him—and the horse he rode in on.

A sharp rap on his door interrupted Mike's review of Appendix 3, Field Sanitation Procedures, to Annex H, Mess Operations. "It's open," he said without looking up. "Come on in, and have a seat."

"I'm not disturbing you, am I?" Lieutenant Colonel Carswell said. "If you're really busy, I can come back later." He stood in the doorway, halfway into the room. "But if you have some time, I really would like to talk to you."

Mike hurriedly stood up and closed the binder containing the SOP. "No, sir. I'm just reviewing the field and the TAC SOPs, but they can wait." He was immediately on his guard. "I wanted to get a look at the SOPs and see how the battalion was supposed to operate," he said warily. "Then I was planning to meet with you and find out how you intend to use me and the rest of the staff."

Carswell entered the room and closed the door behind him. He pulled an overstuffed chair from the corner to a position in front of Mike's desk. As he sat down, he placed a metal thermos and two paper cups on the desk.

"Well, that's partly why I'm here, the second part really." He paused for a moment. "The first part is to apologize for my performance this afternoon when you reported in. "I realized now that I've regained my composure that I was way out of line."

"Apologize, sir? There's no need—"

"Bullshit. Spoken like a true product of Hudson Valley Voc Tech, but still bullshit. I was way out of line this afternoon, and we both know it. Had I said that to you two weeks ago, before I pinned on these silver leaves, you would have decked me. Part of what you heard was jealousy. I tried to get into the Point but never made it. Ever since then, when I see an Academy grad that got out before retiring, I get bullshit. Particularly when I see one who's got all the tickets punched that I need and don't have." He touched an empty space on his BDU jacket above his Airborne wings. In the same place on Mike's jacket, there was a CIB from his service in the Dominican Republic in 1965. Infantry officers took as gospel that success required an officer to be Airborne and Ranger qualified and to have either an Expert Infantryman's Badge or CIB. Lack of any part of the triumvirate was a limiting factor in advancement, particularly at the upper rungs of the ladder.

"There was also a large degree of frustration involved," Carswell said. "I had just returned from Division, where the battalion commanders were told that, within the next seventy-two hours, we will be part of a counterattack to relieve some of the pressure on NORTHAG. During this meeting, the division staff made it quite clear to me that they held 2/66 partly responsible for the breakthrough between Lauterbach and Fulda. As a counterpoint to our dismal performance, the staff told me about the paragons of military virtue and skills of the 805th Support Group. They further informed me that I was lucky enough to get two of those officers who would buck up the performance of the battalion. And, as a side note . . ." He sighed. "I heard all about your football career. How you sacked the quarterback and set up the winning touchdown for Army's upset win in the

Sugar Bowl your senior year. Just what I need, a goddamned recruiting poster—"

"Those dumb fuckers," Mike said, snapping. "This battalion was hit with at least four fuel-air explosive strikes during the Russian artillery prep. That's like being hit with four tactical nukes without the radiation. The big reason we held out at Altendorf as long as we did was that a lot of survivors from Two Six Six rallied on our position and stiffened us up. If those assholes at Division seriously think that CSS troops can take on and defeat line infantry and armor by themselves, they're out of their tiny fucking minds. And my football days ended a long time ago. All I have to show from them is a couple of bum knees and periodic migraines from the hits I took to my head." He shook his head in disgust. "Jesus Christ. Those jerks. Is that really all they have to do up there?"

"Well, at least we agree on that. You want some coffee? The mess steward at HHC informs me that the battalion exec now requires coffee and juice be available twenty-four hours a day for the troops." Carswell opened the thermos and poured two cups of coffee. "Please sit down. Where was I? Right, the two new officers from the 805th, one of whom is a TV star." He suddenly grinned at Mike. "I'm going to have to get your autograph one of these days. I've never known a TV star."

Carswell paused again. He leaned back in his chair and looked down at his coffee cup. "After you left, I thought about what you said about the bond of soldiers who have been shot at together. And I realized that you're right. I don't know what it's all about. Two weeks ago, I was commanding a recruiting station in Omaha. In three days, if we're lucky enough to have the full three days, I will have to take this battalion into combat. I need your help to get our people out of the pit they're in because of Lauterbach. They need to get their self-respect back. You've been shot at before, both here and in the Dominican Republic. You know what combat is like. I don't. You've got your CIB that shows what you've done, not to mention the CNN clip. I'm an unknown quantity to the soldiers. I'm not sure they will be willing to trust me in three days.

"I want us to be a team. You and I, and the sergeant major, will be the spark plug that makes us a success or failure. And failure here means the lives of our troops. I saw the way the two soldiers who came down here with you watched you. We need to create the same kind of bond and trust with our soldiers now. I don't know what you did to inspire that kind of loyalty, but I need to learn from you as fast as I can.

"How I envision you working . . ." Carswell paused to pour two more cups of coffee. ". . . Is as my alter ego or my conscience. You're going to be in charge of support operations. The HHC commander and the S-4 are going to be working directly for you. You'll be responsible for making sure they have their shit together to support the tactical plan the S-3 and I develop. And we'll be developing that with your input from a logistics perspective. You'll also run the staff. I think the Three, Paul White, is pretty sharp. He is the only original staff officer left. I think he's a little weak on tying everything together from a staff viewpoint, though. That's why I want you to be my alter ego and make sure that everything gets coordinated and tied together.

"I want you to make sure that the staff functions as it should. You'll be the primary focus. Therefore, you'll have to know everything I do. We really are going to have to talk to each other so we both have a clear understanding of what the other one is thinking. You have to know my intentions and plans as well as I do. And I'm going to have to know what you're thinking and whether or not we are both clear on what we mean.

"In addition to all this, in your spare time, I want you and Command Sergeant Major Taylor to be my pulse takers and let me know what is going on in the battalion. I don't know how much longer this war is going to last or how it is going to end. I do know that the deciding factor is going to be our individual men and women and how well those soldiers fight. That's what I want you and Taylor to keep tabs on for me, the morale and spirit of the battalion."

The next day, Carswell made a change to the TAC SOP to reflect his mode of controlling the operations of the battalion.

"I'm establishing a jump tactical operations center, two personnel carriers modified with map boards and communications equipment, including a generator to power the radios and several antennas for long-distance communications. This mobile command post will include the S-3, S-2, fire support officer, and a small staff of enlisted soldiers to assist in the TOC operations. The air liaison officer will accompany me in his own track with his set of radios to talk to the airborne forward air controllers. It's just a ground version of the old Command and Control helicopter the airmobile folks use. You must have seen C and C ships in the Eighty-Second, Mike," he said to Mike over coffee at breakfast.

"Yes, I saw C and C ships in the Eighty-Second," Mike answered. "But they were never designed to operate in this kind of environment." He shook his head. "Sir, I don't think you realize how good the other side is in radio electronic combat. They can fix your position in a heartbeat."

"All our commo is secure," Carswell answered. "And if we still use good COMSEC, even if they can hear us, they won't be able to figure anything out in time to affect our operations."

"Their reading our mail doesn't worry me," Mike replied. "You're right. They can't intercept and break our secure gear easily. Their radio direction-finding capability worries me. You're planning on using a lot of radio traffic to make this plan work. If you get sloppy and start talking too much, they'll find you. And once they find you, they'll nail you." In his mind, he saw the remnants of the antenna site in Altendorf. Most of the company's commo section had died when the Russian rocket barrage obliterated the farmhouse they occupied.

Carswell stood up and smiled at Mike. "I promise I won't talk too much. And if I do get loquacious, you can kick me in the butt to remind me to shut up, okay?"

Over the next several days, as Mike worked closely with Carswell, he began to see the colonel as a steady, intelligent, competent professional. The battalion commander was everywhere observing the preparations for the unit's return to combat. Carswell would meet with Mike and the rest of the staff at breakfast and discuss the day's activities. Mike would summarize outstanding staff actions for him. Carswell would provide his guidance and intentions to the staff, answer any questions they had, and then leave to watch the line companies train. On these visits to the field, he took the S-3 and the sergeant major with him. Carswell may not have seen as much action as Mike, but he appeared to know his job.

Historically, the American army has suffered the largest percentage of its losses in its line infantry battalions. This war proved no exception to the historical rule. The losses in killed, wounded, and missing were highest in the infantry battalions, followed by the armor battalions. To rebuild the fighting strength of the rifle and tank battalions, the army resorted to another historical practice—drafting replacements from wherever they could be found.

In this light, Kevin's request for transfer to Second Battalion, Sixty Sixth Mech was accepted with joy and acted on with alacrity. Almost twenty-four hours after he and Ann-Marie had left Mike in Finthen, Kevin found himself back there. He arrived aboard a five-ton truck filled with other replacements and their baggage and rifles. The battalion greeted him far more warmly than the other men he accompanied. The story of the support group's fight at

Altendorf had traveled through the battalion, losing nothing in the telling. Kevin was a proven veteran as well as a volunteer, something the other soldiers were not.

The HHC first sergeant pulled Kevin out of formation and told him he was now the executive officer's driver and sent him over to the *gasthaus* that served as the battalion command post. As the exec's driver, Kevin would live with the battalion command section and work directly for the command sergeant major, along with Lieutenant Colonel Carswell's two drivers, one each for his M-113 carrier and for his Humvee.

As Kevin unpacked his rucksack and duffle bag, Command Sergeant Major Taylor entered the room. "Welcome to the battalion, Specialist Long. I want you to come with me right now. Worry about getting your gear set up later."

"Okay, Sergeant Major," Kevin answered. "But I'm just a Private First Class." He picked up his rifle, web gear, and helmet and followed the NCO out of the room.

"The XO's driver is an E-4 slot," Taylor said, growling. "The S-1 is cutting the orders for your promotion now. Can you drive a Humvee?"

"I'm not licensed for one, but I learned how to drive them in my old unit."

"Well, we'll take care of the license later. What about map reading? Can you read a topo map? How are your radio skills?"

Herb Lovell had drilled the soldiers in his S-1 section incessantly in basic soldier skills—map reading, first aid, weapons, and radiotelephone procedure.

Kevin answered, "I can read maps and talk on radios."

Shortly after Kevin arrived at the battalion, the brigade commander and the ADC/Support, Colonel John H. Warren, visited the battalion for a brief inspection. Warren immediately sent his aide and driver in search of the battalion executive officer. Vicki and Ann-Marie found Mike in the battalion motor pool, helping change a front final drive on a damaged M-113. Vicki walked up and slapped him on the butt as he hung in the engine compartment of the vehicle.

"If you're presentable, there's a briefing for all principal staff officers," she said. "Even if you're not, they'll probably want you anyway. There's just no accounting for some people's taste." Mike had established a reputation for insisting on proper military courtesy, and the crowd around the damaged track waited for the explosion.

They were disappointed. Mike looked over his shoulder and saw who was standing there. He pushed himself out of the engine bay.

"Behave," he said to Vicki with a smile. "Or I'll shake hands. Or maybe I'll hug you instead." He held up his hand and forearms, covered in oil and grease to the elbows. "What are you two doing down here? Slumming to see how the other half lives?"

"A hug is the best offer I've had in a while," Vicki responded. "But I think Dr. McCann has a mean way of getting even." She waved to call Ann-Marie over. "I just brought Annie along. Thought we'd go cruising for some guys."

Ann-Marie walked up and saluted crisply. Mike returned it as crisply and said hello to her. He pulled an old towel out of a box of rags and wiped his arms and hands clean. He told the mechanics he would be back to check on their progress after the briefing and put on his BDU jacket.

"Sir," Ann-Marie asked as the three soldiers walked back toward the headquarters. "Is Kevin around? Can I see him?"

Before Mike could answer, Vicki said, "I'm going over to check on our vehicles, Annie. Then I'll meet you back at headquarters. Why don't you tell the major your news? I'm sure that Kevin won't be busy for long after that."

Ann-Marie blushed furiously as Vicki walked away. Mike looked at the young woman curiously. "Kevin's with the command sergeant major right now. I think they're going over what the CSM expects out of the command group's drivers.

When we get inside, I'll send someone to get him. What's your news?"

Ann-Marie took a deep breath and said in a rush, "Kevin asked me to marry him last week. Before the attack. When I was assigned as Colonel Warren's driver, he tried to come to HHC with me, but they wouldn't approve his transfer. Then he volunteered to come here with you right after I left the group. We haven't seen each other since then." Her voice softened, and she dropped her eyes to the ground.

Mike stopped and took Ann-Marie's hands in his. "Ann-Marie, congratulations. I'm very glad for both you and Kevin." He paused. "I think this meeting is about the counterattack plans we've been making. Life in a rifle battalion is not a good insurance risk. If you want, I'll talk to the battalion commander and get Kevin assigned to Division."

"No, sir," she answered in a soft voice. "We talked about that but decided that we're both soldiers. He wants to be here with you because he respects you so much and wants to be like you." She looked up at Mike, and he could see tears sparkling in the corners of her eyes. "Take care of him for me, sir. Please."

General Staff Bunker
Outside Moscow

The Russian military spends much time and effort studying military history and developing laws and formulas for the conduct of war. They would then take the laws and other results of their studies and project future courses of action.

"One result of our study and analysis is the realization that any land conflict in Europe is decided largely by what happens at sea." The briefing officer was presenting a decision briefing on a new strategy to the Warsaw Pact General Staff in Moscow. "In the Great Patriotic War,

Germany could win the Battle of the Atlantic and still lose the war. The Allies, on the other hand, had to win the Battle of the Atlantic to win the war. This is even truer today than during the Great Patriotic War. Therefore, the defeat of the Western navies in the Atlantic is an important pillar in our plans to fight against the West. You will remember prior to open hostilities that our submarines and surface combatants were surged into the Atlantic to wait for the signal to begin the Second Battle of the Atlantic. The convoy battles began as soon as war started and quickly became bloody and vicious.

"Our surface ships were rapidly sunk or driven into safe ports where they stayed. The submarine forces fared better, but the convoys are still making their way to Europe. In addition, NATO's anti-submarine warfare capabilities are growing in effectiveness. The next step is obvious, gentlemen. If you can't attack the convoys at sea, then attack them in port as they form up."

Intense arguments raged back and forth among the planners, then the ministry staffs, and finally at the highest echelons of the government. A strong and vocal minority resisted any idea of attacking the continental United States. Such attacks might inflame the Americans even more and lift the conflict out of the realm of conventional war into something else. However, NATO was already striking deep targets in Poland, Ukraine, and Russia, so the hawks overrode this opposition. The general staff planned cruise missile strikes against US ports and issued the appropriate orders.

Castle Island Terminal
Boston, Massachusetts

A trace of glasnost and perestroika visited Boston one sunny Thursday afternoon. The Russian missile industry benefited from purchasing many of the components of the guidance systems used in Western cruise missiles. Previous versions of their sea-launched land attack missiles were relatively inaccurate. The new technology furnished to the design bureaus allowed them to develop missiles that could, like the Tomahawk, "score a field goal at a thousand miles."

Boston was an assembly point for the convoys transporting supplies and troops to Europe since its location cut at least one day off the journey from the other East Coast ports. With the increased activity of Russian and other Warsaw Pact submarines, the difference in transit time assumed greater importance. Then, a series of Russian sea minefields laid off the mouth of New York harbor, near Sandy Hook, temporarily closed that port. This made Boston the only major port in the northeast available to load transports for Europe. Aggressive patrolling by the Coast Guard and navy had already sunk one Russian Alpha class attack submarine loitering off Nantucket Island. Traces of other submarines were found, but attacks were unsuccessful.

A Victor class attack boat, armed with SS-NX-26 sea-launched cruise missiles similar to the American Tomahawk land attack missile, fired six of its missiles into the harbor. The missiles flashed over the water at altitudes of five to ten meters above sea level. Their onboard computers steered them around the harbor islands, across the runways of Logan International Airport, and into the docks of the Castle Island Terminal, now occupied by two container ships loading cargo for Europe. The first missile was on track and would have hit its target exactly as planned, but a liquid natural gas tanker entered the channel in the missile's path. The missile struck the tanker amidships, and its thousand-pound warhead detonated in a flash of bright orange light. The liquid natural gas flashed off in a burst of white, and its fireball reached out to either side of the river. Flaming gas immediately spread across the surface of the harbor.

The second and third missiles landed almost simultaneously, several seconds after the destruction of the tanker. The second missile smashed into a container ship loaded with a mixed cargo of supplies. Part of the mix was containers of Patriot anti-aircraft missiles. The Patriot is a "sealed round," shipped from the factory with fuel and warhead already loaded. The SS-NX-23 exploded in the midst of the Patriot containers. Their sympathetic detonation completed the destruction of the container ship. The ship shuddered and died alongside the dock as its cargo blew up in a series of spectacular explosions.

The third missile destroyed the other container ship, but not as dramatically. This ship was not carrying any explosive cargo, but its fuel tanks flashed off as the cruise missile's warhead detonated. The shock waves from the explosions spread outward from the terminal and rolled across the harbor into the heart of Boston. One of the first casualties was the water shuttle crossing the harbor from Logan Airport to its dock at Rowe's Wharf. The blast simply rolled over the small ferry, and it sank like a stone. The second major casualty was a wide-body airliner on short final approach to Logan. The shock wave flipped over the airliner and skidded it across the runway like a Frisbee. Concussion from the blasts shattered every window in the South Station and Chinatown area, adding to the dead and wounded.

The last three missiles flew over the harbor and dispersed their loads of cluster bombs along the center of the city, over the business district and the area known as Beacon Hill.

Elizabeth and Paul Watson, one of the other doctors in the orthopedic clinic, were having lunch at one of the outdoor restaurants in Quincy Market as the missiles struck Castle Island Terminal. The high-rise buildings between East Boston and Quincy Market attenuated the blast waves. The people in the open market could hear the sounds of the explosions. Within minutes, several plumes of greasy black smoke began rising over the skyline.

"It sounds like someone was smoking too close to a gas pump," Paul said.

Both doctors began to stand up when Elizabeth's beeper went berserk. She punched the response button and dialed the hospital, identified herself, and listened intently to the excited voice on the other end of the telephone.

Hanging up, she turned to Paul. "There have been several explosions over at Castle Island," she said in a low, urgent voice to Paul. "No one knows exactly what happened, but three ships have blown up. The emergency response teams are trying to get into the area now. I've got to get over to St. Brendan's right away."

"I'll go with you," Paul answered immediately. "You may need the help."

In the confusion that erupted in Quincy Market following the explosions and shock waves from the missile strikes, Elizabeth and Paul could not find a taxi. By the time they walked across Beacon Hill to St. Brendan's, the wounded were beginning to arrive. Some came in ambulances or other emergency vehicles, some were in private cars and trucks. The emergency room entrance was chaos. People with minor cuts and bruises stepped over and around the more seriously injured to get help for themselves. In one corner of the emergency room, a woman sat silently rocking a young child who stared blankly at its left arm. The arm ended at the elbow. Next to them, a young Asian man squeezed tightly on the stumps of the fingers of his right hand and ignored the ten-inch gash in his side.

Elizabeth took all this in with a single glance. She headed directly for the scrub rooms with Paul following closely. The doctors found organized confusion as the operating teams scrambled to prep themselves for the long ordeal of surgery that lay before them.

The first patient Elizabeth's team received was a black male with multiple wounds and fractures. Once he was stabilized, Elizabeth began examining the most serious wound, a deep penetration of the abdomen. The man's condition precluded any pre-operation x-rays, so she explored the wound by hand. Her probe found an object deep in the wound. She made an incision to open the wound wider.

"Okay, retractors here. Suction here. Now, clamp off those bleeders. I want a lot of suction here," she said, ordering her team in a cold, stern voice that few of her non-medical friends would have recognized. "I've got something. Give me another clamp. Paul, can you give me a hand over here? I don't know what this is, but it feels big."

Paul Watson was treating a compound fracture of the man's right arm. He leaned over the operating table and grasped a large clamp that Elizabeth had attached to the object in the wound.

"Okay, let's pull it out," she said once Paul grasped the other clamp. "Get some sponges ready to put in here."

The two doctors jerked swiftly and pulled out a blood-covered human hand.

"My God. What is that?" the nurse standing next to Elizabeth said. Then he dropped the suction hose he had been holding, stepped away from the table, and became violently ill.

"Somebody take his place," Elizabeth said, snapping.

Paul rotated the hand in his clamp. "It looks like a woman's hand," he said in a matter-of-fact voice. "Probably young and definitely the left hand. Notice the wedding and engagement rings." He dropped the blood-cloaked limb in a basin next to the operating table. "Bomb blast and concussion have strange effects." He had been a navy surgeon at Da Nang, so he had much experience with bomb casualties and blast effects.

Elizabeth sent the nurse to compose himself and proceeded to sew the patient back up. His stomach wound was the most serious, but he had several others besides that one and the fractured arm. The team took two and a half hours to put this patient back together again. And he was just the first of many. Elizabeth lost track of the patients she treated that day. She became numb to the sight of mangled bodies that rolled into the operating theater and worked purely on autopilot.

When she left after the last patient had moved to the recovery room, the sun had set. Unbelieving, she looked at her watch and saw it was almost midnight. The security guard at the hospital's entrance said someone was waiting to drive her home. She turned to find a disheveled Tom Bradley, dressed in BDU's, field gear and helmet standing in the doorway. Except for a soft orange glow low on the skyline, the night hid most of the carnage of the day's attack.

"If you're ready, Doctor," he said as he bowed grandly to her, "your carriage waits. Of course, it's not the BMW you doctors are used to, but my humble Humvee will get you to Concord."

She smiled tiredly. "Tom, it's nice of you to wait. You didn't have to—"

"Ah, but I did. I have further news of some dumb Mick Major in Germany." He produced a torn piece of Teletype paper from inside his jacket. "He has been treated and released from the hospital and further assigned as the executive officer of an infantry battalion."

Elizabeth tore the paper from Bradley's hands and read it intently in the weak light.

> *From: CDR, XXVI US CORPS*
> *TO: CDR, 3077 USAG, FT DEVENS, MA*
> *PLEASE RELAY THE FOLLOWING BY OFFICER COURIER TO DR ELIZABETH MCCANN, 2515 ACTON ROAD, CONCORD MA. MAJOR FITZMAURICE RELEASED FROM HOSPITAL 171700 AUG AND REASSIGNED EXECUTIVE OFFICER, INFANTRY BATTALION. CONDITION EXCELLENT—WOUNDS WERE IN HIS HEAD. SIGNED, BARRETT MAJOR GENERAL USA DCDR*

She crumpled the paper and looked back at Tom. "Does this mean he's all right? What's going to happen to him now? Why did this general send a message to me?"

"I guess he's okay," Tom answered. "Major General Barrett is a good friend of John Warren's and has taken a proprietary interest in some of Warren's protégés, like your husband. I took a similar message to Caroline Warren before I came here to see you. The messages came in about eight o'clock tonight and straight to the garrison commander. He knows you and Mike are friends of mine so he asked me to bring it to you. I think he's been assigned to one of the battalions in the Sixteenth Mech. That division was shot up pretty badly. Mike would be a prime candidate for a replacement officer."

"So he's not coming home then." It was more a statement than a question.

"No, Beth," Bradley answered sadly. "Not for a while yet."

Elizabeth brushed away tears that had formed in the corners of her eyes. "So Mike's staying over there. And you, Tom. If Mike's a prime candidate for a replacement, so are you. Are you going to Germany?"

He nodded in reply. "I got my orders this afternoon. I leave in twenty-four hours."

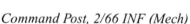

Command Post, 2/66 INF (Mech)
Vicinity Finthen, FRG

Mike was in a conference with Colonel Carswell, Paul White, and John Dugan discussing the current Unit Readiness Report when the day TOC watch officer broke into the conversation.

"Major Fitzmaurice, one of the TOC crew has the BBC on his personal radio. He said they just repeated a Radio Moscow claim that the Russians attacked Boston with cruise missiles. I checked with Division, but they have no information through Intel channels. In fact, they weren't even aware of the report until I called them."

Carswell took in Mike's pale face and stricken look in a glance and asked the watch officer, "Can you contact anyone stateside on the German phone lines?"

"No, sir. The Germans shut down overseas calls as of 0700 this morning. I sent a runner to get the signal officer over here to see if he has any ideas."

Carswell moved the group of officers out into the TOC. Someone had tuned one of the auxiliary radio speakers to the Armed Forces Network's afternoon country-and-western jamboree.

"If we don't hear anything on AFN in the next five minutes, tune the radio to the BBC, and see if they have any more word on what's happening in Boston."

By now, all work in the TOC had come to a stop as everyone stared at the auxiliary speaker. As they stared, the music suddenly stopped, and a somber-voiced announcer took its place.

"The Department of Defense, in cooperation with the Federal Emergency Management Agency, just released the following statement. At 0930, EST, several submarine-launched cruise missiles struck the Port of Boston. Some of the missiles missed their presumed targets in the port area and struck the business district and central downtown Boston. Casualty figures are not available, but they are expected to be heavy. Further information will be released as it is made available."

At the mention of Boston, all eyes in the TOC turned to Mike. The troop bush telegraph spread Mike's biography throughout the battalion. All knew the XO's home and family were near Boston.

"Paul." Carswell's voice cracked like a whip in the silence. "Get on the horn to Division and get more information. I don't care if you drive up there and start slitting throats. Find out as much as you can, particularly casualties and any indication of where the missiles struck."

Paul White looked at Mike. "Didn't you tell me your wife works in downtown Boston?"

"She does," Mike answered numbly.

"Both her office and the hospital she works in are in central Boston."

She's all right, Mike told himself. *Boston's a pretty big target for cruise missiles. Oh my God, Beth. Where are you, and how are you?*

"Major," Carswell said harshly to White, "you have your instructions. Don't speculate on what might have happened. Get us some solid information. The XO and I will be in my office for the next few minutes or so. Someone please bring us some coffee. Sergeant Major—"

"I'm on my way to get Specialist Long, sir. He should be in the motor pool. Shall I bring him to the TOC?"

"Excellent idea, Sergeant Major. Have the S-1 get a list of all soldiers from New England and bring them to the TOC. Gentlemen, carry on."

Carswell grabbed Mike by the arm, led him into a small office, and shut the door. He waved Mike into a chair and pulled a silver flask from his desk, poured two hefty shots into coffee cups, and passed one to Mike.

"Here, Mike. Drink this."

"You think this will help with the uncertainty?" Mike took the proffered cup.

"No, not at all. Just consider this a chance to drink your boss's booze. I'll give Paul White an hour. If we haven't heard any more details, then I am sending you and Long to see your old boss, Colonel Warren. He should have enough mojo to get some information."

Mike tossed off his drink in a single gulp. "I really appreciate what you're doing, sir. But I can't sit here without worrying myself sick, which does no good to the battalion or me. Let me get back to work. I will put a call in to Colonel Warren in a half hour or so."

The TA-312 field telephone on Carswell's desk began chirping, and the commander grabbed the handset. "Bayonet six here."

"This is dragon one three. Who am I speaking to?" Warren's voice came through the handset loud and clear.

"Bayonet six, bayonet five is with me as well."

"Roger, put bayonet five on the line, please."

Carswell handed the phone to Mike. "It's Colonel Warren, dragon one three, for you."

"This is bayonet five. Over," Mike said when he took over the phone.

"Dragon one three, I have further details for you, and they are not good. The office was destroyed in a gas main explosion. There are survivors but not a complete list. Doctor Echo is not accounted for. Status unknown. Break. My contacts are following the situation and will keep us apprised of any new developments. There are some indications Echo was not at the office during the attack but nothing definite. Break. Damage confined to waterfront and business districts in city with nothing outside in any direction. How copy. Over."

"Bayonet five, solid copy. No clear information. Wait for further details. Over."

"Dragon one three, nothing further. Out."

The phone went as dead as Mike's mind. Her office was destroyed, but no one could say if she were there at the time of the explosion. He had seen enough explosions lately to know that some bodies just disappear.

God in heaven, Beth, where are you?

"I couldn't hear all that Colonel Warren said," Carswell spoke into the silence. "Was his news good or bad?"

"Bad." Mike tried to order his thoughts and process what Colonel Warren just told him. "The office where she works was destroyed in a gas main explosion, and Beth is unaccounted for. The authorities are still trying to sort out survivors and casualties."

"Your wife is unaccounted for? Is that what he said?"

"Yeah." Mike nodded his head.

"His law firm is working their connections to get information to all of us. They're not even sure that she was in the office when it was destroyed. For what it's worth, the damage is confined to the city. But then, we already knew that."

Carswell came around his desk and gripped Mike's elbow. "My God, Mike. I wish I could do more to help you."

Mike shrugged off the colonel's grip. "I appreciate all you've done so far, sir. The best thing you can do right now is let me get back to work. I need to do something besides sit and worry about her."

"Then get your sorry ass downstairs and get us ready to move out. And leave my booze alone."

"Roger." Mike gave a half salute and went downstairs to the TOC.

Beth, where are you? How are you? Are you all right? Please, God, let her be safe and unharmed. What will I do if she isn't? She has to be all right. She must be. God, what am I going to do?

Mike entered the TOC with a poker face. "Well, gentlemen, shall we pick up where we left off before the excitement?"

2515 Acton Road
West Concord, Massachusetts

When Tom and Elizabeth arrived at the house in West Concord, they found two police cars, one from Concord and a state trooper, blocking the street in front of the house.

Elizabeth saw a Mercedes in the driveway and recognized Caroline's car at once.

Tom rolled down his window as the state trooper approached. "Is there a problem, officer?"

"Only if you're not Dr. Elizabeth McCann." The trooper shone his light into the car. He saw Elizabeth in the passenger seat. "Are you Dr. McCann, ma'am?"

"Yes," Elizabeth answered angrily. The tension of the day was catching up to her and affecting her temper. "What's going on here? Why are you blocking my driveway and the street in front of my house?"

"May I see some identification, please," the trooper said politely.

Elizabeth handed him her driver's license and military identification card. Tom added his ID card as well. Tom's temper was simmering as well, and he looked to be picking out places to really hurt the officer.

The trooper flashed his light over the cards, checking each with the occupant of the vehicle. "Everything's in order, ma'am." He handed the cards back to Tom. "If you'll wait a moment, I will move my cruiser out of your way."

Tom maneuvered around the cruiser and down the driveway behind Caroline's car. As he shut down the engine, the front door opened, and the twins rocketed off the porch steps into Elizabeth. She knelt down to catch them, and they burst into tears as she swept them into her embrace. The dogs followed two steps behind the children and buried their noses into Elizabeth's coat. Caroline and Maggie followed at a more sedate pace, the younger woman trying to match the gravitas of the older. Maggie finally gave up the struggle and enveloped her older sister in a bear hug.

"Mrs. Warren," Tom said to give Elizabeth and her family some time to compose themselves, "how are you doing tonight? If you need any assistance or support, I will let my replacement know. I've already briefed him on the 805th

Support Group, and he is aware of the high interest in your situation."

"Colonel, thank you for your offer. What I really need is my husband home with me, but I know that's above your pay grade. I am here to find out what happened to our hostess today. I've had several urgent inquiries from overseas."

"I spent the day in surgery at St. Brendan's, Caroline." Elizabeth untangled herself from people and dogs. "I was having lunch with a colleague when the missiles struck, and we both went straight to the emergency department to assist with the casualties. What's all the excitement?"

"My God, you don't know." Caroline gasped. "A cruise missile struck near your office and set off a gas main explosion. Your office was destroyed. No one knew where you were. We all thought you were dead."

Chapter 12

Unto the Breach

Once more unto the breach, dear friends, once more.
— William Shakespeare, *Henry V*, Act III
(1599)

Command Post, 2/66 INF (Mech)
Vicinity Finthen, FRG

Losses of Bradley infantry fighting vehicles caused the Sixteenth Infantry Division staff to consolidate the surviving Bradleys into two of the mechanized infantry battalions as well as the armored cavalry squadron. The remaining three infantry battalions, including 2/66, were reequipped with M-113A2 armored personnel carriers shipped to Europe from storage depots in CONUS. The M-113s were modified with an add-on passive armor kit to lessen their vulnerability to enemy fire. The United States made a large-scale purchase of Milan-2 ATGM systems from the French that allowed one system to be put on each of the new M-113s. In addition to the purchase of the Milans, the army pulled all its remaining M-901 improved TOW vehicles, an M-113 carrier modified to carry a dual launcher and twelve TOW missiles, out of the depots where they awaited disposal as scrap metal. Anti-tank companies were formed from the ITVs and assigned to the

Mech battalions, such as 2/66, that were not equipped with Bradleys.

As Mike walked away from the maintenance shop after inspecting a new shipment of M-113s, Ed Chambers hailed him. Even though the two had arrived at 2/66 together, they had drifted apart in the press of adjusting to their new positions and duties. Ed had taken over Charlie Company and was aggressively establishing himself as a no-nonsense commander who accepted nothing less than total effort from his soldiers. As they walked back to the battalion command post, Ed talked aimlessly about the progress he was making in rebuilding his shattered command.

"Look, Ed," Mike finally said. "What do you really want to talk about? I know you well enough to know that you're not really interested in what I think of how you're setting up your company. What's on your mind?"

"Okay, you're right." Ed stopped and planted his hands on his hips. "You've heard about Baxter and Dumont, right. How come you didn't put me in for anything?"

"What are you talking about?"

"Baxter and Dumont got their medals for the fight at Altendorf yesterday. Dumont got a Bronze Star with Vee. Baxter got an Arcom with Vee. I deserve them as much as they do. Or are they getting special treatment because you and Warren like them better than me?"

"I don't fucking believe this," Mike snapped. "What are you doing, bartering for a medal? You have some kind of hero complex? You and I did our fucking jobs at Altendorf, nothing more and nothing less. We're infantrymen. We're the beady-eyed killers who are trained to take on the other side's tanks and grunts.

"Most of the people who fought and died at Altendorf weren't grunts. They were support soldiers. They did something extraordinary, something above what their job description calls for. You and I just validated our MOS skills. That's all." He paused and reined in his temper. "The group

221

did send a recommendation for a Silver Star forward on you. Apparently, the reviewing authority feels the same way I do. We don't get rewarded for doing what's expected of us."

Unchastened, Ed said, "That's bullshit. I deserve a medal just as much as Baxter or Dumont—"

"You'll undoubtedly get your chance to prove that, Chambers," a new voice interrupted. Both officers turned to find Lieutenant Colonel Carswell standing behind them. "I'm on my way up to Brigade for an orders group, Mike. The warning order just came down. We are to start preparing to move out within the next six hours. I'll be back here as soon as I can."

"I'll alert the company commanders, sir," Mike answered.

Carswell nodded to Ed and said softly, "I sincerely hope that you're as good as you think you are, Chambers. I sincerely hope so."

As Ed sped back to his company area, a bright gleam of anticipation on his face, Carswell turned to Mike. "I heard most of that. Is he good? As good as he thinks he is? Does he deserve something, or is he just trying to punch a ticket?"

"Ed's good," Mike said slowly. "I would take him as a company commander in any battalion I commanded. He's got a hang-up about awards. Baxter and Dumont are female. I guess it offends Ed's view of the world that Baxter was decorated for doing pretty much what he did. Dumont pulled a couple tankers out of an M-1 that was hit. She also knocked out a T-72 with AT-4s. Ed led some counterattacks and backed up some of the tank-killer teams. Yeah, he deserves something. But I'm not on the review board."

"Did you get anything for your little escapade?" Carswell asked with a slight grin. "I mean, besides an Emmy nomination for Best Male Lead in an Afternoon Drama?"

Mike shrugged. "As I was leaving the group to come here, Baxter told me the new group commander killed all the awards. He didn't think anything special had happened during the fight. I just heard about Baxter and Dumont when

Ed told me." He paused and then looked across the town square without seeing it. "The only recognition I want is to go home in one piece. I survived that fight. A lot of good people didn't."

When Carswell returned from the orders group at Brigade three hours later, Mike had the staff and company commanders assembled in the *gasthaus*. Carswell gave a swift, concise digest of the brigade plan. They would be the division reserve and follow the main attack, which would start at 0430 the next morning. The intent of the division commander and the Second Brigade commander was to break through the Russian defenses. Then the division would lunge forward in the general direction of Dresden to seize blocking positions and cut off the enemy's avenues of retreat. The immediate goals of the Sixteenth were not enemy soldiers but key pieces of terrain they could hold against attack and force the other side to break themselves in attempts to escape.

As the troops of the Sixteenth Mech began their movement forward to the line of departure, a dozen MC-130H Combat Talon aircraft lifted off from the Royal Air Force base at Mildenhall, England. The lead aircraft circled the field until all twelve were airborne and then led them east at treetop level. The MC-130s, special operations versions of the venerable Lockheed C-130 transport, had a key role in the NATO counterattack. Each aircraft carried a fifteen thousand-pound BLU-82 "Daisy Cutter" bomb, developed in Vietnam to clear helicopter landing zones. It was effective against personnel, inside bunkers or not. These twelve planes were to blast holes in the Russian defenses that would allow the Sixteenth Mech to pass through the hostile lines and attack the rear areas of the Warsaw Pact forces.

The weather broke as the Allies began their counterattack and the rains of the first part of the month returned. The last half of August became one of the wettest periods in recent memory. Mike sat in his Humvee in the battalion's assembly area listening to the rain drumming on the canvas roof. Water dripped through the roof, onto Mike's helmet, and down the back of his neck. He tried shifting his position, but the drip followed him like a mosquito at a summer cookout. He finally gave up and just suffered.

As he settled uncomfortably in his seat, he glared angrily at Kevin, slumped behind the steering wheel and sleeping like a baby. Kevin easily mastered the old soldier's knack of sleeping anywhere, at any time, under any conditions. Now he slumped against the driver's seat, head leaned backward at an impossible angle while his snores filled the vehicle.

A neutral safety switch, Mike thought grumpily. *He's got a neutral safety switch in his ass. Whenever he sits down, he falls asleep.*

Mike tried sleeping as well but without Kevin's success. Because he couldn't sleep, he ran over the counterattack plan in his mind. The battalion was reorganized as a task force. Bravo Company from 2/66 had been cross-attached to Second Battalion, Ninety-Second Armor, and 2/66 had received Bravo Company of the armor battalion. Part of Mike's planning for the counterattack had been the movement of the vehicles of the task force: 14 M-1A1 tanks, 103 M-113 series vehicles, 43 two-and-a-half-ton cargo trucks, 15 five-ton cargo trucks, 22 Heavy Expanded Mobility Tactical Trucks, eight-wheel drive diesel-powered off-road capable trucks, and 27 Humvees. Somewhere in that crowd, there were sixty-four trailers pulled by other vehicles. And TF 2-66 was only one of nine other task forces in the division. Mike shuddered as he imagined what a target the moving columns could offer the other side's air forces.

A metallic squeal from the radio interrupted Mike's musings as a voice came softly from the speaker. "Victor two victor, romeo four x-ray, papa one november, hotel niner india, mike zero tango. This is charlie five golf three three." It was Paul White calling all stations on the battalion command radio net. "Moonbeam. I say again, moonbeam. Out."

Moonbeam was the code word for the battalion to begin its move forward, toward the enemy. NATO was beginning its counterattack.

As Mike reached over to punch Kevin awake, a brief flash from the southeast was reflected on the bottom of the clouds. Mike passed it off as lightning, but it was the flash of the twelve BLU-82 bombs blasting a hole three miles wide in the Russian defenses.

As Mike watched Carswell operate with the task force, he noticed the colonel had an unconscious habit that could be fatal. When using the radio, Carswell would key the mike for a few seconds before beginning to talk. If the Russian radio intercept teams ever detected Carswell's radio, this delay would give them time to pinpoint his location and attack it with artillery or rockets.

"Sir." Mike cornered Carswell outside the jump TOC after an orders group on the third day of the offensive. "I heard you again on the radio today. You have to watch your transmission time. Once you key the handset, say your piece, and get off the air."

"Right, Mike." Carswell patted Mike's arm. "I know. The radio intercept people are looking for me, just waiting to nab me. However, I usually make all my calls from the jump TOC, and we're always moving. So they can't really fix my location. Don't worry about me."

"It's not just you that I'm worried about, sir," Mike said harshly. "It's the rest of the TOC crew that's with you. I've been on the receiving end of Russian artillery, and it wasn't pleasant, even under a two-story building. A 113 isn't going to do all that much to protect you."

Carswell's mouth tightened to a thin, white line at Mike's tone of voice. Then he relaxed. "Right, Major. Good point. I'll keep it in mind."

Hill 146
Vicinity Prausitz, DDR

Mike was trying to get the battalion combat trains situated. The flute-like Russian jamming of the radio nets was just enough to make coordination extremely difficult but not enough to stop operations. He stood next to the battalion aid station, an M-577 carrier set up as an emergency medical post, where the headquarters company commander, Wally Paxton, had his map out. He and Mike were trying to guess where the rest of the trains, the fuel trucks, and the M-578 armored recovery vehicle had disappeared. Paxton had the ammunition trucks from the support platoon and the battalion mess team with him.

As Mike examined Paxton's map, Kevin called to him from their Humvee. "Major, the old man wants you up forward for an orders group in ten minutes."

Mike waved at Kevin in acknowledgment and told Paxton to follow him. "Leave the rest of the trains to Foxx. He's the support platoon leader and should start earning his pay. Maybe he'll teach his drivers how to read maps now."

The orders group took place on a hill overlooking the town of Prausitz, about forty kilometers northwest of Dresden. The town sat on highway B-6, and in the distance the Americans could see the silver ribbon of the Elbe. Carswell had selected a small nature park, a half-dozen rough pine picnic tables clustered around a small forester's hut. His command track was parked next to the FSO's vehicle, both with their ramps down, facing the hut.

As the staff and team commanders arrived for the briefing, a few members of the TOC crew struggled to erect two radio antennas. The Air Liaison Officer had moved his vehicle about a hundred meters back down the approach trail into the park, below the top of the hill for a clearer radio connection to the airborne forward air controller, aloft in an OA-10 some ten or twelve kilometers away. Those members of the TOC crew not actively engaged in preparing for the orders group moved into the hut with their MREs for a quick meal.

A lovely site for a picnic, Mike thought sardonically as the soldiers cooked their breakfast.

The team commanders straggled in over a fifteen-minute period and parked their vehicles about fifty or sixty meters from the clearing. All were grimy and exhausted; their faces were unshaven and coated with crusted dust and dirt. The task force was moving rapidly. The fatigue showed in the slouched posture and red-rimmed eyes as they gathered around Carswell's command track. The operations sergeant produced a pot of steaming water and a stack of instant coffee, cream, and chocolate packets from some place known only to him and a benevolent God. The officers pulled out metal canteen cups and began making coffee while they waited for the briefing.

Once all the commanders and staff were present, Carswell pointed to his map.

"The mission of the task force has been changed somewhat. We're now to close up along the Elbe in our sector, between the towns of Bahra here and Riesa to the north, and secure any potential crossing sites. We've managed to rupture the Warsaw Pact defenses and force them back toward the German-Polish border. Brigade reports that the forces here in front of us are Russian motorized infantry, mainly category two reserve divisions badly shaken by our attack. G-2 says all they're really interested in is getting home. They're falling back on the major crossing sites to get across the rivers as fast as they can move." He pointed to the large black blotch in the lower right-hand corner of his map.

"In the division's sector, that's toward Dresden. The brigade commander's intent, and mine, is to secure any crossing sites in our zone and be prepared to cross the Elbe on order." He paused and gazed directly at each of his commanders. "Chambers, I want you to orient on Bahra.

You'll be on the right flank of the task force. Make sure that you tie in with 2/92 Armor. Donaldson, Team Alpha will move on the left in the general direction of Riesa, but don't go into the city. Secure the roads into it, and close on the riverbank. Morgan, you follow Donaldson. If he gets tangled up around the built-up area, you're to go around him and close up on the river. Hart, you follow Chambers with your team, but be prepared to switch to support Team Alpha if required. Mike, you and Paxton follow on the right with the field trains. Keep about ten klicks back if you can, but most of all, stay where you can best support us. I'm going to leave the jump TOC here for the time being. Once I get a feel for the way things are going, I'll move behind the axis that's going the best.

"I'm going to give Donaldson the priority of fire initially because he's closest to that built-up area in Riesa. But that may change, depending on who makes contact first. Have your FIST chiefs coordinate fire plans with the FSO. I recommend you have a lot of on-call smoke targets. I'll control the tactical air support myself. If you think you have any targets, call me, and I'll get it for you."

Carswell stopped speaking for a few seconds. "Remember what happened at Remagen in World War II. If you can find a bridge or some way to cross the river, grab it as quickly as you can and then let me know. I believe that, if we can get across the river up here, we can open a bridgehead that will allow the division to get ahead of the Russians and perhaps trap a large number of them inside Dresden. Are there any questions? I want to finish the planning and kick this move off by 0545."

"What about fuel, sir?" Hart, the tank team commander, asked. His M-1A1s soaked up fuel like sponges. "I'd like to get topped off before we start a serious move."

"I'll get the fuel trucks up to you. Have your XO waiting for them so he can show them where you're set up," Mike answered before Carswell could say anything.

The commander grimaced. "Well, we'll have to make sure that anyone who needs fuel gets it before we move out. Give the XO your locations, and he'll have the support platoon's tankers link up with your units. While we're on the subject of resupply, how is your ammo holding out? If you need any class five, tell the XO now, and he can bring it up with the fuel."

As Carswell finished speaking, the operations officer passed pieces of overlay paper to each of the team commanders and Mike. The overlays showed the task force's attack routes and all the associated control measures. After the S-3 explained the concept of the attack and answered questions about the plan, Mike took his overlay over to where Kevin had parked his Humvee, gave his map to Kevin, and told the young man to copy the overlay onto the plastic map case. Once Kevin had the task under control, he returned to listen to Carswell talk to the artillery FSO about the fire support plan for the attack.

When the commander had finished, Mike said to him, "I'm going to take Paxton back now and link up with the combat trains. I'll bring them forward to the woods on the west side of Prausitz and hold them there until you call them forward. I'll have Young find a place in the built-up area for the TOC."

"Okay, Mike," Carswell said with a grin. "Make sure you find us another good *gasthaus* this time. I'm going to call Brigade and let them know that we're ready to move on to the river. Once I get a good feel for how the advance is going, I'll move the jump TOC forward. I'll let you know when we start our move and where I think we'll be stopping."

Hill 146
Vicinity Prausitz, DDR

Mike was about a ten-minute drive from the jump TOC, en route to bring up the fuel trucks, when Carswell called

Brigade to tell them where he was and what he planned to do. Mike heard him key the radio and hold it on while he gathered his thoughts.

"Come on, Brian. Come on," Mike said half-aloud when Carswell finally began speaking. "Say your piece, and get off the air."

Almost on cue, Carswell's transmission was chopped off in midstream. As the Brigade TOC tried to raise Carswell, Mike heard a distant rumbling. He knew no one would be answering the radio.

"Turn around, Kevin," he said, snapping at him. "Head back to the jump TOC."

As Mike's Humvee pulled up to the clump of pine trees that marked the jump TOC, chaos greeted him. The commander's 113 was burning like a blowtorch. The FSO's track lay on its left side with the right track hanging limply from the road wheels like a broken strand of beads. Several lumps of BDUs spilled lifelessly from the open cargo hatch. Shallow craters pockmarked the ground. Several men clustered dazedly off to one side of the splintered forester's hut. One sat next to a tree stump while two others tried to stanch the flow of blood from a head wound. Mike noticed that the smell of pinesap stood out against the stench of high explosive and burning diesel and involuntarily thought of Christmas trees and pine wreaths.

Mike jumped out of his vehicle and ran over to the survivors. "What happened? Where's the colonel?" He grabbed one of the men by the collar of his jacket. He held the battalion S-2, Captain Dave Daniels. The young man looked blankly at Mike without responding. Mike shook him hard and repeated his question.

"Dead. He's dead," Daniels finally croaked in a weak voice. "He was on the radio, and all of a sudden, we got hit with artillery. The first salvo got the command track and the FSO's track, and the second caught us as we got out of the hut."

As Mike stood back to survey the chaos around him, his gaze stopped at the sight of HQ 66, Carswell's command post track. At least one round struck directly inside the armored vehicle, and flame vomited from all the vehicle's hatches, as well as from the rear troop door, which the explosion had wrenched half-open. Shrapnel ripped through the sides, and small jets of fire erupted from the holes in the hull.

The funeral will be a closed casket filled with three fifty-pound sand bags, he thought. *Goddammit, Colonel. I told you not to spend so long on the radio.*

Mike looked around at the devastation and realized he was now a battalion commander, but one who had lost most of his key staff officers. The sole bright spot was that all the team commanders had left before the artillery strike on the TOC.

AutoFahre Elbe
Vicinity Bahra, DDR

Ed scrambled out of his command track and ran up to his first platoon leader, First Lieutenant George Rivera. The lieutenant crouched behind the gutted hulk of a large bus perched on the shoulder of the highway paralleling the Elbe River, about a kilometer south of the town of Bahra. From where they sat, the ground sloped gently down from the highway to the riverbank, a distance of about a hundred meters. The riverbank itself was a stone-faced levee, rising fifteen feet above the surface of the sluggishly moving river.

As Ed squatted next to Lieutenant Rivera, he tugged his map out of the map case hanging over his shoulder. "Okay, George, what are we looking at? You said you had something interesting up here?"

Rivera pointed to a cut in the riverbank about seventy meters north of their position. "There's a ferry site up there, sir. Sergeant Spaulding's got his squad securing it now. And as far as he can tell, there's no one on the other side. The ferry is beached next to the tin shack you can see from here. Spaulding says the engines are fucked up, but there are no holes in the boat itself. I looked at it when I was up there, before I called you, and confirmed it's in one piece. It's got a sign on the cabin that says it's a class fifteen ferry."

Ed put down his map and pulled out his field glasses. He surveyed the far bank of the river, two hundred meters away. The rain stopped earlier in the morning, visibility was good, and he saw no signs of activity.

"Has anyone checked the current? How fast is it?"

"About two and a half klicks an hour," Rivera said. "Spaulding and I did a speed check when I was up there. I've already told my troops to check their drain plugs and hatch seals."

Ed studied the ramp on the far side of the river. It slanted down the bank into the water and looked solid. A small sheet metal building was next to it. Ed decided it was probably a ticket booth and break shack for the ferry crews. Other than the shack, there were no buildings or any other cover within a hundred meters of the site. He put down his field glasses and studied his map. The ground on the far side appeared flat, but the contour interval on the map sheet was twenty meters. Gullies or depressions shallower than twenty meters would not show up. The ground on the near side, where his team was now, was higher than the far bank. Behind him, a small hill covered with pine trees overlooked the river. He recalled seeing a road sign marked "scenic outlook" pointing to the hill. He studied the possibilities and then looked up at Rivera.

"Are you thinking what I'm thinking, George?" he asked.

Rivera, a true product of southern California, grinned in reply. "Surf's up, boss. Ready when you are."

Properly prepared, the M-113 family of vehicles is capable of swimming water obstacles. The preparation involved ensuring that all drain plugs and hatch seals were watertight, the plywood trim vanes on the fronts of the vehicles were installed and operational, and the rubber shrouds over the tracks were present and serviceable. Rivera and his squad leaders had completed these checks before Ed arrived and were ready to cross the river. The current was within safe limits, and the ferry ramps gave adequate entry and exit points into and out of the water.

"Okay, let's do it." Ed said. "I'll get the rest of the platoon leaders up here, and we'll start across in thirty minutes."

Ed went back to his command vehicle with Rivera and called the other platoon leaders to him. Charlie Company was now a combined arms team. One of its rifle platoons was exchanged for a tank platoon from Bravo Company, Second Battalion, Ninety-Second Armored. Ed had also received two improved tow vehicles from the anti-tank company and a Stinger squad mounted in an M-3 Bradley.

When the platoon leaders arrived, he swiftly outlined his plan. Rivera's first platoon would cross the river because they were closest and ready to go. The third platoon would take up firing positions along the highway and be ready to move across the river when Rivera had secured a lodgment on the far bank. The tank platoon would move to the hill behind the ferry site so they could cover the crossing with fire. The ITVs and Stinger squad would join the tankers in their overwatch position. The mortar platoon would put its three 81 mm mortar carriers on the backside of the hill and fire smoke rounds to cover Rivera's crossing.

As the platoon leaders left to move their troops into position, Ed thought briefly about telling the battalion commander his plan and asking for more support. He balanced the time it would take to organize a larger effort against the absence of enemy forces on the far bank.

The longer we wait, he thought, *the greater the chance someone will wake up over there and block the other end.*

He decided to go now with his own Team Charlie rather than wait. He would report his action once he started to move and then ask for permission.

The fire support team chief interrupted Ed's thoughts. The FIST chief, a young artillery sergeant, rode in Ed's command track and believed one of his prime functions in life was educating infantry captains in the value of artillery fire support.

"Is this a private party, sir, or can anyone get in on it?" the sergeant asked. "I talked to the battalion just now, and they're complaining about having too much ammo to hump around. Maybe we could fire some missions and use it up?"

"I'm glad you reminded me, Baskins. I want you to get ready to put some smoke on the far bank when we begin crossing." Ed pointed to where he wanted the fire to go. "Start out right on the bank and work your way back. Get a good curtain of smoke up there. It will take us about ten minutes to get across once we get started. After the smoke goes in, be prepared to fire HE or FASCAM, depending on what we find."

When Rivera was ready to cross, Ed turned on the fire support. The tanks and ITVs began firing at the half-dozen buildings visible on the far bank, a few hundred meters from the ferry site. The team's three 81 mm mortars began firing a mixture of high explosive and white phosphorous rounds to suppress and blind any Russian soldiers hidden on the east bank. The HE rounds burst in dirty gray mushrooms that hung stationary in the still air. The WP rounds exploded into an incongruously bright white smoke bank that slowly rolled over the ground.

As the first APC entered the water, the artillery rounds arrived, building a cloud of hazy gray smoke that blanketed the east bank. The front end of the carrier dipped low into the river, and water surged halfway back over the roof. With a snort from the exhaust, the carrier leveled out and began churning its way across the river. Once it stabilized, the three hatches popped open, and heads and torsos appeared. All but the driver pointed weapons at the far bank in anticipation of enemy action. One rifleman began nervously firing wild shots into the smoke screen until Rivera stopped him. Then, the lieutenant had second thoughts. The .50-caliber gunner began firing into the tin shack next to the ferry ramp, and the rest of the squad opened up with M-16s and SAWs on the still invisible far bank.

Once Rivera was safely on his way, Ed gave his driver the order to move out and start across. The driver leaned forward from his hatch and pushed the plywood trim vane forward. Once the trim vane locked in place, the driver dropped into his seat, released the brakes, and moved out. As his track left the shelter of the road bank, Ed and his crew slammed their hatches shut, making the APC dark and claustrophobic. Ed shook with the vibration of the diesel and the movement over the rough ground leading to the ferry ramp. Even with his headset clamped tightly to his ears, he could hear the growl of the engine and the squeal of the metal tracks. As he clutched tightly to the troop seat that ran the length of the compartment, he was reminded of paratroopers riding a C-130 on their way to the drop zone.

"Coming up on the river, sir," the driver announced over the intercom. "I hope this fucker floats. I can't swim."

"If we start to sink, just open your hatch," Ed said. "You'll pop out like a rocket. At least that's what the book says."

The carrier took a sudden stomach-tightening drop. The periscopes went briefly dark as the river washed over them, and then the carrier floated in the current as it left the ferry ramp. Daylight came back into the APC's interior as it floated in the river.

Ed punched his .50-caliber gunner in the back, and when the soldier looked back at him, he gestured upwards with his left thumb. With his right hand, Ed pulled the chain release and opened the cargo hatch. Light flooded the inside as Ed, his RTO, and the FIST chief jumped up to look around. The carrier floated like a half-waterlogged crate as it butted against the river current. Ed noticed uncomfortably that the carrier had all of about four inches of free board and gave fervent thanks to whichever saint watched over sailors that the Elbe was smooth as glass this morning. Then he jumped about a foot as his .50-caliber gunner began firing. The spent shell casings tumbled down from the gun and bounced over the side into the river. All, that is, but the two or three hot ones that landed on his left hand and down his collar. He swore loudly at the pain of the burns and slapped at the gunner's back in anger. The soldier paused, looked down at Ed, grinned, and continued to shoot.

He didn't have much time to worry about free board, burnt hands, or how the far bank seemed to be receding rather than moving closer as his APC chugged across the river. The radio crackled in his ear, and he heard someone calling him.

"Victor two four. Victor two four. Echo three zero. Where are you?" asked Mike, which was something unusual for the battalion executive officer. As XO, Mike usually operated on the administrative/logistics net and almost never called a company commander directly.

"Echo three zero, victor two four." Ed looked at his map spread on the roof of the carrier in front of him. He found the checkpoint nearest to the ferry site and estimated the distance between the two locations. "I am now three hundred meters east of charlie papa niner seven and moving east. Over."

There was a moment of silence on the radio. From his days in the group's operations shop, Ed visualized the scramble at the map board. First, someone had to locate CP 97 and then figure out where three hundred meters east would put him.

Mike responded with one word. "Why?"

"Victor two four. There's no one across from me. I figured I had better move while I had the chance. Over."

The APC bucked a little, and Ed's RTO became violently and loudly ill. Ed looked up and realized the trip was almost over. He was about twenty meters from the east bank, and one of Rivera's men waved frantically at the driver to guide him onto the ramp.

Ed flipped the intercom switch and told his driver, "Stop when you get clear of the bank and let me off. Then go wherever they tell you to."

Mike came back on the radio. "Victor two four, echo three zero. I just got a call from Bravo five delta about your fire plan. Now I can see what you're up to. I'll discuss the wisdom of this escapade face-to-face. In the meantime, stay where you are. Your location is now Objective Grant. Break. Hotel two four, Romeo two four, Uniform two four, Tango two four, Delta two four, meet me at charlie papa four three ASAP. Over."

The other company commanders answered their calls, and Mike left the air. As he did, Ed's carrier lurched ashore and climbed the concrete ramp. It stopped at the head of the ramp. Ed, the FIST chief, and his RTO, now recovered from his seasickness, jumped out the troop door in the rear ramp of the carrier and ran over to where Rivera stood next to the bullet-riddled tin shed at the head of the ferry landing.

"No disrespect, sir," Rivera said, greeting him. "But I sure could use my second squad a hell of a lot more than I can use you right now."

Ed shrugged. "I'm not about to sit out this party. Besides, they were right behind me. Any sign of life around here?"

"Negative. We can't see or hear anything in the immediate vicinity. But I could do a lot more if my other two squads—"

"Drop it, George. I'm here, and you're stuck with me. I just got a call from the XO. He said to stay here once we get across, and he'll be up to see us in a while."

A heavy thrashing sound came up the river to where Ed and Rivera stood watching the next two APCs cross. The smoke curtain laid by the mortars and artillery was fading, and the Elbe shone naked in the morning sun. The surface was smooth, flatter than Ed remembered it as he crossed fifteen minutes earlier, except where the two tracks bulled their way across. Rivera's second squad was in the lead vehicle, now about fifty meters from the east bank, and his third squad was clearing the entry point. The two officers turned toward the noise. They watched in surprise and dismay as a Polish MI-24 HIND armed helicopter popped above the tree line about fifteen hundred meters downstream from the ferry site. The gunship hovered over the trees like a bloated dragonfly, fishtailing slightly as the pilot surveyed the crossing operation. The nose of the aircraft dipped suddenly, and it began to roll in on a firing pass on the two vehicles swimming the river.

The HIND was designed to carry a full load of six Spiral ATGMs, four 57 mm rocket pods mounted on the stub wings protruding halfway down the fuselage, and a 30 mm Gatling gun mounted in a chin turret beneath the cockpit. In one respect, the Americans were lucky. This particular HIND was not carrying any SPIRALS. A hit by a single Spiral could demolish an M-113. The HIND did have a full load of rockets, and the gunner began firing pairs of the 57 mm missiles at the third squad's APC churning across the river. Puffs of dirty brown smoke trailed rearward from the rocket pods as each pair of rockets was launched. The puffs of smoke gave the helicopter the appearance of a dragon breathing its fire backward. The first two salvos were short. As they exploded in the water, the APCs struggled harder to reach shore and safety.

The third salvo struck the carrier in the roof and punched through the cargo hatch. A geyser of white water swallowed the APC as the warheads detonated fuel and ammunition. When the water subsided, the river was empty. Nine men and a thirteen-ton armored vehicle had vanished. Not even debris or an oil slick marked their resting place. As if the HIND's rockets were a signal, ground fire erupted from both sides of the river. Tracers from .50-caliber and M-60 machine guns wove a bright red web around the gunship. Some ricocheted crazily from the aircraft, but the HIND shook off the ground fire like it was a summer rain. A Stinger rose from the hill behind the team's assembly area on the west bank. The helicopter abruptly dropped to a few feet above the river as it blossomed flares to spoof the SAM's heat seeker. The countermeasures worked successfully as the Stinger vanished into the eastern sky chasing a flare. The gunship passed by Ed's position so closely that he could clearly see the heads of the gunner and pilot and the red and white diamond of the Polish Air Force. In anger and frustration, he emptied a magazine from his M-16 at the helicopter without visible effect. A second Stinger shot across the river after the helicopter. The pilot successfully evaded it by dropping below the trees lining the riverbank. The second Stinger convinced the Pole that his luck was running out so he turned east to safety.

A solid stream of tracers rose from a clump of trees about a thousand meters from the American bridgehead and reached out toward the gunship. Watching the Stinger plunge into the trees, the HIND pilot flew directly into the tracer stream. The HIND staggered to the right like a punch-drunk fighter and immediately began streaming a banner of thick black smoke.

"I don't know who's over there," Ed said to Rivera as they watched the smoking helicopter disappear in the distance. "But I'm going to buy him a case of his favorite booze. He just saved our asses big time."

"You better make it vodka, boss," Rivera said. "My LP says he hears heavy track noises from over that direction. Sounds like lots of big shit. We don't have any tanks on this side so they must be bad guys."

"They must use the same rules we do. Shoot 'em down. Sort 'em out on the ground. Whoever scared off that chopper isn't a bad guy, no matter what kind of uniform he's wearing."

Ed's river crossing continued unabated after the helicopter attack. Within an hour, he had his two rifle platoons and mortar platoons across the river occupying the far bank. His tank platoon and attached ITV section were still in their overwatch position on Hill 841 waiting for a bridge to cross the river. The tank platoon leader reconned alternate positions for his vehicles to play a shell game. Each time one of his vehicles engaged an enemy target, it shifted immediately to an alternate position to escape any incoming counter battery fire.

After the HIND departed the area, trailing smoke from the unknown anti-aircraft gunner, there was a dearth of targets for the tanks and ITVs to engage. The only sign of hostile activity occurred about ninety minutes after Ed started his crossing operation. A Russian BRDM-2 four-wheeled armored scout car poked its nose out of a group of buildings about fifteen hundred meters north of the American position. As soon as it began to move down the river road toward the American infantry, an Abrams tank on Hill 241 smashed it with a single main gun round. The BRDM exploded like a tin can stuffed with a cherry bomb and left only a thin spiral of black smoke in its place.

Ed began sending squad-sized patrols out to feel around the countryside. Other than the smoldering scout car, the only trace of Warsaw Pact forces the patrols discovered was the empty firing position of whatever weapon system had shot at the HIND. The patrols cleared an area within a five-kilometer radius of the ferry. They mainly found civilians huddling in the basements of their homes and praying fervently both sides would go somewhere else to do their fighting.

AutoFahre Elbe
Vicinity Bahra DDR

The task force closed on Ed's position in piecemeal fashion. Team Bravo, the tank company team, arrived first. Captain Paul Hart, the team commander, immediately took control of the friendly side of the crossing site. He pushed patrols upstream and downstream for ten kilometers and scattered outposts—either a section of Abrams tanks or a squad of infantry—throughout the area for security and early warning. He put his attached engineer squad to work improving the approaches to the ferry site.

When Mike arrived, he talked briefly with Hart and then told his track driver to get ready for a swim. As the driver left to begin his pre-crossing checks, Mike turned back to Hart and outlined his plans.

"I've told Brigade what's happening here. They're waiting for more information before they make any major moves. I'm going over to see Chambers in person. While I'm over there, get the combat trains up here and put them in Bahra. It's less than a klick away, so they should be able to support us from there. When Donaldson gets here, have him begin crossing as soon as he's ready. Keep Morgan here with you for the time being. Put some of the ITVs into Bahra, on the south side, close to us so they can cover the far bank. Have Paxton put the heavy mortars on the back side of Hill 241—"

"What about the scouts?" Hart interrupted. "I'd think that you'd need them on the other side. It's a pretty big country, and we don't know shit about what's going on around there. Jesse, my platoon leader with Chambers, told me that a gunship attacked them about twenty minutes before I got here. Somebody on the far side scared him off with what looked like one of those Russian tracked anti-aircraft guns, but he might have told his higher headquarters that Americans were across the river. Anyway, air defense artillery assets normally don't roam around by themselves."

"You've got a point," Mike said. "Send the scouts across when they get here. Keep on the brigade command net so we both know what is going on. If any other infantry units show up, start them across the river. Oh yeah, I just remembered. A section of Avengers is coming up here and maybe some more Stinger squads in M-3s. Put the Bradleys somewhere they can cover the crossing site with their cannons as well as with the missiles. If that ZSU or HIND got word back, we're going to have more company up here."

As Mike's track emerged on the far side of the river, Ed stood beside the bullet-ridden ticket booth and waved the driver over to where he stood. After the driver parked his vehicle in the lee of the building, Mike dismounted over the top and faced Ed.

"I've got patrols out in all directions for about five klicks," Ed began as soon as Mike was on the ground and the engine noise from the APC died away. "We haven't seen much sign of hostiles—"

"What about that HIND that caught you crossing the river?" Mike interrupted.

Ed shrugged. "He made two passes and got one track while it was in the water, and then someone scared him off. Rivera thinks it was a ZSU-23-4, but all we've found are track marks, no vehicle. Everyone else is over here safely. I figure we found a big hole in their lines. Someone forgot to cover this ferry site. If we get the rest of the brigade up here and across the river, we can blow them wide open." Visions of a victory parade through Warsaw led by Captain Edward J. Chambers were dancing in Ed's head.

"Where's Lieutenant Colonel Carswell? I figured he'd be up here in a heartbeat once he figured out that I'd bounced the river."

"Carswell's dead," Mike said bluntly. "He spent too much time on the radio once too often and got clobbered, along with most of the jump TOC. I've brought up the rest of the task force. They'll start crossing once they get here." He turned back to his command carrier and gestured to Kevin for his map case. He opened it and turned back to Ed. "I want you to secure the immediate area, no farther out than ten klicks in any direction. I want you particularly to cover Merschwiede and control the north-south highway that goes through there. Brigade is looking at the situation over the rest of the sector before they decide to commit a large force here."

"Ten klicks! Jesus, that's crazy!" Ed said, exploding. "I'm primed to go. Let someone else secure this place. There's no one in front of me." He pounded Mike's map. "I could go all the way to Dresden."

"That's what I'm afraid of," Mike replied.

"There's no one in front of you, and there's no one in back of you either. Once the other side gets their act together, we're going to have problems. Until I can get enough of a force over here to do something besides piss off a bunch of Russians, I want to keep this bridgehead secure. And Ed, even you couldn't capture Dresden with just one company team."

A call from Paul Hart that the brigade commander was en route to the ferry site to see Mike personally cut Mike's meeting short. Mike headed back across the Elbe, passing carriers from Bill Donaldson's Team Alpha heading east to join Team Charlie. Mike realized he had forgotten to put one person in charge on the far bank to control the buildup of the bridgehead and to ensure that the crossing site was secured. As his carrier climbed the ramp, he radioed back and put Ed, as senior man, in charge of the elements on the east side of the river. He reiterated his instructions to control the north-south highway east of the river.

Hart left a guide waiting to lead Mike to the farmhouse where the TOC was set up. Steve Young, promoted from Assistant S-3 to S-3 by the Russian artillery outside Prausitz, had the operations center functioning smoothly out of its M-577 parked inside the empty barn. Mike's arrival coincided with the brigade commander's.

The colonel dismounted his Bradley and shook Mike's hand vigorously. "You got us a real winner, Fitzmaurice. What's going on over there on the far side?"

"I just visited the team commander, sir. He's got his team, less the tanks, across, and I'm sending the infantry from one other team over there."

"Who's the team commander over there now? Is he a good man?" the colonel interrupted hurriedly.

"Ed Chambers made the crossing with his Team Charlie. I've got—"

"Chambers, Chambers. I know him. Solid man. Any sign of the Russians?"

"He's seen one BRDM and a HIND. The HIND caught his people crossing the river and sank one track. Someone on the east bank fired on the helicopter and drove it off. We think it was a ZSU-23-4, but all we've found so far is tracks. He's run patrols out to an arc about like this." Mike gestured at the situation map and pointed out the general routes of Ed's patrols. "All he's found so far are a lot of frightened civilians."

The brigade commander nodded thoughtfully as he stared at the map. Suddenly, he slapped the map board with his right hand. "Shit, in for a penny, in for a pound. I'm going to send TF 2/92 Armor to secure this side of the crossing. You take back the company you chopped to them and get all your infantry across. I've been on the horn to Division and managed to break loose some bridges out of the engineer battalion. Once they get up, make some rafts, and get your tank team over there. I think this looks like the break we've been looking for. We can tear them a new asshole."

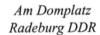

Am Domplatz
Radeburg DDR

The division commander took full advantage of Ed's bridgehead and poured two brigades through it to the east side of the Elbe. The corps commander visited the crossing site as the First Brigade passed over. He followed the Sixteenth Mech with the 287th Armored Brigade and two brigades of the Twenty-Fifth Armored Division. The Americans began spreading south and east like bacon fat melting on a griddle.

The shock of the crossing paralyzed the Russian forces in the division's zone. They limited their reactions to swift, confused firefights as the opposing armies brushed up against each other.

Mike called for an orders group in the town square of Radeburg. The commanders parked their carriers close to the buildings fronting the square and walked to the command post in a small café. Mike moved the group outside to a cluster of benches in front of the building. As the officers found seats on the benches, Kevin and another soldier pulled over a table from the café to spread briefing maps on. Mike heard the rumbling noise of a diesel approaching up a side street. Absorbed in preparations for the briefing, he paid no attention to it.

The boat-shaped nose of a Russian BMP armored personnel carrier poked around the corner of an abandoned bank at the far end of the square. Before anyone could react, the BMP's driver goosed his throttle, and the carrier lurched onto the main street. The turret swung toward the cluster of American APCs and troops. The first shot from the main gun crashed into Mike's command track and shattered it. The 30 mm cannon sprayed the command group like a garden hose. The three light machine guns added their fire to the opening salvo.

The Americans scattered like a covey of quail flushed from a cane break. Mike dove into the shelter of a doorway with Kevin at his heels. As Ed tried to run back to his command vehicle, the Russian gunner caught him with a burst of fire. One of the .50-caliber gunners tried to duel with the BMP as his own track scampered to cover. After his first dozen rounds, the BMP's main gun belched and obliterated the gunner, machine gun, and carrier. The BMP began to roll up the street slowly, alternately firing its main gun and coax into the buildings on either side.

Behind him, Mike felt Kevin struggling to shed his web gear. "What the hell do you think you're doing?" Mike asked.

"I'm going to fix that bastard like we did in Altendorf, sir," Kevin answered.

He had wiggled out of his web gear and now clutched an AT-4. He watched the BMP roll closer to their doorway as he armed the launcher. Then he pushed himself up on one knee, like a sprinter in the starting blocks.

"Cover me, boss," he said to Mike. Then he yelled in a louder voice, "You guys out there cover me. I'm going after him."

He lunged out of the doorway, hunched down and leaning forward, trying to make himself as small as possible. As he ran toward the Russian vehicle, rifle and machine gun fire from all sides picked up in an attempt to distract the crew. The carrier's crew didn't notice him until he stopped some twenty meters from the side of the BMP, stood erect, and swiftly aimed his rocket. The turret started to swerve toward him, and the driver frantically tried to back away as Kevin fired. A small sheet of flame spurted from the launcher as the missile leapt out and crashed into the BMP.

Kevin's shot was a lucky one, the proverbial Golden BB. He was just outside the minimum arming range of fifteen meters. And when the rocket struck the BMP, it functioned perfectly. The AT-4 smashed into the turret just above the ready ammunition rack for the 100 mm main gun. When it exploded, the gas jet from the shape-charged warhead ate through the armor of the turret and into the rack of high explosive ammunition. The main gun ammunition exploded in a massive secondary explosion, even as Kevin turned about to run to safety.

For an instant, the world froze. Mike could clearly see the fireball bloom behind Kevin. It unfolded like time-lapse photography of a blossoming flower. As it grew, its color shifted from white to red to golden-orange to black. Kevin stood spread-eagle, etched against the blast like a crucifix against the door of a church.

Sound and motion returned. The blast wave slapped against Mike, and he flinched involuntarily. Kevin's body was tossed across the street, away from the Russian vehicle. It hit like a rag doll against the side of a building and slowly slid to the ground. Mike heard the solid thump of the body hitting the wall, and it spurred him into action. He picked himself up and ran to where the young soldier sprawled on the sidewalk, oblivious to the possibility of incoming fire.

"Kevin! Kevin!" he said as he knelt beside the body.

The blast blackened Kevin's face, and his breath came raggedly and rapidly. Mike tore open the man's flak jacket and pounded on his chest to begin CPR. Kevin's eyes bulged. His mouth opened wider than a mouth should be able to as he desperately sucked for air. Mike worked harder on his CPR.

"Stay with me, Goddammit. Stay with me."

I can't lose him, Mike thought. *I can't lose him. I promised he'd be okay.*

His world narrowed to focus on Kevin. Then Kevin's body bent like a drawn bow.

"Kevin! Kevin! Goddamn, you! Live!" Mike shouted at his friend.

He pumped harder against Kevin's chest. Suddenly, he was aware of voices in his ears and hands pulling at him.

"Major, it's over. It's no use. He's gone, sir. You can't help him." The senior medic, a tall black soldier with long, graceful fingers and sad eyes, gently tugged away Mike's hands. "Sir, he's finished."

Mike sat back on his haunches and watched as the medic softly closed Kevin's eyes. Then he saw a long, jagged piece of steel protruding from Kevin's groin. Blood coated the ground between his legs like a thick tomato paste. Mike thought absently that he never realized how much blood the human body could hold.

"It was the femoral artery, sir," the medic said. "He was dying when he landed here. You couldn't have done anything to save him."

Tears started unbidden in Mike's eyes. He reached out and touched Long's face. "But I promised Dumont I would take care of him," he told the medic in a weak voice. "He wouldn't have been here if it weren't for me."

Another hand gripped his shoulder, and a voice said, "You have a battle to fight and a battalion that needs you, boss."

He looked up to see Ed standing above him. Ed used his good arm to hang onto Mike's shoulder. The other was strapped tightly to his side, and thick bandages wrapped his chest.

"I'll take care of Kevin now. You get back to work. You made Dumont a soldier. She will understand. Besides, a couple hundred other men here need you."

---∘∘∘◦◉◦∘∘∘---

Hill 347
Vicinity Markersfeld DDR

Mike stared at the situation map and forced himself to concentrate. Dancing lights behind his eyes and the feeling of an ice pick jabbing into the back of his head telegraphed the arrival of a migraine headache again. He alternately cursed plebe boxing four years of football, and the caffeinated coffee the army persisted in putting in its field rations. Trying to massage the back of his neck, he looked again at the map and interpreted its red and blue symbols. Reports from the scout platoon and Team Charlie showed about twenty tanks, or the equivalent of two companies, moving slowly but steadily toward Team Charlie's position. The task force sat on a long fishhook-shaped ridge overlooking the E-40 autobahn, between Bautzen and Gorlitz, the main route to the east and safety for the Warsaw Pact forces now swarming across the Elbe River. The last message from Brigade had told him to hold until relieved. Task Force 2/66 was now the anvil the Russians would be hammered against.

The radio operator monitoring the brigade command net suddenly jerked erect. "Major," he called to Mike, "I've got a flash message from Brigade for you, sir."

"Well, what is it?"

"Juliet two six wants to talk to you direct, sir." The RTO started to pull off his headset and give it to Mike.

"Just put it on the speaker, Perez, and give me the handset." Mike began speaking into the radio handset. "Juliet two six, golf two six. Over."

"Golf two six, juliet two six. Message. Cease all offensive operations, and hold in current positions effective eleven hundred hours Zulu. Limited self-defense authorized only in immediate areas. Acknowledge."

Sound in the TOC ceased. Mike stared at the small, square olive drab loudspeaker. *Did this mean the war was over?* he thought.

"Give me an authentication table," he said, snapping.

The command sergeant major promptly handed him a CEOI open to the authentication table. Command Sergeant Major Taylor had even marked a three-letter challenge and response.

"Juliet two six. Authenticate bravo november."

"Golf two six, I authenticate whiskey." The response was immediate and unhesitant. "Acknowledge my message."

"Golf two six. Roger, message acknowledged."

"Juliet two six. Written instructions to follow. Juliet two six out."

Mike put down the radio handset and gazed unseeing at the wall of the command track. *Maybe we would survive after all*, he thought.

Perez looked up at Mike. "Does this mean it's over, sir? Are we going home now?"

The young soldier's question snapped Mike back to reality. "It means the shooting will be over in about forty-five minutes."

Mike turned back to the map board. He tested his emotions and found nothing, not even a feeling of letdown or elation. The migraine seemed to recede, though.

"Okay, Young," he said to the assistant operations officer, "get me all the commanders on the battalion command net. Once I finish talking to them, I'm going up to Team Charlie's position. Those Russian tanks look as though they don't have the word about the cease-fire yet."

At that moment, another call broke over the loudspeaker. "Golf three seven, tango four three victor. I'm two minutes out from your location. Request you mark Lima Zulu."

"Who the hell is tango four three victor, and why should we mark a landing zone?" Mike asked the room at large.

Steve Young was looking through his CEOI. "Tango four three is the ADC support, and victor is his pilot. Somebody get outside with a smoke grenade and get ready to pop it when the bird appears."

As he spoke, Young pulled on his web gear and helmet and grabbed a green smoke grenade. Over his shoulder, as he exited the TOC, he told Perez to challenge the aircraft. Experience had shown that Warsaw Pact aviators spoke excellent English and a marked LZ could easily become a target. The TOC was inside the barn of an abandoned farm. The faint stuttering sound of the approaching helicopter was becoming louder as the three men stepped into the yard between the house and the barn.

"There it is, off to the west, about nine o'clock." The command sergeant major pointed. "He's low, only about twenty or thirty feet off the deck."

"You blame him, Sergeant Major?" Mike watched the aircraft approach. The black speck grew rapidly into the dragonfly shape of a UH-60. "The main air defense rule around here is if it flies, it dies."

The wheels of the Blackhawk just barely touched ground, and six passengers jumped out. The door gunner gave thumbs-up to the soldiers on the ground as the pilot pulled up his aircraft in a cloud of dust and small debris. He dove for the cover of a wood line about a hundred meters south of the farm.

"Well, Mike," John Warren said as he gripped Mike's hand heartily. "We both seem to have come up in the world lately. Now, if the army will just make the rank and paychecks match the responsibility and position, there may in fact be justice in this world."

"Welcome to our humble home, sir." Mike grinned. "It's not much, but it sure beats an open foxhole. If you all will come this way, we'll get undercover. This neighborhood can be rough at times. Some of the locals aren't too well-disposed toward Americans."

Once inside the barn where the TOC was set up, Warren introduced his party to Mike and his staff. "My aide, Captain Baxter, who has only lately and reluctantly revealed her hidden talent for speaking fluent Russian; Major Goldhammer from Corps G-2, who also speaks Russian; and Mr. Fleming from the State Department. Mr. Fleming is here to oversee the disengagement of our forces from those of the other side."

Fleming was a middle-aged man, running to baldness and a slight potbelly. He looked distinctly uncomfortable and out of place in his BDUs, helmet, and field gear. He carried a battered black leather briefcase in place of any type of personal weapon. He made no attempt to shake hands with any of the officers from the task force.

"Major Fitzmaurice," he said to Mike, interrupting Warren. "I am a senior counselor to the US Ambassador to NATO. This cease-fire agreement took us a lot of hard work and sacrifice to hammer out and make mutually acceptable. Hard work and sacrifice at great cost, I might add—"

In a flash, Mike saw Kevin bleeding to death in his arms and Ann-Marie holding a bloody boot that still contained Sally Grant's foot. "Right," he said in a harsh voice. "I'm well aware of the cost, Mr. Fleming."

Fleming understood his anger. "I'm not deprecating your losses, Major, or the efforts of your soldiers. As badly as you have been battered, you've hurt the Warsaw Pact worse. But so far, we've kept the conflict limited in scope and nature. This agreement gives both sides a breathing space to keep it that way."

Before Mike could answer, the radio loudspeaker squealed, and a voice said, "Golf three seven, Zulu two six bravo. Zulu two six needs to talk to golf two six ASAP. Over."

Mike left the group and strode over to the radio rack. He took the handset from Perez and spoke into it. "Zulu two six, golf two six."

"Zulu two six. Those hostiles I've been watching have stopped moving. They're taking up positions about twenty-five to twenty-seven hundred meters to my front. They're not digging in or anything, just stopping in some half-assed covered positions. I still have some good shots at them, and my FIST can get some fire on top of them no sweat. Shall I engage? Over."

"Golf two six. Negative. Do not engage unless they start something serious by closing on your position or trying to go past you. There is a cease-fire going into effect 1100 Zulu or noon local. I'm on my way up to you now, so hang on until I get there. Break. X-ray, kilo, foxtrot. Did you monitor the cease-fire?"

The other commanders acknowledged they had heard Mike announce the cease-fire and the time it was to take effect.

"Golf two six, foxtrot two six," Paul Hart replied. "Has anyone told the Russians about the cease-fire? We're taking sporadic artillery fire up here.

"If they're going to quit at noon, does it include their gun bunnies?" The tanker ended his message.

"The cease—fire agreement goes into effect at noon our time for everyone, according to someone beside me," Mike answered. Paul Hart. "If they continue firing after 1200, you will return fire, but only in a friendly manner. Golf two six out."

Warren said to Mike as he finished talking to foxtrot two six, "If you have someone in contact, that's where we . . ." He pointed to his party. ". . . Are supposed to be. Under the terms of the cease-fire, senior officers of each side have to meet wherever there are units in contact to verify that the disengagement is taking place and fighting has stopped. My Russian doppelganger is probably on his way forward even as we speak."

Mike pointed to the situation map board. "George Rivera has his Mech team sitting here, sir. The hostiles he mentioned are about eighteen to twenty T-80s moving southeast toward him. We think they're remnants of a tank regiment trying to push George in particular and the rest of us in general out of the way. The only way they're going to get to Gorlitz and farther east is over us. The rest of the task force is overwatching George and can still block the way, but he's the closest to the bad guys. His people forced the river crossing the other day, and they're still looking for scalps for payback. I was on my way up there to keep a lid on the situation when you arrived."

Warren nodded and put his helmet back on. "Sounds good. Let's hit the road." He turned to his companions. "Okay, ladies and gentlemen, pit stop time. Make it quick if you have to go. It may be a long wait once we get up forward, and the facilities available up there will no doubt lack the ambiance you'll find here."

At the mention of ladies, Mike looked closely at the visitors for the first time. He recognized Vicki, now wearing captain bars. Then he saw Ann-Marie standing a few feet behind Fleming and the G-2 Major. Ann-Marie had aged, as they all had, and there was a hardness about her that hadn't been there before. She had lost all her puppy fat that had cost her acting jack stripes after Colonel Porter had replaced Warren. She now wore staff sergeant chevrons and stood taller than she had the last time Mike had seen her.

"Anne-Marie . . . I mean, Sergent Dumont." He stepped forward to greet her. "I'm sorry I didn't speak to you sooner, but I didn't see you. Congratulations on your promotion. The stripes look good on you." His voice trailed away. He remembered his promise to keep Kevin out of trouble. Now that he was closer, he could see a shadow of pain in the back of her eyes.

"Major, it's good to see you again. You're looking well," the young woman said as she stepped around Fleming and Major Goldhammer to shake Mike's hand warmly. "I'm glad you finally got a battalion to command, sir. The people back in the support group would be proud if they could see you now. I know Kevin was." She let go of his hand and moved back toward the entrance to the TOC.

Mike, Warren, and the rest of the party joined Rivera at his CP. Rivera had found a clearing on a logging road that provided a panoramic view of the approaches to the hill that Team Charlie occupied. The valley lay spread out like a giant terrain model bisected by the autobahn. Rivera began pointing out the positions the approaching tanks had occupied when they halted their advance forty minutes before. As he spoke, a Russian BTR-80 PU, a command version of the BTR-80 eight-wheeled armored personnel carrier, appeared from the direction of Bautzen, speeding down the eastbound lanes of the autobahn. The vehicle didn't attempt to conceal itself. It relied for safety on the two large white banners flying from its radio antennas.

The BTR slid to a stop on the road about halfway between the last Russian T-80 and the base of the Americans' hill. As the armored personnel carrier halted, Warren spoke softly to Fleming. Then he said to Mike, "That looks like my visitor. I'll need your carrier and a guide to get us to the bottom of the hill without screwing up the positions here."

"George," Mike said without taking his attention from the Russians at the bottom of the hill, "get someone who can show us how to get down safely without running over the mines you've laid and haven't marked or recorded anywhere. Have him meet us at my track." He turned to Warren. "What kind of markings do I tell my driver to put on the track for us, sir?"

"Us? You're not coming!" Warren started to answer.

"With respect, bullshit, sir." Mike faced Warren squarely.

"If you go down there, I'm going with you. We were together for the start of this thing. Why should the end be any different? Besides, if something happened to you in my area and Major General Barrett missed your promotion party, he'd crucify me."

Warren nodded and gripped Mike's arm tightly.

Team Charlie's senior medic ransacked his medic's aid bags to come up with enough gauze and adhesive tape to produce three crosses on Mike's command track—one on the trim vane and one on each side—and several pennants to hang from each of the three antennas. Rivera sent a team leader from the squad closest to the bottom of the hill to meet Mike and Warren at his carrier. As they boarded the track, Rivera promised Mike he would be watching closely and keeping a loose finger on the trigger. It wasn't quite noon, and the transition from trying to kill someone to trusting him was a difficult shift to make. The guide led them through the team's battle position. Word of their mission spread as they drove through the woods where the team's tanks and APCs were positioned. Soldiers appeared from their bunkers and vehicles to flash peace signs or thumbs-up to the people in the carrier's open cargo hatch.

As he reached the bottom of the hill, Mike stopped just inside the wood line. He and the gunner dismounted the .50-caliber machine gun. After they stored the weapon inside the carrier, the driver started up again. He moved into the open, heading for the BTR and its occupants. Mike told his driver to stop the carrier across the road from the Russian vehicle, kill the engine, and wait for the outcome of the meeting. Once the Americans broke out of the woods and were visible to the watching Russians, the left-side hatch on the BTR opened, and seven men dismounted. They stood clustered tightly next to their carrier and watched the Americans come forward.

Mike's driver parked his vehicle in a small depression in the shoulder of the autobahn almost opposite the BTR-80. The shallow ditch covered most of the 113's bulk, leaving only the machine gun mount exposed. He locked his brakes and then dropped the ramp in the rear of the troop compartment. As the engine died, John Warren crouched under the roof of the carrier and stepped down the ramp. Once outside, he paused to watch the rest of the group dismount. All were empty-handed, except Fleming, who clutched his briefcase tightly in both hands.

As Mike unplugged his intercom to dismount the carrier, his RTO asked from the gunner's position, "You really trust these guys, sir? You think they're going to stay honest?"

"Not much," Mike answered.

"But they know Rivera's up there watching and will shoot if anything goes wrong. Besides, their grunts probably want to go home all in one piece as much as we do."

Mike stepped off the ramp and joined Warren. He nodded silently to the colonel, who then glanced at each of the other six members of his party.

"Okay, people," he said softly. "Let's see what they have to say."

The two groups met in the middle of the median strip. There were seven Russians, six in uniforms and one in a nondescript taupe overcoat carrying a large brown briefcase. One of the uniformed men wore the flat red-banded hat of a general officer. He stepped forward and stopped halfway between the two groups. Warren held up a hand to stop his escorts and walked the rest of the way to meet the Russian officer. The Russian was a tall, slender man. A day's growth of unshaven beard made his dusky complexion darker. He stared coldly at the American and then snarled something in Russian.

Warren answered calmly, "I don't speak Russian, general." He called back without turning away from the Russian, "Captain Baxter, would you come up here and translate?"

As Vicki started forward, a man detached himself from the group of Russians and joined the general. His quiet translation of Warren's remark made it obvious that he was the Russian translator.

"The Russian wants to see your credentials, sir." Vicki translated the opening remark.

With exaggerated care, Warren produced his ID card and flashed it in the Russian's face. When the other man reached for it, Warren pulled it back.

"Not on your life, my friend. Vicki, tell him that, now that I've showed him mine, he's to show me his."

As the two translators spoke, the general reached into his blouse and produced his pay book, the Russian army equivalent of an ID card. He held it up in Warren's face, so the American could see the picture.

Warren nodded sharply. "We're both who we say we are," Warren said to the group at large. "So let's get on with it. Vicki, ask my counterpart here what time it is."

As Warren spoke to the Americans, the Russian general gestured to his group. Two of them stepped forward carrying folded map boards. They opened these and held them between the Russian general and Warren.

Vicki pulled out her own map sheet and began unfolding it as she asked the Russian interpreter the time. The general looked at his watch. The interpreter responded that the local time was three minutes after twelve, three minutes after the cease-fire became effective.

Before Warren could respond, Fleming said in a quiet but firm voice, "I think you ought to introduce me, Colonel. The fellow in the trench coat over there looks like my opposite number. The sooner he and I get talking, the sooner you and the general can get busy doing what you have to do."

Warren nodded. He told Major Goldhammer to introduce Fleming to the Russians and ask if their group included a diplomat.

Fleming guessed correctly. The man in the taupe overcoat was a member of the Foreign Ministry. With obvious reluctance, the general stepped aside and let the diplomat come forward to meet Fleming. Once both men exchanged introductions through their interpreters, they opened their briefcases and began reading documents to each other. Their work engrossed the two diplomats for about fifteen minutes. Then they shook hands and turned to their respective military counterparts. Both sides had coordinated the cease-fire lines, and troop movement could now begin. The two sides would disengage with the Allies moving back west of the Elbe River and the Warsaw Pact forces moving into Poland. Once the area between the Elbe and the Polish border was clear of Warsaw Pact forces, the Germans would move their troops back in.

The Russian general sent most of his party scrambling back into the BTR-80. Mike told his RTO to go back to the command track and call Rivera to reiterate the cease-fire order. He also warned the Americans to expect movement from the Russian forces to their front.

Diesel smoke plumed from behind clumps of bushes and small gullies and hillocks as the T-80s closest to the road started their engines. Mike watched as one tank, evidently the battalion commander's, jerked into reverse, pulled out of its position, and then stopped. With a whine of an electric motor, the turret swung around until the main gun pointed directly over the engine compartment. A hatch on the turret opened. A tanker scrambled out onto the engine compartment. He swiftly locked the gun tube in place in its travel lock. Then he tied a red fluorescent recognition panel over the gun tube and scuttled back inside the turret. As if that were a signal, the other tanks swung their main guns around as well. A man on each tank locked the gun tube in place and put out the recognition panel. The commander backed his tank out onto the road followed by the rest of the T-80s. Once all his tanks were lined up and the individual tank commanders watching him, the battalion commander waved the column into motion. They rolled east, past the cluster of staff officers and others standing silently in the median strip.

Mike left Colonel Warren speaking to Fleming about other aspects of the cease-fire and walked over to join Vicki and Ann-Marie. The two women saluted as he walked up.

"I was just telling Ann-Marie that she shouldn't wear green and brown makeup," Vicki said. "She just doesn't have the right complexion for earth colors. I saw some paperwork the general signed right before we left the DTOC to come up here." Her voice dropped a little and she stepped closer to Mike. "Kevin Long's DSC was approved." She stepped back and returned her voice to normal. "Ed got his medal finally, a Silver Star. He also got his CIB. The CG's policy is that, if a grunt gets wounded before his thirty days of combat time, he gets a CIB anyway."

"And a Purple Heart as well in Ed's case. I wonder if they saved his arm," Mike said. "I put him up for the Silver Star for making that river crossing. I wasn't sure about whether it would be approved or not."

One Russian officer, a motorized rifle major by his shoulder tabs, walked over to where Mike stood talking to Ann-Marie and Vicki. He stared intensely at Mike for a moment and then snarled something in Russian.

Mike shrugged his shoulders. "Sorry, Colonel. I don't speak Russian. I don't have a clue what you just said," he told the man.

The major repeated himself in passable English before Vicki could translate his remarks. "You know, American, I would have forced my way through here. You could not have stopped me. You are lucky."

"You would have tried, Colonel," Mike answered harshly. "You would have tried. A lot of your people wouldn't have made it. Maybe next time we'll find out who's the lucky one, me or you."

He turned his back on the Russian officer. The major spat on the grass and returned to the BTR-80.

As they watched the Russian tanks rolling eastward, Ann-Marie sighed. "Does this mean that it's all over, sir? Both sides just pack up and go home?" she asked softly.

"I don't know, Annie," Mike answered, using her first name unconsciously.

"You heard what Colonel Warren and Mr. Fleming said. We pull back to the west bank of the river, and they pull back further east. That's in our sector anyway. I don't know about the rest of the front, and quite honestly, I don't care. Right now, I'm only thinking about my troops in TF 2/66. The shooting stops here, at least for a while. That's all I need to know."

"So it ends just like it began? Kevin, Herb Lovell, and all the others just died for a tie?" The young woman shook her head and kicked at a clump of grass. "God, what a waste. What a fucking waste."

46th Field Hospital
Bahra, DDR

Mike had visited the last of the battalion's wounded in the field hospital, and he was on his way out the door of the hotel the Forty-Sixth occupied when a vaguely familiar voice hailed him.

"Major Fitzmaurice. Wait a minute."

He turned to find newly promoted Lieutenant General Lincoln Barrett coming up behind him. "We have to stop meeting like this." Barrett shook Mike's hand. "People will begin to talk."

"Congratulations on the third star, sir," Mike said. "It's heartening to see the good guys win one now and then."

"What are you up to now? You're not wounded again, are you?"

"No sir, I'm all in one piece. I'm visiting some of my wounded that haven't been evacuated yet. The task force is still up on the buffer zone, and I'm heading back up there as soon as I can find my command sergeant major. He's trying to get some problems squared away for some of our soldiers."

"Still the battalion commander? You're on the lieutenant colonel promotion list, aren't you?"

Mike shrugged. The subject was a sore one for him. "I'm still the commander for a while, sir. I've been told there are new O-5s due in to take over vacancies in the division, like TF 2-66. I haven't been told directly that I'll be replaced or when, but all the signs are that it will be soon. I guess I'm on the new O-5 list. I haven't heard one way or the other, but I've been a little too busy to follow up on it. Anyway, now that the shooting's all over, we love the other side, and they love us. So I'll probably be demobilized shortly with all the rest of the reservists and guardsmen and sent home. Not that going home would bother me. I'm about all army-ed out, sir."

"Don't get your hopes up about being demobilized anytime soon," Barrett said grimly. "This is just a cease-fire, a truce. It's not the permanent end of hostilities by any means. If you haven't heard, there is a massive build-up of troops stateside. The missile attacks against the States have made people a little less forgiving than might have been the case." He paused and looked at his watch. "Keep that in mind.

Also, realize that these new units forming up stateside need combat-experienced commanders.

"Well, I've got to get back to Corps. This has been fun. We'll have to do it again some time."

Headquarters, 4th Battalion (Mechanized), 48th Infantry
Camp Mackall, North Carolina

The young soldier walked up to the bulletin board outside the recently constructed small frame building that was the headquarters of the Fourth Battalion, 48th Infantry. He had been in the army a total of three months and five days and represented the average time in service of the soldiers assigned to 4/48. The draft was beginning to function and feed conscripts into the training pipeline. The established training centers—Benning, Gordon, Campbell, Dix, and Leonard Wood—accomplished basic training. The advanced training that produced combat-ready infantrymen, tankers, artillerymen, and all the other specialists that went into an effective combat force, was the responsibility of the new battalions and brigades forming up at temporary camps like Mackall. These new battalions received cadres of experienced officers and NCOs to train their soldiers as a unit. Some of these cadres were veterans of the fighting in Europe or the Middle East, and some were not.

As the young man stapled the document that he held in his hands to the bulletin board, he wondered what kind of man the new battalion commander was.

"Hey, man. What's that? Another detail list?" another soldier asked as the clerk stepped away and admired his work.

"Read it yourself, dude," he answered. "It's the new colonel assuming command."

The second soldier stepped up to the bulletin board and read the paper:

Headquarters, 4th Battalion (MECH), 48th Infantry
Camp Mackall, NC
Unit Orders Number 1-001
The undersigned assumes command.
(Signed) Michael P. Fitzmaurice, LTC, IN, USA

GLOSSARY

Abrams	Standard Army Main Battle Tank, first introduced in 1980. There are three variants in service: M1, M1A1 and M1A2. The M1A1 and M1A2 mount a 120mm main gun combined with a powerful 1,500 hp turbine engine and special armor,
ACR	Armored Cavalry Regiment
ADC	Assistant Division Commander
AFN	Armed Forces Network
APC	Armored Personnel Carrier
ARCOM	Army Reserve Command
ARTEP	Army Training and Evaluation Program
ATGM	Anti Tank Guided Missile
AWACS	Airborne Warning and Control System; provides all-weather surveillance, command, control and communications; AWACS is distinguished by the distinctive rotating radar dome above the fuselage.
BDU	Battle Dress Uniform
Bradley	American fighting vehicle platform manufactured by BAE Systems Land and Armaments. The Bradley is designed to transport infantry or scouts with armor protection while providing covering fire to suppress enemy troops and armored vehicles. There are several Bradley variants, including the M2 Bradley infantry-fighting vehicle and the M3 Bradley cavalry-fighting vehicle. The M2

holds a crew of three: a commander, a gunner and a driver, as well as six fully equipped soldiers. The M3 mainly conducts scout missions and carries two scouts in addition to the regular crew of three, with space for additional TOW missiles.

BMP   Soviet amphibious tracked infantry fighting vehicle. BMP stands for *Boyevaya Mashina Pekhoty 1* meaning "infantry fighting vehicle". The BMP-1 was the world's first mass-produced infantry fighting vehicle (IFV) and was armed with a 73 mm gun and a launcher for the AT-5 Spandrel or AT-4 Spigot ATGM

The BMP-2, was equipped with a two-man turret armed with a 30 mm multi-purpose auto cannon and an ATGM launcher capable of firing AT-5 Spandrel or AT-4 Spigot missiles.

The BMP-3 is one of the most heavily armed infantry combat vehicles in service, fitted with a low-velocity 100mm rifled gun, which can fire conventional ammunition or AT-10 Stabber ATGMs, a 30mm auto cannon, and a 7.62mm machine gun, all mounted coaxially in the turret. There are also two 7.62mm bow machine guns.

BRDM   Russian Combat Reconnaissance/Patrol Vehicle" an amphibious armored patrol car armed with a 14.5 mm KPVT heavy machine gun with a coaxial 7.62 mm PKT general-purpose machine gun in a small conical BPU-1 turret

BTR   BTR stands for Bronetransportyor literally "armored transporter"), a series of Soviet or post-Soviet military armored personnel carriers. The BTR-70 is an eight-wheeled armored personnel carrier armed with a primary heavy machine gun and secondary PKT machine gun on a roof mounted turret.

CAP — Combat Air Patrol

CAPSTONE — Program assigning reserve component units to support operational commands and missions.

CAS — Close Air Support

CDR — Commander

CEOI — Communications/electronics operating instructions; a document designed to control communications. Each edition contains the necessary material and information for 1 month.

CIB — Combat Infantryman's Badge

COMSEC — Communications Security

CONUS — Continental United States

COSCOM — Corps Support Command

CP — Check Point, Command Post

CS/CSS — Combat Support/Combat Service Support

DCDR — Deputy Commander

DDR — German Democratic Republic

DISCOM — Division Support Command

EWO — Electronic Warfare Officer

FASCAM — Family of scatterable mines delivered by field artillery munitions or aerial dispensers

FIST — Team provided by field artillery component to each maneuver company and troop to plan and coordinate all supporting fires.

FOUGASSE — Flame weapon, typically a mixture of petrol (gasoline) and oil.

FRG — Federal Republic of Germany

FSO — Fire Support Officer

HEAT — High Explosive Anti Tank

HHC — Headquarters and Headquarters Company

HIND — Russian large helicopter gunship and attack helicopter and low-capacity troop transport with room for eight passengers.

IG	Inspector General
ITV	Improved TOW Vehicle
Klick	Kilometer
LOC	Logistics Operations Center
LBE	Load Bearing Equipment
Milan	portable medium-range, anti-tank weapon
MOPP	Protective gear used by military personnel in a toxic environment, e.g., during a chemical, biological, radiological, or nuclear (CBRN) strike
MRE	Meals, Ready to Eat
MRL	Multiple Rocket Launcher
NBC	Nuclear Biological Chemical
NCO	None Commissioned Officer
NCOIC	Non Commissioned Officer in Charge
NO FORN	No Foreign access to document permitted
NVA	North Vietnamese Army
OER	Officer Evaluation Report
OP	Observation Post
PRC-77	Portable man packed FM radio
RDF	Radio Direction Finding
RTO	Radio Telephone Operator
RWR	Radar Warning Receiver
S-1	Personnel/Administration
S-2	Intelligence
S-3	Operations
S-4	Supply
SACEUR	Supreme Allied Commander, Europe
SAW	Squad Automatic Weapon
SAM	Surface to Air Missile
SEER	Senior Enlisted Evaluation Report
SOP	Standard Operating Procedure
Spetsnaz	Russian Special Forces
Stinger	Man portable infrared homing surface-to-air missile

Strela	Russian man-portable, shoulder-fired, low-altitude surface-to-air missile system with a high explosive warhead and passive infrared homing guidance
T-72	Russian Main Battle Tank armed with 125 mm smoothbore tank
T-80	Russian Main Battle Tank, successor to T-72
TOC	Tactical Operations Center
TOW	Tube-launched, Optically-tracked, Wire-guided anti-tank missile.
TSOP	Tactical Standard Operating Procedures
UH-1	The Bell UH-1 Iroquois is a military helicopter powered by a single, turbo-shaft engine, with a two-bladed main rotor and tail rotor
UH-60	A four-bladed, twin-engine, medium-lift utility helicopter
USAG	US Army Garrison
ZSU-23-4	Lightly armored, self-propelled, radar guided anti-aircraft weapon system, equipped with four 23mm auto cannons